CRAFTSMAN·CHURCHMAN·STATESMAN DUNSTAN Let not the storms of the underworld swallow me up Remember I beg you mercyful Christ to protect Dunstan 988 1988

Michael Murray

DUNSTAN

Saint and Statesman

DOUGLAS DALES

Douglas J. Dales

Ⓛ
Lutterworth Press · Cambridge

Lutterworth Press
P.O. Box 60
Cambridge CB1 2NT

British Library Cataloguing in Publication Data

Dales, Douglas
Dunstan : saint and statesman.
1. England. Dunstan, Saint, 909-988—
Biographies
I. Title
942.01′7′9024

ISBN 0-7188-2704-X

Typeset in Monophoto Photina by
Vision Typesetting, Manchester
Printed in Great Britain by
St Edmundsbury Press Ltd, Bury St Edmunds, Suffolk

To

The Rt Revd Lord Ramsey of Canterbury, PC, DD,
and
The Revd Mother Mary Clare, SLG,
with affection and gratitude

*DEUS auribus nostris audivimus: patres nostri
annuntiaverunt nobis: opus quod operatus es in diebus
eorum: et in diebus antiquis.*
(Psalm 44.1, 2)

*Memoriam fecit mirabilium suorum: misericors et
miserator DOMINUS; Escam dedit timentibus Se.*
(Psalm 111.4, 5)

CONTENTS

PART ONE
GLASTONBURY: AD 909–59

PART TWO
CANTERBURY: AD 960–88

PART THREE
THE LEGACY: AD 989–1023

ABBREVIATIONS

A/S   *Anglo-Saxon England*, ed. P. Clemoes *et al.* (Cambridge, 1972 onwards)

Ad   Adelard's 'Life of Dunstan', in *Memorials of St Dunstan* (MD)

ASC   *Anglo-Saxon Chronicle*, ed. C. Plummer (Oxford, 1892; 1952 edition)

ASE   *Anglo-Saxon England*, F.M. Stenton (Oxford, 3rd edition, 1971)

Asser   *Life of Alfred*, ed. W.H. Stevenson (Oxford, 1904; 1959 edition)

B   'Life of Dunstan' by the anonymous clerk 'B' in *Memorials of St Dunstan* (MD)

C&S   *Councils and Synods: 871–1216*, vol. I, ed. Whitelock, Brett and Brooke (Oxford, 1981)

CS   Camden Society publications

DNB   *Dictionary of National Biography*

DR   *Downside Review*

E   Eadmer's 'Life and Miracles of St Dunstan', in *Memorials of St Dunstan* (MD)

EETS   Early English Text Society

EHD   *English Historical Documents*, vol. I, ed. D. Whitelock (London, 2nd edition, 1979)

EHR   *English Historical Review*

FW   *Chronicle of Florence of Worcester*, ed. B. Thorpe (London, 1848–9)

GA   *The Golden Age of Anglo-Saxon Art*, ed. Backhouse, Turner and Webster (London, 1984)

H&S   *Councils and Ecclesiastical Documents*, ed. Haddan and Stubbs (Oxford, 1869)

HBS   Henry Bradshaw Society

HRH   *The Heads of Religious Houses in England and Wales: 940–1216*, ed. Knowles, Brooke and London (Cambridge, 1972)

HRS   Hampshire Record Society

JAR   *The Times of St Dunstan*, J. Armitage Robinson (Oxford, 1923)

JTS   *Journal of Theological Studies*

JW   *Chronicle of John of Wallingford*, ed. R. Vaughan, CS Miscellany, XXI (London, 1958)

LE   *Liber Eliensis*, ed. E.O. Blake, CS Third Series, XCII (London, 1962)

LVH   *Liber Vitae of Newminster and Hyde Abbey*, ed. W. de Gray Birch, HRS (1889)

MD   *Memorials of St Dunstan*, ed. W. Stubbs, Rolls Series, 63 (London, 1874)

MGH   *Monumenta Germaniae Historica*, ed. G. Pertz *et al.*). SS: *Scriptores*, vols I–XXXII; Epp: *Epistolae*, vols I–VII. (Hanover, 1826; Berlin, 1887)

MO   *Monastic Order*, D. Knowles (Cambridge, 2nd edition, 1966)

MS   Manuscript

O   Osbern's 'Life and Miracles of St Dunstan', in *Memorials of St Dunstan* (MD)

ODS   *Oxford Dictionary of Saints*, ed. D.H. Farmer (Oxford, 1978)

PL   *Patrologiae Cursus Completus, Series Latina*, ed. J.P. Migne (Paris, 1844–64)

RC   *Regularis Concordia*, ed. T. Symons (London, 1953)

RHS   Royal Historical Society

RS   Rolls Series

RSB   *Rule of St Benedict*, ed. and trans. Dom B. Bolton (Ealing Abbey, London, 1969)

S   Number of charter in *Anglo-Saxon Charters*, ed. P.H. Sawyer (London, 1968)

s.a.   *sub anno* (in the year of + date)

SD   *Chronicle of Symeon of Durham: 'Historia Regum'*, ed. T. Arnold, RS, vol. II (London, 1885)

TRHS   *Transactions of the Royal Historical Society*

VD   'Life of Dunstan'

VE   Aelfric's 'Life of Ethelwold'; English translation by D. Whitelock, EHD 235; Latin text in *Three Lives of English Saints*, ed. M. Winterbottom (Toronto, 1972)

Vg   Vulgate

VO   *Life of Oswald*, anon., ed. J. Raine, RS, vol. I (London, 1874)

WMDA   William of Malmesbury's *'De Antiquitate Glastonie Ecclesie'* ed. J. Scott (Boydell Press: Ipswich, 1981)

WMGP   William of Malmesbury's *'Gesta Pontificum'* ed. N. Hamilton, RS (London, 1870)

WMGR   William of Malmesbury's *'Gesta Regum'*, ed. W. Stubbs, RS (London, 1887–9)

WMVD   William of Malmesbury's *'Life of Dunstan'*, ed. W. Stubbs, MD (London, 1874)

FOREWORD BY THE ARCHBISHOP OF CANTERBURY

D UNSTAN was the Archbishop of Canterbury for 28 years, during a period when the foundations of the mediaeval English Church were being laid. It was his misfortune to be somewhat eclipsed, first by the Norman Conquest, then by the martyrdom of Thomas Becket. Though he was remembered as a saint throughout the middle ages, the historical significance of his life was all but lost sight of until Bishop Stubbs collected his 'memorials of St. Dunstan' for the Rolls Series, and published them with a masterly introduction in 1874. Since that time, there has been a wealth of study into the period between the death of Alfred the Great and the Norman Conquest. It is therefore appropriate that in preparation for the millennium of the death of Dunstan, in May 1988, a full-scale life of the Saint should now be available which sets him in the context of the Church and society of which he was part.

As we look back to life and events in our country a thousand years ago, we see many things emerging which were to exercise a profound influence. The unity of England was established, a reconciliation was effected between English and Danes, and more positive relations created with the Celtic peoples of Wales and Cornwall. Contacts with continental Europe, with what became France and Germany, and with Rome itself, tied England into the life of a wider world and Church; and the influences in art and learning and politics were reciprocal and fundamental. It is a time when the special relationship between Crown and Church was deepened and articulated in a way which persists until today; when the Church influenced law and justice in a Christian direction and spoke up for the poor and oppressed. Finally, the period is crowned by glorious and colourful works of art – illuminated manuscripts in particular – of music, and of architecture which attracted the admiration of Europe at the time.

For an English Christian to look into this period of our history is a deeply enriching experience. For we find men and women of great sanctity and learning who are also people of practical ability and sound common-sense. Theirs was a profoundly spiritual achievement, and at the heart of it lay a life of prayer and discipline which was the essence of the renewed Benedictine monasticism for which this period is justly famous. They too had a past to look back to, especially to the age of Bede, whose memory and example broods over the hopes and labours of this generation. For them, as for us, Christian history is very much the experience of a living past nurturing a living present.

I am deeply grateful to Douglas Dales for this comprehensively researched and elegantly written biography. I hope it does much to renew an interest in Dunstan and a period of English church history which has much more immediate lessons for our Christian life now than a thousand years' separation seems to suggest.

+ Robert Cantuar

PREFACE

THE translation and research for this book were accomplished in the two parishes in which I served as a curate, and especial thanks are due to the incumbents with whom I had the privilege of working, Canon Peter Ball, formerly rector of Shepperton, and Canon Neil Munt, formerly vicar of Ely, for the time and encouragement they afforded me in the midst of the relentless demands of parochial life. Thanks also must be expressed to the Rt Revd R.C.O. Goodchild, formerly the bishop of Kensington, and the Rt Revd P.K. Walker, the bishop of Ely, for their kindness and support for this venture. I should like also to thank the staff of the Bodleian Library in Oxford, and of the University Library in Cambridge, for their courtesy and assistance.

This book owes much indirectly to those who introduced me to the study of history: to those who taught me at St Dunstan's College, London, and at Christ Church, Oxford; and more particularly to the Revd Dr Henry Chadwick who, when dean of Christ Church, introduced me to the particular demands of ecclesiastical history. I am grateful too to my colleagues and pupils at Marlborough College for their interest and encouragement, especially to the late G. Kempson, and also to O. Ramsbottom and P. Horden for help with various stages of the text. I should like also to express my thanks to the Dean of Christ Church, the Very Revd E.W. Heaton, for his assistance and encouragement in the publication of this book; also to the Revd R.W. Daniels, and to Michael Murray for their interest and encouragement, and to David Game for his assiduous help as editor.

Finally, I must thank warmly my own parents for giving me a keen sense of the Church's mission in this country, past and present; and the Community of the Sisters of the Love of God in Oxford for their encouragement and support. Without the guidance and help of Sister Benedicta Ward, SLG, this study might never have been completed in time for the millennium of St Dunstan in 1988, and I am very much in her debt for her wisdom, scholarship and friendship. The last note of thanks must go to my dear wife, Geraldine, whose patience and good sense have been an unfailing inspiration.

Marlborough – Michaelmas 1987   *Douglas Dales*

TENTH-CENTURY REGNAL AND ARCHIEPISCOPAL LISTS

Kings of Wessex and of All England

Alfred the Great:	871–99
Edward the Elder:	899–924
Athelstan:	924–39
Edmund:	939–46
Eadred:	946–55
Edwy:	955–9
Edgar:	959–75
Edward the Martyr:	975–8
Ethelred the Unready:	978–1016
Edmund Ironside:	1016
Cnut:	1016–35

Archbishops of Canterbury

Plegmund: 890–923

Athelm: 923–5 (uncle of Dunstan)

Wulfhelm: 925–42

Oda the Good: 942–58 (uncle of Oswald)

Elfsige: 958–9 (nomination not confirmed)

Byrhthelm: 959 (nomination not confirmed)

Dunstan: 960–88

Aethelgar: 988–90

Sigeric: 990–4

Aelfric: 995–1005

Alphege the Martyr: 1005–12

Aethelstan Lyfing: 1013–20

Aethelnoth: 1020–38

PART ONE

GLASTONBURY:

AD 909–59

1

THE LEGACY OF ALFRED THE GREAT

D UNSTAN grew up in a kingdom, Wessex, whose shape and unity had been fashioned by Alfred the Great and his son, Edward the Elder. Within living memory, Alfred had faced his supreme crisis, when in 878 the marauding Vikings had descended upon Chippenham and driven him into flight. From that moment, the whole of Alfred's reign was dominated by twenty years of fighting back to regain his kingdom, to resist the Danes and to reassert the power and influence of Wessex over the English areas still free from Danish control. His son, Edward, carried the attack into the Danelaw: this was the area of England, roughly north of Watling Street, which was firmly under Danish control and undergoing extensive Danish settlement. After the decisive battle of Tettenhall in 909 (the likely year of Dunstan's birth), he brought all the southern Danelaw under his sway. Both kings adopted a clear policy of accommodation and reconciliation towards their new Danish subjects. This may well have been born of necessity; but in part at least it reflected a far-sighted and Christian policy.[1] Asser, for example, records how Alfred sealed his peace in 879 with Guthrum, the Danish leader, by baptising him, and how in due course Danish youths were educated for the Christian ministry at the king's religious foundation at Athelney.[2] Before Alfred's reign closed in 899, missionaries, probably from London and Canterbury, were at work converting the Danes of East Anglia to the Christian faith with considerable success. Around the figure of the martyred East Anglian king, Edmund, who died in 869, a cult sprang up at this time which appealed to both English and Danes in that region, a sign perhaps of their gradual reconciliation.[3]

Alfred's defence of the realm stimulated far-reaching reforms in the way Wessex was organised. His policy of *burghs*, fortified centres, spread evenly throughout the kingdom and dependent on local support, ensured that none of his people was out of reach of organised defence. They were strategically distributed by the king but actually defended by the local inhabitants, not always enthusiastically. Many of these places, for example Oxford and Winchester, became centres of trade and settlement in more peaceful times. Alfred's capture of London in 886 proved irreversible, and the city re-emerged as an important political and trading centre and also as a symbol of the new unity

3

between Wessex and Mercia. The creation of a small but powerful navy further enhanced the position of the king as the focus of military authority, and he committed the shires to its regular maintenance by taxation. The kings of Wessex also asserted strong control over their currency, using it as a means of exerting their authority over all the peoples under their rule. Finally, Alfred was remembered as a law giver. His concern to reiterate the laws of his predecessors in Wessex, Kent and Mercia, and to corroborate them by reference to the teaching of the Bible, demonstrated his conception of Christian kingship. For Alfred believed that a Christian king was in fact Christ's deputy on earth to further the standards of the kingdom of God, but was himself always subject directly to the judgement of God.

This reassertion of strong monarchy in England not only put the Danes on the defensive; it affected too the rulers of the adjacent Celtic lands, especially Wales and Cornwall. Beginning with Alfred's friend and biographer, Asser, who came from St Davids, contacts grew between England and the Celtic Churches. Asser himself records Alfred's generosity towards the Churches in Wales, Ireland and Brittany, and the king's personal devotion while in Cornwall.[4] The reputation of Alfred and Edward spread to the continent also. Regular embassies were sent to Rome, and towards the end of his reign Alfred's daughter married Baldwin II, lord of Flanders.[5] Edward the Elder, around the year 919, married his daughter in turn to Charles the Simple, king of the Franks.[6] Alfred in his childhood had experienced for himself life at the Frankish court and at Rome, and there is little doubt that contacts with the continent were as strong as the troubled circumstances of the period permitted.

Alfred's own commitment as a Christian king plunged him into the reform of the Church. In his view, the state of the Church was weak, and therefore both Church and kingdom were exposed to the judgement of God. The Viking assault had undermined the resolve of many, and the king deplored the decay in learning among many of the bishops and clergy whom he encountered.[7] From at least 838, the kings of Wessex had enjoyed a close working relationship with successive archbishops of Canterbury, however, and by the time of Alfred's reign the primate was in fact appointed by the king of Wessex.[8] Alfred set out to reinforce the role of the diocesan bishops and to spur them into action. Plegmund, whom Alfred appointed in 890 as archbishop of Canterbury, proved the mainstay of this reforming movement throughout the rest of Alfred's reign and that of Edward also; he died in 923.[9] He was a Mercian, 'wise and venerable', respected at home and abroad for his learning. The climax to his endeavours came in 910 when he divided the two Wessex sees of Winchester and Sherborne into five new bishoprics, more closely related to the shires they served: Crediton, Ramsbury and Wells thus came into existence, and Dunstan's uncle, Athelm, became the first bishop of Wells.[10]

The depth of Alfred's Christian commitment expressed itself also in the two religious houses which he founded at Athelney and Shaftesbury. Athelney proved a disaster. It was a lonely and unhappy place, filled with foreign clergy and led by John, a Saxon from Germany. Dogged by scandal, it nearly ended in tragedy, lingering on into the tenth century as an impoverished and insignificant house.[11] Shaftesbury fared better, however. It was a nunnery led by Alfred's own daughter, Aethelgifu, and it remained rich and strong throughout the tenth century.[12] This action of Alfred showed that he and probably some of his bishops regarded the revival of regular religious life as vital to the integrity and welfare of the Church as a whole.

The perennial and underlying weakness of Anglo-Saxon monasticism had always been the way in which the laity regained control of the monastic endowments.[13] It was perhaps inevitable that local families would regard land bequeathed to the Church as a spiritual extension of their own patrimony. This was most obviously true with regard to the parish churches which were beginning to be founded, built and maintained at this time by the local thegns. But it was true also of the older 'minsters', and appointing members of their own kindred to preside as 'abbots' and senior clergy of these ostensibly religious communities reinforced this proprietorial view. The widespread marriage of clergy introduced a further hereditary dimension: their offspring claiming succession to the endowments of the Church. Thus in the minds of reformers and idealists, notably Bede himself, the integrity and spiritual vitality of the Church was continually entrammelled by this 'lay dominion'. Yet tackling this widespread problem effectively posed a real political and psychological challenge.

After Alfred's death, Edward maintained the impetus and founded the New Minster at Winchester according to his father's wishes. This was a royal religious house of clerics, but not a monastery as such. At the same time, Alfred's widow, Eahlswith, founded the Nunnaminster there, and a daughter of Edward, called Edburga, resided there, leaving a reputation of sanctity. Other daughters of the king were remembered as nuns at Wilton and Romsey, and in general the nunneries of Wessex persisted under royal patronage as signs of real continuity with the earlier period of English monasticism.[14] But the two foundations at Winchester confirmed the growing importance of that city as the emerging centre of renewed church life in the early part of the tenth century.[15]

A remarkable feature of Alfred's commitment to the reform of the Church was the way in which he personally contributed to the revival of learning and education in England. He was himself largely self-educated as an adult, and he always lamented his own lack of early and formal education.[16] His biographer, Asser, paints a vivid picture of the king's labours in this regard, and Asser was just one of the scholars from outside Wessex whom Alfred attracted to his court. The king found at Worcester in western Mercia a living tradition of English learning in the figure of Bishop Werferth; and from that bishop's *familia* came learned clergy to assist the king – Athelstan, Werwulf and Plegmund himself.[17] From overseas, and after much negotiation, the king secured Grimbald, a monk from St Bertin's in Flanders, who brought with him John the Saxon who ended up at Athelney.[18] Around Grimbald the germ of a community grew up at Winchester which formed the basis for the foundation of the New Minster.[19]

The tangible result of the king's labours, in concert with his learned helpers, is found in the collection of books translated from Latin into English at this time. The king himself was instrumental in translating the 'Pastoral care' of Gregory the Great, also Boethius' *Consolation of Philosophy*, and some of the *Soliloquies* of Augustine, together with the first third of the psalter. The last three works were clearly of personal value for the king; but the first, the 'Pastoral care', the king intended for his bishops, and copies were circulated for diocesan use.[20] In addition to these texts, the king instigated the translation by Bishop Werferth of Worcester of the *Dialogues* of Gregory the Great. The *Dialogues* include the hagiography of St Benedict, whose rule and cult were the pivot upon which the subsequent renewal of monasticism in the tenth century turned.

Two other works of an historical nature were also translated into English under the king's aegis: Orosius' *Histories*, and Bede's *Ecclesiastical History*. To these may perhaps be added also a leechbook (a medical text), and also a martyrology, which was a register and brief history of selected Christian martyrs, compiled for liturgical use.[21] The purpose of this programme was to make available basic Christian texts to Englishmen in their own language, as the foundation for their education and as a spur to learning Latin. To this end, the king set up schools, one certainly in his own household for his children and for the offspring of the nobility. Literacy was indispensable for good government as well, and throughout the tenth century written documents came to be used more and more as instruments of administration. It is quite likely that the wealth which Alfred bestowed on existing religious houses was used in part for educational purposes, and the 'school' at Glastonbury to which Dunstan went in his youth may well have been revitalised at this time. Certainly the royal policy of educating young men for the service of Church and state was firmly established in the opening years of the tenth century as a consequence of Alfred's foresight and the policy of his heirs.[22]

The translation of Orosius and of Bede reflect also Alfred's interest in history. The way in which the writing of history developed at Winchester at this time, which produced the earliest versions of the *Anglo-Saxon Chronicle*, may well reflect both the influence of the king and the hand of Grimbald of St Bertin's. There is, for example, a somewhat dynastic element in the chronicle, asserting the history of the royal house of Wessex and Alfred's own claim to the throne. There is also a significant component of contemporary continental history, drawn from Frankish sources; and this suggests that Grimbald and his circle may have been emulating earlier ninth-century Frankish history writing. The purpose of the chronicle was both to record contemporary events, often in a dramatic manner, and to place contemporary English history within the long perspective of both national and Christian history. Like Bede, scholars at this time tended to interpret current history in the light of the impending judgement of God and in the light of the Old Testament, using the books of Kings especially as a practical model. The moral aspect of history was coupled to a genuine fascination with the past and to a sense of providence and ancestry.[23]

One of the most important consequences of Alfred's reforms was the flowering of the arts that began to occur early in the tenth century. This was the foundation for all that was accomplished later, and it helps to account for the sophisticated artistic education enjoyed by young men like Dunstan and Ethelwold at Glastonbury and Winchester.

The few surviving manuscripts of Alfred's reign are poor in terms of illumination; they are distinguished by the new and deliberate style of handwriting used. Such rudimentary drawing as occurs looks back to much earlier styles. But by the turn of the tenth century, the first stirrings of continental influences may be detected in manuscripts from places like Worcester and Winchester. However, the reigns of Alfred and Edward saw brilliant artistry in metalwork and jewellery, of which the famous Alfred jewel is the most outstanding example. In all of this artistic influences from the continent are manifest; so too is an interest in complex iconography expressed in elaborate decoration, a feature found also in the stone and ivory carving of the period. Perhaps the most marvellous survival from this time is the embroidery found in the tomb of St Cuthbert at Durham, which comes from Winchester and was carried out early in the second decade of the tenth century. These vestments reflect the richness and intricacy of ecclesiastical taste at that time, and are a unique memorial to all that has since been lost. 'Few as these artistic survivals are, they already indicate the directions in which the subsequent course of Late Saxon art was to go, up to and even beyond the Conquest. Thus Alfred and his successors participated in the creation of one of the greatest and most individual phases of English art.'[24] Throughout the tenth century the artistic and intellectual developments mirror the changes in Church and society almost exactly.

Dunstan therefore grew up as the heir to a strong tradition, and his early life and education were moulded by a clear royal and ecclesiastical policy. The life of the Church in tenth-century England was on the one hand highly traditional, drawing heavily on the past whilst seeking to impose the values and principles of that Christian past upon the present. But, on the other hand, it was also radically clear-sighted, and the policy of bishops and archbishops for 120 years after the death of Alfred was constant and on the whole single-minded. Their goal was the reform of the Church so that a thoroughly Christian society might be created. The revival of monasticism was an instrument of this overall policy; it proved a crucial and a momentous development. Art and culture became the medium through which these Christian values and this over-riding vision were expressed.

At the same time, the life of the Church was deeply rooted in politics. Bishops and archbishops frequently lived longer than kings: they were often political survivors with considerable influence in the king's witan, or council, and also in the localities. As such they were partners, and at times rivals, of the landed nobility in whose hands the good order of the kingdom lay. The laity valued the Church for the spiritual intercessions it could bring to bear upon the normal uncertainties of human life. Against a background of almost continual warfare and the natural brevity of life, the Church was a refuge and sign of more permanent things. The problem for reforming churchmen was to prevent the Church from becoming absorbed in the wrong way into the lay society which it served and upon which it so completely depended. Thus the education of the clergy and the endowment of monasteries were seen as tangible ways of safeguarding the integrity of the Church's spiritual life for more than just one generation.

The fact that a king of Wessex had taken so personal an interest in the welfare and reform of the English Church left an indelible mark upon the ecclesiastical expectations of the monarchy. The profound partnership between kingship and episcopacy stimulated the flowering of a Christian vision of monarchy and society which is peculiar to this period. This theory of Christian kingship, interpreted in the light of episcopacy, developed in England and on the continent throughout the tenth century. It was rooted in earlier English tradition and in the customs and writings of the Carolingian kings and their bishops on the continent in the ninth century, and it was couched in biblical language. As a consequence, the bishops, and especially the archbishops of Canterbury, stood at the heart of the political and judicial process. But at the same time, the English bishops were the nominees of the king. In the light of the later quarrels of the eleventh century, the Investiture contests between secular rulers and the Church's hierarchy, this marriage of secular and spiritual seemed a naïve anachronism. But in the tenth century in England there was no formal separation between Church and state.

The framework for this remarkable ecclesiastical, political and cultural development was a profoundly religious one, a spiritual perspective shared by all people of any education, both clergy and laity. The sense of the past was cultivated to show how the present age also fell under the judgement of God. His divine law stood unchanged, to condemn or to encourage. The turbulence of the times was a sign that the end was at hand. Sincere piety and reform of life, by individuals and by society, would safeguard against evil and prepare men for the final test. This prognosis was not always gloomy; it could inculcate hope, bred from a godly fear. The way of Christ offered an eternal reward, and a way of living in a time of trials in which human existence felt precarious, and culture and order seemed transient and always under threat.

In the light of such vicissitudes, tangible and psychological, the achievements of the tenth century, political, cultural and ecclesiastical, were remarkable and lasting. For it was in this century that the foundations of medieval English Church and society were laid. The life, personality and work of Dunstan emerge at the focus of this whole development.

2

ORITUR PUER STRENUUS

*D*UNSTAN was born around the year 909 near Glastonbury. Earlier historians, including those responsible for the later traditions inserted into the chronicle and the post-conquest biographers of Dunstan himself, took the assertion in the first life of the saint that he 'sprang to light' in the time of Athelstan to mean that he was born when that king began to rule.[1] However, John of Wallingford, a later medieval historian, protested vigorously that to place Dunstan's birth in or around the year 924 made a mockery of the subsequent chronology of his life.[2] The description 'sprang to light' makes more sense if it is taken to mean that Dunstan emerged into the public eye at the court of Athelstan as a young man of promise in the early part of that king's reign, and this conclusion would fit well the testimony of the two earliest biographers.[3]

He was born most probably at Baltonsborough, which lies five miles from Glastonbury, in sight of the Tor. There Dunstan's family owned land, and local tradition affirms that he maintained a lifelong association with his birthplace. The parish church was later dedicated to him, and there is a ditch skirting the village which is said to have been built at Dunstan's behest when he was abbot of Glastonbury. Since 745, Baltonsborough had been the property of the religious foundation at Glastonbury, as it remained until the Reformation.

Dunstan's parents were Heorstan and Cynethrith, and he had at least one brother, Wulfric, who later became the reeve of the Glastonbury estates and a member of the court of Edmund and Eadred.[4] Heorstan's brother was Athelm, the first bishop of the nearby see of Wells and later archbishop of Canterbury. Alphege, bishop of Winchester, called 'the Bald', was a kinsman of Dunstan; so too was Kinsige, bishop of Lichfield. Other kinsmen were among the courtiers of Athelstan who were later to make Dunstan's life at court a misery.[5] It is quite possible, as the later biographers claim, that his family was connected to the royal house in some way. Certainly Edgar's family had roots near Glastonbury, and Edgarsley, a village nearby, was even asserted by John of Wallingford to be the birthplace of Dunstan.[6] Edmund Bishop, in a letter to Dean Armitage Robinson, sums up the family of Dunstan thus: 'It is a family of business, . . . connected by some sort of relationship, however remote, with the kingly line. It is a perfect network. Just this one family: and holding close together. They must

9

have been a capable, a "strong-minded", but also a "having" race.'[7] In short, his was a significant but perhaps typical local landed family, enjoying close connections with the western residence of the royal court at Cheddar, whose forebears may have been among the immediate retinue of Alfred when he was based at Athelney, hard-pressed by the Vikings, in the winter of 878.

Adelard, the second biographer, tells how Dunstan 'sprang forth from holy parents', and recounts a miracle in connection with his birth. His parents were in church, presumably at Glastonbury, for the feast of Candlemas (the Presentation of the Child Jesus in the Temple, on 2 February), and Cynethrith was pregnant. It was an evening vigil service with lights, and suddenly all the candles were blown out. New fire descended upon Cynethrith's taper and from it light was rekindled throughout the church. Thus, in popular memory, was Dunstan's significance illuminated even while he was still in the womb of his mother.[8] On another occasion, according to the first biographer, Heorstan took Dunstan on one of his regular visits to the shrine at Glastonbury. They went by boat and stayed overnight. While he was asleep, Dunstan, who was still a child, had a vision of an old man in snow-white robes who led him through the beautiful narthex to the old church and into the monastic buildings, all of which he, Dunstan, was to build in the future when abbot of Glastonbury. Meanwhile, Dunstan grew up 'and was cherished by God and men'.[9]

Glastonbury clearly exercised a profound fascination over the minds and spiritual lives of Dunstan's contemporaries. The first biographer describes it as a 'royal island',

> spacious and undulating, surrounded by sluggish rivers whose waters are well-stocked with fish, fit to serve many human needs, and best of all consecrated to sacred offices. It was there that the first (English) converts to the Christian religion discovered, with God's guidance, an ancient church, not built (they say) by human skill, but prepared by God Himself for human salvation. Later the Maker of Heaven proved by many miracles and sacred mysteries that He had consecrated it to Himself, and to Mary the holy Mother of God.[10]

In due time, men built there another 'oratory of stone which they dedicated to Christ and to His apostle, St Peter'.[11]

The antiquity of Glastonbury as a religious and monastic site has been confirmed by archaeology in recent times. Traces have been found of the earliest cemetery, with surrounding buildings made of wattle and later enclosed by a *vallum*, or bank, along known Celtic monastic patterns. All these antedate the earliest Anglo-Saxon buildings. The outline of the subsequent church, built by King Ine of Wessex in the seventh century and dedicated to St Peter, has also been discovered. It is assumed that it was linked to the old church, which was built of wattle and dedicated to St Mary. Inscribed crosses from around 700 have been found, with names on them from that period.[12]

William of Malmesbury, in his work 'Antiquities of Glastonbury', which together with his 'Life of Dunstan' was commissioned by the twelfth-century monks of Glastonbury, established a succession of Anglo-Saxon 'abbots' from the time of Ine.[13] The existence of Glastonbury in the eighth century as a religious community is alluded to in the letters of Boniface and in Willibald's life of that saint.[14] Although the existing early charters of Glastonbury are suspect, the tradition of ancient and royal endowment which they represent is supported by the contents of the tenth-century 'Liber terrarum', or land book, to which William of Malmesbury refers.[15] Moreover, the tenth-century chronicler,

Ethelweard, records under the year 866 that Eanwulf, ealdorman of Somerset, and Eahlstan, bishop of Sherborne, who both died that year, were buried at Glastonbury.[16] Alfred gave to Glastonbury, it was claimed, a fragment of the true cross from Pope Marinus,[17] and Athelstan's later devotion indicates the continued importance of Glastonbury as a royal shrine. It was probably under direct royal protection at the time of Dunstan's upbringing and was a popular centre of pilgrimage.[18]

Glastonbury drew pilgrims not only from the west Saxon lands, but also from further afield, notably from Ireland. In those days it was still virtually an island, and for a long time it had enjoyed contact by sea with south Wales, Ireland and even the Mediterranean.[19] By the time of Dunstan, it was believed that the younger St Patrick was buried there, together with the Celtic saints Indracht and Benignus. By the middle of the tenth century, Brigid too was commemorated along with Gildas, the fifth-century historian; and the relics of the Northumbrian saints beloved of Bede, Aidan and Ceolfrid, were believed to lie at Glastonbury.[20] By the time of William of Malmesbury, St David and the great Patrick himself had been drawn into the monastery's cult of its own remote past. The Irish connection was certainly ancient and strong, for there is in a ninth-century Irish martyrology a reference to 'Glastonbury of the Gaels', and in the earliest Glastonbury charters texts from the Irish version of the Latin Bible are cited.[21] The archaeological evidence for the earliest religious settlement at Glastonbury indicates a Celtic pattern, and Ine's own endowment in the seventh century presupposes an existing community.[22] There was also an ancient tradition that Paulinus, the first missionary bishop of York, had restored the ancient wattle church.[23]

The first biographer of St Dunstan records that the Irish pilgrims brought with them many books, and that Dunstan himself derived much of his education from them.[24] Such early literary remains as exist from this period of Glastonbury's history confirm the presence of Irish learning. For example, the so-called 'Liber Sancti Dunstani' contains a great collection of Irish canons added to apostolic canons and early decretals, and was compiled at the time of Dunstan, probably from existing material at Glastonbury.[25] St Dunstan's Classbook, another tenth-century text from Glastonbury, famous for its association with Dunstan, contains numerous Celtic elements and draws extensively on the British text of the Bible. It contains also some of the earliest written specimens of Welsh.[26] 'It was the peculiar lot of Glastonbury to be more thoroughly and successfully exposed to Celtic influences than any other English abbey.'[27]

Glastonbury, therefore, at the time of Dunstan's upbringing was a 'royal island', probably in the king's gift and protection.[28] Its 'abbots' may even have been laymen: Guthlac, Cuthred and Ecgwulf were the 'abbots' under whom Dunstan grew up.[29] It was still, however, a religious community, a familia of clergy who served the ancient church and the many pilgrims who journeyed there. Among these pilgrims were Irish scholars of the type who might be found all over Europe at this time. They added their own learned resources to the existing library at Glastonbury, and probably provided education for the young men attached to the foundation.[30] Athelm of Wells was said to have been educated at Glastonbury, also his successor, Wulfhelm; both men became archbishops of Canterbury.[31] Above all, Glastonbury was a place of strong and ancient spiritual tradition. It was believed to be under the direct protection of heaven itself. It was an island of visions, where men stood in the awe of God and his saints whose relics were enshrined in the fabric of a building believed to be of heavenly creation, and a mysterious sign of the obscure but potent origins of Christianity in Britain.[32]

Dunstan's parents 'set him free for the study of learning', the first steps of which he pursued under the shadow of the old church at Glastonbury. He soon revealed his aptitude for study, and his sharp mind singled him out from his contemporaries.[33] There must, therefore, have been some form of primary education available there, and Adelard envisages him in the tutelage of a nurse at this stage of his life.[34] His progress was such that in due time, perhaps around the age of 12, his parents formally associated him with the community at Glastonbury, and he received the tonsure by way of admission to minor clerical orders. 'Bound thus by divine discipline, he continued there for a long time in the service of God, and of Mary the Mother of God.'[35]

Already his promise and abilities had not gone unnoticed at court,[36] and Dunstan's education fits the pattern laid down by Alfred of training able young men to sustain the government of the country. The resources available to him at Glastonbury were by no means meagre, and the first biographer uses a familiar metaphor by comparing Dunstan to a bee 'coursing over the many fields of sacred and religious volumes'.[37] These were probably biblical texts and commentaries, some patristic writings, law books and penitentials. The Irish wandering scholars who sojourned at Glastonbury had a great influence on Dunstan's education:[38]

> Dunstan diligently studied their books also, meditating on the path of
> the true faith, and always exploring with a critical scrutiny the books
> of other wise men, whose teaching he perceived from the deep vision
> of his heart to be confirmed by the traditions of the holy fathers.[39]

Among these would almost certainly be collections of Irish canons and saints' lives, as well as grammatical and arithmetical material such as that found in *St Dunstan's Classbook*. The first biographer records also how Dunstan perfected the art of calligraphy, and one of the last pictures he paints is of the old archbishop correcting manuscripts at the first light of dawn.[40] He tells too how Dunstan was skilled in design and painting, a craftsman in jewellery and metalwork, and a lover and accomplished performer of both music and poetry.[41] All these gifts must have been nurtured initially at Glastonbury.

In the midst of his studies at Glastonbury, Dunstan faced the first serious trial of his life. According to the earliest biographer, this occurred before he actually took minor orders in the community gathered around the old church. He fell ill for some time with a severe fever, a condition common enough in a place surrounded by undrained fens. It halted his studies and apparently reduced him to the point of death. One night, in his delirium, he arose from his bed, grabbed a stick, and waving it in the air made his way to the old church. He climbed up a ladder left there by some workmen and ascended to the pinnacle of the roof. By divine providence, it was believed, he descended safely to a place within the church, and was found in the morning, curled up asleep between two porters. When he awoke, he remembered nothing of his perilous journey, yet the heavy doors of the church had remained fast shut. In the hands of the later biographers, this story received considerable elaboration, but in the first life it is told as a simple tale of a rather remarkable passage by a youngster who in the midst of sickness had discovered the reality of divine protection. The moral drawn, either by the biographer or by Dunstan himself, was that humble trust in God, proven in the midst of suffering, was the only sure road through the obstacles placed by men; in words echoing the psalmist: 'Let humble patience arise, and may pride collapse.'[42]

It is clear that Dunstan's early spiritual formation at Glastonbury was profound and real. His upbringing in a devout family rendered him sensitive and receptive to childhood faith and vision. 'As he grew more accustomed to the praises of God, so he grew more single-minded in perseverance with his soul.'[43]

To be in minor orders at Glastonbury at that time meant observing the regular round of offices and services, the 'divine praises' just mentioned. It was a relatively disciplined life, dedicated to the service of God and of the Virgin. As Dunstan grew older, 'he grew more fervent in his love for God'. From the Irish visitors he learnt an austere and contemplative Christianity, the Celtic religion so sensitively and vividly portrayed by Bede and elaborated in the lives of the saints. Within this tradition, the sense of the reality and nearness of heaven and hell, visions of saints and a tangible sense of evil in the form of temptations were commonplace, and all these can be found in the later spiritual life of Dunstan. Nevertheless, the formation of his spiritual life was disciplined not only by ascetical practices but also by his studies. 'He so controlled his way of life that as often as he examined the books of Divine Scripture, God spoke with him; and as often as he was released from secular cares to delight in leisure for prayer, he seemed himself to speak with God.'[44]

3

AT THE COURT OF
ATHELSTAN

A THELSTAN was crowned by Archbishop Athelm, the uncle of Dunstan, at Kingston upon Thames on 4 September 925, a little over a year after the death of his father, Edward the Elder. Dunstan went to Athelstan's court for his further education and his experience there proved to be a formative and lasting influence on his life. The achievements of Athelstan, and the rich cultural life fostered at his court, were the immediate background to Dunstan's youth and personal formation.

Athelstan was regarded as the favourite grandson of Alfred the Great. He had been educated in Mercia,[1] and the support which he enjoyed from that part of his kingdom proved crucial to the extension of his power throughout the whole of Britain. The friendship which he cultivated towards his Danish subjects made him in many ways the architect of the unity of England.[2] The death in 926 of Sihtric, king of York, to whom Athelstan was allied by marriage, provoked a rebellion in the north which the new king of Wessex put down vigorously. He captured York in 927, and secured the submission of Northumbria and a recognition of his supremacy from the northern kings. In 934, he conducted a successful campaign against Scotland, supported by the earls of the Danelaw. But in 937, Olaf, the Viking king of Dublin, led a confederacy of the northern kings against Athelstan, invading his domains but meeting defeat at the Battle of Brunanburgh. This was a costly but decisive victory, won by Athelstan and his brother Edmund at the head of an army composed of west Saxons and Mercians. According to the chronicler: 'Never yet in this island was a greater slaughter of a host made by the edge of the sword since the Angles and Saxons came hither from the east, overcame the British, and so won a country.'[3]

Athelstan continued the policy of his father and grandfather towards the Welsh princes. He secured their allegiance at Hereford within the first five years of his reign, and thereafter they appeared at his court as regular signatories to his charters. Hywel the Good, king of Dyfed, became a friend, and imitated Athelstan by issuing silver coins and promulgating a complete code of law. He lived until 950, and during his reign intercourse between the Welsh Church and England became firmly established. The settlement with the Welsh freed

15

Athelstan to subdue Cornwall and to expel the British from Exeter, turning it into a royal fortress.[4]

'In character and cast of mind, Athelstan is the one West Saxon king who will bear comparison with Alfred.'[5] The charters describe him as *monarchus* or *basileus* of Angles, Saxons and Danes. The contemporary chroniclers hail him as the 'glory of his country', and 'dispenser of treasure to men'.[6] Nonetheless, like Alfred, he faced threats of opposition from within his own house, and so most of his courts were held in Wessex. Thither magnates and allies from the north, east and west would come. These, together with the bishops, would corroborate Athelstan's numerous laws and witness his charters, which were being written in an increasingly standard and florid form by the king's clerks. The king's personal influence may be detected in the note of leniency towards the young which enters his codes of law, which are otherwise marked by their severity, especially towards the endemic problem of theft. Athelstan thus depended upon and secured the loyalty and active support of his bishops and leading ealdormen for the governance of his newly enlarged kingdom, and for the maintenance of its precarious unity. Regular attendance at court, a real delegation of government and sustained military activity were the means by which this unity was achieved.[7]

Athelstan's reputation extended far outside the British Isles. He inherited an alliance with the counts of Flanders, which derived from the marriage of Aelfthryth, the daughter of Alfred the Great, to Baldwin II in the closing years of the ninth century. A little later, Eadgifu, the daughter of Edward the Elder, had married Charles the Simple, king of the western Franks. Both these alliances were sustained by ties of kinship and trade and by a common desire to limit Viking settlement along the shores of the English Channel. After the death of Charles the Simple, in 929, his exiled son, Louis d'Outremer, came to England for education and protection. In 926, Hugh, duke of the Franks, proposed a marriage alliance with Athelstan by the hand of Adelolf, count of Boulogne, the king's cousin; in that year Athelstan's sister, Eadhild, was duly given in marriage overseas and became Hugh's wife.[8]

The presence of the Carolingian heir in England and Athelstan's close friendship with Flanders prompted Henry the Fowler, king of the Germans, to secure an alliance with England by means of marriage in 928. Two further sisters of Athelstan were sent: Edith married Henry's son, Otto, who later became the first German emperor; the other sister probably married Conrad, king of Burgundy. English links with the German kingdom of the east were thus opened up, and these remained strong and important throughout the tenth century. Athelstan's involvement on the continent became more tangled after the return of Louis as king of the western Franks in 936. In the year of Athelstan's death, 939, the English sent a fleet to support Louis (ineffectually as it turned out) against Otto in a dispute over Lotharingia.

Athelstan was the protector too of Alan Twisted-beard, the heir of the ruling house of Brittany. In 919 the Vikings had invaded Brittany, expelling many of the leading inhabitants to England. There was an abortive rising in 931. But in 936 Athelstan successfully supported the return of his godson to his hereditary domains in Vannes and Nantes. Alan's reputation as a warrior, together with the size of the English fleet, probably deterred any incursions by the Vikings newly settled in Normandy. Indeed, Athelstan enjoyed good relations with Harold, king of Norway. The king sought his alliance by means of a handsome embassy while Athelstan was sojourning at York, and later in the reign he sent his youngest son, Hakon, to the English court for his education.[9]

These formal ties of diplomacy and kindred mark a pattern of English relations with the continent which remained constant and influential throughout the tenth century. The traffic was two-way. For example, the prior of St Samson's at Dol, in Brittany, wrote to Athelstan for help in the midst of turmoil, reminding him of his father's friendship for their house.[10] German clergy existed at Abingdon, London and Winchester, and it was during Athelstan's reign that the Carolingian minuscule handwriting used on the continent first appeared in England.[11] When Athelstan's brother, Edwin, died at sea, possibly in flight after a failed revolt, the monks of St Bertin's in Flanders buried him, earning Athelstan's gratitude.[12] The most striking example of English ecclesiastical contact with the continent at this time was the visit of Bishop Cenwald of Worcester to the German monasteries of St Gall, Pfäffers and Reichenau. He came bearing generous gifts, as part of a pilgrimage 'throughout all the monasteries of Germany'. He secured the prayers of each community for Athelstan and leading members, clerical and lay, of his court.[13] There is a poem to Athelstan, modelled on one addressed earlier to Charlemagne, from a Frankish admirer; and a tradition that Gregory, later abbot of Einsiedeln, was an 'Englishman of royal descent' may perhaps be connected in some way with this important visitation by English churchmen to such strong centres of Carolingian learning and architecture.[14]

Patronage of foreign churches was part of Athelstan's generosity towards the Church, for which he had a reputation in England in the early Middle Ages second to none. His conquest of Cornwall enabled him to put the care of the Cornish Church on a proper footing. Soon after 926, he endowed the see of St Germans and placed it under the care of a Celtic bishop, Conan. It received financial and moral support from the see of Crediton for most of the tenth century. This was an example of Athelstan's statesmanship, whereby 'kings of the old-English line exercised far-reaching powers of resumption, which enabled them when they saw fit to redistribute the endowments of the church'.[15] It was during his reign that the body of Edmund, the martyr-king of East Anglia, was translated to the church at Bury St Edmunds. This was done by Theodred, bishop of London, who had the care of East Anglia, with an episcopal centre at Hoxne in Suffolk. He, together with the ealdorman Athelstan, popularly called the half-king of East Anglia, built up the faith of the recently converted East Anglian Danes into a Church which was in no way 'behind the rest of England in piety and zeal' by the middle of the tenth century.[16]

William of Malmesbury remembered Athelstan as a generous benefactor of that house, and Milton claimed him as its founder. There are genuine land grants by the king to the churches at Crediton, York, Shaftesbury, Sherborne, Wilton and Winchester. Glastonbury, too, claimed gifts from Athelstan directly, and from his leading thegns: 'the generosity of his household testifies to his pious affection for Glastonbury', wrote William.[17] On his two great journeys north, Athelstan emulated the devotion of his grandfather towards the cult of St Cuthbert by making lavish gifts to the community that guarded his relics at Chester-le-Street. These included a missal, two gospels 'adorned with gold and silver' and a 'Life of St Cuthbert' in metre and prose, the last of which may well have been written at Glastonbury. In the Durham *Liber vitae*, or register of benefactors, Athelstan is given pride of place.[18] An Irish gospel book, now at Lambeth, affords a direct link between Athelstan and Maelbrighde of Armagh, a leading Irish scholar who died in 927, and it was possibly his gift to a king whom the Ulster annalist describes as 'the pillar of dignity of the western world'. Christ Church and St Augustine's, the two religious communities at Canterbury, and also the abbey at Bath, owned handsome volumes which were the king's own gifts, and Winchester possessed the Athelstan Psalter.[19]

'King Athelstan has a unique record among monarchs as a collector of relics.'[20] The letter from Dol in Brittany accompanied relics, 'which we know you value more than earthly treasure' – the bones of SS Senator, Paternus and Scabillion, which were later divided between the religious houses at Milton and Malmesbury. Devotion to the Breton saints came in the wake of the refugees from Brittany in the early tenth century, who left lasting memorials in southern Wessex and Winchester. The later monastery of Westminster claimed relics from the Holy Land, of the apostles, of the Lord himself and of sundry martyrs, all of which came from Athelstan's *haligdom*, or collection of relics. Glastonbury, Abingdon and Winchester all made similar claims. The relic list brought by the embassy of Hugh, duke of the Franks, in 926 gives the best impression of Athelstan's taste in this matter and of the intimate association of these relics with Christian sacral kingship, to which contemporaries drew attention by comparing Athelstan with Charlemagne. The list includes the sword of Constantine, the lance of Charlemagne, the standard of Maurice of the Theban legion, a portion of the true cross and a portion of the crown of thorns.[21]

Such was the court in which Dunstan grew up and was educated. There was a definite cultural and educational programme underway at the court of Athelstan, which was built upon Alfred's provision of a royal 'school'.[22] It drew heavily upon ninth-century Carolingian resources from the continent as Athelstan's reputation and links abroad grew. A group of manuscripts emanating from the court of Athelstan testifies to a small but effective circle of royal *capellani*, or chaplains and clerks, not unlike their continental counterparts at the court of Otto, who 'accompanied their royal master whilst retaining a close relationship with the cathedrals where they had been educated or served, and where they often still held benefices'.[23] Such were Oda, Alphege and Beornstan, the royal 'mass priests' whose signatures are on some of the early charters of Athelstan's reign and who in due course became bishop of Ramsbury, Wells and Winchester respectively; likewise the 'monks' Cenwald and Alphege the Bald, who duly became the bishops of Worcester and Winchester respectively. To these may be added Theodred of London who, with Alphege of Winchester, became an influential prelate at the court of Athelstan and his successors.

Contacts with Germany brought Carolingian models of art and calligraphy into England and these are reflected in the illumination and book writing at Winchester and Worcester at this time. Malmesbury and Glastonbury also flourished as centres of art and learning.[24] From Germany, early in the tenth century, had come the reintroduction of Aldhelm's works into England. Aldhelm was a scholar at Malmesbury at the time of Bede and a man of wide learning. His book, 'On virginity', had great influence in tenth-century church life, especially among the monks. Its reintroduction into England therefore had profound implications both for church life and for stimulating the so-called 'hermeneutic style' of Latin, a style of writing at once florid and recondite which dominated the English scholars of the tenth century. All this, and perhaps more yet unknown, 'was a rich source of the tenth-century intellectual revival: Athelstan's court seems to stand at the centre of a web of learning'. Here an Irish bishop of Bangor could meet a Frankish scholar and a Roman Jew, both renowned for their learning in the gospels.[25] The education of Dunstan and Ethelwold, and others before them like Oda, who became bishop of Ramsbury and then primate in 942, was part of a policy stretching from Alfred to Athelstan to provide the theological, liturgical and intellectual foundations both of their kingdom and of the life and vitality of the Church.

Dunstan's uncle, Athelm, succeeded Plegmund as archbishop of Canterbury in 923. He was formerly bishop of Wells, consecrated there on the division of the two west Saxon dioceses in 909 under Edward. Like his immediate successor, Wulfhelm, who followed him to Canterbury in 926, he was probably educated at Glastonbury. The most notable act of his brief primacy – the coronation of Athelstan in 925 – is confirmed by a charter issued on the day of the ceremony in favour of St Augustine's, Canterbury.[26] According to the second biographer, the monk Adelard, Dunstan, aged perhaps about 14, went to join his uncle on his succession to Canterbury and to live in his *familia* there. One of Athelm's last acts was to introduce his nephew to the court of the new king for his wider education as a courtier.[27] The court was peripatetic, sojourning often in the south west where both Wells and Glastonbury were very close to the royal hunting lodge at Cheddar.[28] Dunstan at court would not necessarily have been far from home, nor would his connection with the clerical community at Glastonbury have been severed. Indeed, his learned and spiritual proclivities seem to have separated him early from some of his peers. Nonetheless, there is a glimpse of Dunstan's life at court in a letter to him at the end of his life from Abbo of Fleury, commending to him a version of the '*Passion of St Edmund*', which Abbo had heard from Dunstan and which he had just put into writing:

> You said then that as a lad you heard the story from a very old man
> who was telling it to king Athelstan. He had been, he said, with king
> Edmund as his armour-bearer on the day he suffered as a martyr.
> You were so struck with the old man's description that you remem-
> bered every detail. He had given it very simply, you said, and in a
> way that carried conviction: it brought tears to your eyes.[29]

At court too, Dunstan learnt the art of poetry, the singing of lays to the harp and the glories and history of his people. This was soon turned against him, however, by his enemies, who accused him of seeking occult knowledge, the magic of the not too distant pagan past![30]

Dunstan seems to have been the victim of a prolonged vendetta conducted by 'some of his own friends and fellow-courtiers, even some of his own kinsfolk'.[31] According to the first biographer, he persisted in the face of hostility for some time. The premature death of his uncle may not have helped his position, though he was not without friends at court. There exists a poem he wrote to and in praise of Wulfhelm, the new archbishop of Canterbury; and Alphege, his kinsman, who signed himself 'priest and monk' at the coronation, remained in favour, becoming bishop of Winchester in 934.[32] Dunstan's brother, Wulfric, and his kinsman, Kinesige, were probably older contemporaries with him at court.[33] Dunstan could ignore animosity; but he could not conceal his ability, nor could he evade the machinations and rivalries of a court full of young men of ambition and connection. They 'incriminated him with some false accusation before the king', seeking his expulsion from court, and before any decision could be taken they took the law into their own hands and tipped Dunstan 'trussed like a patient sheep into a swampy hog-pit'. He made his way to a friend's house to clean up, the dogs charged out barking furiously at him, for he appeared to be 'more monster than man'. The sound of his voice reassured them, and he contrasted ruefully their native friendliness towards him with the animosity of his fellow courtiers.[34] There is no evidence that he was disgraced by King

Athelstan, but John of Wallingford envisaged him returning to Glastonbury for a period of relative obscurity, during which he pursued his studies and cultivated his artistic skills.[35]

The appointment by Athelstan of Alphege, a professed monk, as bishop of Winchester in succession to the saintly Beornstan in 933/4 marks a real turning-point in the life of Dunstan.[36] Sometime after this date, the bishop began to persuade his young kinsman to become a monk like himself. This Dunstan refused adamantly to consider: 'he would rather marry the young girl by whose favours he was daily cherished, than be clothed in sheep's rags after the custom of monks!'[37] He was perhaps aged 25, and there were plenty of married clergy around. Alphege did not remove the pressure; he resorted to prayer. The conflict in Dunstan did not diminish, and its intensity precipitated a severe and humiliating illness.[38] At the height of the crisis, Dunstan resolved to become a monk at the hand of Alphege and join his *familia* at Winchester.

This was no isolated development, for sometime after Dunstan was joined by Ethelwold, a young man of Winchester, who was also being educated at the court of King Athelstan. 'There he learnt from the king's councillors many things useful to him for he was of a keen intelligence,' writes Aelfric, Ethelwold's later biographer, 'and at length by the king's orders he was tonsured and consecrated into the priestly order by Alphege.'[39] According to Aelfric, he and Dunstan were ordained on the same day. Ethelwold remained by the king's order in the bishop's *familia*, and 'greatly benefited by the teaching and example of Alphege'. It is more than likely that it was with Athelstan's approval that Dunstan also settled with Alphege at Winchester, where he 'cleaved fast to him both on account of his wholesome teaching and on account of the bond of kinship'.[40] There is a delightful story of Dunstan accompanying the bishop to the consecration of a new church near the Westgate. On the way back, they stopped at the church of St Gregory to say compline in honour of their 'holy father'. They had just completed the double form of the confession, and the bishop was pronouncing the absolution, when a stone fell out of the roof and narrowly missed both of them! The biographer concludes that it was the work of the devil, who wished to destroy both them and their monastic life together.[41]

This story about the new church in the vicinity of the Westgate of Winchester illuminates also the way in which that city was growing during the first half of the tenth century. Whereas in the ninth century Winchester had been a place of relative obscurity so that even the history of its bishop, St Swithun, was forgotten; under Alfred, and even more under Edward, it had grown up as a thriving and fortified market town, serving the important royal and religious centre which occupied almost a third of the enclosed area. Around the bishop's residence and the king's palace, there gathered the private houses of the aristocracy, ranged along the main street and served by a network of back streets. The restored city walls were lined on the inside by paved streets, geared to the defence of what had become the most important royal *burgh* in Wessex. To cope with the growing population, new churches were founded inside and outside the city walls, and there is evidence of growing trade between Winchester and the neighbouring port of Southampton.[42]

The church at Winchester had also grown in size and importance during this period. Edward the Elder had carried out his dying father's wishes and had founded the New Minster, hard by the Old Minster which was also the cathedral. This was matched by the founding of the Nunnaminster by Alfred's queen and widow, Eahlswith. New Minster was a house of clergy, not monks; a centre of art and learning which revered the memory of Grimbald of St Bertin's and which became the royal shrine where Alfred and his immediate family were buried. These three enclosures, together with the bishop's residence, filled the south-east quadrant of the city, and the three churches, too close at times for comfort, must have made an imposing sight.[43] There is a graphic picture of the rich, cultivated but worldly life enjoyed by the clergy at Winchester at this time in the anonymous first life of St Oswald. Oswald's uncle, Oda, then bishop of Ramsbury, enabled him to buy 'for himself a "monastery" in Winchester for which he paid no mean price'. Oswald lived there like a courtier, dressed in silks, gregarious and popular with the married clergy of the two minsters. 'In those days, men were not monks, nor were the holy rules of monastic life observed in all England. Instead there were religious and most noble clerics who used to give their wealth to their wives rather than to the honour of the church.'[44]

Alphege the Bald came in a good succession of bishops of Winchester. Denewulf, who died in 909, and Frithestan, who followed him, were royal chaplains of good reputation. Beornstan, who immediately preceded Alphege, left a memory of sanctity: he used to wash the feet of the poor and sing psalms in the cemetery for the departed. Yet on his death, the citizens of the city 'sought to obliterate all memory of him in silence'.[45] This makes sense in the light of the fact that Alphege himself was succeeded by a prelate, Elfsige, renowned for his worldliness. Indeed, to judge from the force which Ethelwold later had to exercise against the canons of the Old Minster, it would seem that ascetical Christianity was firmly resisted by the strong and wealthy vested interests, both clerical and lay, in Winchester throughout the first half of the tenth century. Alphege was remembered for his asceticism, however, and Aelfric tells the story of how he enjoined a strict observance of Lent upon his own *familia*, which at the time included Ethelwold.[46] There is also a prophecy recounted in connection with the ordination of Dunstan and Ethelwold which illustrates the rigour with which Alphege regarded the sanctity of monastic and priestly vows; and Wulstan in his metrical 'Life of St Swithun' saw Beornstan, Alphege and Ethelwold as the spiritual heirs of that saint.[47] What was distinctive about Alphege was that, with Cenwald of Worcester, he was one of the first clergy, described as a priest and a monk, to be appointed bishop in tenth-century England. According to Aelfric's 'Life of Ethelwold', he enjoyed royal support in his attempt to establish a monastic way of life in his episcopal *familia*.[48]

'Dunstan was a real monk from the day he took his vows before bishop Alphege.'[49] The memory of St Benedict was far from extinct in England, and news of the continental revival of Benedictine monasticism would have undoubtedly reached Athelstan's court from several sources.[50] Dunstan's first biographer emphasises the resistance which Dunstan put up to the demands of the monastic life and his repugnance towards the name and the habit of a monk.[51] The ordination of Dunstan and Ethelwold is associated by inference with their monastic profession, so much so that the later falling away of their fellow ordinand, Athelstan, is described by Aelfric as 'apostasy' from the 'monastic state', and a confirmation of the prophetic judgement of Alphege himself.[52] According to this prophecy, Alphege foresaw the future episcopates of Dunstan and Ethelwold, but these depended upon the stability of their monastic vocation. The quiet fervour of Alphege the Bald at Winchester fostered a monastic spirit within the episcopal *familia* at the heart of the royal city, probably with Athelstan's support. The measure of its impact may perhaps be discerned in the fact that Oda, bishop of Ramsbury and uncle of Oswald, just before his translation to Canterbury in 942, probably received for himself the monastic habit from the reformed continental monastery of St Benedict at Fleury.[53] He maintained a link with that house of reformed monastic life for the rest of his life, probably by way of a formal association of confraternity.

In the early tenth century, the immediate problem was the complete lack of men committed to living the monastic life. The challenge was to create a community, however small, that actually lived as monks; only then could the endowment of monasteries proceed. To do this was to go against the tide of English church life as it had emerged from the period of the Viking invasions. Yet it was believed, with Bede as an authority, that neither the reform of the Church, nor the education of the clergy, nor the mission to the pagans could proceed and be secured without a strong core of monastic life at the heart of the Church.[54] At another level, the movement towards the revival of monasticism, which is evident in England and on the continent at this time, can be seen as a quest for the identity and integrity of the Church in a world where the life, wealth and patronage of the local church was dominated by, and often hardly distinguishable from, lay society. The bishops themselves were directly appointed by the king, and while royal support was indispensable and often sincere, it was by no means an unmixed blessing.[55] Nonetheless, royal encouragement for Alphege's experiment in monastic living was vital to its success within the life of the wider Church. There may indeed have been a distinct policy on the part of Athelstan, perhaps emulating his kinsmen overseas, to foster a germ of real monastic life. The direction of two of his ablest young noble clerics, Dunstan and Ethelwold, to this end would seem to confirm this, as well as make more intelligible Dunstan's rapid, though not unimpeded, appointment to be abbot of Glastonbury, shortly after Athelstan's death. Alphege's achievement was therefore a real and significant one, and full of promise; he may well be regarded as the father of English Benedictine monasticism.[56]

This was, however, a very small beginning, perceived only with the benefit of hindsight; it was like the mustard seed in the gospel which eventually produced a tree of great size and age.[57] Like the mustard seed of the parable, this beginning signified a spiritual development of great power, yet one which could not be significantly fostered by any external means. It is to the credit of the first biographer of Dunstan that the starkness of this interpretation of what happened in and through the life of the saint is not obscured. Yet spiritual life of that kind needed nurture, and the source of this nurture was the continuing religious life of holy women, conventual and anchorite. 'It is possible that historians have undervalued the contribution made by women to the religious idealism behind the English monastic revival.'[58] A notable example of this occurs in the first life of Dunstan.

Dunstan's links with Glastonbury were not abandoned during his time at Winchester. Alphege, like Athelm and Wulfhelm, the archbishop of Canterbury, had close links with the community there. The first biographer tells how Dunstan had a dream about the future in which he encountered a late friend, 'a certain deacon of the church at Glastonbury, called Wulfred. While he yet lived, he proved both a superior and close friend to Dunstan'.[59] The veracity of the vision was confirmed by a sign: of the burial place in Winchester of a certain priest, who turned out to be the visiting chaplain and spiritual director of 'a certain Aethelfleda, a most noble and religious woman'. He died, and was duly buried in the place which he, and the visionary Wulfred, had indicated. For the biographer this was another sign of Dunstan's holiness – and of his promise, for he concludes with an encomium in verse: 'So Dunstan, perceiving all this, was blessed with humility and wisdom, and he shone forth before God and men throughout his life as a man serene and true, cautious and chaste.'

The biographer is relating a sequence familiar to those who knew Dunstan, the pattern of his own spiritual life as he himself used to relate it. Yet the real significance of Aethelfleda lies deeper. She was a widow of royal lineage, a close friend and mentor of the royal family, and a friend to Athelstan.[60] She lived the life of an anchoress or hermit, in 'a little dwelling at the western end of the town of Glastonbury, where she dwelt constantly, close to the old church'. 'Blessed Dunstan always cleaved there and loved her deeply above all things. On account of his religion as well as of his near poverty, she carefully supported him. It is not within our competence to tell to what extent and in what ways she prepared him for divine service.' If Alphege was Dunstan's spiritual father, Aethelfleda was his spiritual mother. She was renowned for her devotion to Mary, the mother of the Lord, and for the strictness of her ascetical and contemplative life.[61]

Dunstan came to spend long intervals of time living at Glastonbury under Aethelfleda's direction, still part of the community there, studying and teaching, but leading an ascetic life. Osbern claims to have seen the cell which he built there at this time, and it is to this period of his life that the famous story belongs which tells of his tweaking the devil's nose with metalworking tongs![62] This story, though traditional, is interesting: it portrays Dunstan at his metalwork and the devil luring him into distracting memories of former girlfriends! After Dunstan accosted the devil with the red-hot tongs, the monster fled shrieking: 'O what has this bald fellow done to me!'

Aethelfleda's influence was to lead Dunstan deeper into the contemplative life.[63] He cared for her 'as if she were his own mother' during her last illness, and there is a picture of him with his pupils in the church porch, completing vespers there, having missed them on account of these duties. From this vantage point, he glimpsed the descent of the Holy Spirit, in the form of a white dove, into the home of his elderly friend and mentor.[64] On his arrival at the house, the old lady confirmed what had happened and gave instructions for her last rites and burial at the hand of Dunstan. Upon receiving the eucharist the next morning, she died. Osbern asserts that Dunstan was the beneficiary and trustee of her will, and that he made extensive benefactions to Glastonbury itself, reserving the rest of her wealth as a patrimony from which he might endow the five monasteries for which he later had a special care.[65]

'Amidst the study of sacred learning, Dunstan diligently cultivated both the art of writing as well as that of harp-playing and painting.' There occurs the strange story of the harp that played by itself on the wall while Dunstan was designing a stole to be embroidered by 'a certain noble woman and her work-women'.[66] Osbern places this story within the confines of a convent, and he may well be right.[67] Aethelwynn was clearly another wealthy lady and patroness of religion, perhaps even the abbess of a royal nunnery such as Shaftesbury or Wilton. It seems to be more likely that this episode occurred within a religious house when the elaborate and ecclesiastical nature of the work in hand is considered, and also the melody which the harp is purported to have played. It was the tone for the antiphon at the second vespers of the Common of Many Martyrs in the Benedictine breviary: 'Let the souls of the saints who followed the steps of Christ rejoice in heaven: because they shed their blood for His love, they shall reign with Him for ever.'[68]

The identification of the 'white martyrdom' of virginity and celibacy offered to

God in ascetical life with the 'red martyrdom' of actual death for the sake of Christ had a long history in Christian thought and life, going back to the book of Revelation in the New Testament and the ascetic strain in the writings of St Paul.[69] Dunstan himself is described by Osbern as an 'athlete of Christ' in this tradition.[70] Bede and Aldhelm mediated this tradition to the English Church, a tradition exemplified in the lives of St Martin of Tours, Gregory the Great and, of course, St Benedict himself. Aldhelm's work 'On virginity' came into vogue in the tenth century and was one of the most popular and influential books in the whole monastic movement at this time.[71] This was if anything the religious 'idealism' that lay behind the English monastic revival, and to it the Celtic tradition of eremitic life and spiritual conflict added a distinct and potent element.

Athelstan granted two charters towards the end of his reign to one Eadwulfa, a nun, and to Wulfswith, an *ancilla Christi* or handmaid of Christ, and in the brief reign of Edmund there are no fewer than seven similar grants.[72] Clearly therefore Aethelfleda was not alone in leading an anchoritic life. Athelstan too endowed the royal nunneries, notably Wilton and Shaftesbury, whose import-ance and vitality during this period is corroborated a little later by King Eadred's will with its benefactions to them.[73] Romsey and the Nunnaminster at Winchester claimed a continuity of life at this time, also sponsored by the royal house.[74] The sympathy of leading royal and noble ladies, many of them rich in their own right and some of them wont to retire into conventual life upon widowhood, probably accounts for the material strength of these foundations.[75]

There remains one remarkable window into the piety of early tenth-century religion associated with a nunnery. This is the so-called *Nunnaminster Codex*. It is a prayer book from Winchester, possibly the property at one time of Eahlswith, Alfred's queen, or of the saintly Edburga, daughter of Edward the Elder. The Nunnaminster itself had a precarious history after their time and before the reforms of the middle of the century. This codex, however, was already an old book by the beginning of the tenth century, having been written in England in the eighth or early ninth century, possibly under Irish influence.[76] It was almost certainly written for the use of an abbess as the feminine form is preferred in many of the prayers. It is in this book that the original gift to the monastery by Eahlswith of the lands she held in Winchester is recorded.

The prayer book comprises the passion of the Lord from three of the gospels, accompanied by a sequence of seasonal prayers contemplating various episodes in Christ's life and death. These are prefaced by a prayer of St Gregory the Great, another by St Augustine and a prayer about angels. There are also a hymn to the sacrament, sundry devotional and penitential prayers, and also prayers to St Michael, Our Lady and St John the Baptist. There are curious prayer charms against poison and illness, together with the earliest version of the Irish 'Lorica of Lodgen', which is an elaborate prayer for heavenly protection for each part of the body.[77] It is a fascinating collection, of great simplicity and devotion, and it is the closest contact available with the spiritual atmosphere of celibate and contemplative piety associated with holy and noble women, to whom Dunstan and Ethelwold owed so much.[78]

4

ABBOT OF GLASTONBURY

I – the background to the appointment of Dunstan

*A*THELSTAN died in 939, and the accession of his half-brother, Edmund, brought Dunstan back to court,[1] his reputation as a 'man of commendable life and learning in language' being by now well established. He remained as a court cleric 'for a long time', at the heart of Edmund's entourage. 'Some of the thegns living with him began to love him with unmatched sweetness of charity and brotherly love when they saw the constancy of his life.' Others did not, and once again Dunstan fell foul of jealousy and intrigue. They turned the king against him and, while at Cheddar, Edmund 'in a great rage ordered him to be stripped of every office and also deprived of every honour. He commanded Dunstan to procure for himself patronage wherever he chose, only well away from himself and his followers.'[2] In the face of this catastrophe, Dunstan found refuge among some envoys from the eastern part of the Frankish kingdom: 'they took pity on his unhappiness and promised him all the advantages of their kingdom if he went there in their company'.

While Dunstan was thus planning to depart into exile, the king went off hunting in the Mendip Hills. After a long and hard ride, the stag and the king's hounds plunged over the edge of Cheddar Gorge. In a flash, as he contemplated his end, Edmund remembered the wrong he had done Dunstan and repented of it. At the very brink his horse halted by divine intervention, he believed. Edmund returned and immediately summoned Dunstan. Together they rode off to Glastonbury with a small retinue and entered the ancient church. After some prayers, the king embraced Dunstan and they were publicly reconciled. He then led him to the abbot's chair and set him in it, saying: 'Be the head, ruler and occupant of this seat, and the most faithful abbot of this church; whatever you lack for the improvement of divine worship here, or for the support of life according to the holy Rule, I will supply from the royal bounty.'[3]

This momentous development probably occurred in the middle of Edmund's reign. The year, 940, deduced from a charter of the king 'to his faithful abbot

Dunstan'[4] and dated that year, is too early; Oda signs that charter as the archbishop of Canterbury, and he did not succeed to the primacy until the death of Wulfhelm in 942. Nor was Edmund's restoration of Dunstan part of a definite royal policy to restore Benedictine monasticism on any scale at that time, for in 944 the king granted the church and abbey at Bath to refugee monks from St Bertin's in Flanders; they were fleeing from the reforms of Gerard of Brogne, who was reviving a stricter form of Benedictine monasticism in that part of the continent at the time.[5] Florence of Worcester gives the date of Dunstan's appointment as 942; the Canterbury chronicler is more precise when he says that in 943, 'Edmund entrusted Glastonbury to St Dunstan, where he afterwards became its first abbot', words echoed by Osbern.[6] By the end of the reign, in 946, Dunstan was signing charters as 'abbot',[7] and the first biographer portrays Dunstan as a prominent member of Edmund's court during the closing months of the reign.[8] From the language employed in the first life, the king clearly recognised that Dunstan would rule Glastonbury according to the holy Rule of St Benedict. Yet this appointment can hardly have been made unpremeditated, hence perhaps the local opposition. Behind it may be detected the hand of Archbishop Oda, and probably that of Alphege of Winchester as well.

The fraught manner in which Dunstan was disgraced, then rehabilitated and appointed[9] makes sense only against the background of the climate of fear and conspiracy which permeated the court of Edmund. The king was only 18 years old at his accession, and in 940 Olaf, the Viking king of Dublin, having secured York, raided far and wide over the Midlands. Edmund met him at Leicester, but in circumstances that remain obscure; a truce was arranged by the archbishops of Canterbury and of York whereby Olaf obtained all of England north of Watling Street. It was a shattering blow, compounded in bitterness by the treachery of the Danish nobleman, Orm, formerly a member of Athelstan's court.[10] The reign of Edmund was thereafter dominated by the long hard fight back. In 942 Edmund regained the land between Watling Street and the River Humber, and in 944 he expelled Olaf Sihtricson and the rival king, Raegnald, from York, and so liberated the Danish population that had formerly enjoyed the rule of an English king. The next year, the king was strong enough to raid Strathclyde with assistance from his Welsh allies, and to treat with King Malcolm of Scotland. By the early months of 946, Edmund had regained what had been lost at the death of Athelstan, and was able also to intervene in the continental fortunes of his kinsman, Louis d'Outremer. It was against the background of some secret diplomatic negotiations with an envoy from the eastern kingdom in Germany that the sordid murder of Edmund occurred at Pucklechurch in May 946.[11] The first biographer recounts how Dunstan, riding in the company of Athelstan, of East Anglia, saw the devil running amidst the courtiers and enabled Athelstan to see this too. When this happened Athelstan told Dunstan of a dream in which he saw the courtiers turned into goats while the king slept. This Dunstan interpreted as an omen of trouble, shortly confirmed by a sure premonition of the king's death. Edmund died at Pucklechurch, defending his steward from a thief, on 26 May, the feast of St Augustine of Canterbury. Dunstan buried him at Glastonbury.[12]

The death earlier in 944 of Edmund's beloved and saintly wife, Aelfgifu, the mother of Edwy and Edgar, and the duplicity and unreliability of Wulfstan, archbishop of York, would not have helped the king's position.[13] Nonetheless, despite his difficulties, Edmund continued the royal benevolence to the Church, and proved a special friend to New Minster[14] and a generous bestower to

Glastonbury of relics plundered during the wars in Northumbria.[15] He died prematurely, however, at the age of 25, leaving two infant sons.

The most important ecclesiastical appointment which Edmund made during his brief reign was the elevation of Oda, bishop of Ramsbury, to the see of Canterbury in 942. Oda is a figure of crucial importance to the reform and growth of the English Church in the tenth century. It is against the background of his policy and stature that the work of Dunstan and Ethelwold in refounding Benedictine monasticism must be seen.

Oda was of Danish descent,[16] and he had been educated by a certain English thegn, Aethelhelm, with whom he had travelled to Rome. It had been Alfred's policy to train Danish young men with Englishmen to serve the Church,[17] and Oda was related to Oskytel, who became archbishop of York in the later part of Oda's primacy, and also to Thurkytel, abbot of Bedford, both of whom were also Danes.[18] The bishop of Ramsbury was very much a court bishop,[19] and Oda served both as a diplomat to the Franks in 936 and supposedly as a warrior at the Battle of Brunanburgh in 937.[20] His heart, however, lay elsewhere; and at some stage, probably before his succession to Canterbury, he became a monk by association of the monastery at Fleury, a Benedictine house on the continent recently reformed by Oda of Cluny.[21] The first biographer of St Oswald (who was the nephew of Oda) describes him thus: 'This venerable and aged man was full of Apostolic authority, and this glory shone forth so that he adorned his outstanding life by surpassing the honesty of his forebears. He was not only loved by good men with all their hearts, but was also reverenced by the powerful.'[22]

As archbishop of Canterbury, Oda inherited the powerful and unique position of primate. This had been built up by his predecessors in the ninth century, and his immediate forebears had used it to considerable effect in partnership with the kings of Wessex. In the ninth century, [23] the Archbishops Wulfred and Ceolnoth had reacted to the challenge posed by Offa of Mercia in his attempt to move the primatial see to Lichfield by imposing their authority upon their suffragans and extracting oaths of obedience; they also made definite attempts to reform the Church. At the same time, they built up an overwhelming influence in Kent, using their ancient rights over the Kentish minsters to enrich the *familia* at Christ Church, Canterbury. This foundation, at least until the onslaught of the Vikings, was a community under some kind of canonical rule of common life. The ancient see of Rochester was brought very much under their wing also.

Plegmund, who was archbishop from 890 until 923, continued the reforming impulse of Alfred, whom he also assisted in his labours to revive learning in England. In 910, Plegmund divided the two ancient sees of Winchester and Sherborne, creating the new sees of Ramsbury, Wells and Crediton. His successor, Athelm, was close to Athelstan and the royal house, and left his mark on the coronation order. He also abolished the old custom of the archbishops of Canterbury of issuing their own coinage. Wulfhelm, who succeeded in 926, played a prominent role in the councils of Athelstan's reign. His hand and influence may be detected in the legislation promulgated at those meetings. Under Wulfhelm, bishops and archbishops became closely associated with the administration of justice in the shires. This close liaison between king and archbishop was marked by Athelstan's generous gifts of precious books to the community at Christ Church.[24]

Oda himself played an important role as a figure of continuity and stability during the chequered reigns of Edmund, Eadred and Edwy. He continued the reforming and legislating work of his predecessors, and his influence may be detected in the first and second codes of law issued by Edmund.[25] Here ecclesiastical and secular laws stand together. At some time also in Edmund's reign, Oda issued a letter to all his bishops reasserting the primacy of Canterbury. With it came a short body of canons drawn from earlier English ecclesiastical sources, notably the legatine decrees of 786.[26] These constitute a document of exemplary clarity, simplicity and breadth, unusual in this period. In ten brief chapters, Oda asserts the basic freedom of the Church, calls rulers and nobles to obedience and urges impartiality in the administration of justice. He is adamant about a bishop's duties, and insistent that the clergy should be learned and live according to their vows. His sixth chapter addresses 'monks', who are to remain faithful to their vocation, living in stability and under rule. He forbids illicit marriages and makes special provision for the protection of nuns. He concludes with an appeal for unity in the Church; with prescriptions concerning fasts, alms and tithes and the observance of Sundays and festivals; and a condemnation of the practitioners of magic. This is a formidable statement of intent and accounts for the remarkable consistency and purpose with which he sustained his primacy. It enabled him to accomplish much of abiding worth in the life of the Church, in which the appointment of Dunstan as abbot of Glastonbury proved an important and auspicious part.

During the primacy of Oda, the Church was formally re-established in East Anglia. Theodred, bishop of London, worked from an episcopal centre at Hoxne in Suffolk, probably assisted by a circle of German clergy of whom only the names are known, from Theodred's will.[27] Sometime in the 950s, a proper see was set up at Elmham in Norfolk, and the profession of obedience rendered by Athulf, the first bishop there, is still in existence.[28] This venture needed not only the moral and material support of the king: it rested also upon the willing assistance of Athelstan, of East Anglia, and his family. His support probably secured the appointment of Oda's kinsman, Oskytel, to the see of Dorchester, from which the Church reached out into the Danelaw. Towards the end of his life, in 957, Oda secured a substantial grant of land at Ely, probably with a view to founding a monastery there.[29]

Oda engaged in a partial rebuilding of Christ Church Cathedral in Canterbury, assisted by the king. He raised a clerestory of 20 ft in height, and it was said that no rain fell during the time when the church was without a roof.[30] The community there prospered as a centre of learning, adorned by the scholarship of a German, Frithegod, a deacon under whom the archbishop placed his young nephew, Oswald.[31] Frithegod wrote a verse 'Life of Wilfrid'; Wilfrid was the Northumbrian bishop from the time of Bede whose relics Oda brought south to Canterbury from Ripon after it had been sacked by Eadred in 948.[32] It is quite likely that monastic life of some kind was fostered at St Augustine's, Canterbury, under Oda, for an abbot, Eadhelm, appears towards the end of Oda's reign as a signatory to the charters.[33]

Oda's personal commitment to Benedictine monasticism lay behind Dunstan's reforms at Glastonbury. He later used his own connection with Fleury to secure a welcome there for Oswald and his companions, who lived as members of that monastic community under Abbot Wulflad for some while,[34] during which time the archbishop evidently kept in regular contact. At the close of his days, Oda summoned Oswald back to England, though he died before his nephew arrived. The language of his sixth canon, the one which regulates monastic life, is couched in terms drawn from the Rule of St Benedict, and the eventual founding of Abingdon under Ethelwold would have needed Oda's active support.[35] Oda was venerated at Canterbury for his sanctity and political courage. He was in many ways the primate by whom Dunstan came to be measured; remembered for his miracles, his devotion to the eucharist and his gift of tears.[36] Dunstan himself later used to genuflect before Oda's tomb at Canterbury and hail him as 'Oda the Good'.[37].

II – the reform at Glastonbury

The appointment of Dunstan to be abbot of Glastonbury did not occur in a vacuum. It was supported by the generous benefactions of the king, of Aethelflaed of Damerham, his second queen, and of leading members of his court. William of Malmesbury, in his 'Antiquities of Glastonbury', records the scale of this operation:

> the king gave to Dunstan 20 hides at Christian Malford, 8 hides at
> Kingston, 5 hides at North Wootton, 4 hides at Whatley, and retur-
> ned to him 21 hides at Wrington . . . 'These lands', he said, 'I do
> confer in the old church of the blessed Mother of God on the hill of
> Glastonbury to wipe away my sins and those of my grandfather
> Alfred and my father Edward.'[38]

The memory of Edmund's devotion to Glastonbury was such that the monastery later claimed an extensive privilege and liberty supposedly granted at his hand in 944.[39]

The benefactions of the court were no less significant: Edward's widow, Queen Aelfflaed, led the field with a grant of 42 hides; she was followed by Wilfrid (who may in fact have been Dunstan's brother, Wulfric); Athelstan, a courtier; Alfheah and Elswithe, the king's kin; Sigewulf, Wulfheah and Aethelnoth, the king's retainers. In all, William reckoned up a grant totalling 368½ hides, though not all the grants would have come to Glastonbury immediately, many reverting only on the death of the donor or his widow. This pattern of endowment, pledged to take effect over many years, laid the foundations for the future prosperity of the abbey at Glastonbury.[40] It established the enterprise as a major political development, to which leading families and bishops could direct their religious generosity in concert with the royal family.[41] This prominence was enhanced by the king's deposition of relics from the north, the spoils of war, in the new abbey.

> These lands testify to the marvellous devotion of the king and his fol-
> lowers towards the monastery at Glastonbury and its protector, the
> most glorious Dunstan. Moreover, in order to distinguish the place
> with greater gifts, the king, with pious generosity, conferred upon
> Glastonbury many relics which he had sought throughout Northum-
> bria and even in regions across the sea . . . attracted by the sanctity
> of the place he even vowed his own body to it after his death.[42]

Foremost among these lay benefactors was Athelstan of East Anglia, whose family held substantial lands in the south west also. He was at this time virtually regent of the eastern Danelaw, holding over 200 hides, an endowment unmatched by any other layman, and he was a figure of crucial political and military importance throughout the reigns of Edmund and Eadred. He and his brothers were among the early benefactors of Glastonbury and, in due course, Abingdon, and Athelstan himself retired as a monk to Glastonbury at the end of his life. His personal friendship with Dunstan must have guaranteed the security and continuity of the reform and restoration of Glastonbury. It is interesting that Glastonbury scribes produced the charters which Athelstan used to secure his influence over the newly reconquered Danelaw,[43] an influence which may well account for the appointment in 949 of Dunstan's kinsman, Kinsige, as bishop of Lichfield.

The second biographer, Adelard, describes Glastonbury under Dunstan as a 'school of monks', an image drawn directly from the Rule of St Benedict.[44] The first biographer portrays this completely:

> Dunstan, the servant of God, assumed this dignity by command of the king and ruled with great grace. By following the health-giving Rule of St Benedict, he shone forth as the first (or foremost) abbot of the English nation. For his service sprang spontaneously from the disposition of his heart: he vowed to give back everything to God.

> First and foremost, this most prudent pastor firmly secured on all sides the enclosure of the monks with monastic buildings and other provisions, so that it was now even as it had once been described to him in the dream. This was where he would enclose those sheep of the Lord gathered from far and wide, lest they be slain by the invisible wolf. Then the same teacher from God began to feed with the nourishment of the divine word the monastery committed to him, and from the eternal spring within him to water them with the honey-sweet instruction of Holy Scripture, teaching them how they ought to pass through the painful paths of this life to the celestial banquets.

> It was obvious to nearly all the faithful around about after a passage of a few years, how Dunstan had sown the Lord Christ by his labour in the disciples who had come to him young and void of full faith, so that they grew abundantly and bore fruits of good works with a compliant beauty. So that thereafter even until now, many pastors of churches were instructed by his teaching and example, and were sought after for different cities and other holy places, and were elected because they had been recipients thence of the holy Rule and the standards of justice. Thus they became notable men: deans, abbots, bishops, even archbishops, as well as foremost in other orders of clergy.[45]

The determination with which Dunstan sought to establish a proper Benedictine enclosure is reflected in a passing remark of the first biographer: 'Dunstan had a brother, called Wulfric, whom he made reeve outside the monastery to attend to the business of their farms, so that neither he nor anyone else in monastic vows should wonder abroad, being unsuited to the pursuit of secular affairs.'[46] Probably the version of the rule used was closer in form to the eighth-century 'Ordo qualiter' than to the more elaborate developments of contemporary continental reformed life. [47] Archaeology has recently confirmed the extent of the building programme which Dunstan planned and supervised.[48] The enclosure of the ancient cemetery, reported by William of Malmesbury in his 'Life of Dunstan', has been confirmed, and some of the footings of the monastic buildings surrounding the cloister have been discovered.[49] It would appear that the cemetery and the church were separated from the monastery itself: thus the pilgrimage centre would not have disturbed the life of the monks. The chapel to St John the Baptist which Dunstan later built,[50] a small four-square construction, may well have served as an entrance chapel to this area. In the course of this major rearrangement, the ancient cemetery itself was covered by a thick layer of clay excavated presumably from the foundations of the monastic buildings, creating a mound and meadow in which the relocated bodies of the saints there 'might rest in peace'.

William of Malmesbury also describes how Dunstan added to Ine's stone church, lengthening it and adding aisles and porticus so that it was virtually square. Adelard records a miracle from this time when Dunstan checked a beam which was about to fall from the top of the church.[51] This may have occurred when Dunstan was building the great tower, in the course of which operation the ancient eastern crypt had to be filled in and the bones removed and carefully placed in a stone coffin. At the east end, to the north, lay the chapel of St John the Baptist and to the south lay the chapel of St Andrew, both of Dunstan's creating. In many ways this important reshaping foreshadowed the rebuilding of Old Minster at Winchester by Ethelwold later in the century. It created a church 89 ft long and 85 ft broad.[52] By the standards of the day, it was an impressive structure, connected to and sheltering the ancient wattle church which was still preserved, and making a fitting focus for pilgrimage. Yet it was a monastic church, full of side chapels dedicated to various saints and with a choir where the Benedictine office would be sung throughout the day. To this renovated and venerable church Dunstan himself made many gifts of permanent worth:

> organs and two notable little bells, an altar cloth and a bell in the refectory on which were the verses: 'Dunstan ordered this bell to be cast for himself, etc.' On the holy water vat on the altar could be read: 'Archbishop Dunstan ordered this stoup to be cast. May the Almighty grant him eternal salvation.'[53]

He also provided the gospel book, 'elegantly adorned', in which gifts to the monastery were recorded, a book which he probably first obtained as a gift from the king.[54]

The archaeological reports afford only a limited and rather confused picture of the monastic buildings erected by Dunstan. But behind the enclosed cemetery and extending to the south of the church he created a full monastic establishment, similar to that alluded to in the later 'Regularis concordia',[55] and recorded for educational purposes in Aelfric's 'Grammar': namely, a dormitory, refectory, guest house, cellar, vestry, kitchen, bakehouse, storeroom and latrines; also an infirmary, chapter house and warming house.[56] Archaeology has, however, confirmed the existence (so far a unique discovery at any Anglo-Saxon monastery) of bronze-working hearths and glass furnaces. This would corroborate Dunstan's own reputation as a metalworker and master craftsman, and imply that Glastonbury became a centre for these and related activities.[57]

Glastonbury under Dunstan was both an educational establishment, a centre of learning and a place where genuine monastic life following the Rule of St Benedict was cultivated. Dunstan's reputation as a teacher is not confined to the monastic biographers; it is confirmed also in a charter where, as in the first life, Dunstan is styled as 'dogmatizator' (i.e. teacher).[58] This educational emphasis is borne out by several of the early stories: for example, when Dunstan narrowly missed being killed by a falling stone while waiting for the funeral of his brother, Wulfric, it was a small schoolboy, who later became a bishop, who remembered the incident.[59] Of Dunstan's own learning tantalisingly little remains: there is an acrostic poem, a popular device in those days, in a manuscript at Trinity College, Cambridge,[60] written by him while abbot. There is the beautiful picture attributed to him, where he kneels, a tiny figure of a monk, at the feet of Christ the Wisdom of God, in the book called *St Dunstan's Classbook*,[61] and that is about all. Of his lifelong standing as a wise and learned man there can be no doubt, and the foremost scholar of the reformed monastic life, Abbo of Fleury, later hailed him as one of the most learned men of his generation.[62]

Aelfric, in his 'Life of Ethelwold', says that:

> Ethelwold went to Glastonbury and placed himself under the instruction of that glorious man, Dunstan, abbot of the monastery. Profiting much from his supervision, he at length received from him the habit of the monastic order, giving himself up with humble devotion to his rule. For he learnt there the art of grammar and metrics, and the sacred books and authors, devoting himself exceedingly to vigils and prayers, subduing himself by abstinence, and always exhorting the brothers to higher things.

The other biographer, Wulstan, says that in due course, Dunstan made Ethelwold the dean of the monastery.[63] This is a fascinating glimpse of the life at Glastonbury, both intellectual and spiritual. It would appear that Ethelwold went seeking learning, and seeking too to test his vocation, which in due time he accepted. It is not unlikely that many others entered the monastery in the same way and progressed in a similar manner. In addition to these mature recruits, there were also children and young men being educated in the monastic way of life, and perhaps others also not intending to become monks.

Such books as remain from this period which are associated with Dunstan at Glastonbury illuminate the kind of education that was available there. They are a haphazard but interesting selection. There is a copy of Smaragdus' 'Exposition of the Rule of St Benedict', a ninth-century continental work, copied early in the tenth century and bearing corrections which are almost certainly Dunstan's.[64] At the end of a copy of Caesarius of Arles' 'Commentary on the Apocalypse' stand the words: 'Dunstan the abbot ordered this book to be copied'.[65] Associated with both these books is a copy of Primasius' 'On the Apocalypse', which was annotated by Dunstan while he was at Glastonbury.[66] This in turn would indicate that Dunstan probably handled a text of Aldhelm, brought to England from the continent along with this work. Aldhelm was by far the most popular and influential author among tenth-century monks in England; his style was emulated by Frithegod at Canterbury, and probably at Glastonbury also, 'in an attempt to show that English learning was as profound, and English writing as sophisticated as anything produced on the Continent'.[67] The so-called 'hermeneutic style' dominates most of the monastic literature of the period, including the earliest biographies of Dunstan and Oswald. Aldhelm's 'On virginity' is, however, the key to understanding the peculiar fervour of the monasticism which Dunstan helped to revive.[68] Virginity and martyrdom, asceticism and expectation of the end constituted the spiritual framework in which Dunstan and Ethelwold lived. This is confirmed by the typical spiritual trials which the first biographer records as afflicting Dunstan during this period.[69]

The remarkable volume called *St Dunstan's Classbook* was probably compiled from existing material at Glastonbury at this time. It illustrates well the range and limitations of monastic learning. The codex contains a grammatical treatise of Eutyches, probably of Breton origin from the ninth century, also a computistical tract and the first book of Ovid's *Ars Amatoria*, both texts of which are of Welsh origin and contain 'some of the earliest specimens of written

Welsh'.[70] It was evidently compiled in England by the middle of the tenth century by a scribe who made annotations and restored lacunae in all three parts. (At a later date, an Old English homily on the invention of the cross was added.) 'The hand is that of a person taught originally to write the insular script, who later learned to write Caroline minuscule.'[71] This hand also added the couplet above the kneeling figure of Dunstan at the foot of Christ:

Dunstanum memet clemens rogo Christe tuere,
Tenerias me non sinas sorbsisse procellas.
(Remember, I beg you, merciful Christ, to protect Dunstan, and do
not permit the storms of the underworld to swallow me up.)[72]

It seems almost certain that the hand was Dunstan's and that the couplet was modelled upon the opening lines of Hrabanus Maur's 'De laudibus sanctae crucis',[73] as was the style of the drawing. Buried in this fascinating codex are 'the lessons and canticles (in Greek and Latin) of the Roman Easter Vigil just as they were at the time of the reform of Gregory the Great, probably in 592'.[74] The computistical material contains a paschal table for 817–32, and the biblical material is drawn from the Old Latin version, not the Vulgate.[75] In the words of Stubbs, 'it is one of the most curious volumes in existence, and would go further to prove the antiquity of Glastonbury and its connexion with early British as well as Anglo-Saxon history than all the forged charters even if they were genuine'.[76]

With these books should be placed the so-called 'Book of St Dunstan'. It is a collection of canon law written abroad, in two parts but with the first seven leaves replaced in a hand which is in 'transitional English Caroline minuscule, and dating from the time of Dunstan'.[77] The older part is a collection of apostolic canons and decrees from the early church councils. The later part is a copy of a body of Irish canons, together with the canons of Adamnan, selections of Roman and Frankish law books and regulations governing degrees of kinship in marriage. If this were collated at Glastonbury under Dunstan, it would corroborate the more practical training in law and justice for which Dunstan himself and his pupils became respected. 'The impression one gets from all these books is that Dunstan was making the most of what he found to hand; and in this way they lend support to the view that his monasticism was largely of native growth',[78] though at no time immune to resources brought over from the continent.

Something of the wealth of material available to Dunstan while at Glastonbury can be detected in the quality of the few lines of Latin verse inscriptions attributed to him by William of Malmesbury, which he found on the artefacts given by the saint to the monasteries at Glastonbury and Malmesbury.[79] A ninth-century text of Boethius' De Consolatione Philosophiae from France, for example, passed through Dunstan's hands and was collated by him, having been brought perhaps to Glastonbury at the turn of the ninth and tenth centuries.[80] Certainly the scriptorium at Glastonbury continued to exert a distinctive and powerful influence on the cultural life of the tenth-century English Church throughout the rest of the century. Not only was the continental Caroline minuscule handwriting probably introduced and popularised there; line drawing also flourished, of which the Christ figure in St Dunstan's Classbook is the most striking example. And this skill in line drawing influenced taste in such matters at Canterbury also, where this aspect of tenth-century art reached its climax in the illustrations for the Utrecht Psalter. The Christ figure in the classbook is a harbinger also of the iconographical alliance between the demands of monasticism and the Christological understanding of kingship promoted by the reforming churchmen of the tenth century. This reached its apogee in the Benedictional of St Ethelwold, but the pattern was beginning to be established already in the manuscripts and illuminations emanating from Glastonbury. The rod of wisdom in the picture in the classbook is also the rod of kingship, and the psalm quotation is drawn from the Roman version of the psalter, use of which persisted at Glastonbury and Canterbury throughout this period while the new monasteries generally were moving to the Gallican version brought over from the continent. Later Canterbury manuscripts which reflect elements drawn from Glastonbury, such as the Psalter (Arundel MS 155) and the miniatures of St Gregory from a Canterbury pontifical of the early eleventh century, demonstrate a decisive and complex iconography – 'word-illustrations' which are 'pictorial manifestos of the ideas of the English Benedictine reform movement of the time of Dunstan'. This tradition complemented the more famous Winchester school of the second half of the tenth century, and 'Dunstan himself now has a good claim to be considered as an iconographically inventive artist and patron'.[81] The art of the period was also powerful and memorable propaganda for the distinctive vision and values of the monastic reform movement.

The regular life of the Benedictine monks acquainted them with comprehensive selections from the Latin Bible and from the fathers, both in the lections during the divine office and in the readings in chapter and refectory. Meditation on such texts, and even closer familiarity with them through copying in the scriptorium, wove the very language of scripture and tradition into the lives and thinking of the monks. This is clearly reflected in the language of many of the charters and in the style of the hagiographies of the period: Frithegod's 'Life of Wilfrid', for example, and the first lives of Dunstan, Ethelwold and Oswald. In the production of books, the monastery at Glastonbury began to exercise an influence comparable to that of the traditional centres such as Worcester, Winchester and Canterbury. Moreover, by the very selection and acquisition of texts, this influence was a definite monastic one and the wider availability of such texts was fundamental to the revival of monasticism. This is particularly evident in the kalendar of Glastonbury Abbey which is contained in the Bosworth Psalter[82] and confirmed in its character and provenance by comparison with that in the Leofric Missal.[83] The Bosworth Psalter was almost certainly drawn up early in Dunstan's primacy for his own use at Canterbury, and as such contains some additions suitable to that milieu. The Roman psalter used is divided into the Benedictine divisions, with 100 hymns for use in the divine office. The kalendar, which was added shortly after Dunstan's death, is distinctive in commemorating saints precious to Glastonbury both before and during the time of Dunstan: for example, the two Patricks and Brigid, redolent of the Irish traditions before the tenth century; Aidan and Ceolfrid, whose bones came south to Glastonbury either during the first Viking raids in the eighth century or by the hand of King Edmund; Gildas, the British historian; Paulinus and Wilfrid, bishops of the era recorded by Bede; saints of the eremitic tradition, like Guthlac and Neot; and Benignus, a member of the martyr throng; a characteristic of the Glastonbury kalendar and those calendars descended from it.

It is hard to gauge the size of the community at Glastonbury by the time it was well established under Dunstan. From the remaining sources, nearly two dozen likely contemporaries and monks of Dunstan's can be named; these are, of course, those who became prominent in later years. In addition to the abbot, Dunstan, and the dean, Ethelwold, there were Osgar, Foldberht and Frithegar, who later went to Abingdon with Ethelwold; Aethelgar who, having been a monk both of Glastonbury and Abingdon, became abbot of New Minster; Wulfric (Dunstan's brother), the lay reeve; Ceolwy, later a prior of Glastonbury; and the cellarer, Aelfsige (the last three all lay brothers who appear in stories in the first life of Dunstan); Sigeric and Aelfric and possibly also Alphege, each of whom was to hold the post of archbishop of Canterbury after Dunstan; and Elfwold, Ordberht, Wulfsige, Cyneward and an unknown schoolboy, all of whom became bishops. To this list can be added those who became bishops while Dunstan was still abbot: Bryhthelm of Wells, Aelfwold of Crediton and possibly Daniel of Cornwall; perhaps also Elfric, the second bishop of Elmham. There was also Sigfrid who went to Norway as a missionary bishop; and possibly Aelfstan, bishop of London, and Wulfsige, bishop of Cornwall as well.[84] Some of these men would have started off as youngsters in the monastery, and the tradition of Glastonbury providing trained clergy and monks for the English Church continued well into the first part of the eleventh century. The whole community at Glastonbury may well have totalled around fifty members at any time, not including schoolboys and novices, craftsmen and other labourers.

Under Dunstan, Glastonbury grew to be an institution and enterprise of a scale quite unparalleled in recent Anglo-Saxon history. As a wealthy centre of learning and religious life it was an impressive and significant entity, and the ramifications of its influence, whether in terms of land holdings or of personnel, were beginning to touch and to change the life of both Church and society in Wessex.

However, it remained pre-eminently a spiritual enterprise, founded upon an ancient tradition which had been brought to new life by the example, vision and teaching of one man. Dunstan was a remarkable abbot, capable of exerting a profound influence on those who came under his authority, because he was seen to be an 'athlete of God', who strenuously practised what he preached. The vigils and austerities of monastic life were the hidden centre of it all. Glastonbury was a school of prayer, and Dunstan and Ethelwold were remembered as men of prayer, champions of Christ who in their lives overcame evil.[85] In the words of Adelard: 'By his care, holy religious life emerged there, and the excellence of the monastic religious life was spread by Dunstan from that place throughout the whole world of the English.'[86]

III – the founding of Abingdon

Edmund was succeeded by his brother Eadred on account of the infancy of his two sons, Edwy and Edgar. Eadred was probably a contemporary of Dunstan's; he was a man of resolute and warlike spirit, but prone to physical illness.[87] His tenuous hold over the north of England was shattered by the invasion of Northumbria late in 947 which established the formidable Eric Bloodaxe as king.[88] Eadred promptly raided the north, sacking the church of Ripon on his way, and after a narrow victory at Castleford he secured the expulsion of Eric. In 949, however, Olaf returned from Dublin and ruled at York until he was in turn expelled by Eric in 952. Eric ruled with impunity for at least a further two years, and the real limits to Eadred's power were demonstrated by his need to arrest Wulfstan, archbishop of York, in 952 'because he had often been accused to the king'.[89] Sometime in 954, in circumstances shrouded in obscurity, Eric lost his kingdom and Eadred regained control of the north, entrusting the province to the English earl, Oswulf, the high reeve of Bamburgh. Then in 955, on the feast of St Clement (23 November), Eadred died suddenly at Frome.[90]

Eadred and Dunstan were close friends:

> he loved the blessed Father Dunstan with such an ardour of love that
> he made him his chief adviser. For his part, the man of God, in order
> to repay from the depths of his heart such a measure of love shewn
> to him, used to hail the king as most dear to him above all others.
> On the grounds of this loving trust, the king committed to Dunstan
> the best of his belongings, many deeds of property, and even the an-
> cient treasures of earlier kings, as well as divers of the wealth be-
> longing by personal right to him, all of which were to be faithfully
> kept in the security of his monastery.[91]

Osbern rightly perceived that this reign was the time when Dunstan emerged as a figure of considerable political importance, even if his account is coloured by an exaggeration born of hindsight.[92] Dunstan's position as treasurer to the king, 'an official position somewhat like that of later chancellors',[93] is confirmed by the will of Eadred where as abbot of Glastonbury he is to take charge of the money set aside by the king in the event of Viking raids in Somerset and Devon.[94] This document affords a fascinating insight into the composition of the royal household and the fervour of Eadred's own religious devotion. The gifts to the old royal houses at Winchester – Old Minster, New Minster and the Nunnaminster – and the nunneries at Wilton and Shaftesbury come first. Then £1600 is set aside to benefit the people in the event of famine or raids, with the archbishop of Canterbury, the bishop of Winchester, Oskytel, bishop of Dorchester (and effectively archbishop of York at this time), and Dunstan the abbot as the trustees. As the king's death approached, Dunstan and the other guardians of the king's treasure were sent away to retrieve the royal property. The king died before they could accomplish their mission, although Dunstan received a divine premonition of the king's death, and in due course Eadred was buried at the Old Minster in Winchester.[95]

Dunstan enjoyed a prominent position at court because of his close personal friendship with the king. But his political influence rested also upon his relationship with Athelstan of East Anglia, whose control over the eastern Danelaw was the indispensable base for all Eadred's campaigns in the north.[96] Both Dunstan and Athelstan were also closely associated with the royal family, and especially with Eadred's mother, the powerful Queen Eadgifu, widow of Edward the Elder. Athelstan's own wife nurtured the infant Edgar, the younger child of Edmund and Aelfgifu, after Aelfgifu's death in 944, and Dunstan may have helped to foster her cult at Shaftesbury, having received divine intimation of the birth of Edgar.[97] According to the anonymous biographer of Oswald, 'Dunstan used to praise Athelstan's wife as a blessed woman and blessed in her offspring'.[98]

Queen Eadgifu's political sway over the court of Eadred is confirmed by stories in both the early lives of Dunstan. According to the first biographer, Eadred wanted to offer the see of Crediton to Dunstan on the death of Bishop Aethelgar in 953.[99] This Dunstan refused, saying that he did not wish to leave Glastonbury. The king turned to his mother who tried to persuade Dunstan over dinner, but to no avail. Instead, Dunstan suggested Aelfwold, who may have been a member of the community at Glastonbury, and who duly became bishop of Crediton and remained there until 972. Adelard, the second biographer, gives a slightly different version of this story: Alphege, bishop of Winchester, had died on St Gregory's Day (12 March) 951, and the king asked Eadgifu, again over dinner, to persuade Dunstan to become the new bishop of Winchester. Dunstan refused, saying that he would not become bishop while Eadred reigned: 'he loved the king, and did not wish to be absent from him because of episcopal duties'.[100] Certainly if Dunstan had become bishop of Winchester then, he might have avoided considerable trouble in the future; Elfsige, the new bishop, proved an implacable rival and, after the death of Eadred, an adversary. This may give the clue to the curious story of the dream in which Dunstan was rebuked by St Andrew, in the company of St Peter and St Paul, for refusing the episcopal yoke. Adelard gives a different form of this story again and recounts how Eadred interpreted it as a prediction that Dunstan would become archbishop of Canterbury. But the primitive story of the rebuke by St Andrew, Dunstan's patron saint, has the ring of truth to it; after the death of Eadred and while he was in exile, this decision to refuse a bishopric may have seemed to Dunstan to have been a real mistake. It is of some passing interest that in this dream Dunstan is approaching Rome itself on a pilgrimage, which may indicate that he had once made a journey there, like Oda before him, long before he became the archbishop of Canterbury. This story of Dunstan's refusal to become a bishop illustrates his real and personal commitment to the life of the community at Glastonbury in the midst of his duties as a member of Eadred's court. Nonetheless, he was very much associated with the inner circles of that court, travelling with the king to the north where he saw the body of St Cuthbert,[101] and receiving from the king a land grant at Badbury in Wiltshire at the very end of the reign.[102]

By 954, Eadred was in a strong enough position to take active steps in the ordering of the Church in the northern Danelaw. Sometime around the year 950, Eadred had appointed Oskytel, the kinsman of Oda the archbishop of Canterbury, to be bishop of Dorchester, a see which stretched out into the eastern Danelaw. After the arrest of Wulfstan, archbishop of York, in 952, what was left of the northern church was without its primate. When Eadred regained control of the north in 954, it appears that he appointed Oskytel effectively to be archbishop of York, while Wulfstan remained as a kind of suffragan bishop at Dorchester. Wulfstan died soon afterwards, in 957, and the circumstances behind this irregular arrangement were forgotten; Oskytel remained as archbishop of York for sixteen years, dying in 972. From the first life of Oswald it is clear that Oskytel and Dunstan were firm friends, and Oskytel's appointment as archbishop of York was to prove of crucial importance in securing the eventual return of Dunstan from his exile.[103] It was while Oskytel was bishop of Dorchester (near Oxford) that the foundation of the monastery at Abingdon occurred.

According to Aelfric,

when a long time had passed after he had received monastic orders, Ethelwold determined to go to lands across the sea, to train himself more perfectly in sacred books and monastic discipline. But the venerable Queen Eadgifu, King Eadred's mother, prevented his attempts, advising the king not to let such a man depart from his kingdom. It then pleased King Eadred by his mother's persuasion to give to the venerable Aethelwold a certain place, Abingdon by name, in which a little monastery was situated in ancient days. But it was then waste and deserted, consisting of poor buildings and possessing only 40 hides. The rest of the land of this place, namely 100 hides, the king was holding by royal right. It was brought about with Dunstan's permission and according to the king's wish, that Ethelwold took charge of that place, in order that he might ordain monks serving God according to the Rule. That servant of God therefore came to the place committed to him, and at once certain clerics from Glastonbury followed him, namely Osgar, Foldberht, Frithegar, and from Winchester Ordberht, and from London Eadric, submitting themselves to his instruction. In a short space of time he collected there a flock of monks, over whom he was ordained abbot by the king's orders. The king also gave to the abbot and the brethren the royal property which he had owned in Abingdon, namely the 100 hides, with excellent buildings, to augment the daily provisions, and he assisted them greatly with money, but his mother did so even more.[104]

Abingdon, like Glastonbury and Ely, was an ancient religious site held in trust by the king as part of the royal patrimony. It had been a small west Saxon foundation of the seventh century, on the borders of Mercia. Sometime after 788, however, it had been endowed by the king of Mercia, Offa the Great, and some kind of community existed there into the ninth century when Abingdon was in the diocese of Leicester. Although Berkshire was a Mercian shire in the middle of that century, Abingdon enjoyed close links with the west Saxon royal family, and after its devastation by the Danes Alfred sequestrated the main endowment of 100 hides 'jure regale'. Under Athelstan, there was a German cleric, Godescalc, to whom the king granted land, at the head of a small church community and there was perhaps a school there. This probably existed under the shadow of the royal manor where Athelstan met the embassy from Hugh, duke of the Franks, in 926. But by Eadred's time, it was a poor and neglected place, dependent totally on the small endowment of 40 hides which was probably the lands at Uffington which Athelstan the half-king had given around the year 931.[105] Archaeological investigation has confirmed the existence of the earliest foundation, though it has shed little light upon the buildings erected by Ethelwold.[106]

Eadred himself took a keen personal interest in the rebuilding of Abingdon. On one occasion, he actually came and measured out the footings himself, before proceeding to dine with Ethelwold in the refectory. He brought with him some Northumbrians, and Aelfric records how the whole party drank mead for the rest of the day 'until the Northumbrians were intoxicated after their fashion'! But the biographer admits that it was not until the reign of Edgar after 960 that the main rebuilding and the refashioning of the church were completed. Nonetheless, Abingdon was a foundation close to the heart of Eadred and his mother, Eadgifu. It was a royal creation, set amidst royal lands which had been granted to Ethelwold for the express intention of creating another Benedictine monastery after the pattern initiated by Dunstan at Glastonbury. Ethelwold emerged as a man of wealth and consequence, with a circle of followers and a style of monasticism that was very much his own.[107] After Dunstan was exiled by Edwy in 956, it was Ethelwold who took on the education of the young Prince Edgar, and both men exerted a formative influence upon him.[108]

The founding of Abingdon nevertheless marked an important development in the growth of monasticism in England. Ethelwold, it is said, desired a stricter life, more simply monastic than that which pertained at the monastery at Glastonbury, which was also an educational and political centre. He was a man of singular gifts, and this Dunstan recognised. Wulstan, in his 'Life of Ethelwold', recounts a vision which Dunstan had while abbot of Glastonbury of Ethelwold's future promise and role as a father of monks,[109] and Ethelwold confirmed later that he had had a similar vision of his mission. Abingdon was thus founded with the full support of Dunstan, and he and Ethelwold remained firm friends to the end of their lives.[110]

Aelfric records that initially Ethelwold had desired to go overseas to one of the reformed monasteries on the continent. In due course, he sent one of his monks, Osgar, who had come to Abingdon from Glastonbury, 'to the monastery of St Benedict at Fleury, there to learn the customs of the Rule and then expound them by his teaching to the brethren at home'.[111] Fleury had been reformed around the year 930, under the influence of Cluny. It may have been the place to which Ethelwold himself had yearned to go before the king gave him Abingdon, or he may have wished to go to Corbie, a house from which in due course he drew men skilled in singing the monastic chant according to the reformed manner; they taught the monks gathered at Abingdon from various parts of England a standard way of singing the psalms.[112] Discipline was Ethelwold's strength and his leadership and rigorism drew many to him. It was a measure of Dunstan's achievement at Glastonbury that in less than a generation men were seeking so disciplined and simple a monastic way of life. Yet, in the words of F.M. Stenton:

> The history that began when King Edmund gave the abbey of Glaston-
> bury to Dunstan would have followed a very different course had not
> King Eadred granted the 'monasteriolum' of Abingdon to Dunstan's
> follower, Ethelwold. It was at Abingdon that English monastic life was
> first affected directly by the example of discipline which prevailed in
> the religious houses of Flanders and Burgundy.[113]

Oda, the archbishop of Canterbury, had already sent his nephew Oswald to Fleury with the sanction of the king in order to live the monastic life undistracted by the worldliness of Winchester. This was probably around the year 950, for the anonymous biographer gives the impression that Oswald became an established and well-loved member of the community at Fleury. His reputation for sanctity, obedience and humility left a lasting impression, and Oswald was able to count on the active friendship of the monastery at Fleury for the rest of his life after his return to England in 959. He was ordained priest there, and was renowned for his melodious voice when singing the offices. Oda had evidently sent him there in order that one day he might return to England, possibly to lead the new community that Oda may have been planning to found at Ely.

> Oswald began to learn by memory the custom of the holy monastic
> law, and to retain the ecclesiastical offices by heart. For he desired,
> with the merciful consent of the Lord, to teach it to his fellow compat-
> riots at home, who had only been taught what was proper hitherto by
> foreigners.[114]

To this end, Oda summoned him back just before he died. This last reference to foreigners is interesting, and may allude to the tradition that Oda drew monks from Fleury to England, including possibly the young Abbo of Fleury, who later became a life-long friend of Dunstan.[115]

At no stage in the revival of Benedictine monasticism in England had developments occurred in isolation from what was happening on the continent. The whole movement had the same roots, used the same resources and attracted the patronage of kings, nobles and bishops for similar reasons. Athelstan and Alphege the Bald must have known about the early moves to revive monastic life abroad, and Athelstan was remembered at home and abroad as a patron of religious houses. To England German scholars had come, bringing books and contacts with them, and to Fleury and elsewhere English churchmen like Oda looked for practical guidance and inspiration. After the initial foundations had been safely established, in England and on the continent, the monastic movement generated its own momentum, politically and spiritually. The sense of monastic confraternity was strong and real and the thirst for and exchange of scholarship created special bonds. There was also a desire for uniformity in the sense of sharing in the riches and heritage of the whole tradition, and between houses and their rulers there began to emerge that sense of zeal and rivalry that drew the monasteries together. With the founding of Abingdon, the intermingling of English and continental monastic traditions became imminent.

5

EXILE AND RETURN

E *ADRED* was succeeded by Edmund's elder son, Edwy, who was crowned at
Kingston upon Thames in January 956: 'he for his great beauty got the
nickname "All-Fair" from the common people . . . and deserved to be loved'.[1]
This favourable verdict by his kinsman, Aethelweard, is corroborated by the
preface to the *'Liber vitae'* of New Minster, the place where Edwy was eventually
buried after a brief and unhappy reign which lasted just four years.[2] His
accession saw certain significant changes in the political life of England.
Wulfstan, archbishop of York, died; he was succeeded by Oskytel, who had been
appointed by Eadred to care for the northern church and to whom Edwy granted
lands with extensive rights at Southwell as a basis for his operations in the
north.[3] Athelstan the half-king of East Anglia also died, having retired to be a
monk under Dunstan at Glastonbury, and four ealdormen emerged at this time
who would survive Edwy and remain prominent into Edgar's reign: Aethelwold
of East Anglia, Athelstan's son and heir; Bryhtnoth of Essex; Aelfhere of Mercia;
and Aelfheah of Hampshire.[4] Two bishops assumed increasing importance at
court: Elfsige, bishop of Winchester, and Byrhthelm, the king's kinsman and
chaplain, whom he made a bishop early in his reign.[5] Edwy was a generous
benefactor to churches: Wilton, Bath Abingdon, Shaftesbury and New Minster
all benefited at his hand; and to Oda, the archbishop of Canterbury, the new king
granted extensive lands at Ely, the site of the foremost monastery in East Anglia
before the Viking invasions whose lands now lay in the king's gift.[6] No fewer
than twenty-four out of the eighty-five land grants made by Edwy were to
religious ends, though some of these are spurious; Edwy was remembered at
Bath, Abingdon and New Minster as a notable benefactor, and in his first grant
to Abingdon, which Dunstan witnessed as abbot, there occurs the striking
dedication to 'blessed Benedict, the most noble patron of the monks'.[7] Edwy
appears, however, to have been almost over-generous: sixty of these grants were
issued within his first year as king, probably in the wake of the coronation itself.
This had long been regarded as a sign of either political weakness or
inexperience, or both.[8] Edwy was only just 15 years old when he began to reign,
and 19 when he died. It is against this background that the famous story of
Dunstan's clash with the new king at his coronation feast must be seen.

41

Edwy, the son of King Edmund, succeeded, who being young in years, started to rule with little prudence, although as the elected monarch, he ruled by right over both peoples. A certain foolish woman, noble by birth, with a daughter ripe and alluring, attached herself to him. She pursued him and enticed him into intimate relationships, clearly in order to ally either herself or her daughter with him in marriage. It is said that the king consorted with them alternately, and shamelessly.

When the time came, as appointed, for him to be anointed and con-secrated king after the common election of all the English nobles, on the very day after this solemn occasion, he suddenly rushed out, full of lust, leaving the merry banquet and those of his nobles who were sitting with him as was meet, straight for the arms of that whore. When Oda the Archbishop saw the petulance of the king – and on this the day of his coronation too – and how it displeased all the council sitting round him, he said to his fellow-bishops and the other nobles: 'I beg you, let someone go from among you to bring the king back to this company so that, as is only fitting, he may be a joyful companion at this royal banquet.' But they, fearing either to incur the animosity of the king or the complaint of the woman, each began to make excuse and to draw back. Finally, they chose two from among them all whom they knew to be most constant in mind, Dunstan the abbot, and Kinsige the bishop, a kinsman of Dunstan's, who, conform-ing to the command of them all, would lead the king back, whether he wished it or not, to the seat he had left.

They entered, thus commanded, and they found the royal crown, which shone forth in a splendour of wonderful metal-work, gold, silver and gems, far from the king's head and lying carelessly tossed to the ground. The king was with them both after his evil custom, pres-sed close in with desire, like pigs wallowing in a pit. They said to him: 'Our peers have sent us in to ask you to come without delay to your seat at the decked table, and not to spurn your nobles by being absent from their joyful feast.' Dunstan became the first to challenge the folly of this woman, for when the king would not arise at the sign of his hand, Dunstan dragged him from his adulterous repose, placed the crown back on his head, and led him by the hand back into the royal company, thus snatching him by force from his women.[9]

It was an inauspicious beginning to the reign, and from this time on, Dunstan became the target for the hatred of the elder woman, Aethelgyfu.[10] The young king married her daughter, Elfgyfu, and she was in due course commemorated at New Minster as Edwy's queen.[11] Aethelgyfu's ascendancy at court led to the ousting and despoliation of the old queen mother, Eadgifu, and her retinue.[12] She, with the late Athelstan and Dunstan himself, had been closest to the former king, Eadred. John of Wallingford even asserts that Edwy, while heir presumpt-ive, had fomented discontent towards Dunstan, insinuating dishonesty on the part of the king's treasurer.[13] There is the story too in the first life of Dunstan of the vision which Athelstan the half-king imparted to Dunstan in which he saw the king's councillors turned into goats, which Dunstan interpreted as presaging future discord.[14] William of Malmesbury records a tradition that when Dunstan reached the body of the dead Eadred at Frome, he found it deserted by the courtiers; it fell to Dunstan and his monks and clergy to bury it at Winchester, in the Old Minster.[15] It may well have been the case that opposition

to Dunstan was simmering on account of his prominence under Eadred, and the
death of Athelstan, and the precipitate eclipse of the old queen mother, Eadgifu,
would have left him exposed to the calumnies of the woman, Aethelgyfu, and
her entourage. Adelard envisaged Dunstan returning to Glastonbury at this
point to supervise the building of the great tower there, during which he
checked the fall of a beam in a miraculous way.[16]

While at Glastonbury, Dunstan in his prayers encountered yet another
conflict with evil, which he overcame with the famous words: 'Let God arise and
let his enemies be scattered, and let those who hate him flee before his face'
(Psalm 68: 1).[17] This memory may well allude to a tangible crisis within the
community at Glastonbury, for Aethelgyfu was able to suborn certain of
Dunstan's own brethren, which led to a plot to evict him from the abbacy.
Perhaps Dunstan's many absences on royal business under Eadred had
distanced him from some of the community, or perhaps his custom of permitting
clerics to mingle with the monks proved fatal at last, especially if some of them
were related to families now antagonistic to him at court. Either way, the 'new
Jezebel' was able to harry Dunstan at court and in his monastery, finally
persuading the king and his council to proscribe him and to seize both his
personal property and the abbacy and monastery at Glastonbury.[18] This action
is a graphic example of 'the difficulty men found at that time in grasping the
distinction between lands belonging to monasteries which could not be forfeited
by individuals in charge of them, and lands in private ownership'.[19]

Life at Glastonbury continued under a new 'abbot', a royal nominee called
Aelsige to whom Edwy made some small grants of land.[20] The initial strength of
Edwy's political position in 956, which lay behind this action, rested upon the
loyalty of the west Saxon noble families, a loyalty which never wavered
throughout the reign. Before this apparently inevitable development, even Oda
the old archbishop had to bow, and both he and Edgar, the king's brother, sign
the charters recognising the new regime at Glastonbury. Dunstan, meanwhile,
was hardly safe among his friends, for by harbouring him they fell under the
king's wrath. In the autumn of 956, fearing for his safety and his very life,
narrowly escaping capture, and braving the storms of the Channel, he fled
abroad.[21]

> Dunstan, counted an exile for justice, crossed the sea and came to a
> great man of royal descent called Arnulf. At this time, this nobleman
> had restored in great elegance a certain monastery called Blandinium,
> which had been built by St Amandus, whither Arnulf had translated
> that great priest of God, Wandrille and his fellow-bishops. There
> blessed Dunstan remained for some long while, and left an example of
> light to be imitated.[22]

Thus wrote Adelard, the second biographer, a monk of the very house,
Blandinium, at Ghent, where Dustan took refuge. Arnulf, count of Flanders, was
the son of Baldwin II and Aelthryth, the daughter of Alfred the Great. He had
ruled from 918 and had long enjoyed close links with the English royal house
and its affairs.[23] It is possible that Dunstan was a distant kinsman of Arnulf's,
since Dunstan may have been descended from the family of Aethelwulf, Alfred's
father.

Arnulf and his family were at the forefront of the reformation of the
monasteries of Flanders, a reformation which drew its inspiration from the work
of Gerard of Brogne and John of Gorze, but which depended for its active impulse
upon lay patronage, both noble and royal.[24] Brogne was founded around the

year 920, and Gerard's influence as abbot spread directly into Flanders. John of Gorze was an outstanding spiritual figure, of great asceticism, who was still alive at the time of Dunstan's exile. Gorze was founded in 927 and brought completely under Benedictine rule in 933.[25] When Dunstan arrived at Blandinium, Arnulf's royal monastery there had but recently received renewal under the direct influence of John himself.[26]

John of Gorze and Gerard of Brogne looked back to Benedict of Aniane, the father of Benedictine monasticism as such. Benedict grew up under Charlemagne and flourished under Louis the Pious, Charlemagne's successor. He was of noble birth, but a hermit of strict life whose monasteries at Aniane and Inde were considered model institutions for the whole empire. Benedict was commissioned to reform monasteries far and wide, and in 817 regulations which were to govern monastic life throughout the empire were issued from a synod of abbots at Aachen. In these *capitula* Benedict aimed to establish the Rule of St Benedict as the authority and norm of monastic life, and to support it by a thorough collation of monastic traditions and customs.[27] The death of Benedict of Aniane and the collapse of the empire put an end to this attempt at monastic uniformity. Nonetheless, the memory remained: monasticism in the west meant Benedictine monasticism; reform and renewal, when it came, could legitimately call upon the active support of the temporal powers. Thus in England and on the continent, monastic renewal in the tenth century built upon this two-fold tradition.

The part played by temporal authority in the reformation of the monasteries was not without its hazards for the monks. Lay endowment threatened lay domination, the very phenomenon which had done so much to undermine and destroy earlier monasticism in England and on the continent. Bede, in 734, had complained bitterly to Archbishop Egbert of York about the way so-called 'monasteries' deteriorated into secular and lay establishments, often of ill repute.[28] Ethelwold, writing late in the reign of Edgar, singled out secular dominion of monastic lands as the greatest threat to the renewed Benedictine life.[29] In concert with the work of John of Gorze and Gerard of Brogne, but with slightly earlier beginnings, there arose at Cluny in 910 a fully reformed Benedictine monasticism based upon the rule as amplified by Benedict of Aniane, and characterised by a very full liturgical life. Cluny was distinct in seeking complete independence from all local lay control, and to that end it was put under the protection of the apostolic see. The second abbot, Odo (924–42), exercised a wide reforming role, visiting Rome itself in 936 to this end, 'although as late as 950 there is no certainty that any of the Roman monasteries were Benedictine'.[30] This was one of the darkest periods in the long history of the papacy, when the charisma of the successor of St Peter was all but obscured and the authority of the apostolic see more myth than reality.[31]

One of Odo's striking achievements was the reform of the monastery at Fleury sometime after 930. Fleury claimed to possess the body of St Benedict himself, supposedly transported thither from Monte Cassino to escape the ravages of the barbarians. It became a place of intense devotion to the cult of St Benedict, a place of pilgrimage for those who, like Oda and Oswald in England, looked to St Benedict and his rule for their spiritual guidance. The text of Pope Leo VII's privilege of 938 to Fleury captures well the firm attitude which the Cluniacs took towards lay domination of monasteries: 'neither shall the place or any property belonging to it ever be put under any (outside) authority, except that of the king; neither shall the king or any prince ever give the place to the lordship of any bishop, canon, abbot, layman, or any other person'.[32] The monastic community would elect its own abbot. Indeed, the abbot, Wulflad, under whom Oswald trained, was renowned for his wisdom and energy as a builder.[33]

Nonetheless, the new Benedictine monasteries did depend, for good or ill, upon local royal and lay support. The activities of Arnulf of Flanders are a notable example of the way monastic reforms were accomplished in the early tenth century. Blandinium itself was first endowed by Arnulf's father, Baldwin, and his wife (Alfred's daughter) as a royal burial place and shrine, rather like New Minster at Winchester.[34] The translation thither in 944 of the relics of St Wandrille and his companions by Arnulf marked another important stage in its growth as a royal monastery. This occurred in the same year that Arnulf turned his attentions to another monastery which had hitherto been the hereditary property of his family: St Bertin's. His son, Adelolf, count of Boulogne, a familiar emissary to the English court, had been lay abbot of St Bertin's until his death in 933.[35] In 944, Arnulf summoned Gerard of Brogne to reform St Bertin's, and this he did, despite local and popular opposition and against the wishes of the community itself. The refugees from this community eventually found their way to England where King Edmund granted them Bath Abbey.[36] Wulfgar, the 'abbot' of Bath, to whom Edwy granted lands, may have been one of these foreign refugees; he is described as the king's mass priest.[37]

St Bertin's prospered under its abbot, Hildebrandt, and by 954 he and Arnulf had restored Benedictine life in the neighbouring monastery at St Vedast. Blandinium, after some upheavals in 947, was ruled by Abbot Womar to whom Arnulf made many gifts of precious relics. When Dunstan arrived there, the count was on the verge of endowing a great rebuilding of the monastery which began in 960 and continued until Arnulf's death in 964.[38] The nearby monasteries at St Omer and at Corbie were associated with this process of reform; all these houses enjoyed regular contacts with England.[39]

Although Dunstan missed his own community at Glastonbury and recalled in exile 'what a peak of religious life he had left behind in that monastery',[40] he was clearly welcome at Blandinium in a community ordered along congenial lines. Arnulf proved a trusty and powerful protector, and this direct personal contact with the reformed monastic life on the continent proved of lasting influence in the life and work of Dunstan. Meanwhile, he was not out of touch with affairs in England, either political developments or the change of regime at Glastonbury. The first biographer recalls how in a dream Dunstan saw the Glastonbury monks in choir unable to complete an antiphon at vespers: 'How forcible are the words of the upright: do you imagine that you can reprove my words and make merchandise of your friend? Now therefore . . .' The closing words were: 'be pleased to look upon me', words which stuck in the throats of those who had betrayed their own abbot.[41] According to Adelard, it was at this time that Dunstan's own devotion to the apostle, St Andrew, was greatly deepened.[42]

William of Malmesbury asserts that Dunstan resided at Blandinium, 'not as an exile and stranger, but as an inmate and "abba" – father-in-God'.[43] This is confirmed by a document which is itself a singular monument to Dunstan's sojourn there. In 964, Edgar, at the behest of Dunstan, granted to the monastery of St Peter's (Blandinium), Ghent, lands at Lewisham and other places in Kent.[44] Despite a later interpolation alleging that this was a restoration of lands originally granted by Alfred to his daughter on her marriage to Baldwin of Flanders, the charter states that the king is granting the land to the monastery where Dunstan resided during his exile, and which enjoyed his rule and patronage at that time. From this it would appear that Dunstan may have functioned as prior of the community at Ghent, under Womar, the abbot. The context for this remarkable grant, the first known grant of land in Anglo-Saxon times to a foreign house, is provided by the letter of Arnulf to Dunstan, when newly archbishop of Canterbury. It was sent probably in 961 to assist the embassy of Adelof, abbot of St Bertin's, to the court of the new king of England, Edgar.[45] If so, the land grant came as a tangible expression of Dunstan's own personal gratitude, of his political influence with Edgar and as a token of the new king's friendship for his elderly kinsman.

The friendship with the religious houses in Flanders continued throughout Dunstan's life and beyond,[46] and Womar, abbot of Blandinium, retired at the end of his life to be a member of the community at New Minster. His death is recorded in the chronicle under the year 981.[47]

Edwy's new regime did not last long:

> It came about that this king was in due course wholly deserted by the northern people, being despised because he acted foolishly in the government committed to him, ruining with a vain hatred the shrewd and wise, and admitting with loving zeal the ignorant and those like himself.[48]

There is no evidence, however, that Edwy was motivated by feelings of hostility to the new monasteries, for Ethelwold remained at court throughout the reign. The new building programme at Abingdon came to a halt, however, during this period, no doubt because of the troubles which would have affected the community there, close as it was to the borders of Mercia and Wessex.[49] The verdict of Dunstan's first biographer is the same as that of Ethelwold himself: Edwy forfeited support because he behaved in an arbitrary manner, unsettling leading families in the localities and ignoring the susceptibilities of the various peoples under his rule. 'Through the ignorance of his youth he dispersed his kingdom and divided its unity, and also distributed the lands of the holy churches to rapacious strangers.'[50]

Osbern, in his biography of Dunstan, records the tradition that civil strife ensued and that Aethelgyfu, popularly regarded as the source of the trouble, was lynched at Gloucester.[51] Sometime in the later part of 957, Edgar left his brother's court and was chosen by the Mercians and Northumbrians to be their king in place of Edwy.[52] The west Saxons, as William of Malmesbury rightly observed, remained as ever loyal to the rightful heir.[53] If the reign of Edwy was a period when certain west Saxon families regained an ascendancy over the representatives of Mercia and the eastern Danelaw who had prevailed under Eadred, then this might well account for the manner in which the kingdom was divided along the River Thames 'with the agreement of all'.[54]

Edgar owed his position not only to the support of the Mercian and East Anglian aristocracy, men like Bryhtnoth of Essex, Aethelwold of East Anglia and Aelfhere of Mercia; he ruled too with the active support of Oswulf of Bamburgh, the powerful lord of the northern marches.[55] The venerable Bishop Cenwald of Worcester switched his support from Edwy to Edgar shortly before his death in 957, and Bishop Kinsige of Lichfield, Dunstan's kinsman and no friend of Edwy's, would have been prominent at the court of the new king. The figure of crucial influence and importance in this whole development was Oskytel, the bishop of Dorchester, who upon the death of Archbishop Wulfstan in 956 formally assumed the leadership of the northern church. The jurisdiction which he enjoyed in the lands only recently granted to him by Edwy 'set him in the exact position which the king himself had held'.[56] Stenton concludes that: 'it is probable that the permanent establishment of religious order, and of the civilisation which was its accompaniment, in this part of England, was due to the character, energy and ability of Archbishop Oskytel . . . among the greatest churchmen who have ever held the see of York'. Oskytel, and others of the Danish nobility like his own kinsman Thurkytel, abbot of Bedford, came to enjoy a singular influence over the way Edgar ruled his Mercian kingdom.

Meanwhile, England laboured under a dual rule: both kings issued charters, and at least one charter sheds light on the way petitioners were able to set the verdict of one king against another.[57] Edwy's position was further undermined by a public rebuke from Oda, the ageing archbishop of Canterbury, over the conduct of his private life. The chronicle asserts that Oda actually separated Edwy and his young wife, Elfgyfu, because they were too closely related; the earlier tradition in the anonymous 'Life of Oswald' alleges that Oda personally ousted the king's mistress from his company.[58] Clearly there was some scandal, and it would appear that Oda absented himself from Edwy's court for most of the last year of his life until his death in June 958.[59]

The weakness of Edwy was demonstrated by the fact that one of Edgar's earliest acts was to recall Dunstan 'the reverend abbot from the hateful exile in which he was languishing, remembering how much he had been revered by his predecessors, to whom he had rendered untiring service and loyal obedience with sound counsel'.[60] So, by the end of 957, Dunstan returned from his stay at Blandinium, 'with honour and glory'.[61] Edgar 'maintained him with every honour and dignity as was due to such a father'. He recompensed Dunstan and his family for the lands which they had forfeited in the kingdom of his brother, and for the temporary loss of Glastonbury itself.[62] Dunstan enjoyed close links with the East Anglian noble families, and with Oskytel of York, and these together with his kinsman, Kinsige, bishop of Lichfield, were undoubtedly instrumental in securing his return.

Soon after his accession and Dunstan's return, Edgar held a great council at Brandanford (possibly Brentford in Middlesex), 'and there by the choice of all Dunstan was ordained bishop, that he might constantly be in the royal presence on account of his farseeing and prudent counsels'.[63] Cenwald of Worcester may still have been alive, for it was only afterwards that Dunstan was designated to be bishop of Worcester. If the Canterbury tradition which commemorated Dunstan's ordination on 21 October recalled his consecration as a bishop, then this would have occurred on that date in 957.[64] Dunstan was then approaching the age of 50. Adelard records that it was Oda who came from Canterbury to consecrate Dunstan.[65] The primate could not name a see, for at this stage Dunstan was to serve as a court bishop; then in a moment of divine inspiration, he named him to be the next archbishop of Canterbury, to the wonder of some and the embarrassment of others!

Sometime early in 958, Oda the archbishop, sensing that his end was nigh, summoned his nephew Oswald back from Fleury. Oswald complied, though not without regrets, but he no sooner reached Dover than he learnt that his uncle had died before he could reach him. 'Having completed his devout journey to Canterbury, Oswald the monk went on to Oskytel, the Archbishop of York, who was his earthly kinsman.'[66] Oskytel proceeded to commend the young monk to 'the venerable bishop Dunstan, who was foremost in those days . . . and who loved Oswald with a divine charity'.[67] The death of Oda posed an immediate crisis in the affairs of the Church in the divided kingdom, and according to

Eadmer, Oskytel went to Rome, taking Oswald with him, to receive the *pallium*, and to regularise his position after the demise of Wulfstan.[68] Oswald apparently made another visit on the way back to Fleury, leaving his friend and companion Germanus there when eventually summoned to return to England by Oskytel. In the course of 959, Byrthhelm, bishop of London, died, and because London was a Mercian town Edgar appointed Dunstan to hold the see in plurality with Worcester.[69]

Upon the death of Oda, Edwy appointed Elfsige, bishop of Winchester, to be the new primate. Elfsige left an unhappy memory: he was no rigorist, and he left a son who fought against the Danes under Ethelred, falling in battle in 1001.[70] According to the anonymous 'Life of Oswald', Elfsige detested Oda and received a dire warning from the saint for insulting his grave.[71] William of Malmesbury suggests that he secured the see of Canterbury by simony.[72] With great haste he made his way to Rome to secure the *pallium*, but his party got caught in a severe snow storm crossing the Alps, and there the would-be archbishop died of cold, despite having his feet plunged into the belly of his horse![73] Thereupon, Edwy, in the closing months of his reign, appointed Byrhthelm, bishop of Wells, who probably also held Sherborne at this time[74] and who was a kinsman of his, to be the new archbishop; this is confirmed by a charter of Edwy's, which is signed by Byrthhelm, '*Dorobernensis ecclesiae episcopus*'.[75] About this time, Edwy appointed another kinsman, also called Byrthhelm, to the see of Winchester.[76]

Edwy died at the beginning of October 959, and according to Osbern, Dunstan interceded in a vision for the dead king's soul.[77] Edgar immediately acceded to the throne of the now reunited kingdom.

> He proceeded to restore Dunstan to the position & property he had formerly enjoyed and of which he had been deprived; and also his own grandmother [Eadgifu, the queen mother] and some others whom his late brother had caused to be plundered by an unjust judgement while he yet reigned.[78]

Within the month, Edgar dismissed Byrhthelm from the see of Canterbury. 'He was a man mild, modest, humble and kind', and incapable of exercising authority,[79] so he returned to his former see at Wells, where he remained as bishop until his death in 973.

'Then, in response to God and on the advice of his wise men, the king made Dunstan, whom he knew to be steadfast, Archbishop of Canterbury.'[80] He was probably enthroned on 21 October 959,[81] the twenty-sixth successor to St Augustine.

PART TWO

CANTERBURY:

AD 960–88

6

ARCHBISHOP OF CANTERBURY

*I*N 960, as soon as the winter was over, 'Dunstan went, by the long-drawn-out journeyings to which archbishops were accustomed, to the city of Rome, and arrived there finally by a propitious route'.[1] The scale of such a journey is recorded in the itinerary of one of Dunstan's successors, Sigeric, who travelled to Rome in 990. It describes a route through Italy, over the Alps and across the middle of France, of eighty stations from Rome to the English Channel near Witsand.[2] Dunstan stayed at the monastery of St Bertin's near St Omer, as did his later successors,[3] and so long a journey depended upon monastic and episcopal hospitality for its success. There is a delightful story in the first life which illustrates well the strength of these connections and the haphazard nature of such a journey. After many days of travelling, the supplies were running low, and Dunstan's steward chided him for the lavish way he had given so much away in alms. As Dunstan went off to say vespers, having tried to reassure his harrassed companion, the steward retorted: 'Just you go off and adore this Christ of yours who pays no attention to our needs!' The story concludes:

> Now there were in that same town, where the man of God was staying with his companions, messengers from a certain venerable abbot, who for three days had been waiting the arrival of the blessed bishop. Just as Dunstan was beginning to sing the office of Vespers, they arrived to greet the bishop and his faithful company with rich provisions of gifts and other delicacies from all the places around about, as a gift by the kindly prayer of that abbot and his brethren. Dunstan gratefully accepted their gifts of alms, and returned greeting to the gracious abbot and to the devoted community of brethren living under vows with him.[4]

From the beginning of the Roman mission to England, the successors of St Augustine had received the *pallium* directly from the pope himself, and by the tenth century it had become the regular custom of the new primate to make the dangerous journey to Rome to receive this badge of metropolitan authority. The *pallium* itself is a band of white wool worn by the pope; it was conferred upon the archbishops of Canterbury *in partem sollicitudinis*, and was the symbol of their

51

direct relationship with the apostolic see itself.[5] In the Sherborne Pontifical, a liturgical book intimately associated with Dunstan's primacy at Canterbury, there is a detailed account of how the archbishop received the *pallium* from the altar of St Peter, having first accepted a written privilege from the pope himself. The text of this privilege is preserved also in the Sherborne Pontifical, and it enjoins Dunstan to be a faithful bishop and specifies the occasions upon which the *pallium* might be worn by him.[6] These include the feasts of Our Lord and of the Apostles, as well as the occasions when the primatial authority was exercised in the consecration of bishops. The personal nature of the privilege is reflected in the provision that Dunstan might wear the *pallium* on his birthday. It is also significant that the Feast of the Assumption of Mary (15 August) is singled out by the pope as another suitable occasion. Dunstan remained throughout his life singularly devoted to Mary in a century which saw the steady increase in the formal prominence accorded to the Virgin by the western Church.[7]

The pope from whom Dunstan received his *pallium* and privilege was John XII, who had reigned since 955. The papacy stood on the verge of an acute crisis, caught between the pressing threats of Berengar, king of Italy, and the rising pretensions of the German ruler, Otto the Great. Less than two years after Dunstan's visit, John XII invoked the aid of Otto, creating him emperor in February 962, during which ceremony the pope handed him an ornate copy of the infamous 'Donation of Constantine'. This marriage of convenience soon collapsed amidst acrimonious wrangling and in the autumn of 963, after a revolt in Rome, John was deposed and replaced by a layman, Leo VIII, at the direct instigation of the emperor, who insisted that thereafter future popes should swear fealty to him. John, however, engineered his return as soon as the emperor had left, and deposed Leo and his entourage most cruelly. John was murdered in 964 and was succeeded by Benedict V, whom the emperor duly deposed, replacing him with the hapless Leo! Leo in turn died, in 965, and Benedict returned to reign briefly again. The emperor once more intervened and appointed John XIII, and in 967, at Christmas, Otto's son was crowned by the pope as co-emperor. But this imperial ascendancy was more apparent than real, and for forty years the papacy languished under the corrupt sway of the Roman Crescenti family. John XIII survived until 972, but his successor, Benedict VI, was murdered in 974. His heir, Benedict VII, reigned until 983; the next pope, John XIV, was murdered and replaced briefly by Boniface VII (who had made a brief appearance as pope in 974). He too was murdered, whereupon John XV reigned until 996, when he summoned the new young emperor, Otto III, to his aid, with momentous consequences for the history of the papacy and Europe.[8]

Despite this sordid and complex history, the papacy continued to exercise an influence upon European, and therefore English, affairs far out of proportion to the real power and personalities of the popes. Remarkably, the machinery of the papacy continued to operate, and rulers sought papal approval and privileges for their religious foundations. Rome remained the 'eternal city' and pilgrims flocked to the tombs of Peter and Paul and the other venerable saints and martyrs buried there. The very weakness and corruption of the Roman Church laid it open to Frankish and German ecclesiastical influence and liturgical usage, to the extent that it has been claimed that 'it was the Franko-German church which, at this critical epoch, saved the Roman liturgy for Rome and the western world'.[9] The symbol of this development was the fact that during the sixty years after 962, five German kings were crowned as emperors of the Romans at St Peter's Basilica. This elaborate and impressive ceremonial not only elevated the

German emperors, it emphasised the crucial and indispensable role of the pope, or more precisely of the institution of the papacy, without which there could be no emperor in the west.[10]

Dunstan too came to Rome as a pilgrim: 'he made offerings at the shrines of the saints, and ministered to Christ's poor, and so he returned in peace from his journeyings to his native-land'.[11] Again, the record of Sigeric's itinerary in 990 affords details of the likely objects of Dunstan's devotions: St Mary's of the *scola Anglorum*,[12] the churches of St Valentine, St Agnes and St Laurence outside the walls; St Sebastian, St Anastasius, St Paul, and St Mary *scolam Graecam*, St Cecilia, St Mary across the Tiber and St Pancras. These saints and martyrs, many of whom were commemorated in the English kalendars, epitomised the awesome tradition of the Roman Church to which English Christians showed peculiar devotion.[13] The Blickling Homilies, collated during Dunstan's primacy, reflect this clearly.[14] In the chronicle, the pilgrimage of Aethelmod the priest to Rome is recorded in 962; Bishop Cyneweard of Wells, formerly abbot of Milton, may well have made a similar journey at the end of his life in 975.[15] Oswald, on his appointment as archbishop of York in 972, travelled as Edgar's emissary to Rome, carrying large gifts and disbursing generous alms.[16] Among the miracle stories narrated by Aelfric in his 'Life of St Swithun' is the tale of how a certain rich English thegn went blind, travelled to Rome seeking a cure but was disappointed there and remained blind for four more years until Swithun came to his rescue.[17] Dunstan's own dreams, recorded by both the first biographer and by Adelard, testify to the deep impression which Rome made on his mind and spirit, an impression which abided throughout his life.[18]

During his primacy, Dunstan maintained the traditional pattern of links with Rome, and these appear to have been both financial and judicial; the restoration of the monasteries also occasioned appeals for papal authority and protection.

Edgar's second code of law, issued at Andover shortly after Dunstan's return from Rome, places the traditional methods of raising financial support for the Church on an organised footing. Having prescribed the tithe, it enjoins the payment of Peter's pence, with the following penalties for delay: 'He who has not rendered it by the appointed day is to take it to Rome, and 30 pence in addition, and then to bring back a document showing that he has handed over that amount there. When he comes home, he is to pay 120 shillings to the king.'[19] So stern a penalty probably reflects the difficulty encountered in raising such church taxes; nonetheless it stands as a measure of royal and episcopal commitment to this ancient financial obligation to the apostolic see. Evidence of judicial appeals is sketchy, but Adelard recounts the fascinating story of how Dunstan:

> rebuked a certain noble-man often for his illicit marriage; but because he could not correct him he finally cut him off with the sword of the gospel of Christ [i.e. excommunication]. So the noble-man went off to Rome and prevailed upon the prince of the apostles to write on his behalf to Dunstan. Dunstan, true to his name ['stone' or 'rugged'], as an unmoveable mountain, or as a stone fixed into the Corner-stone, could not be moved. Instead he persisted firm in his mind and superior in judgement to the mind of the apostle [i.e. pope], saying to his 'legate', 'Know that only the authority of my Lord will move me, not the threat of punishment!'[20]

When Edgar came to authorise the expulsion of the 'canons' from the Old Minster at Winchester in 964 (in order to introduce monks)[21] at the behest of the new bishop, Ethelwold, he could claim direct papal approval for his policy in the form of a remarkable and probably unique document, which was later preserved by Archbishop Parker.[22] Such a direct appeal must have been channelled through Dunstan, the archbishop of Canterbury, and may well have been initiated by him in order to resolve a peculiarly difficult political challenge to the royal policy towards the monasteries.[23] What is striking about this document is that its language resembles closely the prologue to the *'Regularis concordia'* in which the influence of Dunstan is clear and explicit. It may well be that the papal decree, which endorsed and facilitated the royal action at Winchester, was actually drafted by Dunstan before being sent to Rome.[24] Glastonbury also claimed a privilege, probably from John XII (and if so, obtained perhaps by Dunstan as a result of his visit in 960), in which the pope received 'that place into the bosom of the Roman church and the protection of the blessed apostles'. This decree was duly ratified by Edgar, the Glastonbury monks claimed, at London in the twelfth year of his reign.[25] Such papal acts of protection and exemption for monasteries grew apace during the latter half of the tenth century,[26] and were not without precedent in England. What such papal involvement might mean, and the nature of the spiritual power it was believed the pope could wield on behalf of a threatened house, can be seen in an unusual letter, probably from John XV (after 985) to the ealdorman Aelfric (either of Mercia or of Hampshire).[27] Here the pope rebukes the nobleman who has abused his relationship as a near neighbour of Glastonbury, having seized estates and villages belonging to it. Threatening excommunication unless Aelfric desists, the pope admonishes 'your love to cease pillaging that place, for fear of the Apostles Peter and Paul, and out of respect for us'. Shortly after the death of Dunstan in 988, there is another letter from the same pope, John XV, confirming a peace treaty between Ethelred of England and Richard of Normandy which had been brought about by papal mediation; this is an interesting if rare example of the diplomatic role of the papacy at this time.[28]

No clearer picture can be drawn of relationships between Rome and England given the paucity of remaining material. But it is beyond doubt that the archbishop of Canterbury was the principal channel for all such communications, and he in a very real way represented the patriarch of the western Church to the English, and indeed to much of north-western Europe at this time. During Dunstan's primacy, the weakness of the papacy and the strength and prestige of Edgar bolstered this prominence, and added influence and some real power to an office already surrounded with an aura of antiquity and sanctity.[29]

Dunstan inherited bishops who had been appointed by Oda, many of whom continued to serve during the first half of his primacy. There can be little doubt that Dunstan was regarded by many as the natural successor to Oda, and Osbern recounts the strange but moving story of how on the day that Dunstan came to celebrate the mass in the cathedral at Canterbury for the first time, the Holy Spirit hovered over him in the form of a dove throughout the consecration:

> When the Mass was ended, it rested on the memorial to blessed Oda
> which had been constructed in the form of a pyramid to the south
> side of the altar. From that day, Dunstan the archbishop always rever-
> enced the merits of that man of God, and he never passed by without
> bending the knee and calling him a good man, saying: 'Here lies Oda
> the Good.'[30]

The appointment of Dunstan to Canterbury thus secured a great measure of continuity, and there is a very real sense in which Dunstan's achievements rested upon the foundations laid by Oda and his bishops.

Foremost among these bishops was Oskytel, who remained archbishop of York until 971 and was the keystone to royal and ecclesiastical policy in the north, East Anglia and the eastern Danelaw. Dunstan enjoyed the support of his own kinsman, Kinsige of Lichfield, for the crucial opening years of the new reign until 963/4. The sees of Crediton, Elmham, Chester-le-Street, Hereford, Dorchester with Lindsey and Ramsbury were served also by men whom Oda had appointed and who remained as bishops into the 970s.[31] A more difficult inheritance, perhaps, was the legacy of Edwy: the handful of bishops, mainly kinsmen of the king, whom the late king had appointed – Byrhthelm of Wells; another Byrhthelm, of Selsey; yet a third Byrhthelm, who succeeded Elfsige at Winchester; also Aelfweald, who went to Sherborne and remained there until 978. All these were Wessex sees, closely associated with the areas and families which had lent their support to the regime of Edwy. Opposition to the appointment of Dunstan, and to the policies of reform and monasticism for which he stood, certainly persisted at Winchester, and perhaps elsewhere in Wessex too.[32]

Nonetheless, the archbishop of Canterbury enjoyed a unique ascendancy over the Church in England, and over the appointment of its bishops. These appointments were always made in conjunction with the wishes of the king, and it would appear that Dunstan exercised a decisive influence over the young king, Edgar. In a letter written much later by Dunstan to Ethelred concerning the state of the Cornish see, the way in which this collaboration operated can be glimpsed: 'When King Edgar ordered me to consecrate Wulfsige [before 963], he and all our bishops said that they did not know who might own the estates [in dispute] with greater right than the bishop of the diocese, when he was thoroughly loyal and preached God's faith rightly and loved his lord.'[33]

Dunstan's first move was to appoint bishops to the two sees which he had held in plurality during the division of the kingdom, London and Worcester. To London he appointed Aelfstan, who was to serve for over thirty years until 995/6 and who exercised a decisive political influence during the troubled years of Ethelred's reign. To Worcester Dunstan sent his young friend, Oda's nephew, Oswald, recently returned from Fleury.

> Dunstan asked the powerful king, Edgar, to give Oswald the apostolic
> see which was vacant at Worcester, which he duly acquired from the
> king by this request. Oswald was commended to the earthly monarch
> by the bishops of that region . . . and was later elected and
> honourably consecrated by the bishops as one fitted for the care of
> such an office.[34]

This was probably in 961, and in the light of subsequent developments was a highly significant move, for Oswald was a practising monk and one of his first actions as a bishop was to found a small monastery at Westbury.[35]

In 963, Byrhthelm of Winchester died, and the most powerful see in the kingdom after Canterbury itself lay vacant. 'In that year Abbot Ethelwold succeeded to the bishopric of Winchester, and he was consecrated on the eve of St Andrew's day. That day was a Sunday.'[36] This was a decisive political move by Dunstan and the young king. At the heart of the Wessex religious establishment was placed the man who, after Dunstan himself, most represented the monastic reform movement in the Church, and did so in a vigorous and uncompromising way. Moreover, Ethelwold enjoyed an influence over Edgar comparable only with that of the archbishop himself.[37] With the sees of Canterbury and York, London, Worcester and Winchester in the hands of such men, and with the active zeal and support of the king himself, the reform of the

Church could proceed. In 964, Dunstan completed his circle by appointing Aelfstan, who was a close friend of Ethelwold and of the archbishop, to Rochester.[38]

> For the reformers were aiming at something more than a revival of
> strict monastic observance. They were endeavouring, partly by per-
> sonal influence and partly through the medium of their cathedral
> churches, which became centres of learning, to rouse the enthusiasm
> of the laity and to raise the standards of the secular clergy.[39]

Dunstan's first biographer rightly observed the manner in which men were drawn from Glastonbury to become 'deans, abbots, bishops, even archbishops, as well as foremost in other orders of clergy',[40] and Adelard actually avers that 'Dunstan would not permit any but outstanding abbots or religious monks to serve in the hierarchy of the church'.[41] This last observation is not strictly true: the see of London was never occupied by a monk in Dunstan's time, and Dunstan made non-monastic appointments to Lichfield in 963 (Winsige), and to Selsey in 967 (Ealdhelm). The mission sees of Chester-le-Street, Elmham and Cornwall could hardly support a monastic appointment or establishment at this time, and so they were served by non-monastic bishops.[42] Nonetheless, during Dunstan's time, 77 per cent of the episcopal appointments were of monastic clergy, and this tendency persisted long after Dunstan's death. Just over half these appointments were drawn from the circle of men associated with Dunstan himself at Glastonbury; the remainder came from the circle of Ethelwold at Abingdon and Winchester, a few being protégés of Oswald, who became archbishop of York in 972.[43] This was a bold and sustained policy, and one of its immediate consequences was that some cathedral communities began gradu- ally to assume a monastic character, in part at least. The directions and intentions which Dunstan laid down for these monastic bishops in the 'Regularis concordia' were clear:

> Where monks live the monastic life in a bishop's see, the election of
> the bishop shall be carried out in the same way as that of an abbot, if,
> by the Lord's grace, a monk of sufficient worth be found in that place.
> . . . As for him who is chosen to be bishop, he shall live with his
> monks, unceasingly and with exceeding diligence and care, keeping to
> the monastic life in everything, as would the abbot of a monastery.

All this was to be discharged 'with the consent and advice of the King and according to the teaching of the Holy Rule'.[44] After Dunstan's death in 988, although the pre-eminence of the monks among the bishops was never quite the same, a clear tradition remained. Almost all the monks appointed to sees in the years up to the conquest were drawn from the Dunstan circle; and from 988 until 1038 the six archbishops of Canterbury were monks from Glastonbury, in a real way, therefore, the spiritual heirs of Dunstan himself.

There are several glimpses of the close-knit character of Dunstan's circle of monastic clergy and bishops. Both the early biographies of Dunstan sprang out of this milieu, and although both writers were foreigners, it was to the memory of this circle of Dunstan's friends that they appealed.[45] The close friendship that existed between Dunstan, Oswald and Ethelwold was clearly of crucial importance to the whole reform of the Church. Both men owed much to Dunstan, both personally and in terms of their appointments, and Dunstan retained his hold over even as strong a character as Ethelwold to the end. There is a story, for example, in the 'Life of Ethelwold' of how Dunstan alone could persuade and order Ethelwold to mitigate the severity of his fasting.[46] According to Adelard, it was Aelfgar, Dunstan's chaplain (not a monk), later bishop of Elmham, who had the vision of the heavenly summons to Dunstan immediately prior to his death.[47] Adelard also relates how Dunstan learnt in a vision of St Andrew that he was to appoint his old friend, Alphege, abbot of Bath, to be bishop of Winchester in succession to Ethelwold, who died in 984.[48]

The two early lives of Ethelwold also illuminate the spirit of monastic cameraderie which pervaded among these bishops. There is an alarming story of the extremes to which Ethelwold's idea of monastic obedience could run when he commanded one of his monks, Aelfstan, while at Abingdon, to plunge his hand into a cauldron of boiling water; this he did, and the hand survived unharmed as a sign of his virtue. Aelfstan moved on to Old Minster, Winchester, and in due course became bishop of Ramsbury in 970.[49] Another important member of Ethelwold's circle of friends was Aethelgar, who became abbot of the New Minster and, in 980, bishop of Selsey; it was he who succeeded Dunstan as archbishop of Canterbury in 988.[50] In 992, Ealdwulf, whom Ethelwold had made abbot of the renewed monastery of Peterborough, became archbishop of York in succession to Oswald.[51] Aescwig, who became bishop of Dorchester in 979, was a close friend of Oswald's also;[52] originally a monk from Old Minster, he was warlike in more than a spiritual sense, for in 992 he took a hand in leading an abortive naval operation against the Danes.[53] A charming letter from Elfweard, abbot of Glastonbury, to his erstwhile pupil Sigeric, now (in 990) the new archbishop of Canterbury but formerly Dunstan's choice as abbot of St Augustine's, Canterbury, reveals how this tradition of common dedication, learning and discipline continued to hold fast into the next generation of bishops.[54]

In 980, at the rededication of the newly-enlarged Old Minster, Wulstan in his 'Life of Ethelwold' paints a dramatic picture of the monastic bishops in action: there were nine of them: Dunstan and Ethelwold, Aelfstan of Rochester, Aethelgar of Selsey, Aelfstan of Ramsbury, Aescwig of Dorchester, Alphege of Lichfield, Aethelsige of Sherborne and Athulf of Hereford.[55] With the exception of Aethelgar (who had until recently been abbot of the adjacent New Minster), all these are listed in the Hyde 'Liber vitae' as episcopal brethren of the Old Minster whom the community remembered in their prayers.[56]

The importance of so cohesive an episcopate cannot be underestimated, and it was Dunstan's achievement to create and to lead this team of bishops, many of whom were united by a common discipline and vision. Dunstan himself was archbishop of Canterbury for twenty-eight years. Dunstan presided in a highly traditional manner, so much so as at times to seem almost invisible, especially in the reform and renewal of the monasteries; constancy, determination, and diplomacy, qualities without which no such major reform could have prospered, proved to be the hallmarks of his primacy. The strength of his own position, and that of his leading fellow bishops, notably Oswald and Ethelwold, made possible the profound changes in custom and land tenure which had to occur throughout the shires as churches and monasteries were endowed. It was Dunstan's particular political task as primate to carry the king, Edgar, with him, and to commend the Church's policies to the leading lay nobility. In the enforcement of justice in the shire courts, the integrity of the local bishop was indispensable, and it was in a judicial capacity also that Dunstan and his fellow bishops made their presence felt, not only by the exercise of ecclesiastical penalties. Further afield, the steady expansion of the Church in the north, and the consolidation of its position in East Anglia and eastern

Danelaw, required the strong co-operation of leading magnates, the king and the bishops, led by Dunstan, Oskytel and, in due time, Oswald. Likewise, the partnership between king and archbishop lay behind the extension of the influence of Canterbury into Wales and the other tributary kingdoms, and overseas by way of the missions to Scandinavia. The great renewal of monastic life was the crown to this whole movement of church reform and influence within political and national life. Such was the relationship between Edgar and Dunstan that, despite inevitable differences and some difficulties, Church and kingdom were remarkably at one in policy and operation, a unity symbolised in the prominence accorded to Edgar's coronation in 973, but whose fragility was highlighted by events immediately after his death.

Much of Dunstan's time as archbishop was spent in his own diocese of Canterbury, which he may have administered with the assistance of a suffragan at St Martin's in the see city.[57] He perambulated the various manors held by the archbishop elsewhere in Kent and southern England, using them also as bases for his occasional visitations to the religious houses with which he was particularly involved or for attending court. The archbishop of Canterbury was the leading magnate in Kent, giving judgement at the south door of the cathedral in causes which could not be tried or resolved elsewhere. The cathedral of Christ Church was an imposing and venerable symbol of the archbishop's office: the eastern end was in the form of an apse containing the altar to Christ and the tomb of Oda, and behind that was the shrine of Wilfrid. From this altar the new primate received again his *pallium* and processed westwards to the altar of Our Lady in the western apse, behind which stood the *cathedra* on which he sat. In this position he would celebrate the mass, facing east, with the people also facing east, their backs towards him.[58]

The community of Christ Church was an ancient body; its members were the custodians of the precious relics and archives of the cathedral which were kept in the baptistery off the eastern end of the building, and of the tombs of the archbishops. They were probably a body of clergy living under some kind of canonical rule, though they were hardly monastic in the strictest sense.[59] Under Oda and the foreign scholar, Frithegod, learning had revived to some extent, centred on the ancient library where Dunstan himself spent many hours correcting manuscripts at first light.[60] Dunstan undoubtedly introduced some monks into the community, but there is no reason to suppose that Christ Church did not remain a mixed community of clerks and monks throughout his episcopate, as perhaps Glastonbury had been, though in rather different circumstances. Dunstan's own chaplain, Aelfgar, later bishop of Elmham, is described as a 'cleric',[61] and that was at the very end of Dunstan's life; it was to his 'monks and clergy' that he taught the music of the anthem that had occurred to him in a heavenly dream.[62] It was only under Archbishop Aelfric in 997 that Christ Church became fully monastic. Under Dunstan it became the archbishop's own *familia* of clergy and monks devoted to him, where foreigners and strangers might come and feel immediately at home.[63] But with his monks he maintained a fully monastic way of life, observing the Benedictine offices in full in choir,[64] and keeping, for example, the summer siesta, prescribed in the 'Regularis concordia' and the rule, to the end of his life.[65]

Dunstan safeguarded the material interests of the community also. His friendship with Eadgifu, the old queen mother, secured two properties in Kent for Christ Church, perhaps in thanksgiving for the restoration of her property by Edgar.[66] The generosity of thegns and other nobility remained important for the prosperity of the cathedral community. The most striking example of this is the bequest sometime after 973 of the manor at Meopham in Kent, together with a lavish gift of gold and two silver cups, by the thegn, Byrhtric, and his wife, Aelfswith.[67] There is some evidence too that Dunstan continued Oda's work of rebuilding the cathedral and its community buildings, possibly reordering the crypt in anticipation of his own burial there.[68] The library and scriptorium were also prime concerns of Dunstan, and its likely composition was highly traditional. The fire of 1067 destroyed much, but at least thirty-seven volumes remain from the pre-conquest library; from the time of Dunstan only splendid gospel books, Frithegod's poetical 'Life of Wilfred' and Dunstan's own Sherborne Pontifical and Bosworth Psalter;[69] otherwise many of the traditional monastic texts were similar to those alluded to in Bede or listed by Alcuin as being in the library at York.[70] Although some of these books were probably written after the sack of Canterbury by the Danes in 1011, by which time Christ Church had been monastic for two decades, there is evidence that some were written as early as about 990, possibly during Sigeric's primacy. The impetus for the formation of such a monastic library and scriptorium was almost certainly Dunstan's: 'He would correct erroneous books & erase false writings as soon as he could study them by the first light of dawn.'[71] Within a decade of his death, he was regarded by the community as 'foremost of all the saints who rest at Christ Church'.[72]

The other monastic community at Canterbury in which Dunstan maintained a keen interest was St Augustine's, the ancient foundation which lay just to the east of the cathedral, outside the city walls, where some form of regular monastic life may well have persisted into the tenth century.[73] Its abbots remain shadowy figures: Eadhelm, a likely contemporary of Dunstan while still abbot of Glastonbury; Aelfric, who was abbot when Dunstan became primate and remained until 971; Aethelnoth, about whom nothing is known; and finally Sigeric, Dunstan's pupil from Glastonbury, who was abbot from around 980 until becoming bishop of Ramsbury in 985. He was succeeded by Wulfric, who sent the first life of Dunstan to Abbo of Fleury to be turned into verse just before Abbo's death in 1004.[74]

Dunstan himself was in the habit of praying at St Augustine's, keeping the night vigils and reciting the psalter:

> While he was offering himself up there in holy prayers, he moved to
> the eastern church to pray to the Mother of God. He was approaching,
> singing the psalms, when suddenly, in a quite unexpected way, he
> heard unusual voices of sweet singing in the night, echoing in the
> church with subtle melodies. Peeping through a hole in the perforated
> screen, he saw that the church was completely filled with a shining
> light, and a crowd of virgins was going around in order singing as a
> choir this hymn of the poet Sedulius: 'Cantemus socii Domino, etc.'[75]

St Augustine's at that time was really a complex of three churches: the main one was dedicated to Peter, Paul and Augustine and contained the tombs of the first archbishops; to the east of this stood the church of the Virgin; and beyond that was the chapel of St Pancras. There is evidence of rebuilding and extension during the time of Dunstan, both of the church and of the monastic buildings, although the scale and the shape remain unclear.[76] There is a late tradition in William of Thorne's Chronicle that in 978 Dunstan conducted a great service of rededication for the reformed and enlarged monastery and church.[77]

The advent of Dunstan's pupil, Sigeric, in 980 may have crowned this refurbishment of St Augustine's. Certainly it was at this time that the library of the monastery was enriched by the work of its own scriptorium. Sigeric himself may have been the instigator of this development; he may also have been the instigator of the comparable but later developments at Christ Church when he was archbishop. T.A.M. Bishop writes of these manuscripts produced at St Augustine's:

It is a group of manuscripts of comparable size [to the Christ Church group] whose epicentre seems to be earlier than the Christ Church group. The St Augustine's group includes specimens of excellent late square minuscule handwriting; it seems to be preceded by a kind of square minuscule that can be placed about the middle of the 10th century; and its Caroline minuscule seems to be allied, to be in not exactly immediate succession to a specimen of Caroline minuscule written at Glastonbury. If this excellent but clearly primitive specimen of English Caroline was written by St Dunstan, then the evidence of the manuscripts concurs with the charters in placing the introduction of this script about the middle of the 10th century.[78]

The precise dating of manuscripts is fraught with hazard, but this thread of continuity in style between Glastonbury and St Augustine's may be a precious indicator of Dunstan's impact upon the intellectual life of that house. Certainly it was at St Augustine's that the first historical interest in preserving the memory of Dunstan was kindled, and this expressed itself in the revision and transmission of the first life of the saint.[79]

Kent was divided ecclesiastically into two dioceses, Canterbury and Rochester, and from the beginning Rochester had tended to fall under the penumbra of the archbishop of Canterbury, sometimes to the extent that it appeared to function as a suffragan see to the mother church. It was, of course, a venerable see, dating back to the mission of St Augustine himself; but on the whole it was an impoverished bishopric, and there is no evidence of organised monastic life there in the tenth century.[80] The close friendship between Aelfstan, the bishop of Rochester, and Dunstan has been remarked upon and is attested more than once.[81] Adelard is the first to attribute Dunstan's special care for Rochester, whose cathedral is dedicated to St Andrew, to his devotion to that saint who, he believed, had assisted him at various crises and turning points in his life: 'The sword proffered him by St Andrew [in the vision after he had refused a bishopric] contains the see of Rochester, in which although he never sat as bishop, he shewed care and concern.'[82] The later historians duly elaborated this tradition in the interests of Canterbury. But the reason why Dunstan was remembered as a staunch defender of Rochester was more prosaic. In 986, during the upheavals of the early part of Ethelred's reign, the king fell out with the bishop of Rochester, distrained some land belonging to the see, and actually besieged the bishop in his cathedral city. Dunstan rebuked the young king for his rashness, but to no avail; he had to resort to other means, and finally bought Ethelred off. Later, the king restored the lands, lamenting the follies of his youth.[83]

In two remarkable documents,[84] Dunstan can be glimpsed restoring land to Rochester which for various reasons, good and bad, had passed out of the ancient patrimony of that church. The first was ratified before Edgar's witan in London towards the end of his reign; the other was ratified before Dunstan himself, as archbishop, at his manor at Wrotham in Kent, in the company of Aelfstan of London, the clergy of St Paul's Cathedral and Aelfstan of Rochester, together with the complete community of Christ Church, Canterbury, who had an interest in the case. The king's interest on this occasion was represented by the priest, Wulfsige, who was the *scirman* (shire reeve). 'All Kent, east and west, was there', and the judgement of Dunstan in the favour of Rochester was solemnly and publicly acclaimed, and published throughout Sussex, Wessex, Middlesex and Essex. The occasion gives a clear picture of the way in which the archbishop of Canterbury presided over Kentish affairs as a justice and as the arbiter of the various ecclesiastical interests in both dioceses.

It was, however, as a diocesan bishop that Dunstan was best remembered in Kent, and in his own diocese of Canterbury in particular.

> Thus having become archbishop of the English, Dunstan was filled
> with all spiritual gifts, and he who was superior to all other orders of
> the clergy began first to submit himself to the higher service of Christ.
> Not only did he administer the comforts of the true faith to others, but
> he also demonstrated the right path to heaven by his salutary preach-
> ing. . . . So Dunstan began to renew that which was cast down, to
> vindicate that which was neglected, to enrich holy places, to love the
> just, to recall the erring to the way, to build the churches of God, and
> so to live up to the name of a true pastor among all men.[85]

Two of the miracle stories associated with his work as archbishop of Canterbury, recounted in Eadmer's life, took place in connection with the dedication of new church buildings. On one occasion he called forth a spring of water at the inauguration of a new church built by a 'noble and religious man'; on the other, Dunstan himself realigned the new wooden church at Mayfield in Kent.[86] These episodes were simply the memorable incidents in a whole programme of provision for the parochial ministry, according to Eadmer. In this way did the parochial system begin to supplement the older pattern of minster churches and their archaic 'mission' areas. This development relied on the support of the lay nobility, and more especially of the thegns, and was expressly provided for in the laws of Edgar prescribing the tithe.[87] Dunstan, for example, purchased land for the benefit of St Martin's in Canterbury and 'those who serve God there'.[88] It was his example as a diocesan bishop that gave his occasional visitations to other dioceses and monasteries their particular effectiveness.

The power of Dunstan's own example as a bishop, either in his own day or in the memory of those who came after him, cannot be overestimated. Like Oda before him, he was the living embodiment of the Anglo-Saxon 'good bishop': 'an unshakeable pillar of the Church, distinguished in deed and doctrine, of angelic countenance, bold in acts of mercy and words of prophetic judgement'.[89] 'Dunstan was a faithful bishop, oak-like in hope, and joined to Christ in Divine Love, and familiarity with true justice: he took care to pray to the Lord always.'[90] Perhaps Wulfstan of York, a bishop of the succeeding generation, had Dunstan in mind when he described the ideal bishop in his 'Institutes of polity':

> First to his prayers, & then to his book-work,
> Reading or writing, teaching or learning,
> And to see the canonical hours in their due time,
> And to all things that pertain to them;
> To wash the feet of the needy and to distribute alms,
> And to give instruction where it is needed.
>
> Also good craftsman's work is proper to him,
> And that men in his household should know such skills,
> So that none shall remain too idle!
> And also it is seemly that he teach God's Law,
> Portion it to the folk,
> Often and frequently at the courts.[91]

Certainly, to judge from the later miracle stories associated with Dunstan's tomb at Canterbury, he was remembered as a bishop who was approachable by all sorts and conditions of folk: the blind, both men and women; the crippled and handicapped; poor women; old and young; even visiting foreigners and schoolboys fearing a whipping! Perhaps his first biographer, who knew Dunstan in his closing years as archbishop of Canterbury, should have the last word:

> I think that I am able to elucidate what I have seen and heard myself
> . . . out of love for him. . . . He was always fervent in church affairs,
> & sweated at his labours; yet he was equally assiduous in spending
> the night in vigils, overcoming sweet sleep. . . . He could discern with
> a wise & astute judgement what was true and what was false between
> men, & could bring agreement & peace by his peaceful words to the
> troublesome and quarrelsome. He would aid widows and orphans, pil-
> grims and strangers, in their several needs with a pious assistance. He
> used to separate unsuitable and unjust marriages by a just sequest-
> ration, and so he strengthened by his timely word and the example of
> his life the complete three-fold order of human life: either by just cen-
> sure and enquiry, or by supporting people with a quiet probity to the
> enrichment of the Church of God. He provided for the unskilled of
> both orders, both men and women, who came to him day and night,
> the salt of heaven, and so he established them in the teaching of
> health-giving wisdom.[92]

7

THE MONASTERIES

I – the heart of the reform

M ONASTIC reform was for Dunstan as archbishop of Canterbury only one side of widespread activities.[1] Nonetheless the massive and decisive policy of monastic renewal and endowment, for which Dunstan's primacy is justly remembered, was at all times close to his heart and utterly dependent upon him as archbishop of Canterbury for its success. Both Osbern and, later, William of Malmesbury regarded Dunstan as the virtual founder and patron of a circle of at least five monasteries, not including the two Canterbury houses and Glastonbury itself.[2] In Kent there is no evidence of any effective reform of the ancient monasteries or 'minsters'; Reculver may have been defunct, as may have been Minster-in-Sheppey, while Minster-in-Thanet lingered on into the first decade of the eleventh century under the penumbra of St Augustine's at Canterbury.[3] Certainly conditions in Thanet appear to have been quite unstable, for in 969, and again perhaps in 974, the king ordered punitive raids in retaliation for the islanders' lawlessness.[4] Rochester also remained impoverished and too vulnerable to enjoy any monastic renewal before the Norman Conquest.

It is uncertain whether Dunstan ever fully relinquished the post of abbot of Glastonbury. Certainly Edwy's appointment, Aelsige, who may even have been a layman, was swiftly removed upon Edgar's accession.[5] It seems likely that by 964 there was a new abbot, Aelfstan, probably Ethelwold's friend and a monk from Old Minster and Abingdon, who later became bishop of Ramsbury.[6] In 970, or thereabouts, Sigegar succeeded; he was also an Old Minster monk and he remained as abbot until his consecration as bishop of Wells some five years later. The next abbot, Elfweard, outlived Dunstan by some twenty years.[7]

Nonetheless, there is sound evidence for Dunstan's continued and active interest in the life of the monastery at Glastonbury. The first biographer tells how the prior, called Ceolwy, visited Dunstan when he was on a visit to Bath. This was apparently a custom, valued by both bishop and community, and its significance is emphasised by the story of Dunstan's premonition on this occasion of the death of a little boy at Glastonbury, a death which the visiting prior confirmed at the saint's prompting.[8] This story is followed by another in

63

which Dunstan foretold the imminent death of the cellarer, Aelfsige, while he was on a visit to Glastonbury itself, 'taking stock of their possessions'.[9] The first story also indicates the continuation of educational work at Glastonbury, for the boy who died was a *scolasticulus*, a pupil of the monastery. Dunstan was well remembered as a generous benefactor to Glastonbury. According to William of Malmesbury, he donated organs, bells, an altar cloth and a holy water vat for the altar; and the first biographer records how Dunstan ordered the building of a little square chapel, dedicated to St John the Baptist, at the western end of the old church.[10] For Glastonbury Dunstan secured both a papal privilege and the lavish gifts of the king, Edgar, who was finally buried there and subsequently revered as a principal benefactor.[11] During the troubles of Ethelred's reign, Dunstan's efforts to protect Glastonbury did not falter; he secured papal intervention and even divine vengeance against predatory neighbours.[12]

Dunstan's visit to Bath was just one instance, says his first biographer, of his habit of 'going round the country visiting the monasteries in his care'.[13] In the case of Bath, Dunstan enjoyed a close relationship with its abbot, Alphege, whom he later made bishop of Winchester; he also took the waters there for the sake of his health. Alphege was a contemplative with a considerable following, who had come from his cell at Deerhurst to lead the renewed monastery at Bath.[14] Bath itself was an important town, on the borders of Mercia and Wessex, and in 973 it witnessed the coronation of Edgar on Whitsunday in the fine new minster church which had been built there. The circumstances of its conversion into a Benedictine monastery are not clear; it appears to have been a gradual but decisive development which began in 963.

A clutch of lesser Wessex foundations claimed connections with Dunstan and Glastonbury. Muchelney and Athelney were virtual dependencies of the mother house, though their history at this time is obscure; Athelney later claimed to possess a book given by Dunstan.[15] Milton, reformed by the king in 964, and Exeter, founded in 968 with Sidemann, the tutor to the royal princes and later bishop of Crediton, as its first abbot, received monks from Glastonbury.[16] But these were all minor foundations, never greatly endowed.

The two great houses which claimed Dunstan as their founder were Westminster and Malmesbury. William of Malmesbury claims that 'Dunstan, while still bishop of London, made Wulfsige abbot at Westminster where he had already gathered together a dozen monks'.[17] This tradition is corroborated by a charter of Edgar's, probably drawn up in 959, restoring land to the community at Westminster.[18] From this genuine base, a whole farrago of spurious charters claiming Edgar's patronage and Dunstan's involvement was later generated by the monks of Westminster. Wulfsige's was an important appointment: for twenty-five years he ruled as abbot of Westminster; then he became bishop of Sherborne, where he was responsible for introducing monks in 993.[19] Formerly a monk under Dunstan at Glastonbury, he was regarded as a saint after his death in 1002.[20] The historian of Westminster, Sulcard, writing a century later, definitely regarded Dunstan as the instigator of monastic life there; and Eadmer records a miracle which occurred in connection with Dunstan's chasuble, which was kept as a relic at Westminster.[21]

The early history of Malmesbury was of particular interest to its own historian, William of Malmesbury, and he was quick to establish the great antiquity of that house. It had a history, like that of Glastonbury, which stretched back beyond the tenth century to the time of Aldhelm and Bede.[22] The first abbot of the new regime was a certain Aelfric, who later may have succeeded Sidemann as bishop of Crediton in 977. According to Abbo of Fleury he was an intimate friend of Dunstan's,[23] 'a man of learning and piety, of complete single-mindedness and industry' which he expressed in a great programme of rebuilding.[24] To Malmesbury, Dunstan gave an organ; this, together with a beautifully wrought holy water stoup, the archbishop dedicated to St Aldhelm, whose relics he caused to be translated for safety. William of Malmesbury was quite certain that it was Dunstan who had reformed the community at Malmesbury, probably in the year 965.

At Malmesbury, Dunstan apparently had to drive out the clergy who had been appointed in the days of Edwy in order to create a new monastic community there.[25] At Bath, some accommodation with the former regime may be indicated by the existence of an abbot called Aescwy who appears to have ruled for a time with Alphege. But at Milton, the *Anglo-Saxon Chronicle* speaks of expulsion of clerics,[26] and the restoration of Glastonbury can hardly have occurred without some conflict. Westminster was a new creation over which Dunstan watched carefully for the rest of his life. Resistance to these strictly monastic communities was never far from the surface, and the sheer political weight which the archbishop was able to wield on their behalf was clearly crucial to their survival. It may well be significant that in the heartlands of Wessex relatively little progress was made in setting up major monasteries, Glastonbury, Malmesbury and the Winchester houses apart. Nonetheless, the patronage of Dunstan attracted generous and steady benefactions, from the king and his family and from the lay nobility. William of Malmesbury's list of gifts to Glastonbury is illuminating: 215 hides, given by members of the court, were confirmed by the king.

> Moreover he had a cross made to be put above the greater altar, which was woven throughout in gold and silver; and also some impressive little bells. He also presented the most precious royal robe in which he had been crowned to serve as an ornament for the altar. He gave a large shrine, covered with gold and silver and decorated beautifully with ivory images, which contained the relics of St Vincent and the head of St Apollinaris; in which shrine the king himself now rests. He also commended to the monastery of Glastonbury many relics acquired by him in all the lands he had traversed, including the remains of two of the Innocents, translated from Bethlehem.[27]

From Edgar the monks of Glastonbury claimed to have received an extensive privilege which the king confirmed by the gift of an ivory staff, 'decorated with patterns of gold lines', which the king marked and laid upon the altar. Upon the basis of this privilege, the abbey claimed jurisdiction over the surrounding 12 hides near Glastonbury. By the time of the 'Domesday Book', Glastonbury had become the wealthiest abbey in England.[28]

There is another common link between these houses of the 'Dunstan connection'. Each could claim some link with Athelstan and the memory of his piety and generosity. Milton actually claimed to have been founded by him and Malmesbury received his body, regarding him as its singular benefactor. Westminster later claimed a collection of relics which had once been Athelstan's.[29] Glastonbury too claimed 'innumerable outstanding relics, as noted in St Dunstan's Gospel Book' from Athelstan's collection.[30] Later, Exeter was to make a similar claim. To Bath too went a book from Athelstan, with a later dedication similar to those in corresponding gifts to Christ Church and St Augustine's, Canterbury, but notable in carrying a reference to St Benedict. It may well be that Dunstan 'had part of Athelstan's treasury of relics at his disposal', and distributed them to these particular monasteries in his care as a way of perpetuating the memory of the king under whose patronage the very first seed of Benedictine reform had been sown, the king who could now be regarded as the epitome of successful kingship, rich in possessions, power and piety.[31]

The appointment of Ethelwold at the end of 963 to be bishop of Winchester marks the beginning of the full scale reform and renewal of the monasteries. This appointment was a decisive political move, introducing the most rigorous exponent of the new monasticism to the heart of the old Church establishment of Wessex. Ethelwold had just completed building the great church at Abingdon, and the monastery there was at the height of its development. He had sent his disciple Osgar 'across the sea to the monastery of St Benedict at Fleury (where Oswald had sojourned), there to learn the customs of the Rule and then to expound them by his teaching to the brethren at home'.[32] He had also summoned monks from Corbie to instruct the brethren in the correct manner of chanting the psalms.[33] He was therefore well placed to draw on resources from continental monasticism. Ethelwold also enjoyed a relationship with the young king as close as Dunstan's and in some respects more immediate inasmuch as the court was frequently at Winchester during Edgar's reign. Edgar had been educated by Dunstan and Ethelwold, and it was during Ethelwold's time at Abingdon that the king's zeal for monastic renewal had been kindled.[34] The appointment of Ethelwold, only lately recovered from a serious injury sustained in the course of the building works at Abingdon, brought the king to the fore of the struggle to re-establish monasticism. Ethelwold's course of action bore the imprint of the royal wishes and of active royal support. The consequence was a political revolution of far-reaching and profound significance. This revolution, which was to transform the life of the Church, disturb traditional patterns of land holding and increase the authority and prestige of the royal house, was perhaps what men feared would happen when Dunstan was appointed to be archbishop of Canterbury.

Aelfric, in his 'Life of Ethelwold', paints a black picture of life at the Old Minster, Winchester; of proud, decadent clerics, some married, leading a thoroughly irregular life.[35] In fact, Old Minster, and for that matter, New Minster, were wealthy establishments, full of noble clergy, cultivated and politically powerful, enjoying the good life. Even under Alphege the Bald, Winchester did not lend itself to a strict monastic life, as Oswald had found out,[36] and Elfsige, Alphege's successor (briefly archbishop of Canterbury before Dunstan) was hardly an example.[37] Within months of his appointment, Ethelwold expelled the clergy from the Old Minster with the king's permission and under the watchful eye of the king's minister, Wulfstan of Dalham. In their place he put monks drawn from Abingdon, formed a proper monastic chapter and became its abbot as well as its bishop. The expelled clergy were invited to become monks and rejoin the community; only three did so.[38] Osgar returned from Fleury to become abbot of Abingdon and Brihtnoth became prior of the Old Minster.[39]

There was an immediate backlash to this development; the ousted clergy and their allies attempted to poison the bishop at dinner in his hall. He survived the bitter draught as if by a miracle.[40]

After that, Ethelwold spread his wings, and expelled the clerics from the New Minster as well, with King Edgar's consent, ordaining his pupil Aethelgar as abbot there, with monks under him leading a life according to the Rule. Aethelgar was afterwards made Archbishop in Kent.[41]

The chronicle gives a wider perspective to this move:

In this year [964] King Edgar drove the priests in the city from the Old Minster and from the New Minster; and from Chertsey and from Milton; and replaced them with monks. And he appointed Abbot Aethelgar as abbot of the New Minster, and Ordberht for Chertsey, and Cyneweard for Milton.[42]

Ordberht was probably the cleric who had come from Winchester to be a monk at Abingdon, and who later became bishop of Selsey.[43] Ethelwold's biographer associates the lavish endowment of Abingdon by the king with this development. In all, this was a striking demonstration of royal resolve and episcopal policy behind which stood the determination and authority of Dunstan, who had expressly sought the pope's approval for such a move.[44]

There is in the 'Liber de Hyde' a somewhat garbled account of a great council at Winchester around this time which authorised this most momentous of developments.[45] This was probably the assembly described in the 'Life of Oswald'[46] which may have assembled at Easter 964. The king decreed the founding of fifty monasteries:

complete with monks, for he loved Christ the Lord above all things, as well as his most worthy warrior St Benedict, whose fame he knew through the telling of holy Oswald the bishop, even as he had been instructed in the knowledge of the true King by Ethelwold the most holy bishop of Winchester. For it had been Ethelwold who had provoked the king to this great deed, so that he might expel the clergy from the monasteries, and found our orders, because he was the foremost counsellor to the king.

Some echo of this decision as it affected the future of the Old Minster may be discerned in a charter of Edgar to that monastery[47] in which there is a lengthy contrast drawn between the old way of life of the 'canons' and the new duties of the monks. They are set apart for the salvation of the king and of his realm, and for the prosperity of his successors. They are not to fall into the insubordination of their predecessors, who respected neither their bishop nor their earthly king. There is also a document which records the substance of a speech by the king to his bishops urging the reform of the Church through the monasteries:

You have the sword of Peter in your hand, I that of Constantine: let us join hands, sword to sword, to expel the lepers from the camp, that the sanctuary of the Lord may be purged, that only sons of Levi may minister in the church, who are prepared to say to their parents, 'I do not know you', and to their brothers, 'I disregard you'.[48]

The mention of Alfred and Edward as benefactors of the Church may well indicate the imminent reform of the New Minster. This highly rhetorical piece captures something of the ferment behind this political development.

The great monument to this decision is the famous New Minster Charter,[49] dated 966. In itself it is a landmark in the development of manuscript art, being the first example of what has come to be known as the Winchester style. It is written in gold, in the king's name, and is prefaced by a full-page miniature showing Edgar between the Virgin Mary and St Peter, offering the codex containing the charter to Christ. It is witnessed by Dunstan, who signs after the king, and before the two *aethelings*, Edmund and Edward, Queen Aethelthryth and the old queen mother, Eadgifu, who had been instrumental in founding Abingdon. The witness list contains the principal bishops, abbots and nobility of the land; and Ethelwold, the likely author of this remarkable document, refers explicitly to his band of disciples whom he is commending to the king. 'Does it not look as if the whole thing were a creation of Ethelwold, made after the event; a solemn commemoration to be preserved on the altar as a memorial?'[50] It is likely that this solemn commemoration occurred in 966 in the presence of those whose signatures appear on the witness list.

The content of the New Minster Charter is no less striking. It is a virtual manifesto of the new monastic movement. It begins with a theological dissertation upon the fall of man from the state of paradise, the hatred of the devil for mankind, the calamities of this world and the coming of Christ and his passion which opens again for men the way to heaven. The king's benevolence has arisen out of his meditation upon this theme and his desire for a change of life. Quoting the authority of St Gregory the Great, and fearing divine judgement, the king now explains why he has acted to purge the canons and clergy and institute regular monastic life. The task of the New Minster monks is to intercede for the welfare of the king, his family and his realm, and to live subject to their abbot. There follow two anathemas against those who would subvert the monks and a blessing upon those who will reverence and assist them, mentioning the 'Liber vitae' into which their names will be inscribed (which still survives). There follow various prescriptions for the monastic life, very similar in content and tone to the proem of the 'Regularis concordia'. The monks are to live according to the rule and to obey their spiritual fathers; to remove themselves from secular life and values; and to lead an ascetical life. They are forbidden intercourse with the city and its social life, and they must eat together in refectory unless one be ill. Caution is to be exercised with regard to hospitality, which is to be at the abbot's discretion, and strangers are not to be admitted to eat in refectory; but the poor are to be received with open arms. Life according to the Rule of St Benedict is enjoined – study, prayer and charity – and the abbot is to be elected by and from the community. Edgar's successors are to provide for and respect the abbot and the monks, and the community by its life and prayers is to thwart all the designs of the evil one on behalf of the king. They are his spiritual warriors, whom he in return will defend from their temporal adversaries. The possessions of the monastery are privileged and sacrosanct, and cursed be they who usurp them.

In the two lives of Ethelwold, a clear picture of monastic life at Winchester under this formidable bishop begins to emerge. Both lives were written by Winchester men: Aelfric the Homilist wrote a terse and penetrating biography, which was probably the basis upon which Wulstan the Cantor wrote his slightly expanded life shortly afterwards.[51] Both men portray Ethelwold as enjoying completely the king's confidence, a picture confirmed by the 'Life of Oswald'. The bishop was a great preacher, a campaigner for the monastic cause and, with Dunstan himself, a tireless strategist in promoting new foundations.[52] 'He was a father of the monks and nuns, a comforter of widows and a restorer of the poor, a defender of churches, a corrector of those who strayed, a receiver of pilgrims, and a helper of orphans.'[53] He was not averse to selling church treasures to assist the starving, and as a great educator in Latin and English he was a spiritual father to many young men who later rose to eminence in the life of the Church.[54] As an abbot he had a remarkable, even ferocious, hold over his chapter, yet he found time and energy for nocturnal studies; his austerity and the depth of his spiritual life became a byword and a powerful example to those who lived with him.

In the Hyde 'Liber vitae', the book of remembrance of the New Minster, there is a notable list of brethren from the Old Minster, Ethelwold's own community, whom the brethren especially remembered. It includes as well as Ethelwold and his successor, Alphege, ten bishops and several abbots, including Womar, the retired abbot of Ghent (where Dunstan had stayed in exile), who had come to Winchester and whose death there is noted in the chronicle in 981.[55] The list of monks and clergy which follows contains many of the names of those mentioned in the lives of Ethelwold, and the picture emerges of a strong and lively community at the hub of Ethelwold's activities.

The appointment by Ethelwold of his pupil, Aethelgar, a monk of both Glastonbury and Abingdon, to be abbot of the reformed New Minster was an important move. Old Minster and New Minster stood so close together that friction between the two communities was almost unavoidable. Even under Aethelgar, Dunstan had to adjudicate a settlement with Ethelwold that would ensure 'that the two institutions should be as one in all holiness', a settlement modelled apparently on arrangements made by an earlier bishop of Winchester, Frithestan, for the clergy there long before the monastic reform.[56] There is another document remaining in which the king reordered the boundaries of Old Minster, New Minster and the Nun's Minster in the presence of Ethelwold and Aethelgar to ensure peace and concord.[57] Ethelwold had revived the Nunnaminster, appointing the elderly holy woman, Aethelthryth, who was a friend of his family from his youth, as its first abbess.[58] With close friends like these as monastic neighbours, Ethelwold ensured that religious life at Winchester would be united, exemplary and strong. The opening pages of the Hyde 'Liber vitae' describe Aethelgar in glowing terms as an outstanding abbot, full of energy and spiritual vigour. He later became bishop of Selsey before succeeding Dunstan as archbishop of Canterbury in 988.

Ethelwold and Aethelgar were both energetic builders, whose first aim was to place the three minsters within a single monastic enclosure. To the east of New Minster lay the Nunnaminster and the monastic buildings of New Minster lay between these two churches. In so cramped and complex a site, the layout of the several monasteries remains unclear.[59] It is assumed that the monastic buildings of the Old Minster lay to the south of the cathedral. The Hyde 'Liber vitae' opens with a careful account of the way in which Aethelgar reordered the New Minster during the reign of Edgar and in the reign of Ethelred rebuilt the church in great style, with turrets and tower, to the solemn dedication of which Dunstan himself came.[60]

Meanwhile Ethelwold was personally supervising the radical rebuilding and enlargement of the Old Minster itself.[61] Recent excavations have confirmed the scale and significance of this operation.[62] The first thing Ethelwold did was to construct a vast westwork over the site of St Swithun's grave, linking the old church to the existing St Martin's Tower. To the north and south of this spot, he created apsidial chapels full of altars to saints which, in the words of Wulstan the Cantor, 'keep the entry of the threshold doubtful, so that whoever walks in these courts with unfamiliar tread, cannot tell whence he comes or whither to return, since open doors are seen on every hand, nor does any certain path seem clear'.[63] This labyrinthine structure was complicated by the building immediately afterwards of a square westwork around the old tower of St Martin's, rising to 150 ft and possibly containing galleries. This great and imposing work was dedicated by Dunstan in 980, in the company of all the monastic bishops, as well as of the king and his court. Wulstan has left a vivid and moving account of this great day, both in his 'Life of Ethelwold' and in his metrical 'Life of St Swithun'.[64] No sooner had this work been completed than Ethelwold embarked upon the reconstruction of the east end of the cathedral. He died in 984 before completing it, but Alphege, his successor, continued the task, vastly enlarging the church with side chapels and a number of crypts. Around this time, a huge and powerful organ was built which needed seventy men to pump it! Wulstan provides a lengthy description of the refurbished minster and its grand rededication by Archbishop Sigeric around the year 994.[65] Nothing remains of the interior decoration, but in the light of the art of the Winchester school manuscripts it must have been magnificent. A fragment of a frieze which may come from this time has been found, used perhaps on the tower like the friezes described in the account of the new tower of the New Minster.[66] In all, these ambitious and beautiful buildings, and the scale and complexity of the monastic buildings surrounding them, constituted one of the most impressive church sites north of the Alps.[67]

At the heart of this redesigning of the Old Minster lay the revived cult of St Swithun, a hitherto obscure bishop of Winchester who had died in 862 and whose tomb had lain, exposed to the elements, outside the old cathedral in the space between the west door and St Martin's Tower. In the words of Ethelwold's biographers: 'His preaching was greatly assisted by St Swithun, who was translated at this time [on 15 July 971]; because what Ethelwold taught by words, Swithun wonderfully adorned by miracles.'[68] It was the unanimous opinion of Wulstan, Aelfric and the foreigner, Lantfrith, that little which was certain was known or remembered about the saint before this time, which Aelfric blames on the appalling state of learning in ninth-century England.[69] It was his notable and public miracles at Winchester during Ethelwold's episcopate that brought him to prominence, provoked his double translation in 971 and 974 and brought hordes of pilgrims to the Old Minster. Ethelwold and Edgar and their followers regarded this as a divine endorsement of their religious policies and the cult served also to unite the life of the monastic communities at Winchester with popular religious sentiment in the diocese and farther afield in a remarkable and timely way.

The story is told by Aelfric in his 'Homily on St Swithun': he was an eyewitness of much that happened, being educated at Winchester, and as he was a scholar of great sagacity and caution his account bears careful examination and respect. It affords a fascinating insight into the religious temper of the period, both within the monastery and among the populace at large; it is also a startling record of the way such a cult emerged in early medieval society.

There is an ironic but moving beginning. In 968 a smith had a vision of St Swithun, who commanded him to approach Eadsige, one of the clerics whom Ethelwold had expelled, saying: 'Truly bishop Swithun has commanded him to go to bishop Ethelwold and say that he is to translate his bones into the church.' The saint duly gave him a sign, to pull out an iron ring fastened to his tomb. The smith's faith quailed at the prospect, and Swithun had to appear to him three times! The smith only acted when he had himself tested the sign at the bishop's tomb, whereupon he met a serf of Eadsige, who was then living at Winchcombe, and sent the message.

At that time this Eadsige shunned bishop Ethelwold and all the monks who were in the minster because of the ejection . . . and would not obey the saint's command, though the saint were of worldly kindred to him. Yet within two years he retreated (as Swithun had commanded him in the vision) to that same monastery, and became a monk through the grace of God till his life's end.[70]

This act of repentance and costly human reconciliation was the first miracle wrought by the resurgent saint; a very real and tangible miracle in human relationships, given the recent circumstances! The next miracle relieved a poor churl of his humpback, even though the monks, ignorant of Swithun, were wont to attribute the cure to another saint. For the next man it was a choice between the relics of St Judoc at New Minster or the tomb of Swithun, where in curious circumstances he was healed of blindness; and several others were also healed prior to the formal translation. In the light of this, Edgar ordered the translation of Swithun's relics, and Ethelwold 'with abbots and monks' complied with all pomp and chanting. Within ten days 'two hundred men were healed'. Mass healings ensued, beyond counting, both of men and women, many of them blind or crippled, from all levels of society. Ethelwold ordered the monks of Old Minster to sing 'Te Deum' 'as often as any sick man should be healed'. This had to happen so frequently, by night and day, that it soon palled on the monks and they left off 'because the bishop was busy with the king'; thereupon the saintly bishop sent a warning upon which Ethelwold acted, and ordered the immediate resumption of the singing of 'Te Deum', even though he himself was still at court! Aelfric was one of those who was in the monastic choir at this time. A chain of other miracles is recorded, including the story of how a rich thegn, struck blind, made a pilgrimage to Rome and stayed there for four years uncured; on hearing of Swithun's fame he hurried home and was healed at Winchester. At Ethelwold's command, 'Lantfrith the foreigner set down in Latin' the miracles, and his cautious letter to the monks of Old Minster is a reminder that not all was credulity and superstition in those days.[71] (He refers also to the European reputation of Swithun, and there are still some churches dedicated to him in Scandinavia, as well as fifty-eight ancient dedications in England.[72]) Aelfric concludes his homily with a salutary caution against relying on visions and dreams in the Christian life and a sally against sorcery. Swithun's clemency embraced prisoners as well as the sick. 'The old church was hung all round with crutches and with the stools of cripples (from one end to the other on either wall), who had been healed there, and not even then could they put up half of them.'[73]

To Aelfric this was the great sign that all was well in England, 'when King Edgar furthered Christianity, & built many monasteries, and his kingdom continued in peace', aided by 'worthy bishops, Dunstan the resolute, in the archbishopric, & Ethelwold the venerable, and others like them'.[74] To Wulstan and Lantfrith it confirmed the reality of the saints and their intercession, a sign of renewal and life in the Church. The cult of Swithun did much to reconcile the people of Winchester, including perhaps some of the old clerical regime, to the new order in the cathedral and the minsters, for 'Swithun had come from the very class of clerics whom the monks had so violently displaced',[75] and yet had endorsed the new monasticism.

The cult and its attendant miracles could not fail to impress and fascinate the royal family and nobility assembled at Winchester, giving considerable spiritual 'muscle' to Ethelwold's presence at court. The scale of popular devotion and pilgrimage provided a welcome and timely boost to the revenues of the Old Minster at a time of great rebuilding. The scale of that rebuilding with its radical changes of plan and three-fold development must have been planned partly with such pilgrimages in mind. The two-fold translation of Swithun's remains entailed the separation of his skull into another shrine in the sacristy, and this may have been the reliquary which Alphege took with him to Canterbury in 1005.[76] It can only have served to heighten the devotion and mystique surrounding him in the Old Minster. For the monks and nuns, and for their cause, it was without doubt a powerful and providential manifestation; the entry in the list of bishops of Winchester in the Hyde 'Liber vitae' makes this quite clear: 'The holy and most merciful bishop Swithun was revealed in our times by the ineffable mercy of God: his most holy nativity is celebrated on the second of July.'[77]

II – the widening circle

Winchester and its powerful monastic centre became the base for Ethelwold's wider activities. The chronicle associates the reforms at Winchester in 964 with reforms at Milton and Chertsey. Milton received as abbot a certain Cyneweard, of unknown provenance, who later became bishop of Wells: he may have had a connection with Glastonbury. Chertsey, a very ancient foundation, received Ordberht as abbot; he may have been the cleric who joined Ethelwold at Abingdon in the early days and later became bishop of Selsey.[78] Abingdon itself continued to flourish under Abbot Osgar, receiving privileges and lavish bequests. Aelfric, Ethelwold's biographer, continues:

There is a place called Ely, greatly ennobled by the relics & miracles of St Etheldreda the virgin, and her sisters; but at that time it was deserted and given up to the royal treasury. Ethelwold bought this from the king and stationed in it many monks, over whom he placed as abbot his pupil, Brihtnoth by name; and he endowed the place most richly with buildings and lands. He acquired another place from the king and the nobles of the land, situated on the banks of the river Nene, which of old was called Medehamsted in English, now usually Burh [Peterborough], where in like manner he assembled monks, placing over them as abbot Ealdwulf, who afterwards obtained the arch-bishopric of the city of York. Also he acquired by purchase a third place, close to the aforesaid river, named Thorney in English, which he committed to monks under the same conditions; and when he had constructed a monastery, he appointed an abbot to it, Godemann by name, and enriched it abundantly with possessions.[79]

The Hyde 'Liber vitae' records the strong bonds of monastic confraternity which existed between these new houses and their abbots and the community at Winchester.[80] With this development may perhaps be associated the revival of the ancient church at St Albans.[81] All these new abbots were pupils and friends of Ethelwold, and over each of these monasteries the bishop of Winchester exercised a close and formative influence.

The immediate impression gained is of the immense wealth and influence which Ethelwold was able to wield in order to endow these foundations. Among the Peterborough documents is a list of his gifts: ornaments, a gospel book, candlesticks, bells, vestments and twenty-one books. In conjunction with the energetic abbot, Ealdwulf, extensive lands were acquired by exchange, purchase and negotiation.[82] This could only occur with the co-operation of the local landed nobility and, of course, of the king himself. It is most significant that all this occurred in the eastern Danelaw where, after relatively recent reconquest, the king may have had lands at his disposal. Moreover the leading families were known supporters of the monastic movement: the family of Athelstan led now by his sons Aelfwold, Aethelsige and Aethelwin,[83] and also Bryhtnoth of Essex. Thurkytel, a kinsman of Oskytel the archbishop of York and bishop of Dorchester, founded monasteries at Bedford and Crowland about this time.[84] The formation of this chain of foundations, each amassing to itself substantial holdings of land and patterns of local patronage, would have strengthened indirectly royal influence in these parts, as well as strengthening the control and prestige of the leading local families.

Ely emerged by the time of the Norman Conquest as the second richest monastery in England, the richest being Glastonbury. Refounded around the year 970, it was placed under the control of Brihtnoth, who had been prior of the Old Minster.[85] The story of its foundation and endowment is recorded in the remarkable 'Liber Eliensis', a twelfth-century compilation which draws heavily on tenth-century sources then available at Ely.[86] It gives an invaluable picture of the way in which, often quite ruthlessly, Ethelwold and Brihtnoth set about building up the resources of the abbey.

In 957, Edwy had granted the lands of the ancient shrine at Ely to Archbishop Oda. Perhaps the archbishop had intended to found a monastery there himself to be led by his nephew Oswald, then at Fleury; Edgar later offered Ely as a possible site for a monastery to Oswald.[87] Early in Edgar's reign, Ely had become the focus of litigation between a Greek bishop, Sigewold, and a Dane (perhaps a kinsman of Oda's) called Thurstan. It was the intervention of Wulfstan of Dalham, the East Anglian minister of Edgar who had been instrumental in removing by force the clergy from the Old Minster in 964, which secured Ely as a site for a monastic refoundation to be led by Ethelwold.[88] The friendship of Wulfstan, and later of Bryhtnoth, ealdorman of Essex, was of critical importance to the sustained success of this enterprise.[89] Ethelwold's devotion to Ely knew no bounds, and he endowed it handsomely out of his own patrimony, some of which he had received while a courtier under King Athelstan.[90] His own piety towards the cult of the virgin Queen Etheldreda, whose story was recorded in Bede, is reflected here and in the glorious portrait of her in his benedictional, drawn for him by Godeman, his chaplain and later abbot of Thorney.[91]

Ethelwold and Brihtnoth adopted a businesslike approach to building up a composite body of lands around the monastery, and it was Ethelwold himself who prompted the delineation of the estates in the Isle of Ely.[92] Although the king had authorised the expulsion of the clergy remaining in the old church, Ethelwold had actually to buy from the king the lands pertaining to the shrine and other lands which he required before he could build his monastery.[93] From Ethelwold's treasury came much of the stuff with which the church and its services were to be adorned: vestments, gold and silver ornaments and the like. From Edgar, the monks of Ely also claimed to have received an extensive privilege.[94] When the day for the consecration came, and the new abbot was to be installed, Dunstan came to Ely and with Ethelwold inaugurated the new monastery. Brihtnoth himself adorned the renewed church with images of virgins, two each side of the altar, encrusted with gold, silver and precious gems.[95] The 'Liber Eliensis' records at length the manifold possessions of the monastery and the story of how they were acquired by Ethelwold and Brihtnoth, a sustained if piecemeal process stretching over the quarter-century of Brihtnoth's abbacy. In due time, Edgar himself became devoted to the place, lavishing upon it many valuable and beautiful gifts.[96] Brihtnoth rebuilt the old church around the shrine of St Etheldreda, to which he and Ethelwold translated the remains of Sexburga and Withburga, two of the early saintly kinswomen of Etheldreda and her successors as abbesses of Ely. The renewed church was dedicated by Dunstan himself.[97] Carved above the monks' door from the cloister into the Norman abbey at Ely there are the figures of two monastic bishops, an early twelfth-century remembrance based perhaps upon manuscript illuminations of Dunstan and Ethelwold, the two founding fathers of that great monastery.[98]

Ely became the object of Ethelwold's particular devotion as bishop of Winchester in a way comparable to Oswald's devotion to Ramsey. Oswald succeeded Dunstan to the see of Worcester in 961 and ruled there for over thirty years, dying in 992. For the second half of his episcopacy he ruled the see of York as well, having been appointed by Edgar in 972, upon the death of Oskytel his kinsman and the speedy resignation of his successor, Ethelwold, who wanted a quieter life.[99] As a kinsman of Archbishop Oda, who was a Dane, and a close friend of Dunstan's, Oswald was well suited to being bishop, first of western Mercia and later also of the northern Danelaw, and his biographer records the welcome he received in York.[100] As a bishop, Oswald was a great pastor, renowned for his care of the poor, 'mindful of their fragile humanity'; 'he was not tardy with justice, but was mighty in kindness'. Nonetheless, his heart was set on founding a monastery which would compare with Fleury, where he had received his formation as a monk. From Fleury he summoned his friend and companion, Germanus, formerly from Winchester, and immediately ordered him to instruct those who came to him seeking the monastic life. Very soon there were more than the dozen which Oswald wanted in his own familia, so he set up a small monastery for them at Westbury in his diocese, endowing it carefully from episcopal lands. It was a strictly contemplative house, withdrawn, simple and stable. Nonetheless, after a few years, Oswald began to fear what would happen to this community were he to die, and at the famous Easter synod when the formation of the monasteries was authorised (in 964 or 965), he approached the king, to whom he had earlier taught the Benedictine way. What Oswald sought was a site for a monastery from the royal patrimony, duly protected by the aegis of the king himself and presumably outside his own diocese. Edgar, 'like another Constantine', offered him three places: St Albans, Ely and Benfleet. While he was still surveying the possibilities, by accident or, as Oswald believed, by providence, while at a funeral he outlined his hopes and plans to one of the sons of Athelstan, Aethelwin, a friend of Dunstan's. He was a devout man who immediately caught the vision Oswald held out to him and took the venture under his own personal protection, offering to the monks the island of Ramsey on the edge of the Fens, north west of Ely.[101] Oswald seized the opportunity, and committed the task of raising the monastery there to his follower, the venerable Eadnoth (later bishop of Dorchester). The Fens were in those days a semi-cultivated wilderness, whither hermits and others had gone since the days of Bede, and the monks hailed Ramsey as an ideal retreat. The first biographer of Oswald was himself a monk there, and he gives an ample picture of its situation and life. Uniquely among the English tenth-century foundations, it was dedicated solely to St Benedict, and it became in the minds of its inmates a second Fleury. Fleury was the fount of the cult of Benedict, claiming to possess his body as well as offering the most spiritual application of his rule. Devotion to Benedict is a particularly prominent feature of the first life of Oswald,[102] which provides the fullest picture of what life in a tenth-century monastery was like. For both Oswald, the bishop, and Aethelwin, the lay protector and benefactor, Ramsey became a spiritual home; Oswald remained its abbot until his death, endowing it generously not least with a wonderful library,[103] and summoning thither, from Fleury, Abbo, the foremost scholar of the monastic movement on the continent, certainly on one and possibly on two occasions.[104] From Ramsey came Byrhtferth, one of the most interesting and educated minds of the later tenth century, author of scientific treatises and possibly the author of the anonymous first life of Oswald.[105]

Oswald's unease at the likely protection such a foundation would receive in his own diocese is interesting and confirms the reputation of the leading East Anglian families as protectors of monasticism. It indicates also some of the undercurrents of difficulty and outright opposition which were never far from the surface during Oswald's time as bishop of Worcester. Shortly after the foundation of Ramsey, the monasteries of Winchcombe and Pershore were founded in western Mercia. Germanus, who had been prior of Westbury and then of Ramsey, went to be abbot of Winchcombe. To Pershore went Foldberht, one of the early followers of Ethelwold from Glastonbury to Abingdon and a man renowned for his severity.[106] Around this time a monastery was founded at Evesham, possibly by Ethelwold and Oswald together, with Frithegar, another of the early companions of Ethelwold, as its abbot. Deerhurst, the cell of Alphege, now abbot of Bath, may also have become a monastic house at this time.[107] The ties of monastic friendship were thus close and strong. But immediately after the death of Edgar in 975, these west Mercian houses became the immediate targets of assault by the ealdorman of Mercia, Aelfhere.[108]

As bishop of Worcester, and in his attempt to convert his episcopal *familia* into a proper monastery, Oswald was engaged in a long and arduous campaign to protect the landed endowment of the see and its cathedral community from lay appropriation. Whether Oswald had to resort to force to eject clergy from the cathedral at Worcester is unclear. From the many charters of his episcopate, it would appear that there was a gradual conversion of the chapter into a monastic community, similar to the process underway at Canterbury under Dunstan.[109] Over this community he placed Wynsige, a noble parish priest from Worcester who had gone to Ramsey to train as a monk and who returned at Oswald's behest in the company of some other Ramsey monks. Somewhere between 969 and 977, he became prior of the community there, perhaps in 972 when Oswald assumed new duties as archbishop of York. Wynsige may have represented some kind of continuity with the old days, but probably he became prior only after the conversion of the Worcester community into a monastic one was well underway. There is a mention in Florence of Worcester (*sub anno* 969) of some measure of forcible conversion upon Oswald's own testimony, and this is alluded to in a lawsuit in the time of Wulfstan of Worcester, bishop in the eleventh century.[110] Towards the end of the first life of Oswald the writer asks: 'What shall I say about the place wherein he had his episcopal seat? Did he not cause monks to serve God where once only deacons and birds had lodged?'[111] If this applies to Worcester rather than to York (as is likely, York hardly being able to support a monastery at this time, hence the plurality in which Oswald and others held it), then some firm action by Oswald, when local political conditions permitted, seems likely, and it would be consistent with the actions of Dunstan and Ethelwold elsewhere.

What is quite clear is that early in his episcopate Oswald built a new and larger church alongside the ancient cathedral of St Peter. This was dedicated to the Virgin, like the other west Mercian foundations, and like the majority of monastic dedications at this time. The reason for this was that the old cathedral, though venerable, was too small, and Oswald was a great and popular preacher. Indeed, initially, Oswald preached at the cross outside in the cemetery to the assembled crowds. The old church was spared until well into the next century, but the new church was indicative of the new regime, both architecturally and liturgically. It became in due course the seat of the bishop and of his monastic community.[112]

Although Oswald was loved and respected for his sanctity and humility, he was a singularly effective administrator as well as a pastor. The monument to his labours is the numerous charters which he issued as he organised the Oswaldslaw, the lands supporting his see and its monastic cathedral community; the lands actually remained church property, capable of reverting after 'three lives' and capable too of rendering the military and naval dues to which so large a 'liberty' was liable.[113] 'The number of charters issued by Oswald has no parallel for any other church':[114] thirty between 962 and 969, seventy-seven in all. Three irregular hundreds made up Oswaldslaw; but there is evidence that Ethelwold was building up similar privileges of jurisdiction for Ely and Peterborough, and himself enjoyed immunities in his great manor of Taunton.[115] In return for this privilege, Oswald was liable for the administration of justice and of some taxes, and the provision of military and naval service. This elevation of the bishop's juridical authority, and the real restrictions now placed on the way in which church lands were to be held, affected the local landowners in an immediate and adverse way. No longer were the lands of the Church a disposable extension of lay private property; no longer would a local lay magnate enjoy sole sway settling matters affecting the hundred. Instead, a body of land books now existed, claiming royal and divine authority in no uncertain terms. This entrammelled everything in the mesh of episcopal authority, whose pretensions were now backed up by threat of penalty and forfeiture.

This was a most thorough and ambitious assault on the old enemy of secular rule over the lands of the Church. It was widely believed by the reformers that the lay appropriation of Church endowments had been, with the Viking assaults, the principal cause of the Church's decline through earlier generations.[116] Nonetheless, some of Oswald's own kinsmen benefited from the new leases: there are at least nine examples;[117] and this can hardly have endeared local people to the new arrangements. But behind all this lay the direct intrusion of royal authority which sanctioned the new manner of land holding, royal authority to which the monks and their bishops appealed in every charter. This was the heart of the political revolution underlying the reformation of the monasteries. It is hardly surprising that ambivalence and direct hostility lurked in the hearts of many as the sacred and time-honoured conventions of land holding, which were the very foundations upon which Anglo-Saxon society rested, were set aside for the convenience and well-being of the Church and its monasteries. Veneration for a bishop like Oswald might seem to ease the situation in part, but it could not eradicate the tension and even ill-feeling; paradoxically, it might even exacerbate it. But under a powerful king like Edgar, there could be no lasting resistance.

There is ample evidence to show that many of the lay nobility did not merely acquiesce in the formation of the monasteries, they actively promoted them. Reluctance in some quarters there undoubtedly was, and some real resistance, but unless a sizeable part of the landowning class had been sympathetic to the cause, the monasteries could never have been established at the rate they were. Within the fifteen years of Edgar's reign, some twenty-two monasteries were established, either in existing foundations or on new or ancient sites;[118] and there were the nunneries besides. This was a revolutionary development, for Church and society. Clearly the example set by the king and the royal family was of great importance, and royal encouragement and endorsement for bequests to the Church continued to be sought, as had always been the case in Anglo-Saxon society. The king's approval was the best guarantee that land bequeathed to the Church would actually be respected as an inalienable endowment. Moreover with the king so actively committed to establishing monasteries in the localities, lay patronage was an important way of counterbalancing such influence from the centre. It became a matter both of fashion and prestige for local families to espouse and assist a monastic foundation; and, of course, there were benefits to be accrued from having some degree of influence over such an ascendant landowner.

Yet underlying these mundane and practical considerations lay a real groundswell of piety. People believed that endowment of the Church would strengthen their claim to life in heaven; that the prayers of the Church could assist them and their ancestors; and that the favour of God was their best guarantee of peace, prosperity and protection. Perhaps they believed and hoped that these new monastic communities would prove more effective instruments of intercession and spiritual well-being than some of the older clerical establishments; and that land granted to these formidable corporations would actually remain as land set aside for spiritual purposes and would not revert to lay ownership or sink under clerical mismanagement and corruption. Undoubtedly the sheer force of personality and conviction of Dunstan, Ethelwold, Oswald and their colleagues helped to carry the day. Yet despite their avowed determination to rid the Church of 'secular dominion' and assure it of real integrity and relative independence, the proprietary instinct towards the local church, whether by king or lay landowner, was never far from the surface. For this was the way men related to the Church: 'their church' meant what it said; it was the focus of their local loyalty and devotion, to be provided for, in personnel and kind, as part of the web of kinship which bound their society together. In no way could this be eradicated, and it is true to surmise that men tolerated the monks and their ways because they sprang from their own ranks and were never far removed from the society they served. It was believed, and proclaimed by the reformers, that they were better spiritual warriors and more disciplined intercessors than the clerics they replaced, and, for many of the laity, that was enough to secure their support. There were those, like Athelstan, who retired from public life to become a monk at Glastonbury, and Aethelwin, the devout patron of Ramsey, who espoused the Benedictine way for themselves and shared the more spiritual vision of the great reformers; even the king himself, in his better moments, may have shared this hope. Yet as in any generation, those with solely spiritual motivation were inevitably a small minority.

The open agreement of the king's witan was clearly indispensable, and was forthcoming, according to the first life of Oswald and the 'Regularis concordia'.[119] To Dunstan and Ethelwold must go the credit for securing this decisive political support and for sustaining it throughout the whole of Edgar's reign, till 975. The ear of the king was crucial, and Ethelwold clearly had it; but behind the scenes much skilful, patient but firm diplomacy on Dunstan's part must have gone on, perforce unrecorded.

The list of benefactors to Glastonbury names seven prominent members of Edgar's court, including the queen; and the local ealdormen are given pride of place as principal donors.[120] The Hyde 'Liber vitae' of New Minster, which was the solemn list of benefactors placed on the altar at mass, gives lists of many of Edgar's prominent ealdormen and nobility, as well as royal and noble womenfolk, all of whom it commemorated for their generosity.[121] The East Anglian family of Athelstan the half-king, and the Wessex family of Ordgar, both of which had close links with Edgar by marriage, emerge as prominent patrons of the new monasteries.[122] A little later, Aethelweard, a cousin of the king, and his family who lived in Wessex were to play an important part in keeping up the momentum of monastic foundations after the death of Edgar.[123] Aethelwin, the protector of Ramsey, and Brihtnoth and Wulfstan, the protectors of Ely, figure prominently in the records of those houses, and without their respective assistance neither place would have fared so relatively securely and well. The speed with which the monasteries were established, and the scale on which the greatest of them were endowed, reflect the wealth and generosity of these great landed families. Some of the charters by which these gifts were made, or ratified by the king, have survived in the archives of the monasteries, and in their cartulary rolls.

The wills surviving from this time afford the closest glimpse into the minds and intentions of these varied benefactors.[124] Some twenty-four examples remain, drawn up by people great and small who had grown up or lived in the second half of the tenth century, which specify bequests to no fewer than twenty of the monastic communities, including some of the later foundations. A frequent variant upon the direct gift of land to a church or religious house was the gift of a final reversion after the life of the immediate beneficiary and his heirs. Thus the process of ecclesiastical endowment may well have been more gradual than appears at first sight. Sometimes gifts were made personally to Ethelwold or other abbots and bishops, presumably to be used at their discretion for religious ends, often for the care of the poor. Specific gifts of vestments, books and ornaments are not unknown; and many family treasures as well as land books and documents came to be lodged at the monasteries for safe keeping. By these channels, and the many personal ties of kinship and friendship which developed as members of families became monks and nuns, the new monastic communities were grafted into the fabric of English society.

The attention of the king, Edgar, and of his family, was of central importance to the reform and renewal of the monasteries, and the dependence upon the king's initiative and the patronage of the royal family left its mark in a profound way upon the whole enterprise. Edgar, by a unique combination of circumstances in his childhood, was very much the protégé of all three of the great reformers: Dunstan, Ethelwold and Oswald.[125] The king's devotion to the monastic cause was personal and unwavering; and as the strength of his political position grew, so he pursued the wishes of the reformers with great vigour. Glastonbury, where he was finally buried, regarded him with especial honour, and he was revered there as a second Josiah.[126] An analysis of his many charters reveals his great generosity towards the Church, and he made many other lands available for purchase by bishops like Ethelwold and Dunstan as well. The number of spurious charters claiming his patronage, generated in later times by the monks, reflects his reputation as a benefactor of the Church second only to Athelstan. Religious communities overseas approached him for assistance: St Ouen, St Genevieve in Paris and St Peter's at Ghent, where Dunstan had stayed.[127] The pope too wrote to him as an ally in the reform of the Church.[128] The personal scandals of his reign in no way detracted from his memory in this regard.

Edgar's queen, Aethelthryth, was an active partner in this process. Despite her later bad reputation among the monks, arising out of the murky circumstances which surrounded the accession of her son, Ethelred, in 978,[129] the queen proved an active benefactress of the monasteries. Glastonbury, Ely and Winchester all remembered her generosity, and it was she who commissioned Ethelwold to translate the Rule of St Benedict into English in return for a gift of land intended finally for Ely;[130] the translation being intended, it would appear, first and foremost for a nunnery.

During this period, the queen emerges principally as the protector and patron of the nunneries.[131] As in Germany, her role as *adiutrix* to the Church, in succession to such royal figures as St Etheldreda, was much emphasised, and the parallel between the king as the representative of Christ and his queen as the representative of the Virgin, to whom the monks and nuns of England were especially devoted, was often drawn.[132] This was rooted in the long tradition whereby the nunneries had persisted due to the influence of royal women. Alfred's sister had founded and led the nunnery at Shaftesbury, the only new monastic community of that time to flourish and survive; Edmund's wife, Aelfgifu, was venerated there as a saint.[133] It was believed that the daughters of Edward the Elder had become abbesses of the Nunnaminster and of Romsey, where they were remembered for their sanctity.[134] Wilton and Wareham also existed as monuments in Wessex to the monasticism of an earlier age, and it was from this living tradition of female religious life that the first nurturing impulses towards the full scale revival of monastic life had sprung.[135]

During the primacy of Dunstan, many of these existing nunneries took on a new lease of life, most of them falling within Ethelwold's immediate care as bishop of Winchester. Nunnaminster in Winchester he reformed personally.[136] The ancient foundation at Barking was substantially endowed and renewed by Edgar, and new houses were created at Amesbury and Wherwell in Hampshire by Queen Aethelthryth herself.[137] The abbesses of Wilton, Romsey and Shaftesbury (and of the later houses at Reading, Berkeley and Horton) are listed in the Hyde 'Liber vitae' as illustrious devotees of New Minster, and the community there as a body enjoyed links of confraternity with the sisters at Romsey.[138] The Salisbury Psalter remains as a fine relic of a tenth-century nunnery, probably Shaftesbury itself, reflecting the growing continental influence towards the use of the Gallican version of the psalms (rather than the older Roman one) in the English monasteries.[139] Houses of nuns may have existed in Exeter and Minster-in-Thanet also, but their history is shrouded in obscurity.

Nunneries by their very nature were peculiarly vulnerable to predatory clergy and nobility, and in the 'Regularis concordia' Dunstan himself categorically insisted, 'that no monk, nor indeed any man whatever his rank, should dare to enter and frequent the places set apart for nuns; and that those who have spiritual authority over nuns should use their powers not as worldly tyrants but in the interests of good discipline'.[140] This passage takes on poignant significance in the light of the way the nunneries were in fact treated by the royal family at this time. Indeed, it is doubtful whether the nunneries were ever properly reformed at this period. The very fact of their existence prior to the monastic renewal, and their peculiar nature as retreats for royal and noble ladies, probably made them as intractable in some respects as any of the old minsters.

At the Nunnaminster, Ethelwold's appointed abbess, the venerable and holy lady of his youth, Aethelthryth, appears to have been set aside by the king in favour of his own daughter, Eadgifu, who was still a child.[141] This might make sense in the light of Goscelin's 'Life of Wulfhilda', written in the eleventh century, which tells how Wulfhilda, while a nun at Wilton, was pursued by King Edgar and nearly trapped by her aunt, the abbess of Wherwell. She escaped the king's passion and took refuge at Wilton. The king, duly frustrated, then made her abbess of Barking. She was later expelled from there for twenty years by Queen Aethelthryth, presumably out of some personal jealousy. An unedifying tale, compounded by the fact that Edgar proceeded to take Wulfhilda's cousin, another nun of Wilton, called Wulfthryth, as his concubine (he was already married, either to Aethelflaed, his first wife, who died young, or, more likely, to Aethelthryth). This liaison did not last long, and the hapless nun returned to Wilton as its abbess.[142] According to Osbern, in his 'Life of Dunstan', Edward, the son of Edgar who succeeded him, was the child of this relationship, and in response to this behaviour Dunstan imposed a substantial penance upon the young king.[143] This is unlikely to be true, but clearly there was some deep scandal, from the baneful consequences of which these royal nunneries were not immune, even if the details of Goscelin's story are incoherent and plagued by anachronism.

From this last unhappy and sordid affair, there was indeed a child, Edith, who was brought up by her mother as a nun at Wilton, where she flourished as a rose among thorns. Her life and sanctity are recorded in the next century by Goscelin, who had been for a time chaplain at both Barking and Wilton.[144] She received her nun's habit from the hand of Ethelwold, who was a spiritual father to her.[145] At one stage Edgar tried to make her abbess of the Nunnaminster, Amesbury and Barking, but Edith refused, electing instead for the obscurity of the cloister and nominating others in her place. On the death of Edgar, and in the crisis over the succession, she was even approached to become queen, it was said, after the murder of Edward, her putative brother. Instead, Edith built an oratory in honour of St Denis, adorned with pictures of his martyrdom; these were executed by Benno, her chaplain from Trier, who, with the other chaplain, Radbod of Rheims, had been responsible for her education. Dunstan came to dedicate the new chapel and predicted both her impending death and the incorruptibility of her finger. She died soon after, aged only 23, and Dunstan buried her in the chapel of St Denis. In the porch of the chapel, thirteen paupers were daily provided for in her memory.

After her death, she apparently appeared to her mother in a vision and also to Dunstan; he examined her relics and found her partially incorrupt. Later the relics were formally translated in 997, and her cult spread from Wilton to many English monasteries. Even King Cnut's scepticism about the likely sanctity of any of Edgar's progeny could not diminish her fame. She fulfilled in the minds of the monastic reformers and their disciples exactly the requirements of a royal and holy virgin. Such consecrated virginity was the apogee of monastic life; and it was at this time that devotion to the Virgin and her assumption grew apace, with Ethelwold also promoting the cult of the conception of Mary at Winchester and the houses influenced by him.[146] The shady circumstances out of which such a life grew enhanced rather than diminished its significance in the minds of men like Dunstan and Ethelwold, for thus was the work of divine grace the more evident.

III – The 'Regularis concordia'

Within a decade of the great council at Winchester of 964 which had commissioned the widespread founding of monasteries in England, there had grown up a plethora of such institutions, scattered throughout southern England, Mercia and East Anglia. They fell into roughly four groups: those revived and guided personally by Dunstan; those founded and managed by Ethelwold and their dependencies; Oswald's own monasteries; and the royal nunneries, in a peculiar position of their own. To these might be added a fifth group, whose composition is relatively obscure; independent foundations like Crowland, Chertsey and perhaps Barking. While the key to the success of the monastic enterprise lay in the friendship and co-operation of Dunstan, Ethelwold and Oswald, backed by the king, this was inevitably too personal an alliance to provide a sure foundation for unity and good government in the future. Indeed the very enthusiasm behind the movement, the scale of it and its dependence upon individual bishops and lay protectors made it vulnerable to fissiparous and centrifugal tendencies, with the danger that the proprietorial element in Anglo-Saxon church life would gain the upper hand again as each house or group of houses went its own way.

Shortly after 970, therefore, a great council was summoned to Winchester, attended by the monastic bishops and most of the heads of religious houses, to settle the way in which the Benedictine life would be observed throughout the land. The monument to this meeting is the 'Regularis concordia',[147] the formal agreement between the monasteries as to how they would together observe the great Rule of St Benedict. This solemn occasion, over which the king presided in name if not in deed and summoned in the national interest at his behest, mirrored a similar occasion in 817 at Aachen; then Benedict of Aniane at the behest of Louis the Pious formulated with the agreement of his fellow abbots the pattern of Benedictine life to which the tenth-century reformers, in England and the continent, looked for their example.[148] To the synod at Winchester came representatives from Fleury and Ghent, the two foreign houses with which the English reformers had personal contact, and which each represented the main traditions of Benedictine renewal on the continent.[149] Thus for the first time, openly and publicly, the English monastic revival was to be associated with that on the continent from which, in part, it had drawn inspiration. The 'Regularis concordia' does not stand alone; there is an account of the formation of the monasteries, probably from the pen of Ethelwold himself, appended to the very translation of the Rule of St Benedict into English which he made at the queen's request. There is also a fragment of an English translation of the 'Regularis concordia', itself adapted for a nunnery.[150] Many years later, Aelfric compiled a summary of the 'Regularis concordia' for the monks at Eynsham in which he attributed the composition of the great agreement to Ethelwold himself.[151] It stands as a great act of statesmanship, and an act of uniformity demonstrative of national unity. As a judicious but firm political settlement it probably represents the climax and expression of Dunstan's patient diplomacy and leadership as archbishop.[152]

The proem and the brief epilogue[153] illuminate the political background precisely. King and archbishop are afraid lest the new-found enthusiasm for the monastic life burn itself out, or by scandal discredit itself. They believe also that the well-being of the Church is the key to the prosperity of the state, and therefore have to expel lax clergy and plan to introduce monks and nuns throughout the country. So the king 'as Good Shepherd' took the monasteries under his own protection and placed the nunneries under the queen's care, in order to safeguard them from any suggestion of scandal.

The problem had arisen that, in their following of the Rule of St Benedict, the new communities were full of enthusiasm but were not united in their usage of the rule. The king summoned the heads of houses and commanded them to be united in their interpretation of the rule, fearing that a multiplicity of interpretations within one country would bring the newly revived monastic life into disrepute.

To secure an authoritative basis for a national consensus, and to ensure that English Benedictine life should be in harmony with the monastic life on the continent, monks from Ghent and Fleury were present to testify to their several traditions. Thus on the clear instruction of Gregory the Great to Augustine, recorded in Bede, the English Church and its monasteries should ever be eclectic in the absorption of the best in the traditions of others. In this way the 'wickedness of boasting, weariness or grumbling' might be banished as the English monks saw themselves as partners in a great tradition. The whole assembly of abbots and abbesses then vowed, compacting their vow with a spiritual pact, that they would follow the customs enshrined in the 'Regularis concordia' with a uniform observance. Any other customs were for private use only.

There then follows a number of precise prescriptions 'to confirm the deliberations of the Synodical Council' which were added by Dunstan, 'moved by a spirit of prophecy', according to the proem. All these address situations particular to the circumstances of the English monastic reform, and were of obvious and urgent importance to its continued life.

First comes the instruction concerning the protection of the nunneries, already discussed; it is based on the provision of Isidore at the second council of Seville in 698.[154] Then it is made clear that the manner of monastic observance agreed at the council was always to take precedence over local custom. Then the council turned its attention to the sensitive but important issue of how heads of communities should be elected. It was agreed that elections should be carried out following the custom of the rule and with the 'consent and advice' of the king.

This was a delphic utterance which meant that appointments of abbots and abbesses were placed on a par with those of bishops, vastly enlarging royal patronage of the Church, and plunging the abbots particularly into the heart of national life, where they sat with the bishops in the witan.[155] The clear intention of the reformers is evident in their next provision – for monastic bishops presiding over religious communities living the Benedictine life in the cathedrals. Once again the patronage of the king is expressly permitted to play a crucial part in securing a suitable nominee, if the cathedral monastery could not provide one of its own. Although at the time of the council only Winchester and perhaps Worcester were monastic cathedral communities, this was a clear statement of policy for the future which was in part fulfilled, giving birth to that unique English institution – the monastic cathedral community, headed by a monk-bishop.[156] Drawing on their own example and experience, Dunstan and Ethelwold enjoin very explicitly a fully monastic life for the bishop, who is to fulfil the monastic ideal in an exemplary way.[157]

The council categorically denounced 'secular dominion' by lay nobles over the life of the Church and its monasteries, turning instead to the king and his consort 'for the safeguarding of holy places and for the increase of the goods of the Church'.[158] While abbots and abbesses were assured of ready access to the king, they were forbidden 'to meet persons of importance, either within or just outside the monastery for the purpose of feasting together'. A similar measure is found in the New Minster Charter.[159] It is a reminder of the ease with which religious life could revert to being secular in all but name. To guard further against this inevitable tendency, the king, in the epilogue to the 'Regularis concordia', 'with all the might of his royal power strictly forbade abbots & abbesses to gather together an earthly treasure-store to enable them to pay, as secular persons do, the customary tax or "heriot" which it is usual to offer the King on the death of notable persons in this country'.[160] Instead they were, living or departed, to devote their wealth to the care of the poor.

The proem to the 'Regularis concordia' concludes with various provisions, all of which reflect the lives and characters of the three great reformers, Dunstan, Ethelwold and Oswald. The strict observance of the divine office is enjoined, even on journeys, and the reciting of psalms is to replace gossip.[161] Let them dismount, and pray on their knees! The care of the young being educated in the monasteries is of particular concern. They are not to be embraced or kissed, nor taken away on journeys; no monk is ever to be alone with a young boy under any circumstances, but the youngsters are to be under the care of their master, as a disciplined body or *schola*.[162] Monks 'shall not gad about visiting the properties of monasteries unless great necessity or reasonable discretion require it'.[163] 'Neither prelates or their subjects should ever think of presuming to be present at worldly feastings, unless perchance in case of unexpected hospitality when travelling.'[164]

At the heart of it all there is to be the simple monastic life:

we purpose to uphold by every means within our power those things which have been handed down to us from our Father Benedict, and which we have freely taken upon ourselves: victuals according to weight, measure and number; clothing, fasting, abstinence, vigils, silence, the virtue of obedience. ... We shall set forth plainly in writing those customs of the Holy Rule which have been constantly and everywhere observed, both by the aforesaid Benedict and by his holy followers and imitators, after deep consideration and examination. This we shall do in loving care for brotherly unity, relying on the advice of our King, and trusting in the commandments of the fathers; and we pray that all who observe these customs in peace and thanksgiving may receive the reward of eternal life.[165]

The 'Regularis concordia' gives the fullest picture now available of Benedictine life in the tenth century, whether in England or on the continent. There is nothing comparable remaining from this period for Ghent or Fleury, the two houses from which much of the English settlement was derived, for example.[166] It is an eclectic summary of the monastic customs built round the Rule of St Benedict which were fairly widely known and available in England at the time.[167] It gives a carefully worked out and very full timetable of life in a monastery, built around the divine office: nocturns, matins, prime, the first or morrow mass, terce, meeting of the chapter, sext, sung mass, none, vespers and compline.[168] In between these liturgical activities which were the primary *raison d'être* of the community, the meals, work and sleep were fitted in. It was a life minutely prescribed for, with precise instructions as to how the various necessary customs of the house were to be arranged. The abbot, assisted sometimes by a dean or prior, ruled every detail of a monk's life, and complete obedience was required at all times. It is not clear whether monks engaged in manual labour or whether the period assigned to work was really reserved for the necessary chores, preparation for services in church and intellectual activity. The monks ate only twice daily for most of the year, only once daily in the winter and in Lent. Hospitality towards the poor and strangers is especially enjoined and monks were expected to wash the feet of some of the poor daily, following Christ's example. This is a particular insistence of the *'Regularis concordia'*, unparalleled elsewhere, and reflecting no doubt the habits of Dunstan, Ethelwold and Oswald, each of whom was remembered for his care for Christ's poor. The contemplative side of the monastic life is emphasised in the requirement for silence in the house; conversation was restricted to the strictly necessary. Private property was forbidden; humble obedience was the inner core of a monk's life.

The *'Regularis concordia'* did not claim originality: it claimed the authority of tradition and experience to regulate individual fervour. Thus it is an amalgam of Benedictine traditions, mainly drawn from the continent, and distinct English customs which were regarded as of special value. It also bears the stamp of the particular circumstances which gave it birth, notably the singular devotion to the royal house of Wessex.

Monks from Fleury and Ghent were present, perhaps even Abbo of Fleury himself, to testify to the traditions and customs of each of the two main strands of monastic reform and renewal on the continent at this time.[169] Although the corresponding customary of Ghent is not known, those of other houses of the Lotharingian reform movement initiated by Gerard of Brogne are: Einsiedeln, where there was an abbot, Gregory, related to the English royal house,[170] Trier and Verdun. The customs of Fleury can be discerned only from much later sources. Underlying both traditions, and that of the *'Regularis concordia'* itself, were the great reforms at the beginning of the ninth century of Benedict of Aniane, to whom all the tenth-century Benedictines looked as their principal authority. Behind these are the most venerable customs drawn from the earliest years before the ninth century and stretching back to Benedict himself.[171] Nonetheless, 'the *"Regularis concordia"* itself is often extremely difficult to understand owing to its silence on many points that were perfectly clear to those for whom it was written'.[172]

The Rule of St Benedict was fundamental to the whole settlement. But perhaps of equal importance, and reflecting probably the pattern of life observed at Glastonbury and Abingdon prior to Edgar's reign, was a book called *'Ordo qualiter'*, an ancient guide to living the monastic life in accordance with the Rule of St Benedict, but antedating the reforms of Benedict of Aniane. The *'Ordo qualiter'* was extensively used throughout the *'Regularis concordia'*. Several sources from the ninth-century reforms may also be discerned: Amalarius' 'Rule for Canons', the *'Capitula'* of Benedict of Aniane and Smaragdus' *'Via regia'*; but these are cited in an eclectic manner, as elements in a common tradition in tenth-century monasticism.

The *'Regularis concordia'* is typical of tenth-century Benedictinism in the way it weaves additional liturgical and monastic customs around the relatively simple framework provided by the Rule of St Benedict. Here the influence of continental practices is paramount. From the ninth-century reforms, additional practices like the 'Trina oratio' and the gradual psalms before nocturns spring. The services for Holy Week and Easter actually cite the 'ordo romanus primus', the first time this is known to have been used in England but a custom common to the monasteries of the Lotharingian reform. From that source too came additional Holy Week rites, the earliest form of Easter drama recorded and the habit of replacing the monastic office with the secular office of the clergy in Holy Week and Easter Week and at nocturns on Whit Sunday. Offices of All Saints and of the dead and many other smaller uses are common to tenth-century monastic life on the continent; some details spring from Fleury and the Cluniac reform, but most come from Ghent and the Lotharingian reform of which it was a part. 'Here, in this Ghent connection, we may recognise perhaps the influence of Dunstan, who had first hand experience of the observance of St Peter's, Blandinium some years before.'[173]

The way in which the 'Regularis concordia' preserves distinct English customs sheds much light on the character of monasticism under Dunstan and Ethelwold and the degree to which it was rooted in the established life of the English Church. Foremost among these are the repeated prayers and psalms for the king and his family, for whom the first or morrow mass was usually said. 'The "Concordia" practice is unique: nowhere else is there to be found anything comparable to it.'[174] In all some eighteen psalms and twenty-three collects are specified as the content of this ceaseless intercession. The convergence of interest between king and Church, expressed in the monastic enterprise, could not be more strongly emphasised.

There are other distinctly English features: the use of Roman psalms and of chasubles in Lent; prayers at the veneration of the cross; the psalm 'Miserere' after matins, vespers and compline; and mass in honour of the cross on Fridays and of the Virgin on Saturdays. The ringing of bells is enjoined, 'as is the custom among people of this country' at Christmas time; processions are to be made to local town churches to venerate the patron saint; and the local laity are to assist at the offertory on Sundays and feast days. 'For we have ordained that the goodly religious customs of this land, which we have learned from our fathers before us, be in no wise cast off but confirmed on all hands.'[175] Most notable of all is the emphasis placed upon frequent confession in preparation for the eucharist, which is to be received daily:

Let them bear in mind the words of the blessed Augustine in his book 'Of the sayings of our Lord', namely, that in the Lord's Prayer we ask for daily not yearly bread. There also he declares that it is as easy for a Christian never to receive the food of life, that is the Body and Blood of Christ, as to receive it no more than once a year. 'So live,' he says, 'that you may be worthy to receive daily; he that is not worthy to receive daily is not worthy to receive once a year.'[176]

This may have rested also on the authority of Bede's letter to Egbert. 'Possibly the "Concordia" is here giving official recognition to a devotion that had originated in some monastery in the early fervour of the English reform movement.'[177] Dunstan at his death, as in his life, revealed his own deep devotion to the frequent reception of the eucharist, and he may well be the moving spirit behind this requirement of the monks.

It was the view of St Anselm, writing to Lanfranc when archbishop of

Canterbury, that Dunstan's authority lay behind the 'Regularis concordia': 'I have heard that St Dunstan drew up a rule of monastic life: I should like, if it be possible, to see the Life and "Instituta" of so great a father.'[178] As an act of statesmanship and wisdom it bears all the hallmarks of his primacy and personal influence. As a monastic tract it seems almost certainly to have been composed under the direction of Ethelwold, 'the father of the monks'. In its more contemplative and spiritual elements, and in its insistence on the care of the poor, the influence of Oswald may perhaps be discerned. It stands as the most comprehensive and fitting memorial to their unique friendship and alliance.

8

THE STATESMAN

EDGAR came to the throne of the reunited kingdom in 959 when he was aged around 16. He was probably born in 943; his mother, Aelfgifu, had died while he was still a baby in 944. She was buried at Shaftesbury, where she was regarded as a saint.[1] Edgar had for a time been brought up with the East Anglian family of Athelstan the half-king, and both Dunstan and Ethelwold took a keen interest in his education.[2] The circumstances of his accession, first to Mercia and the Danelaw, then to Wessex itself, rendered him peculiarly behoven to the Mercian and East Anglian noblemen who had secured his succession: to Aelfhere of Mercia and the sons of Athelstan; and also to the Danes, especially the Danish primate, Oskytel of York, and his kindred. Oskytel did not receive his *pallium* until 959, and because of the confusion at Canterbury after the death of Oda, it is likely that the formal consecration of Edgar as king was delayed at least until 961, when Dunstan returned from Rome with the pope's blessing as archbishop of Canterbury.[3] Meanwhile Edgar had contracted his first marriage to Aethelflaed Candida (known to her friends as 'the Duck'!), who almost certainly died before she could be anointed queen; from this union sprang Edgar's first son, Edward, who would later succeed him.[4] Early in his reign over the united kingdom, Edgar married Aethelthryth, the youthful widow of Aethelwold, ealdorman of East Anglia, and daughter of Ordmaer, ealdorman of Devon. This match balanced the interests of Wessex and eastern Mercia exactly. Aethelthryth functioned as Edgar's anointed queen and as patroness of the Church and its monasteries (especially the nunneries), and she bore him two sons, Edmund, who died around the year 971, and Ethelred, who would later be king.[5] As early as 965, Edmund was regarded as the *aetheling*, the likely successor to his father.[6] Dunstan himself had a close relationship with Edgar and his family dating back to the time of Edgar's birth near Dunstan's family lands at Glastonbury.[7] He placed the royal children under the care of Sidemann, a monk of the Old Minster, who in 970 became bishop of Crediton.[8]

Despite the relative silence of the *Anglo-Saxon Chronicle* for this period, Edgar enjoyed a reputation in the tenth century, at home and abroad, second only to the great Athelstan. In many ways his accomplishments mirrored those of his famous uncle: he was remembered as the great peace giver, the beneficiary of a prolonged pause in Viking attacks from the north; and also as a fearless warrior, 'bold in battle', capable of marshalling formidable forces and holding sway over all the princes of the British Isles.[9] The chronicle alludes briefly to his forceful policy towards the north: in 966 a raid on Westmorland is mentioned together with the ealdormanship of Oslac, who became the king's leading presence in Northumbria.[10] Nearer home, in 969 (or perhaps in 974) the king devastated the Isle of Thanet as a punishment for despoiling merchants from York, possibly Danes, of their goods.[11] York under Edgar became a thriving trading city; when Oswald became archbishop there, he found it 'filled with activity and with the treasures of merchants who came thither from all parts, but mostly from Danish lands'.[12] Later historians, like Florence of Worcester, writing with hindsight after the disasters of Ethelred's reign and the Norman Conquest, tend to regard Edgar's reign as a golden age.[13] Nonetheless the writer of the encomium inserted into the chronicle under the year 959, possibly Archbishop Wulfstan of York writing at the end of Ethelred's reign, could record with candour the strengths and weaknesses of Edgar's time:

> In his days, things improved greatly, and God granted him to remain in peace as long as he lived; and to this end, he laboured zealously, as indeed he was obliged to do. He exalted God's praise far and wide, and loved God's law; and he improved the peace of the people more than any of the kings who were before him in the memory of man. God in turn supported him so that kings and earls willingly submitted to him and were subjected to him. Without battle he brought under his sway all that he wished. He came to be honoured widely throughout foreign countries . . . and continually & frequently directed all his people wisely in matters of Church and state. Yet he did one ill deed too greatly: he loved evil foreign customs and tactlessly encouraged heathen manners within this land, and attracted hither foreigners and enticed harmful people to this country. But may God grant that his good deeds may prove greater than his ill-deeds, for the protection of his soul.[14]

Behind the homiletic and minatory style, typical of Wulfstan and his contemporaries, and the clear overtones from Old Testament royal exemplars, David and Solomon, there stands here a careful and balanced appraisal of the reign, at once shrewd and fair.[15] The relative stability of Edgar's rule rested on the way he secured the united co-operation of the leading ealdormen: Oslac of Northumbria, Aelfhere of Mercia, the East Anglian families and the nobility of Wessex. Behind this also stood the strong and united episcopate, led by Dunstan and Ethelwold and, in due course, Oswald.

Edgar inherited an alliance by marriage with the newly crowned emperor, Otto I, who had married a sister of Athelstan, an aunt to Edgar. The English royal house sustained a lively interest in her family, although she herself died in 946.[16] Florence of Worcester records that early in the reign, Otto sent lavish gifts to Edgar to cement the alliance, and when Otto died Edgar in turn sent a handsomely endowed embassy to his heir and successor.[17] 'Edgar was generous in his bounty, for which he was praised by kings of other races.'[18] A cautious letter to Dunstan from Arnulf of Flanders, seeking good relations with Edgar the new king, paved the way for an embassy led by the abbot of St Bertin in 961 and for the first known grant of land to an overseas monastery, the house at Ghent where Dunstan had sojourned in exile.[19] Edgar maintained good working relationships with the papacy: the letter from John XIII, which authorised the restoration of the monasteries at the expense of the existing clergy, regards Edgar as a reformer and ally of the Church,[20] and when Oswald became archbishop of York in 972, the king sent with him generous gifts to the apostolic see.[21] Edgar's reputation for generosity also attracted the attention of churches overseas; letters remain from St Ouen in Rouen and St Genevieve in Paris seeking his assistance for the restoration of their churches.[22]

It was within the British Isles that Edgar's sway was felt most, and the chroniclers regarded him as the last of the *bretwalda*, those English kings who had exercised an *imperium* or overlordship over the Celtic and other kingdoms of Britain. The style of Edgar's charters describe him as king of all 'Albion', a title and view of his rule which is confirmed in many of the monastic texts of the period; according to the first life of Dunstan, Edgar 'subdued to himself the kings and petty rulers around him'.[23] From the Welsh chronicle for 965 comes notice of Edgar's strong policy towards his western neighbours and intervention in their affairs, like that of Athelstan before him; and in the law codes of Hwyl Dda can be discerned the impact which English law and culture had been making since that earlier reign.[24] Edgar's death is recorded in the Irish and Welsh chronicles, and the 'Life of St Iltud' saw it as divine revenge for a raid on Glamorgan![25]

According to Roger of Wendover, and before him Symeon of Durham, Edgar contracted an alliance, shortly before his death, with Kenneth, king of the Scots; Kenneth, in return for rendering homage, received Lothian and sundry lands in England, together with handsome and lavish gifts.[26] Aelfric, a virtually contemporary source, tells in his 'Life of Swithun' how Edgar maintained supremacy in Britain by his fleet, which was unmatched, and how 'all the kings who were in this island, Cumbrians and Scots, came to him, eight kings on one day, and they all submitted to Edgar's direction'.[27] The chronicle asserts that shortly after his solemn coronation at Bath in 973, these kings 'came to meet him and all gave him pledges that they would be his allies on sea and on land'. This was at Chester, where Edgar had assembled his formidable fleet and where, according to Florence of Worcester, the English king was rowed by his vassals up and down the Dee.[28] Stenton has shown that the names of the eight kings given by Florence fit remarkably the political situation in the Celtic kingdoms at that precise time.[29] This combination of homage, influence and mutual self-defence demonstrated decisively the meaning of the pretensions of Ethelwold's New Minster Charter, where words from Jeremiah were ascribed to Edgar: 'Behold, I have set you over peoples and over nations'; representatives of these would all be present in 973 at Edgar's great coronation at Bath.[30]

The impact of Edgar's political hegemony may be discerned also in the life of the Welsh Church. In 962, Edgar intervened to resolve a dispute concerning land belonging to the see of Llandaff. This apparently occurred against the background of a disputed succession and some attempt to impose clerical celibacy on the clergy of the diocese, an attempt which utterly failed.[31] It was later claimed too that from 972, the bishops of Llandaff, like some bishops of St Davids before them, had been consecrated by the archbishop of Canterbury.[32] Edgar was remembered as a founder of monasteries, including the one at Bangor; there were Saxon monks at Llanilltyd, and probably in other Welsh monasteries, early in his reign.[33]

Evidence for English church influence in the other Celtic regions is fragmentary. Of the Church in Cumbria little is known at this time; a Scottish bishop intervened in English church affairs shortly after Edgar's death, perhaps as a consequence of the alliance with Kenneth.[34] In Cornwall, the reign of Edgar saw a consolidation of the relatively new and impoverished see at St Germans under Wulfsige, its bishop.[35] The manumissions of slaves, inserted into the margins of the Bodmin Gospels, reflect both Edgar's presence and interest in Cornwall and the influence of Saxon clergy in a British monastery.[36] From Cornwall at this time came the cult of St Neot, whose relics were appropriated around the year 974 by the founders of the monastery in Cambridgeshire, which bears his name.[37] Of unusual interest is a tenth-century Breton litany (of eighth-century origin, possibly from York) which prays for the English king, archbishop and clergy.[38] The strength of Edgar's position in Church and state had many ramifications.

At home, Edgar was revered as a law giver. Within a generation, both Ethelred and Cnut regarded Edgar's laws as the fundamental component and basis of their own law codes, and to Edgar was later attributed the code of ecclesiastical law in fact drawn up by Archbishop Wulfstan and called the 'Canons of Edgar'.[39] Edgar, of course, stood in a long and distinguished line of law givers, stretching back before the reign of Alfred the Great. Law giving was fundamental to monarchy as the Anglo-Saxons conceived it, and the English Church from the beginning had provided a steady impulse towards the formation and writing down of the laws. Justice and its sure administration was permanent common ground between Church and king, and Christian kings had a special duty to ensure that their laws conformed with Christian morality. Alfred prefaced his code of laws with the decalogue, and the influence of biblical law is often evident and specific.[40] Within the body of English law, the place and privileges of the Church and its clergy were clearly established. From the times of Ethelbert of Kent, the penalties for injuring church property or persons were severe. As time progressed, church influence secured laws to enforce the payment of ecclesiastical taxes, to mitigate the severity of secular penalties and to decree the observance of saints' days and the like. Increasingly in the tenth century, the Church had a part to play in the administration of justice, and bishops sat with ealdormen in the shire courts, supervising both secular and spiritual causes.[41] Edgar's laws reflect that developed interpenetration of Church and state which is the salient feature of this period of English history, a subtle expression of what emerged by the end of the century as a sophisticated system of Christian political theory. Within this body of law there lay two particular areas of royal justice: the administration of a sound currency and the granting of relative autonomy to the Danish population – the Danelaw. In both these areas too, the Church had a crucial interest and influence, and the policy adumbrated during Edgar's reign was of lasting importance for the unity and stability of England.[42]

It is striking that apart from the 'Regularis concordia' there are no ecclesiastical canons surviving from this reign. There is no evidence that Dunstan emulated Oda, who twenty years before had issued a succinct but comprehensive body of canons to the English Church.[43] On the other hand, there is a strong reinforcement of the tradition that secular law might enforce ecclesiastical interests and, if need be, penalties too. Indeed, the first part of Edgar's code of law issued at Andover at the beginning of his reign is purely ecclesiastical (II Edgar).[44] It confirms the entrenched rights of the Church, as indeed did the 'Promissio regis' which Dunstan later extracted from Edgar at his coronation in 973.[45] The payment of tithe is the main concern of this code, with specific provisions and penalties to be enforced by the king's reeve, the bishop's reeve and the priest concerned. The interests of the old minster churches are safeguarded, but provision is also made for the financial support of newer and proprietary churches in the emerging parishes. The ancient customary payment of hearth penny (later Peter's pence) on St Peter's Day for the support of the Roman see is enjoined with severe (and probably impractical) penalties. This may reflect Roman pressure on Dunstan when he went there to collect his *pallium*; the holy see was hard pressed within and without at this time.[46] Finally, the full observance of Sunday, together with the other church festivals, is firmly reiterated.

The other part of this code (III Edgar) demonstrates how deeply church influence permeated the administration of law and justice, just as the first part shows what a vital interest the institution of the Church had in the protection which the law afforded it. The king upholds the essential impartiality and importance of justice for all men, 'whether poor or rich', with right of appeal to the king himself. Clemency in the mitigation of penalties, and severe punishment for unjust judges, who fall under the purview of diocesan bishops, stand out as priorities. 'In the shire-meeting the bishop and the ealdorman are to be present, and there to expound both the ecclesiastical and the secular law.' (5.2) Perjury is singled out for harsh treatment, and there are firm measures to ensure uniform currency and also weights and measures. To curb crime, sureties are called for: open and regular attendance at local courts and meetings are mandatory to check outlawry and treason.

The spirit of this law code is best summed up in the terms of the *'Promissio regis'*, which, from the time of Dunstan, became an integral part and prelude to the solemn rite of coronation:

> In the Name of the Holy Trinity I promise three things to the Christian people and my subjects: *first*, that God's church and all Christian people of my dominions hold true peace; *second*, that I forbid robbery and all unrighteous things to all orders of men; *third*, I promise and enjoin in all decrees justice and mercy, that the gracious and merciful God of his everlasting mercy may forgive us all.[47]

To this three-fold promise stands appended a brief homily from Dunstan on the nature and duties of kings in this regard. Its tone is the key to what is distinct about Edgar's later code of law (IV Edgar), issued after the plague of 962, perhaps in 973 near the time of the Bath coronation:[48]

> The Christian king who keeps these undertakings earns for himself worldly honour, and the eternal God also is merciful to him, both in this present life and in the world to come. But if he violate that which was promised to God, then shall immediately grow worse among his people, and the end is destruction, unless he in this life first amend it.
>
> . . .
>
> The duty of a hallowed king is that he judge no man unrighteously, and that he defend and protect widows, orphans and strangers; that he forbid thefts, and correct immorality, and annul and prevent incestuous marriage; that he extirpate witches and sorcerers, drive out of the land kin-slayers and perjurers, feed the needy with alms; and have old, wise and sober men for his counsellors, set upright men for stewards. For whatever they do wrong by his fault, he must render account of it all on Judgement Day.

This minatory and homiletic approach by an archbishop to royal justice and law making is normally associated with Wulfstan of York in the reign of

Ethelred. But it was by no means his invention, and Dunstan here is in the long tradition of popes and bishops, notably Carolingian bishops like Hincmar of Rheims, who, drawing on Old Testament prophetic tradition, addressed kings in this fearless manner.[49] IV Edgar similarly begins with a doom-laden assumption arising in response to plague throughout the land: 'It seemed to the king and his councillors that a calamity of this kind was merited by sins and by contempt of God's commands, especially the withholding of the tribute which Christian men ought to render God in their tithes.'[50] Clearly the ambitious programme of church taxation, outlined in the earlier code at Andover, had broken down in many places. The alarm of the king and the bishops may be detected in this remarkable clause: 'I and the Archbishop command that you do not anger God, nor merit sudden death in this present life or indeed the future death in everlasting Hell by any withholding of God's dues.' (1.4) The king emphasises the universal application of this rule throughout his dominion. Yet this fear of divine wrath is not far removed from the desire to secure a favourable intercession for the well-being of the king and the realm, which also underlay and justified the reform of the monasteries. Indeed, before this code turns to strictly secular matters, there is a dark hint at the unacceptable side of clerical life, the kind of loose living that Edgar expunged at Winchester:

> And those servants of God who receive the dues which we pay to
> God, are to live a pure life, that through their purity they may inter-
> cede for us to God. And I and my thegns shall *compel* our priests to
> that which the pastors of our souls direct us, namely our bishops . . .
> that through that obedience by which we obey them for God's sake,
> we may merit the eternal life to which they draw us by teaching and
> by example of good works. (1.7,8)

Whether this edict signifies the imposition of clerical celibacy among the non-monastic clergy remains an open question; but it is doubtful, given the silence of other evidence.[51]

Edgar's legislation bears the impress of episcopal influence, and this was nothing new. The archbishop of Canterbury led the bishops in their judicial capacity; Oda, for example, had performed just such a role during the reign of Edmund.[52] The entrenched position of the Church emerges clearly, to secure its needs as the parochial system began to take shape at this time, and the internal reform of the secular clergy began to gain momentum.[53] The king was not averse to enforcing certain ecclesiastical sanctions and taxes; indeed the bishops expected him to do so, for collecting the tithe on so widespread a basis was well nigh impossible without royal authority and active support. Even then it was only partially successful, and the dire penalties reflect real problems here. Feast days and fast days were difficult to establish fully in an agrarian society, yet in the Church's eyes they were indispensable if the worship of God was to be faithfully and fully carried out. They were indispensable too to the welfare and protection of the poor and slaves. The emphasis on equity and clear justice, free from violence and private retribution, was the main concern of king and bishops. Here principle bolstered expediency and the ultimate self-interest of an ordered community. Yet theft, often with violence, remained endemic in early medieval society. Similarly, the Church's campaign for Christian marriages, regularised, monogamous and free of incest, ran against the grain of society, noble and peasant. The kings themselves were rarely exemplary in this, although Dunstan, like Oda before him, had a reputation for severity over this issue.[54] Sound coinage and proper standards of measurement had a moral dimension too, for it was the poor who were robbed most by corrupt coinage and measures. To secure non-fraudulent trading in the burgeoning boroughs and ports of the land posed a major challenge to which Edgar and his heirs rose successfully. The partnership between ealdorman and bishop, and on a more practical level between their officials, meant that the mingling of spiritual and secular requirements in law had a practical effect. Bishops were expected to be learned in justice: Glastonbury under Dunstan had trained clergy precisely for that task.[55]

Dunstan's personal influence as archbishop of Canterbury upon Edgar's legislation should neither be overemphasised nor played down. By virtue of his office, he was expected to play a leading role in the witan, clarifying and formulating laws, and his own reputation as a law giver and judge at Canterbury became proverbial.[56] Moreover, his influence as one of the principal advisers of a youthful king obviously fitted him for the role of an 'old, wise and sober counsellor'; Edgar was in his 20s, Dunstan in his 60s. He presided over and led a formidable company of bishops, like Oswald and Ethelwold who used the law to the full to secure the foundation of the monasteries and the interests of their own sees. Nonetheless, Dunstan did embody a potent tradition of the statesman-archbishop, like Hincmar of Rheims, whose works Dunstan would probably have read, at the court of Charles the Bald a century earlier.[57] The iconography of the famous picture of Christ, drawn by Dunstan, gives the clue: Christ is portrayed as the wisdom of God, and also the true ruler of men; two psalm-couplets juxtapose equity and education.[58] This is the model upon which Dunstan and his contemporaries styled their vision of kingship, and in the 'Regularis concordia' Edgar is hailed as a type and representative of the Good Shepherd.[59] At the same time, good order in the Church, like the royal patronage of the monasteries and clerical and episcopal co-operation in the administration of justice, vastly extended the practical authority of the king, especially with regard to the local nobility upon whom government ultimately depended. Nor should the moral impact, even the sheer terror, upon the laity, noble and peasant, of divine sanctions and ecclesiastical supervision of trial by ordeal or oaths on relic boxes and altars be overlooked. The Church at the same time offered mercy and judgement; but it was a judgement that could turn against a ruler or a nobleman if he proved himself unjust, cruel or wicked.

Florence of Worcester paints a picture, not unconvincing, of Edgar 'perambulating his kingdom, winter and spring, enquiring diligently how his laws and statutes were being observed by the ealdormen & judges, lest the poor be oppressed by the prejudice of the powerful'.[60] The king's own personal commitment to the cause of justice seems to have been both real and exemplary.

IV Edgar is of great interest also because of the light it sheds on Edgar's policy towards the Danelaw. He owed his accession, during his brother's reign, to the loyalty of the northern people, and Oskytel, the Danish archbishop of York, was instrumental in securing both the young king's position and also Dunstan's own return. Moreover, the policy of evangelising East Anglia, which had been pursued by archbishops of Canterbury and bishops of London since the time of Plegmund and Edward the Elder, had borne fruit in a remarkable degree of harmony between Danes and English in that region.[61] The success of the monastic plantations in East Anglia and the southern Danelaw, in which Oswald, of Danish descent, and Thurkytel, also a Dane, played a prominent part, must have depended in part at least on the goodwill of the local Danish nobility. Edgar in his fourth code grants virtual autonomy to the Danes within his domain: 'It is my will that secular rights be in force among the Danes according to as good laws as they can best decide on.' (2.1) Later in the code, this is reiterated, in the words: 'I have ever allowed this, and will allow it them as long as I live, because of the loyalty you have always shown me.' (12) Nonetheless, the king is not averse from decreeing elaborate provisions and penalties to cope with theft and stolen property which are to be 'common to all the nation, whether Englishmen, Danes or Britons'. (2.2) So this is not autonomy granted out of weakness, but as a matter of policy.[62] It is to be seen in conjunction with the appointment of Earl Oslac to lead in the north, and the continuation of the policy begun under Edwy of building up the position and wealth of the archbishopric of York, both by grants of land (like Southwell) and by holding Worcester in plurality. Oskytel and, later, Oswald, being Danes and men of great character and capacity, proved ideal for this end. After the treachery of Archbishop Wulfstan, a Northumbrian was never again appointed to the northern primacy.[63] The task of building up the northern church was not easy, and Edgar's sympathy towards the Danes may not have been popular elsewhere; it probably accounts for the criticism of his toleration of 'foreign customs & manners' in the chronicle.[64] Nevertheless, it secured the unity of the kingdom in a lasting way; it also opened the way for the Anglo-Saxon missions to Scandinavia which probably had their beginnings at this time.[65]

Roger of Wendover sheds further light on the reference to a standard coinage in III Edgar 8: 'Edgar ordered a new coinage to be made throughout the whole of England, because the old was so debased by the crime of clippers that a penny hardly weighed a half-penny on the scales.'[66] Archaeology has produced numismatic evidence that in 973, the year of his coronation in Bath, Edgar thoroughly reformed the English coinage, laying the basis for the pattern of minting for the next 150 years. Standard coins were issued, replacing all others. The issue lasted for a limited number of years, then the process was repeated. To this end the number of mints increased from forty to sixty, though the dies were produced centrally and under strict royal control. On one side of the coin was a portrait of the king and the words 'Rex Anglorum'; on the other side was a sign indicating the mint from which it came. The mints were for the most part located in the boroughs. Penalties for forgery were extremely severe. The result was a coinage unrivalled in Europe whose reputation spread from Ireland to Rome. Despite the decentralising of the mints, a sophisticated administration not only kept the coining as a royal monopoly; it also enabled the king to regulate the silver content of the coin without undermining its standard value. No foreign coins were allowed to circulate, and the manipulation of the weight of the silver in the coin not only made a profit for the crown, it also regulated the balance of trade between England and the continent. This was, in all, a remarkable achievement.[67]

Dunstan was remembered as a formidable supporter of the royal policy towards the coinage. In an earlier period of history, archbishops of Canterbury had minted their own coins, but by the tenth century this had died out. According to Athelstan's second code, there were to be seven moneyers at Canterbury: 'four of the king, two of the archbishop, and one of the abbot (of St Augustine's)'.[68] According to Osbern, Dunstan refused to celebrate the mass of Pentecost until false coiners had been duly punished, and Eadmer inserts a solemn homily by Dunstan concerning this affront to divine and natural justice, this exploitation of God's poor.[69]

In his thirtieth year, Edgar was crowned at Bath, at Pentecost 973, at a solemn gathering to which men came from far and wide: 'from west to east, from the north to the sea, the command of the king [*imperatoris*: cf. Luke 2.1] went forth that all should come to him'.[70] The anonymous 'Life of Oswald' affords a vivid account of this unusual and much remembered occasion. Oswald's visit to Rome in 972, as the king's emissary as well as on account of his appointment as archbishop of York, was apparently a prelude to this, as was Edgar's courting of the new emperor, Otto II. This was hardly a delayed coronation as writers since the time of Osbern have conjectured. Stubbs' verdict, based on the work of Robertson, corrects this erroneous conclusion:

> Edgar's coronation at Bath was a solemn enunciation of the consummation of English unity, an inauguration of the king of all the nations of England, celebrated by the two archbishops, possibly with special instructions or recognition from Rome, possibly in imitation of the imperial consecration of Edgar's kinsmen, the first and second Otto, possibly as a declaration of the imperial character of the English crown itself.[71]

The choice of Bath, a city redolent of the Roman past with substantial remains, 'the crowning city of a far-flung kingdom', provided also a strategic meeting-point for Wessex and Mercia, and for the Welsh princes.[72] Bath also possessed a fine new abbey church, as much a sign of the new ecclesiastical order underpinning Edgar's regime as the ranks of the clergy and religious who swelled the congregation on that occasion. These were the great king's spiritual warriors, their intercession his strength, their order a tangible reflection of the king's own power and priorities.[73] To meet the needs of his allies and retainers a special 'circumscription' issue of the coinage was made at Bath itself in 973.[74] The chronicle makes it quite clear that immediately after this notable event, Edgar proceeded to Chester for the naval display and homage by the Celtic kings described by Florence of Worcester.[75] Like Charles the Bald in 869 and King David in the Old Testament, Edgar celebrated in this solemn consecration his new *imperium* throughout Britain; he was a *ducatus* leading a defensive confederacy from a position of considerable military, naval and diplomatic strength.[76]

It was when he was 30, the canonical age for ordination and consecration, that Edgar underwent this solemn inauguration, and the whole occasion was hedged around by a religious aura which culminated in the vision of the king as 'God's anointed' and his deputy over Church and state. At this time, elaborate westworks were being built both at Bath itself and at Winchester; these may have emulated similar buildings on the continent set apart for the cult of the king within the liturgy of the Church.[77] The iconography of the great Benedictional of St Ethelwold, drawn at exactly this time, portrays Christ as the king of kings whose rule sheds light and glory upon the reign of the earthly king of England. This picture is echoed in the *'Regularis concordia'*, where Edgar is described as the imitator of the good shepherd, a teacher of the Church and the sole fount of its good order. He is, in the later words of Archbishop Wulfstan of York, 'Christ's deputy in a Christian people' (VIII Ethelred 2.1).[78] Indeed, the promulgation of the *'Regularis concordia'*, perhaps in the year preceding the Bath coronation or possibly even in the same year as a consequence of that event, can be seen as a mirror too of Edgar's position as 'glorious, by the grace of Christ illustrious King of the English and of the other peoples dwelling within the bounds of the island of Britain'.[79]

The picture of the great coronation which is described in the anonymous life of Oswald is confirmed in almost all its details by a surviving 'Ordo' of this coronation, which was copied at the monastery of St Vedast in Arras around the year 980 and acquired by Abbot Ratoldus of Corbie who died in 986.[80] It became a fundamental basis for later French coronations with all its English peculiarities. It is not an original *ordo*; it almost certainly rests upon traditional patterns for coronation dating back to the time of Charles the Bald and Hincmar of Rheims in the ninth century, and beyond them to early English customs in the eighth century.[81] Consequently, even in its revised form, it 'reflects the continuity of English kingship and of the independent traditions of the English church' over at least 200 years.[82] It is a monument too to the mutual influence of Carolingian and Anglo-Saxon ideas of kingship.

The Whitsun coronation began with an episcopal admonition to the king urging him to obey the law and to uphold justice. Then two of the bishops showed the king to his people to secure their consent, a vestigial election. They then led him into the church to the antiphon from Psalm 89, which included the words: 'Righteousness and judgement are the foundation of thy throne.' At the altar, Dunstan removed the king's crown and intoned the *'Te Deum'*, and then extracted the three-fold promise[83] upon which his Christian rule was to be based. The traditional prayers followed, led by both Dunstan and Oswald. The solemn consecration followed, leading up to the sacred anointing with oil, to the words from the Old Testament: 'Zadok the priest and Nathan the prophet anointed Solomon king',[84] to which the people cried out, 'May the king live forever!' 'After the anointing, Dunstan the archbishop gave the king a ring, and girded him with a sword; then he placed the crown on his head and blessed him. He gave him also a sceptre and a rod.'[85] The solemn mass of Whitsun followed, after which the king was enthroned, accompanied by the queen, who was almost certainly anointed in a similar manner on that occasion.[86] Great celebrations ensued, after which 'everyone went home, blessing the king and the queen, and desiring only the peace which their ancient kings had promised them'.[87]

The Ratoldus 'Ordo' is rich in theological association and imagery, as well as in direct political assertion. The very occasion, Pentecost, a feast which united the power of the Holy Spirit with a vision of the unity and universality of the Church (and of all men), was appropriate to such a display of spiritual and 'imperial' hegemony. Emulating however distantly the great Byzantine emperors, 'the political intention was identical, to show the ruler as Christ's vicegerent on earth. Ceremonies involving the ruler on feast-days proclaimed his God-given character'.[88] It was at a similar Easter gathering that the momentous decision to renew the monasteries on a wide and irreversible scale was publicly taken.[89] Edgar's age, and its association with ordination and consecration, suited precisely the sacral associations which the anointing of the king had in the minds of Dunstan and Oswald. The endowment of the Holy Spirit is prayed for again and again in the rite, also a spirit of wisdom and a pastoral charisma to enable the king to uphold the right and defend the poor.

The long line of Old Testament antecedents is related as a remembrance of God's assistance for kings long ago, and a reminder too of his purpose in history, impinging either as blessing or as judgement. Abraham, Moses, Joshua, David and Solomon are the five outstanding figures to whom reference is made.[90] Then, at the heart of the consecration prayer itself, comes Dunstan's distinct insertion, describing Edgar as king of 'all Albion', king over the 'Saxons, Mercians, and Northumbrians', whose rule would unite all these peoples. Later in the service, at the giving of the sceptre, the prayer asks God to honour him above all the kings of Britain too.[91] Then follows the actual anointing, an act associated with the anointing of 'priests, prophets and martyrs', and a divine enabling which assured spiritual victory over the 'powers of the air'.[92] The subsequent prayer prays that the 'dove of peace' may descend on the king's people as the king himself receives divine blessing.

Each item of apparel is also charged with theological significance which is in turn applicable to the well-being of the Church. The ring represents orthodox faith, the foundation of the kingdom and the scourge of heresy and sedition. The sword is the symbol of the power of the Holy Spirit to defend the Church from all its enemies. The crown embodies the blessing of God which is the true glory of a king and inspires the justice of his rule. The sceptre is the token of power to be wielded in the best interests of Church and people, a veritable sign of the kingdom of God; whereas the rod is the rod of 'virtue and equity', the pledge of true discrimination and clemency.

The final solemn and prolonged prayer of blessing seeks divine protection for both king and kingdom, and bears the stamp of Dunstan's own predilection by invoking the prayers and merits of the saints, especially 'St Mary, St Peter Prince of the Apostles, and St Gregory Apostle of the English'.[93] From Dunstan too may come the description of the king as 'mediator between clergy and people'. Attached to the Ratoldus 'Ordo' are the propers of the mass for this occasion, in the course of which God is invoked as the protector of 'all kingdoms, and especially of Christian empires' (christiani imperii). 'Christian liberty' and victory over spiritual adversaries are specifically mentioned, and there is a prayer at the end for the blessing of a royal standard for which the intervention of Michael the archangel is sought. Of especial interest, however, are two collects: the daily collect for the king is that found also in the 'Regularis concordia';[94] and the collect 'ad complendum' not only weaves together 'imperial' and spiritual themes completely but may also indicate another dimension to the missions to Scandinavia which probably had their beginnings during Edgar's reign: 'God Who did prepare the Roman Empire for the preaching of the Gospel of Your eternal kingdom, extend heavenly protection for your servants our rulers, that the peace of the churches may be disturbed by no upheaval of war.'[95] It is also a sharp reminder of the political uncertainty and violence of the age, which was never far from men's minds and would sweep England again within a decade of this event.

The coronation of Edgar at Bath in 973 was by episcopal initiative and shrouded in theological imagery and thought. It was a supreme act of 'sacral kingship' whose significance has stretched down to the present day. It reflected the great trust placed in the king by Dunstan and his fellow reformers throughout the monastic renewal. It represented too a real union between Church and state; not quite a theocracy, but an identification of action, role and interest between king and Church that only a century later would seem hopelessly anachronistic. The Church was not subservient to the king, nor the king to the Church; there was a partnership which smacked of a marriage, but a partnership which would always need a strong archbishop and an amenable king for its success. Behind it lay a formidable if hidden ideology, later to be enunciated by Wulfstan, of a kingship by divine election and sacred anointing, but bound by law and justice and obligation to the people. This was expressed in a formidable coalescing and articulation of ancient tradition which on this occasion was rendered capable of discharging an 'imperial' political function, never to be repeated and the apogee of the Anglo-Saxon 'British empire'.[96]

9

TWO KINGS

I – Edward the martyr (975–8)

*E*DGAR died unexpectedly, aged 32, on 8 July: 'this noble monarch generous with gold left his lifeless body, he who sprang from the race of the Saxons, Edgar the king, Monarch of Britain: in the Latin tongue his fortunate folk gave him the name of "contim beatam" [i.e. blessed spear]'. So Aethelweard, his kinsman, concluded his chronicle,[1] and plaudits resound from all the other chroniclers. Florence of Worcester goes so far as to compare him to Romulus, Cyrus and Alexander, and also to Charlemagne.[2] He was buried at Glastonbury, probably by Dunstan himself.[3] He had proved a generous benefactor of that house and was revered there as a saint for more than a hundred years William of Malmesbury tells the gruesome tale of how the king's uncorrupted body was translated forty years after his death to the reliquary he had donated to Glastonbury for that purpose, where he might repose along with the head of St Apollinaris and the relics of the martyr St Vincent.[4] Dunstan had buried him 'in the chapter house near its entrance to the church'; but his final resting place was a fine shrine 'covered with gold and silver and decorated with ivory images', a fitting accompaniment to the other gifts he had made, which included 'the most precious royal robe in which he had been crowned to serve as an ornament for the altar'.[5] Immediately after this translation, a lunatic and a blind man were cured at Glastonbury, apparently at Edgar's heavenly intercession.[6]

The kingdom Edgar relinquished was immediately plunged into crisis because his first son, Edward, came to the throne in circumstances that remain obscure. Edward was the child of Edgar's first marriage, which was terminated by the death of Aethelflaed before she could be consecrated as his queen. Consequently, as early as 965, it would appear from the New Minster Charter that Edward was being passed over as a likely successor in favour of the first son of Queen Aethelthryth, Edmund, the *aetheling*, who died around the year 971. The charter quite explicitly styles Edmund as '*clito legitimus filius*', whereas Edward is merely '*clito procreatus*'.[7] The premature deaths first of the youth Edmund and then of Edgar himself left Edward with the clear advantage of seniority in age over Ethelred, the younger son of Queen Aethelthryth. Edward was perhaps 16;

Ethelred hardly 10.[8] According to Osbern, Dunstan's personal intervention was crucial to Edward's peaceful accession;[9] but a charter of Ethelred's emphasises that his half-brother succeeded 'by the unanimous election of all the leading men of both orders',[10] and Dunstan and Oswald crowned the young king at Kingston upon Thames. However, there is reason to believe that this may have been delayed until as late as March 976.[11]

The anonymous 'Life of Oswald' sheds some light on the circumstances and difficulties surrounding Edward's succession and brief reign. Although Edgar apparently indicated his preference for Edward as his successor,[12] he was resented personally in many quarters: 'he inspired in all not only fear but also terror, for he scourged his retainers not only with words but truly with bitter blows'.[13] This may lie behind the assertion by John of Wallingford that there was some grumbling grievance within the court against Edward, fomented perhaps by the retainers of the queen and her son.[14] The feeling ran very deep, so that 'there began to approach on all sides dissension and tribulation, which neither bishops nor leaders in ecclesiastical and secular affairs could allay'.[15] To judge from this writer, incipient civil war was at hand and a divided kingdom in prospect, its security jeopardised further by renewed external threats.

For some reason now unfathomable, Edgar's faithful and powerful earl, Oslac, who ruled Northumbria, was exiled: 'a grey-haired man, wise and skilled in speech, he was bereft of his lands'.[16] A memorandum of Archbishop Oswald of York refers to the plundering of the northern Church, a likely consequence of this upheaval.[17] Aelfhere of Mercia emerged as the most powerful force in the land, and in the confusion, which he to some extent fomented in and around Mercia, his ascendancy seemed assured. He not only plundered some of the monasteries, newly founded in western Mercia by Oswald and Ethelwold, on a tide of popular resentment and support, he challenged also the position of the great East Anglian family of Aelfwold and Aethelwin. Aethelwin, the protector of Ramsey Abbey, took up arms against Aelfhere to protect his position in eastern Mercia. With the active support of Bryhtnoth of Essex and backed by a show of force, he attracted the support of other unspecified members of the nobility; a stand-off was secured and Aelfhere's pretensions contained.[18] Against this uneasy background, Edward began to rule. His position was not made happier by the appearance of a comet which with hindsight was regarded by many as a harbinger of trouble, for within a year of his accession great famine raged throughout England and the unrest continued.[19] Few charters of Edward remain, five in all, and all are land grants in Wessex. Perhaps, like Edwy before him, Edward was thrown back upon the heartland of his kingdom for any reliable support. According to John of Wallingford, the young king gave over Dorset to the queen mother, Aethelthryth, as a virtual fiefdom, though with unhappy consequences.[20] In a grant to his kinsman, the chronicler and ealdorman Aethelweard, Edward disposes of a large holding in Cornwall; but the military emphasis is clear and the charter opens with a frank admission of the uncertainty and fragility of the times.[21] The witness list reveals, however, some semblence of unity and normality, with Dunstan and Ethelwold, Aethelwin and Aelfhere signing together.

Both the anonymous 'Life of Oswald' and the various versions of the chronicle emphasise the attacks on the monasteries of Mercia as the most scandalous feature of this disturbance. Aelfhere is singled out as the principal culprit and adversary. 'In these days, because of Edward's youth, the adversaries of God, Ealdorman Aelfhere and others, broke God's law and hindered the monastic life, destroyed monasteries and dispersed the monks.'[22] The biographer of Oswald goes further and hints at greed for the revenues of the Mercian monasteries under the cloak of popular outrage, so that 'those monks who earlier used to ride on caparisoned horses, and join their fellows in singing the psalms of David, had to bear their own burdens . . . walking with companions or friends, without scrip or shoes, and thus involuntarily fulfilling the words of the holy gospel'.[23]

There is indeed irony in the last remark, for it touches on the paradox of substantial landed endowments for monks whose way of life was supposed to be apostolic. The writer himself goes on to admit that many of the monks and their abbots had placed too much trust in noblemen like Aelfhere. Vast and organised endowments like the Oswaldslaw disrupted the delicate and subtle web of land holding in the shires, much of which went back for generations. There is, for example, a charter of Ethelred's which illuminates the way in which Edgar's own generosity, in this case to Abingdon, had diminished the patrimony of the heir to the throne. Consequently, at the accession of Edward the lands in question were returned to Ethelred the *aetheling* 'by the decree and order of all the leading men, from the possession of the monastery'.[24] Only very much later did Ethelred make amends to Abingdon from his own patrimony. The endowments of the monasteries on so wide a scale had only been secured with the backing of a strong king. The ruthlessness with which Oswald, Ethelwold and other abbots had pursued their interests had won them many local enemies. Aelfhere of Mercia, who had been a pillar of Edgar's rule, was nonetheless threatened by a formidable revolution in land tenure and jurisdiction in the Oswaldslaw which had grown up in the midst of his own homeland. His reaction and action may also have been a blow at Dunstan's alliance with the East Anglian families, a weapon in his rivalry with Aethelwine; it may have contained an element of Mercian chauvinism and independence; but it may simply have been an urgent and opportunist attempt to secure his power base in western Mercia.[25] His patronage of Abingdon would belie a simple antagonism to monasticism as such. The ambivalence which many felt towards the new monastic houses is nowhere better exemplified than in the behaviour of the great Aethelwine towards Ely. Ramsey may have been the apple of his eye, his *eigenkloster*; but Ely regarded him as its pre-eminent enemy and a ruthless litigant.[26] It is clear that monasticism as such was not the sole issue.

There was, however, another ecclesiastical dimension to this challenge to the endowments of the renewed monasteries which was exploited with some success by the parties concerned, both clerical and lay. The biographer of Oswald asserts that 'abbots, with their monks, were expelled; clerics, with their wives, were introduced; and the latter error was worse than the first'.[27] Oswald's friend, Abbot Germanus of Winchcombe, suffered this fate. Osbern, in his 'Life of Dunstan', sheds more light on the background to this upheaval. Although Edgar exerted political force to eject clergy from Winchester and elsewhere, their claims upon the endowments which they enjoyed did not subside, for this direct assault on the hereditary and proprietorial habit of the English clergy was a profound revolution in principle and effect. The fact that Dunstan, and probably Oswald also, showed caution in their own cathedral chapters about the implementing of this policy reflects this, but it in no way diminished the strength of feeling on the part of those who felt aggrieved.[28] The issues came to a head in the reign of Edgar at a synod at Winchester, over which Dunstan presided, but which was convoked at royal request as a result of the clerical lobby against Dunstan and Ethelwold.

> When they saw that they would not overcome Dunstan by force of ar-
> gument, aided by the king and his nobles they turned to pleading
> with him, and urgently pressing him to reinstate certain people whom
> they introduced as having been expelled from their livings.[29]

As Dunstan demurred, he received assistance from an unexpected quarter: the crucifix on the wall spoke forth, miraculously but unequivocally denouncing any such deal. Before such a thing, both king and nobles drew back, aghast and outmanoeuvred; their kinsmen, the clergy of noble birth and others were apparently powerless to reverse their fate.

The issue did not go away, and was revived after the death of Edgar by their sons. The complainants secured a Scottish bishop, Beornhelm, as their advocate and at a synod at Calne towards the end of Edward's brief and unhappy reign they bearded Dunstan again. It was clearly an occasion of some importance at which, according to the chronicle, the whole witan was present. Dunstan was ill and obliged to attend on a stretcher, confined to lying on his back for all business apart from his prayers. In his frustration he refused to judge the issue, handing it over to God. Thereupon the floor collapsed under the feet of the entire assembly, leaving only Dunstan and his immediate entourage unscathed! Osbern, writing long after,[30] regarded it as a decisive judgement from God. It may have been; but it was also a major calamity, for according to the chronicle, 'some were severely injured there, and some did not survive it'. If this occurred towards the end of 977, it was the second such synod to settle the affairs of the Church and its endowments. At an Easter synod at Kirtlington, Bishop Sidemann of Crediton, the young king's former tutor, died suddenly and had to be buried by Dunstan at Abingdon.[31] It was probably at this synod that the position of the monasteries was secured against further depredations, thanks to the forceful leadership of Aethelwin of East Anglia. 'He stood up in synod and said that he could in no way suffer while he lived that the monks, who maintained all the Christianity in the kingdom, should be expelled.'[32] His brother, Aelfwold touched on a raw nerve when he said in support: 'How can we guard our own property without Christ's help?'; for quite apart from the supernatural dimension, there were enemies stirring abroad and at home and sustained lawlessness against monastic property threatened the very rights by which all property was held.

So, in the end, the scale of the monastic endowments secured their position; the renewal of the monasteries under Edgar was proving to be irreversible. Nonetheless, without the protection of a strong king they were peculiarly vulnerable to lay depredations and claims, and the monks did not enjoy the unanimous support of their fellow clergy. The claims of the displaced clergy would and did wane with time. But the dubious precedent of lay reappropriation of monastic estates had been re-established, and even in more peaceful times abbots were obliged, with bishops, to spend a lot of time and energy in lengthy litigation to secure their lands. But there is no evidence to suppose that the life of the monks did not, on the whole, proceed as normal throughout this difficult time. Apart from in the Mercian monasteries, Winchcombe, Pershore, Evesham and perhaps Deerhurst, the disruption was not as severe as the monastic historians would make out; but the picture they paint reflects their acute fear and anxiety. The landed endowments of monasteries were ever a mixed blessing: a protection and buttress without which stable monastic life could hardly proceed, but also a bane and a paradox that threatened both the material and the spiritual well-being of the monasteries.

Edward's brief reign came to a premature and bloody conclusion. On 18

March 978, he was murdered while visiting his stepmother at Corfe in Dorset. The biographer of Oswald gives the earliest account, and attributes the blame to the over-zealous thegns in Ethelred's retinue.[33] There is no hint of ill will between Edward and his half-brother and Ethelred's mother; quite the reverse, for 'the revered king indeed had with him very few thegns, for he feared no one'. As he was being formally welcomed at Corfe, he was seized from his horse and brutally murdered. According to one version of the chronicle, it happened in the evening, and Edward was subsequently buried 'at Wareham without any royal honours. No worse deed than this for the English people was committed since first they came to Britain. . . . His earthly kinsmen would not avenge him'.[34] It was an appalling crime, an act of sheer treachery that offended all notions of kinship and of hospitality. Oswald's biographer, and later Archbishop Wulfstan in his 'Sermo Lupi', evade naming the culprits, but both hint at treachery and both, together with one version of the chronicle, describe Edward as a martyr.[35] The biographer of Oswald tells of the personal 'calamities of those who killed him', victims of divine judgement.[36] Despite the relief expressed by many at Ethelred's succession, the circumstances by which he acceded cast a baneful shadow over his reign, and in the minds of later historians Queen Aethelthryth became the villain of the piece, the cruel architect of Edward's fate. Osbern, in his 'Life of Dunstan', directly accuses the queen, and the 'Liber Eliensis' casts another aspersion on her memory.[37] The Icelandic 'Dunstan saga' actually makes her the murderess,[38] while John of Wallingford more judiciously suggests that the king's visit may not simply have been personal, but rather to enquire into abuses in Dorset perpetrated by the queen's retinue.[39] Thus a real quarrel possibly lay behind that tragic day. According to this last source, the deed was suppressed and the body initially concealed in the River Stour for some days before its hasty and furtive burial at Wareham.

There is no hard evidence that either Aethelthryth or her young son Ethelred were privy to the conspiracy or colluded in the act. On the other hand no one was apparently punished for the royal murder. Instead the body of Edward received a stranger and more lasting memorial. In 980, 'the Ealdorman Aelfhere fetched the holy king's body from Wareham and bore it with great honour to Shaftesbury'.[40] According to a later chronicler's insertion, Dunstan participated in this translation.[41] The biographer of Oswald again affords a fuller reminiscence; the body of the late king was apparently incorrupt, and 'they placed it, clothed in new vestments, in a casket-shrine; and carried by noble thegns on a bier, he was buried honourably, where masses and sacred oblations were celebrated for the redemption of his soul, by the Ealdorman Aelfhere's orders'.[42] One of Dunstan's successors as archbishop of Canterbury, Aelfric, later vouched for the miracles that laid the basis for the cult,[43] and around that time King Ethelred endowed the royal nunnery at Shaftesbury with land at Bradford-on-Avon, commenting on the manner of his half-brother's death and the miracles he had wrought.[44] In his laws of 1008, the feast of 'St Edward' was enjoined throughout the land for 18 March.[45]

It is a strange development, adding pathos to the chequered reign of Ethelred. Yet there is no evidence that the cult of the dead king was a reaction to Ethelred's rule or a threat to it. Indeed Ethelred seemed in a way to benefit from it, for a connection between anointed kingship and martyrdom lay in the coronation rite itself.[46] About this time, Abbo of Fleury wrote up the life of another martyr-king, Edmund of East Anglia, who was killed by the Vikings in 870, for the clergy at Bury St Edmunds. He turned to Dunstan as his source, and made great play of the fact that Dunstan had vouched for the like incorruption of Edmund's body on the grounds that he himself had touched the still undecayed corpse of St Cuthbert![47] This is a curious parallel, and may indicate that Dunstan himself had a hand in fostering the cult of the murdered monarch as a way of strengthening the 'divinity that doth hedge a king'.

II – Ethelred: early reign

Ethelred may have been 13 when he came to the throne and he was crowned by Dunstan at Kingston upon Thames a fortnight after Easter, probably in 978 but perhaps in 979.[48] A slightly later version of the chronicle asserts that 'Ethelred succeeded to the kingdom, and very quickly afterwards he was consecrated king at Kingston with much rejoicing by the councillors of the English people'.[49] If this were so, it would perhaps underline the gravity of the crisis, for the date would be 14 April, less than a month after the murder of Edward. According to the biographer of Oswald, Ethelred was 'a youth young in years, elegant by habit, of attractive appearance and fitting demeanour'; Oswald duly assisted Dunstan at the joyous occasion.[50] Nonetheless, it may well have been for this very coronation that Dunstan composed the admonition which stands appended to the 'Promissio regis' given by the new young king at his coronation. The warning against 'violating that which was promised to God' lest decay set in and 'in the end all turn out for the worst', and the plea for 'old, wise and sober counsellors' may well allude to the troubles of the previous reign, and particularly to their effect on the Church.[51] In the light of some of the problems which were to arise during the reign of Ethelred, it is easy to see how later the tradition grew up that Dunstan had actually threatened the young king with dire maledictions because of the circumstances of his accession.[52] But this is the verdict of long hindsight, coloured by the more recent calamity of the Norman Conquest. Nonetheless, there were deep wounds to be healed in the body politic, and the solemn translation of Edward's body to Shaftesbury may have been a step to this end; so too may have been the great rededication of the Old Minster at Winchester in 980, to which the new king and his court came, together with the leading bishops and their monastic entourage. Wulstan the Cantor composed a lengthy *carmen* in commemoration, and at the end it comments on how the secular nobles and the judges, gathered from far and wide, 'who had hitherto seemed so contrary and resistant to the way of God, payed deep devotion, suddenly (& miraculously) turning from wolves into sheep!'[53] Their submission may have proved temporary and opportune; but the scale of the occasion and its location seem to represent some act of national reconciliation.[54]

During the king's minority, the country was effectively governed by a small group of nobles led by Aelfhere of Mercia, until his death in 983, together with the queen mother, Aethelthryth. Bishop Ethelwold also seems to have sustained some control over royal policy and the situation at court until his own death in 984.[55] 'Certainly there are no signs of upheaval in the composition of the king's council' before this latter date.[56] Despite this apparently stable beginning to the reign, the chronicler remembers that in the year of Ethelred's coronation 'a bloody cloud was often seen in the likeness of fire, especially towards midnight, composed of various shafts of light, but at dawn it disappeared'.[57] At this stage in Ethelred's long and varied reign, the immediate threat was from without. In the very year of the translation of Edward and the rededication of the Old Minster, the town of Southampton, by now an important port and market,[58] was sacked by a Viking naval force. They attacked and harried Thanet also, and raided far and wide in Cheshire, in this last instance coming from the north. The following year Devon and Cornwall were ravaged, and the monastery at Padstow (or else Bodmin) was destroyed. In 982, 'three ships full of vikings arrived in Dorset and raided Portland'; it was a year of disaster, for London was burnt down in a fire too. Ethelred also lost two senior members of his witan, Aethelmaer of Hampshire and Edwin of Sussex, by natural death.[59] Clearly Edgar's naval policy had been neglected, or had failed to deter the raiders. But the reasons for their mobilisation did not lie in England alone. After the death of Otto the Great in 973, the imperial containment of the Vikings weakened at the same time that a strong Danish hegemony under Harold 'Gormsson' had generated centrifugal forces. The disaffected Viking leaders rejected his leadership and control, and also his attempt to impose Christianity by force. So they left in pursuit of adventure and booty elsewhere.[60] The impact of these attacks was, however, strictly limited, and there is little evidence of disruption to administration, justice or the coinage during these years.[61]

During his early reign Ethelred proved a steady and conventional patron of the Church, perhaps at Ethelwold's behest, for up to 984 the Winchester houses benefited especially, together with Malmesbury, Abingdon, Shaftesbury and Bath.[62] Ethelwold and Aethelgar, now the new bishop of Selsey, were also personal beneficiaries of royal generosity. There was continuity too in the appointment of bishops, most of them monks, a sign of Dunstan's sure hold over the Church, and a letter from Dunstan to Ethelred remains, clarifying the position and endowments of the bishop of Cornwall, whose see had historically been under the wing of the see of Crediton.[63] Dunstan's last notable appointment was that of Alphege, abbot of Bath, to replace Ethelwold as bishop of Winchester after Ethelwold's death in 984.[64] It is a measure of the close web of friendship which bound the monastic episcopate together that Dunstan not only predicted the impending death of Ethelwold on his last visit to Canterbury in the company of the bishop of Rochester[65]; he also received a divine intimation concerning the appointment of his friend, Alphege, to the vacant see.[66] According to Adelard, who records this last tradition, Ethelred was persuaded only by the sheer weight of Dunstan's own authority.

The death of Aelfhere of Mercia in 983 and of Ethelwold in 984, together with the waxing ambitions of the young king, now aged about 18, opened the door to rapid and disastrous changes. In 985, Aelfhere's son and heir, Aelfric, was banished from the land;[67] and from 984 until 993 the queen mother, Aethelthryth, appears not to have witnessed charters.[68] According to later charters of restitution, a clique of unscrupulous young nobles gained the king's ear, notably Bishop Wulfgar of Ramsbury, Ealdorman Aelfric of Hampshire and a certain Aethelsin.[69] As a consequence of their influence, certain Church lands were plundered or misappropriated; and the height of their insolence was reached when they secured the appointment of Edwin, Aelfric's brother, to be abbot of Abingdon by simony.[70] He remained there for five years until 990. There is a letter from Pope John to the same Ealdorman Aelfric castigating him for his depredations against Glastonbury itself, for the monastery claimed papal protection.[71] There is another story peculiar to William of Malmesbury which refers to this period; a certain Alwold, a monk of Glastonbury, wanted to relinquish the religious life and regain his property. To this end he sustained quite a quarrel with the abbot and chapter, enlisting Ethelred's help in his favour and raising a rabble to invade the properties of the monastery. In despair the monks turned to Dunstan who was powerless to help, except to curse Alwold, who died shortly after and was devoured by foxes.[72] Charters also tell how Bishop Alphege of Winchester was obliged to foreswear land properly his own, and how Muchelney sustained losses which Ethelred later restored.[73] In his later charters of restitution, Ethelred deplored the folly of this course of action, but at the time a real element of lawlessness had crept into the heart of the king's counsels.

There is a letter to Dunstan, probably from abroad, which alludes to the political and personal difficulties he was having in maintaining control and good order, 'pushed to the limits by calumnies and insolence'.[74] In 986, matters reached boiling-point: 'In this year the king laid waste the diocese of Rochester; in the same year the great murrain first occurred in England.'[75] Sulcard, the historian of Westminster, corroborates Osbern's account of Ethelred's quarrel with the bishop of Rochester. It arose over a property of the bishop's which the king and his henchmen wished to obtain. The bishop refused to deplete the patrimony of the see, so the king laid siege to the town of Rochester; in his frustration at its defence he laid waste the episcopal lands. Dunstan remonstrated with the king, but to no avail, so he resorted to bribery and bought off the king and his army with 100 pieces of silver.[76] Dunstan's fears, expressed in his short homily at Ethelred's coronation, had been confirmed, and he wrote to the king in no uncertain terms:

> Because you have preferred the money of God and the silver of the apostle to my will in this matter, and all because of your greed, the evils which the Lord has spoken concerning you will swiftly befall you; ills of such a gravity as have never been from the time when the English race began to rule until this time. But while I yet live, this will not occur, for the Lord has told me this.[77]

Ten years later, in a charter of restitution to Rochester, Ethelred would admit his guilt quite frankly, blaming his rapacity on his erstwhile friend, Aethelsin, 'an enemy of God and the people', who encouraged the king to act 'more out of ignorance than cruelty'.[78] But it was an act of remorse wrung out of him at a time when Dunstan's prophecy appeared to be coming true and the kingdom and empire he had inherited were in all but ruins.

III – the last days of Dunstan

If Dunstan's final years were clouded by the uncertainties and turmoil of Ethelred's conduct, his own life at Canterbury appears to have been steady and assured unto the end. He maintained contact with friends overseas; the letter from Abbo of Fleury concerning the life of St Edmund the martyr-king dates from this period, between 985 and 988, and there is also a personal letter from Wido, the abbot of Blandinium, the monastery of Dunstan's exile, seeking help to meet a crop failure.[79] From this very house would come one of the two earliest biographers of the saint, the monk Adelard, who addressed his brief life to Dunstan's friend and successor, Alphege.[80] About this time too, it is likely that the first biographer of Dunstan actually joined his *familia* at Canterbury as a guest and protégé; probably a kinsman or pupil of Ebracher, bishop of Liège, he was a visitor to England.[81] This would account for the intimate, personal and spiritual character of the final stories about Dunstan, which are anecdotes which he himself had shared with his inner circle of monks and clerics as his life drew to its close.[82]

Both these early biographies were written for people who had known Dunstan and his circle at the end, and the picture they afford is of a venerable and lovable bishop, a great teacher and pastor and a man of God. Perhaps most striking are two features of Dunstan's inner life which were already apparent and well-developed during the Glastonbury years: his profound love of music and his deeply contemplative spirituality. The second biographer tells how Dunstan heard in a dream the hosts of heaven singing 'Kyrie eleison', and in due course a special musical tone for the Kyries became associated with Dunstan's memory and passed into the plainsong tradition of the English Church.[83] The first biographer gives a fuller story of how during Dunstan's vision of his late mother's heavenly marriage he was taught a melody by an angel for the antiphon, 'O King of the nations and Ruler of all things, from the throne of your majesty grant us, O Christ our King, forgiveness of our sins. Alleluia!'[84] He tells how 'Dunstan ordered that it be kept in memory and be written down before it be lost in oblivion, so it was noted down by a monk at his dictation. Then he made all his subordinates, both monks and clerks, learn to sing it in the morning'. Apparently, 'Dunstan often learnt by spiritual vigilance and divine intuition the melodies of sacred songs and other fitting praises to God, even while his human faculties slept'.[85] It was while he was reciting the night office at the shrine of St Augustine that he perceived a crowd of heavenly virgins singing the great hymn of Sedulius 'Let us sing, O friends, to the honour of the Lord: let the sweet love of Christ sound through pious lips'.[86] Always, 'while laboriously engaged in the tedium of living out this life, his highest occupation was in holy prayers and in frequently pursuing the notes of the "ten-stringed" psalter of David'.[87]

Dunstan's contemplative life and heartfelt discipline of regular prayer gave him a visionary and prophetic reputation within his own lifetime. It was in fact the hidden thread throughout his whole life, and the source of his spiritual authority and strength.

> And so the whole of this land of England was filled with his holy doctrine, and it shone before God like the sun and the moon. When he fulfilled to Christ the Lord the due hours of divine service, and at the celebrations of the Mass, he discharged them by intoning with such integrity of devotion and of mind that he seemed to talk with the Lord Himself face to face, as if not irritated at all by the upheavals and quarrels of people beforehand. Like blessed Martin of Tours, he used always to lift up his eyes and his hands to heaven, and his spirit never relaxed from prayer. Whenever he was engaged in any work of dignity or perfection or praise, either at ordinations to the sacred priesthood, or consecrations of churches or altars, or in whatever institutions of divine affairs, he always shed copious tears, which the Holy Spirit who ever dwelt within him drew forth mightily from the streams in his eyes.[88]

The circumstances of his death were surrounded by testimonies to this two-fold interweaving of music with contemplation. Dunstan's own chaplain, Aelfgar, who later became bishop of Elmham, saw in a vision 'Dunstan sitting on his episcopal throne, accompanied by his clergy, uttering canon law. Suddenly, as he watched, the host of heaven, shining with crowns of gold and gleaming in white robes, burst through all the doors of the church in great numbers'.[89] It was the feast of the Ascension, and they summoned Dunstan to heaven. He demurred, protesting his pastoral duty to his church on such a day, so they told him: 'Be prepared to come with us next Sabbath day to Rome itself, there to sing eternally the "Sanctus" before the Pope himself.' This was an utterance whose very strangeness conveys the ring of truth.

Consequently, Dunstan preached on Ascension Day 988 at Canterbury, 'as he had never preached before'.[90] Three times he spoke forth: the sermon itself which set forth the gospel of man's salvation by the Son of God who on this day returned openly to share the eternal unity with the Father and the Holy Spirit; then he added a homily to his solemn pontifical blessing; finally he spoke again for the last time after the peace and the 'Agnus Dei'.[91] Those present 'gazed on him as if he were an angel of God'.[92]

After eating the midday meal with his brethren, he retired to his bed for the afternoon siesta prescribed by the Rule of St Benedict. He never rose from it,[93] lying there, 'his bald head gleaming with light'.

From the day of the Lord's Ascension [17 May], this pillar of God began slowly to lose his strength; weariness prevailed and he took to his bed, and for the next days and nights, he was intent on heaven, coming and going in the Lord, and thus comforted. On the morning of the Sabbath [i.e. Saturday 19 May 988], when the mattins hymns were now finished, he bade the holy congregation of his brethren to come to him. He again commended his spirit to them; then he received from the heavenly table the viaticum of the sacraments of Christ which had been celebrated in his presence. Then he gave thanks to God and began to sing the psalm: 'The merciful and gracious Lord hath so done his marvellous works that they ought to be had in remembrance. He hath given meat unto them that fear him . . .' [Psalm 111. 4–5]. Thus with these words in his mouth, he rendered his spirit into his Maker's hands, and rested in peace. O how happy him whom the Lord found thus watching! He was buried in a grave of his own preparing, in the place where he had taught his people while living as a bishop among them.[94]

PART THREE

THE LEGACY:

AD 989–1023

10

THE SUCCESSORS

OSWALD, bishop of Worcester and archbishop of York, outlived Dunstan by just under four years. He died on 28 February 992 at Worcester, having been bishop of that see for well nigh thirty years.[1] He was an assiduous pastor who divided his residence between the two sees under his care, while maintaining close supervision of his own monasteries in Worcester and at Ramsey. He never lost contact with Fleury either, and his death was duly noted there by the chronicler Hugo, probably at the behest of Oswald's old friend and admirer, Abbo, abbot of Fleury. The last journey which Oswald made was to Ramsey for the dedication of the new tower there. At a solemn celebration he bade farewell to his brethren and to his old friend Aethelwin for the last time, after a sojourn of some three months over the summer.[2] He remained healthy to the last, 'wracked only by gout'.

The story of Oswald's death is movingly told by his first biographer, probably Byrhtferth, a monk of Ramsey.

> It was the annual custom of this most noble man to wash the feet of twelve poor men out of love for Christ throughout the whole of Lent. While he was performing this deed, he used to sing the fifteen psalms of Ascent [Psalms 120–34] . . . That morning, Oswald got up and as a good 'athlete of Christ' completed his prayers, the hours and psalter of the day. Then not sparing his elderly frame, he stooped down to wipe the feet of the poor, not only with a cloth but also with his own hair, mindful of the words of Christ. With water in his hands, he sang the fifteen psalms. At the end, he bent the knee with the brethren at the feet of the Lord. The venerable bishop recited: 'Glory be to the Father, and to the Son, and to the Holy Spirit', and at that instant his holy spirit, even as he bent down, left his body by some secret sign from the Lord, and was lifted up to heaven.[3]

His funeral procession was thronged by the whole populace of Worcester who wept for the loss of such a spiritual father, and it was believed that the divine light of the Holy Spirit hovered as a sign over his remains. For in the words of his pupil, Byrhtferth, 'the Spirit of the fear of the Lord shone through Oswald'.[4]

With the passing of the last of the three great reforming bishops and founding fathers, men marked the end of an era. Aelfric, concluding his 'Life of Swithun' less than ten years after Dunstan's death, could write of Edgar's reign:

> At that time there were worthy bishops, the resolute Dunstan in the archiepiscopal see, and the venerable Ethelwold, and all the others like them. But Dunstan and Ethelwold were chosen by God: they led men to do God's will, and established all manner of good to the satisfaction of God, as He testifies by the miracles He now works through them.[5]

The course of public affairs during the long reign of Ethelred tended to reinforce the habit of regarding the age of Edgar and Dunstan as a recent golden age.

From the death of Dunstan in 988, England was assailed by warfare almost continuously, and attacks were of increasing seriousness. Oswald's biographer records a sharply contested battle in the south west in 988, in which the men of Devon only just prevailed.[6] By 990, the collusion between the Duchy of Normandy and the Viking raiders provoked such tension between Normandy and England that the pope, John XV, had to intervene, apparently successfully.[7] In 992, a major Danish raid culminated in the tragic English defeat at Maldon, where Bryhtnoth of Essex made a heroic stand to the last, a feat recorded in the famous poem and also by Oswald's monastic biographer. He was buried at Ely in the church he had endowed and which he loved.[8] So devastating were the raids of this year that the southern shires were obliged to buy peace from the Danes through the mediation of Archbishop Sigeric and the two leading ealdormen, Aelfric and Aethelweard.[9] Although this was hardly without precedent, it was in fact the first of the several payments of Danegeld for which the reign of Ethelred became notorious. Raids in 993 on the north-east coast heralded a massive invasion in 994 led by Olaf Tryggvason from Norway and Swein, the son of Harold of Denmark. Some English nobility defected, but the alliance fell apart before the war could be concluded decisively, and Ethelred bought peace again. However, Aethelweard, together with Bishop Alphege of Winchester, acted as mediator to bring Olaf to meet Ethelred at Andover; there the Norwegian prince was confirmed in the Christian faith and promised never to return as an enemy.[10]

Between 997 and 1002, England was systematically raided along its entire southern coast, year by year, until the English lost control of the Channel and were forced to sue for peace at a price of some £24,000.[11] The same year, 1002, saw two momentous acts by Ethelred. He married Emma, the sister of Richard, duke of Normandy, an alliance pregnant with unforeseen significance for the not too distant future; and on 13 November he ordered a massacre of the Danish population. In Oxford the Danish citizens were shut up in refuge in St Frideswide's minster, but in vain, because the mob burnt it down. The king's own chilling account and justification of this atrocity is extant.[12] It was a fatal move, alienating the population of the Danelaw, reversing at a stroke the royal policy towards —the Danes of 100 years and provoking the wrath of Swein, whose sister was caught up in the violence and killed.[13] From this time on, Ethelred's grip on his kingdom began to slip as each year brought new and heavier raids and a demoralising trickle of defections and acts of treachery. The administration of the land stood firm, however, and in 1008 there was a vast overhaul of the fleet, organised on a national basis. But treachery again thwarted its effectiveness when the great invasion of 1009 was launched. The Danes burnt Oxford, besieged London and overcame the resistance hitherto afforded by Ulfkell Snilling in East Anglia. In 1011 they besieged and burnt Canterbury, taking Alphege, the archbishop, as a hostage. In the spring of 1012 they were bought off for £48,000, but Alphege, refusing a ransom, was brutally killed.[14] The defection of Thorkell the Tall to Ethelred's service prompted a renewed invasion in 1013, led again by Swein. After a brilliant campaign, Oxford, Winchester and finally London itself fell to his control. Ethelred fled his kingdom and took refuge with his family in Normandy.

Swein died unexpectedly in early 1014, and his younger son, Cnut, took control of the northern forces. But in the hiatus, the English nobility negotiated the return of Ethelred 'if he would govern them more justly than before'.[15] To this condition, and others similar, the hapless Ethelred agreed, and on his return he led a brutal campaign of pillage against the people of Lindsey, who had supported Cnut's retreating army. But Thorkell the Tall defected to join Cnut, and in 1015 trouble broke out for Ethelred in Mercia and the Danelaw, which led to a rebellion there led by his own son, Edmund. The ealdorman of Mercia, Eadric, submitted to Cnut soon after his invasion, and thus the battle was fought between three competing sides, at a time when Ethelred was already succumbing to a fatal illness. In the spring of 1016, father and son rejoined for the defence of London. Ethelred died at last on 23 April, and Edmund led a spirited defence of his new kingdom during which Cnut besieged London, but in vain. Edmund harried Cnut's retreat at Otford in Kent, but at Ashingdon in the autumn both kings sued for terms after a stiff fight and a virtual English defeat. England was divided by settlement: Edmund kept Wessex; Cnut ruled everywhere north of the Thames. The precarious nature of this treaty, resting as it did upon a transient balance of forces and, more ominously, upon divided and shifting loyalties among the English nobility, was evident; it was, however, never tried, for on 30 November 1016 Edmund Ironside died and Cnut acceded to the whole kingdom. In a note of complete pathos, the chronicler observes: 'Edmund's body is buried in Glastonbury along with his grandfather Edgar.'

While the country reeled under poor political leadership, the basic fabric of administration and justice remained intact, as did the currency. Indeed the very way in which considerable taxes could be levied to meet the demands of the Danes is testimony to the basic strength of the English system and economy.[16] The life of the Church is an accurate reflection of this situation. Individual churches, sees and monasteries did suffer real depredations, and probably the loss of precious ornaments of gold and silver as well, but the basic position of the Church was not undermined. Indeed, it was strengthened during this turbulent period, not least because, unlike the state, it was effectively led by bishops and scholars who articulated and acted upon the principles laid down in the Dunstan era. The great achievement of Dunstan, Ethelwold and Oswald was that they in no way inhibited the steady development of the leadership required in the next generation to maintain and deepen the life and work of the Church. Men might look back to their times; but they did so for inspiration, not out of nostalgia.

Dunstan's immediate successor at Canterbury was Aethelgar, the bishop of Selsey, formerly Ethelwold's great ally and friend as abbot of New Minster in Winchester. He may for a time have been a monk at Glastonbury.[17] Aethelgar was also a close friend of the king.[18] However, he was an elderly man, and within two years he was dead. On his appointment, he made the arduous journey to Rome for the *pallium*, and renewed contact with the great Flanders monasteries of St Vedast and St Bertin; letters remain to him from both these houses.[19] In 989 Aethelgar convened a great synod at London, and a document remains from this occasion revealing the judicial functions of an archbishop of

Canterbury at the king's witan.[20] To Aethelgar's *familia* came the foreigner from Liège who became the first biographer of St Dunstan. Aethelgar would have been well-placed to inform him about Dunstan's earlier days.[21]

Sigeric, who succeeded Aethelgar in 990, reigned for four years.[22] A monk from Glastonbury, then abbot of St Augustine's, Canterbury and bishop of Ramsbury he embodied the Glastonbury tradition completely. The abbot of Glastonbury, Elfweard, wrote him a pastoral letter of some length which sets out in full the monastic vision of a bishop.[23] It is an exacting and highly traditional admonition, after the example of Alcuin or Bede, emphasising the pastoral duties and the need for constant study of scripture and the 'Pastoral rule' of St Gregory the Great. It became something of an exemplar, for another similar letter remains, sent probably by Sigeric as archbishop to the new monk-bishop of Sherborne, Wulfsige, shortly after his appointment in 992.[24] Elfweard of Glastonbury presided as abbot from 975 to 1009, a remarkable span; he is probably a figure of real importance in accounting for the steady continuity of monastic episcopal policy during these years.[25] Sigeric was a patron of learning, at Canterbury and further afield, and Aelfric dedicated both series of his homilies to him as a direct contribution to the archbishop's work of pastoral education in the Church.[26] During Sigeric's time, first at St Augustine's and then at Christ Church in Canterbury, the monastic scriptoria received fresh impulse, and to Christ Church Sigeric left a handsome bequest of books.[27] Meanwhile, Sigeric was plunged into public affairs at a particularly difficult period. His unhappy reputation as the instigator of the Danegeld in 991 needs to be set against the real vulnerability of the see of Canterbury to Viking depredations. In 994, Sigeric himself had to buy off a raiding army threatening Canterbury with a loan from Bishop Aescwy of Dorchester of £90 in pure silver and 200 mancuses of pure gold. For this, the bishop of Dorchester gained an outlying Canterbury estate at Risborough.[28] The upheavals of the time probably account also for the extraordinary delay in making Ealdwulf, bishop of Worcester, the archbishop of York in succession to Oswald, an event which apparently did not occur until 995.[29]

Sigeric died at the end of October 994, and it was not until Easter 995 that his successor was appointed.[30] This was Aelfric, bishop of Ramsbury and formerly abbot of St Albans, and before that a monk of Abingdon.[31] Aelfric proved a prelate of substance, and became a figure of stability during his ten-year pontificate. There is a letter of Pope Gregory V to Abbo of Fleury enquiring after the safety of the archbishop on returning from Rome with his *pallium*.[32] To him the first life of St Dunstan was dedicated and sent for correction, and it was during his lifetime also that the first biography of St Oswald was composed; at one point it appeals to his authority.[33] It was believed that Aelfric finally succeeded in converting the community at Christ Church into a thoroughly Benedictine monastery.[34] Certainly Aelfric continued the policy of appointing monks as bishops, together with his fellow archbishop, Ealdwulf of York, himself formerly abbot of Peterborough. By far his most significant appointment was that of Wulfstan to the see of London in 996, and to York in 1003.[35] Aelfric was a wealthy man and a pluralist who retained his abbacy while bishop of Ramsbury and the see of Ramsbury while archbishop. He could on occasion wield great influence with Ethelred in the interests of his see and its endowments,[36] and his will affords a fascinating mirror of the interests of an archbishop during Ethelred's time.[37] Among bequests to Christ Church, Abingdon and St Albans, 'he bequeathed to his lord his best ship and the tackle with it, and 60 helmets and

60 coats of mail'. In addition to a 'heriot' in cash to the king, he also 'granted a ship to the people of Kent and another to Wiltshire', and relieved the people of Kent, Middlesex and Surrey of their debts to him, presumably incurred as a result of the Danegeld. The military flavour of this episcopal will may be compared with that of another monk-bishop, Aelfwold of Crediton, one of Dunstan's last appointments and apparently a monk of Glastonbury,[38] who died at the end of Ethelred's reign.

Upon the death of Aelfric in 1005, Alphege, who had been bishop of Winchester for over twenty years, became the archbishop of Canterbury, and the next year he duly made the long journey to Rome and back.[39] He was a close friend of his predecessor who had left him a crucifix in his will. His reputation was one of being an effective bishop and administrator under whom the rebuilding of the Old Minster at Winchester had been completed. He was also a bold and skilled negotiator, as his dealings with the Norwegian Prince Olaf in 994 had shown. To him the second brief life of St Dunstan was dedicated, and he did much to advance the cult of his old friend and mentor in the cathedral at Canterbury.[40] Alphege represented in his old age an embodiment of the ideals of monastic episcopacy, having a reputation as a contemplative, an ascetic and a spiritual father.[41] Of his primacy little is actually recorded and the manner of his dying overshadowed all that was remembered of him at Canterbury after the conquest. Osbern records the death of Alphege at the hands of the Danes in 1012 as a martyrdom, both in his life of the saint and in his 'Life of Dunstan' at the end. The story told by the chronicler is stark and simple:

> In this year [1011] they besieged Canterbury between 8th Sept and
> Michaelmas [29th], and they got inside by treachery, for Aelfmaer,
> whose life Archbishop Alphege had saved, betrayed it. [Florence of
> Worcester adds that Aelfmaer was the archdeacon, and that the city
> was partly burnt.] They captured there the Archbishop, and the
> king's reeve Aelfweard, and Abbess Leofrun [of Minster-in-Thanet]
> and Bishop Godwine [of Rochester]; but they let Abbot Aelfmaer [of
> St Augustine's] escape. So they took captive there all the ecclesiastics,
> men and women [and Christ Church was plundered and burnt, adds
> Florence]. . . . After they had ransacked the whole burgh, they went
> to their ships, and took the archbishop with them. [1012] The Witan
> assembled at London for Easter, and stayed until the tribute had been
> paid. Then on the Saturday, the army became greatly incensed
> against the bishop because he would not promise them any money
> and forbade that anything should be paid for him. They were also
> very drunk, for wine from the south had been brought there. They
> seized the bishop and brought him to their assembly on the eve of
> Low Sunday, the 19th April, and shamefully put him to death there.
> They pelted him with bones and ox-heads, until one of them struck
> him on the head with the back of an axe, and he sank down and
> died. In the morning, his body was carried [from Greenwich] to
> London . . . and buried in St Paul's minster where God now reveals
> the powers of that holy martyr.[42]

There is a virtually contemporary record of this event, which the writer says he learnt from an Englishman called Sewald, in the chronicle of Thietmar of Merseburg.[43] According to this source, the Danes employed torture and Alphege as a feint proffered terms, committing himself to ransom by a certain date and giving himself time to prepare for death. When the day of reckoning came, the

Danes suspected duplicity as no money was forthcoming, probably for the reasons given in the *Anglo-Saxon Chronicle*. Alphege had sought to protect his people from further demands while proffering false hopes to his captors; in his words: 'It is not my wish, but dire poverty, that makes me seem a liar to you.' This stung his enemies, and they were not dissuaded by the sudden intervention of Thorkell the Tall on Alphege's behalf; it was after Alphege's death that Thorkell defected to the service of Ethelred. It was a shattering moment for the English Church, a measure of the nadir of the nation's fortunes, as the chronicler laments, and it was believed by Eadmer later that the community at Christ Church never really recovered from the blow.

Of Athelstan Lyfing, who was appointed archbishop of Canterbury by Ethelred in 1013, the little that is known about his activities belongs properly to the reign of Cnut whose accession he oversaw. With Archbishop Wulfstan of York, he was responsible for the settlement of the kingdom under Cnut, with the Church very much at the centre of power and the law based firmly upon the legislation of Edgar's reign.[44] His obituary notice in the chronicle is terse and discreet: 'In this year [1020] died Archbishop Aelfstan, who was called Lyfing, and he was a very prudent man, both in matters of Church and state.'[45] He fell within the clear Dunstan tradition; he was possibly a monk of Glastonbury, certainly abbot of Chertsey and probably bishop of Wells before his elevation.[46]

The last archbishop of Canterbury who can in any way be regarded as part of the Glastonbury tradition was Lyfing's successor, Aethelnoth, who presided over the English Church from 1020 until 1038. According to the chronicle, he was a monk and 'dean' (or prior) of Christ Church, Canterbury, not previously a bishop. William of Malmesbury claims him too as a monk, first of Glastonbury, which may mean that that was where his education and early monastic life began. He recounts a charming tale establishing a family connection between Aethelnoth and Dunstan himself:

> About Aethelnoth, a monk of Glastonbury who became Archbishop
> of Canterbury, the story has spread that when he was being baptised
> by Dunstan himself, he held his hand aloft after the manner of a
> bishop blessing the people, whereupon Dunstan, as though aware of
> his excellence, prophesied that he would be an archbishop! He was
> indeed archbishop in the time of Cnut, by whose assistance and
> decree he translated the relics of the martyr Alphege to Kent from his
> place of rest in London. Aethelnoth gave a copy of Hrabanus' 'In
> Praise of the Cross' and a prayer-book illuminated in gold to
> Glastonbury.[47]

According to Florence of Worcester, Aethelnoth was the son of Aethelmaer, the founder of Cerne and patron and friend of Aelfric, who may well have instructed the young Aethelnoth.[48] Certainly he was well regarded in church and monastic circles, and also at court, where he stood up to Cnut and was acclaimed by Emma, the queen, as a man of 'outstanding virtue and wisdom'. His was an unusual appointment, direct from the monastic chapter at Canterbury and not from the episcopate, but it was very much in the spirit of the *'Regularis concordia'* and a tribute to a man who by his death had received the simple epithet of Oda and Dunstan before him: 'Aethelnoth the Good'.[49]

A survey of the existing religious houses confirms the picture of steady consolidation, despite individual set-backs.[50] The wills of the period indicate the confidence felt in the new foundations by members of the laity and some of the clergy.[51] Wulfwaru, a woman otherwise quite unknown, left to Bath Abbey an estate, an annual food-rent and 'an armlet of 60 mancuses of gold, a bowl of $2\frac{1}{2}$ pounds [of gold?], two gold crucifixes, a set of mass-vestments, the best dorsal and set of bed-clothing with tapestry and curtain'.[52] Aelfwold, bishop of Crediton, left an estate to his see, together with 'three service-books, a missal, a benedictional and an epistle-book and a set of mass-vestments'. He also gave the nuns at Wilton a chalice and paten worth 117 mancuses of gold.[53] The *aetheling* Athelstan, son of Ethelred, who died in 1014, gave estates to each of the Winchester houses, with some of his fine weapons and silverware. He bestowed gifts on Christ Church, Canterbury, and on Shaftesbury and gave a food-rent to feed 100 paupers at Ely annually.[54] These are but three examples of a pattern confirmed in lists of benefactions preserved by some of the major monasteries.

Royal patronage did not abate, and Ethelred for all his faults was devout and generous to the Church. He gave lands after the death of Dunstan in 988 to Abingdon, Wilton, Muchelney, St Albans, the Old Minster, Shaftesbury, Westminster, Wherwell, St Frideswide's at Oxford, St Davids in Wales, Ely, Athelney, Sherborne and Evesham; and these gifts are spread throughout his long reign.[55] Some of Ethelred's grants were by way of restitution for losses incurred in the earlier part of his reign or as a result of the Viking upheavals. Rochester received back land in 998 with an apology from the king for his earlier folly;[56] so too did the Old Minster at Winchester and the monasteries at Abingdon and at Evesham.[57] Edmund Ironside, during his brief reign and in the midst of the fighting, granted land in the Danelaw to New Minster and to Thorney Abbey.[58]

Documents from the main monastic centres convey a similar impression. Christ Church, Canterbury, became fully monastic for a while under either Sigeric or, more probably, Aelfric, but the picture is one of continuity and growth rather than radical change. The liturgical psalters used the Roman rather than the Gallican version of the psalms, a conservative habit, and the Canterbury kalendar only reflected the wider habits of the Winchester monasteries with the arrival of Alphege in 1005.[59] It is hard to form a reliable picture of life at Canterbury before the Norman Conquest directly from the writings of Osbern and Eadmer, both Christ Church monks but of a later generation. The important achievement at Canterbury during this period was the setting up of a firm educational tradition, based on a scriptorium which produced some of the finest books of the time, both for its own library and elsewhere.[60] At the earliest stage, and perhaps later, there was interchange with the scriptorium of the nearby monastery of St Augustine's. 'Christ Church during the pontificate of Aethelnoth was one of the most outstandingly creative and productive centres of manuscript illumination in the eleventh century.'[61]

William of Malmesbury's investigations at Glastonbury in the twelfth century record some of the treasures bestowed on that shrine. Ethelred and Edmund, and later Cnut, feature as benefactors, but it is the gifts of the clergy that are most interesting.[62] Sigeric gave seven altar cloths decorated with white lions and Sigfrid, a monk who went to Norway as bishop, gave four copes, two with lions and two yellow. But the bequest of Bishop Brihtwold, for forty years bishop of Ramsbury (1005–45) was truly amazing:

> He sent a most precious alb of silk, 10 copes with palls with gold &
> gems. Sundry vestments, two chalices, one of 20 marks of silver and
> 4 of gold, and the other of less weight but greater value; two Gospel-
> books, a large censer of gold and silver, an altar worth 20 marks, a
> processional cross and 25 other crosses! A Book of collects illuminated

in gold, a pall of gold, 9 other palls, & two candlesticks. He also
bought back all the monks' lands in Wiltshire for them.[63]

This last comment is interesting, and William amplifies it to refer to lands
mortgaged to pay Danegeld and later redeemed by the bishop for the monks.

The 'Liber Eliensis' conveys an impression of lengthy and tangled litigation to
secure the vast endowments of the monastery at Ely, which came into especial
favour in the reign of Cnut. There is a long list of treasures bestowed during this
period which matches amply the generous benefactions of Edgar and Ethelwold,[64] and the generosity of Athelstan, bishop of Elmham, is particularly
striking.[65] The first life of St Oswald recalls at length the careful preparations by
Oswald and Aethelwin for the future prosperity of Ramsey,[66] and after the
intrusion of Edwin between 985 and 990 Abingdon prospered under regular
monastic rule.[67] At Winchester a strong tradition of scholarship, education and
craftsmanship was maintained,[68] of which Aelfric the Homilist was the
outstanding representative, and the New Minster 'Liber vitae', which was
compiled in 1031 but draws on earlier documents, affords a fascinating picture
of the way in which the Winchester monasteries found themselves woven into
the very heart of court life.[69] Finally, at Worcester, although the temporal
endowments of the monastery had been vulnerable since the days of Oswald and
the position of the see was compromised by its being held in plurality with that of
York, the ancient tradition of learned monasticism was strong enough to raise
up Wulfstan as bishop as late as 1062. A kinsman by descent from Oswald, and a
studious admirer of him and of Dunstan, he represented the ideal of monastic
episcopacy with great effect into the reign of the Conqueror and died a saint.[70]

There are two striking features of English Church life during the reign of
Ethelred the Unready. The first is the spate of new monastic foundations made
by prominent members of the lay nobility, and the second is the sending of
missionaries to help convert Scandinavia to Christianity.[71]

The deaths of Aethelwin, the patron of Ramsey, and of Bryhtnoth, the friend
of Ely, in 992 did not diminish the impetus to found new religious houses.[72]
Already in 987, Aethelmaer, son of the ealdorman, Aethelweard, had founded a
monastery at Cerne Abbas in Dorset with estates passed to him by his father,[73]
and the life of this new house was carefully nurtured by Aelfric, whom
Aethelmaer summoned from Winchester.[74] In 1005, Aethelmaer founded
another monastery at Eynsham, near Oxford, to which Aelfric went as abbot.
The foundation charter is extant together with a letter of Aelfric's which
provides a summary of the 'Regularis concordia' for the monks.[75] In 997, the
abbey founded by another family, that of Ordgar and his son Ordwulf of Devon,
at Tavistock, was burnt by the Danes. But it was apparently refounded quite
swiftly, and drew its support from Glastonbury, whence came its first two
abbots.[76] To Ordwulf, Bishop Aelfwold of Crediton left a book by Hrabanus
Maur, and also a martyrology.[77]

Lay lords were not the only moving spirits behind new foundations. In 993,
the new bishop of Sherborne, Wulfsige, formerly abbot of Westminster,
converted the chapter there into a cathedral monastery. He also was a friend
and patron of Aelfric, who sent him a collection of canons for the instruction of
the clergy. The famous Sherborne Pontifical, which was created at Winchester
for his use, remains and to it is appended a letter from either Sigeric or Aelfric as
archbishop of Canterbury to the new bishop. Wulfsige was regarded after his
death as a saint; he was a man of simple austerity of life, who died in 1002.[78]
When Oswald died in 992, Eadnoth, a monk from Worcester, became abbot of

Ramsey, having been its prior,[79] and he was responsible for founding a nunnery at Chatteris in the Cambridgeshire Fens. He was a relative of Oswald's family, and his sister became the first abbess of the new house. The substantial landed endowments they inherited on their mother's side passed to the new house at Chatteris, and some later passed to the small monastery they founded at St Ives. Others of their kindred were drawn into the endowment, and when Eadnoth became bishop of Dorchester in 1006, he was able to further the interests of this house with which his family had such close ties. This is an interesting example of the way in which a local family network was able to establish the endowments necessary to support a small house of nuns in the course of one generation.[80] The date of the foundation was probably just after Eadnoth left Ramsey to become a bishop, but the preparations must have been made for some time beforehand. Chatteris was only the second nunnery in East Anglia, after the ancient house at Barking in Essex.

The will of Wulfric Spott sheds fascinating light upon the attitude of a leading and devout landowner towards his own foundation at Burton upon Trent. This was an outpost of monasticism in the north of Mercia, founded perhaps around the year 1004.[81] It is clearly a document designed to draw in as many of his friends and kindred as possible to protect the future life and integrity of the religious house. He grants to every bishop 5 mancuses of gold, and to each of the archbishops 10. To each monastic foundation he gives a pound, and to each abbot and abbess 5 mancuses of gold. He earmarks an estate specifically for Archbishop Aelfric of Canterbury 'in the hope that he may be a better friend and supporter of the monastery which I have founded'. He divides the bulk of his estates between his two sons, on condition that they pay 3000 fish annually to the monastery. Various friends are granted land to secure their support for Burton, and there are several reversionary grants in favour of the foundation. His actual endowments to the new religious community range across his extensive holdings in the Midlands, and he concludes his grants with these words:

> I desire that the king be lord of the monastery which I built and of
> the estates which I bequeathed to it to the glory of God and the
> honour of my lord and the good of my soul; and that Archbishop
> Aelfric and my brother Aelfhelm be protectors and friends and advo-
> cates of that foundation against any man born, not as their own
> possession, but as belonging to St Benedict's order.

Later records suggest that the first abbot of Burton, a monk called Wulfgeat, was drawn from Winchester.[82]

The last phase of these further monastic foundations occurred during the reign of Cnut.[83] Close on his victories of 1016, Cnut commemorated his fortune and the unity of his new kingdom by dedicating in 1020 a church and foundation at Ashingdon, the site of his decisive battle.[84] Around the same time he endowed two monasteries in East Anglia: he founded St Benet at Hulme, on the edge of the Norfolk Broads, and undertook the great refoundation at Bury St Edmunds, where the relics of the martyr-king of East Anglia had been venerated since the time of Edward the Elder.[85] A foundation charter is still extant,[86] and the wealth showered upon St Edmundsbury by Cnut and his entourage made it one of the six wealthiest houses in England by the time of the Domesday reckoning. Bury was placed on a par with some of the most prestigious of Edgar's foundations, Ely and Westminster, and became comparable in wealth with the ancient houses at Canterbury, Winchester and Glastonbury. It was a tangible sign of the Danish king's commitment to the values of the monastic episcopacy of the English Church so effectively inculcated by Archbishops Aethelnoth and Wulfstan.

The missionary activities of the Anglo-Saxon Church in the tenth century stretched northwards to Norway and Sweden, and in a more limited way to parts of Denmark also. Conducted in the teeth of the Viking raids and continuing into the new political situation of Cnut's reign, they are a remarkable tribute to the vision and vitality of the Church in England. They are yet another example of the power of the Christian past to inspire and guide the reformers of the tenth century; for this wave of mission was modelled very much upon the famous missions of men like Boniface and Willibrord in the eighth century.[87] The missionaries were drawn from the monasteries and operated with the full support of the English bishops.

English Church interest in Norway probably dated back to the sojourn of Hakon at the court of Athelstan, his godfather,[88] and there were many nobility in the Danelaw who would have had close family ties in Scandinavia. Indeed, the missionary impulse towards Norway may well have arisen out of the successful and prolonged work of evangelisation among the Danes of East Anglia and the Danelaw, which dates back to the primacy of Plegmund and was the basis for the foundation of the great monasteries in the Fens and East Anglia. Nor indeed was this great enterprise of home mission completed in the northern province by the end of the tenth century, as the labours and writings of Wulfstan of York indicate.[89] The trade routes centred on York, crossed the narrow seas to Flanders, the Low Countries and Denmark and afforded ready means of contact and exchange for Danes living in England. Hakon may well have sent for bishops and monks from England in the time of Dunstan, and if this were so, the confirmation of Olaf Tryggvason in 995 at Andover, with the English king as his sponsor, would make more sense. During his reign, which ended in 1000, English missionaries were at work in Norway. The principal witness to this development is Adam of Bremen,[90] and his stance reflects the unease of the archbishops of Bremen and Hamburg later in the eleventh century towards this encroachment on their primacy in the north. More tangible remains of these missions remain in the form of sixty standing stones in western Norway, of distinct design and runic inscription and dating from the last half of the tenth century. William of Malmesbury records the death of 'Sigfrid, bishop in Norway and monk of Glastonbury' and a benefactor of that house, who may have worked during the reign of Olaf.[91] Olaf's successor, Swein, received a mission led by a monk called Gotbald soon after 1000. Through Norway, the missionaries passed on into Sweden; Gotbald worked in Scania as bishop, and David in Västmanland. Some of them met martyrs' deaths. But the work continued well into the eleventh century.

The accession of Cnut in 1016 opened the way for sustained contact between the English and Danish Churches. In 1022, Archbishop Aethelnoth of Canterbury consecrated three bishops of German extraction for Denmark.[92] One of them, Gerbrand of Zealand, was captured by the archbishop of Bremen and obliged to profess canonical obedience to him. But those consecrations were really the result of Cnut's dual kingdom rather than evidence of a true metropolitan jurisdiction by the English primate. They were more on a par with the continued consecration by English archbishops of bishops for the Welsh sees of Llandaff and St Davids, which reflected the immediate state of political power and influence.

Around the same time, Olaf of Norway (St Olaf)[93] began a programme of advancing Christianity, if need be by force. In this task he was assisted by the Englishman, Grimkell, who later became bishop of Trondheim. In due course, Cnut was able to exploit the resentment in Norway towards Olaf's policy of Christianisation, and in 1029 Olaf lost his throne; in 1030 he was killed while attempting to return. However, alien Danish rule, and the memory of the austere king's life, turned him into a national hero. The Church duly found evidence of his sanctity, and his cult began to appear in the Viking regions of Britain and in some of the English monastic kalendars.

Contacts and influences flowed both ways between England and Scandinavia. Many of the Church institutions, even buildings, in Sweden and Norway were modelled on English examples.[94] Norwegian service books show clear monastic influences from England and include direct fragments from the 'Regularis concordia'; English manuscripts from Winchester came to rest in Oslo and Stockholm.[95] A memory of Dunstan stretched as far as Iceland, reaching its finished form in a saga written in the thirteenth century.[96]

The interest of certain English monasteries in the life of the Scandinavian Church was maintained by the return of missionaries and others to their midst. For example, by 1006 a bishop, Siward, and a monk from Ramsey called Wulfred returned to live at Ramsey.[97] Later in the eleventh century, two Scandinavian bishops retired to England: one of them, an Englishman, became abbot of Abingdon in 1051; and the other, Bishop Osmund from Sweden, came to settle after a rather chequered career at Ely, where he lies buried.[98] Even after the Norman Conquest, Evesham, St Albans and Canterbury retained strong ties with the Danish Church; in the twelfth century Englishmen became bishops in Sweden, and one became leader of a mission to Finland.[99] It is a paradox that the Church at York does not appear to have played a more prominent part in this missionary activity, despite its position in the principal city of the Danelaw and its many contacts with the north. Its relative impoverishment, together with its effective status as a missionary area within the English Church for most of the period, may well account for this situation.[100]

It is especially remarkable that the English Church should have laboured to evangelise the lands from which the scourge of their century, the Vikings, had emanated. It may well be that many of the missionaries were of Danish or even Norse extraction, but they had the backing of English bishops and the support of major monasteries. The roots of this phenomenon must lie in the strong memory of the mission origins of the English Church recorded by Bede and the example of the eighth-century missionaries to the continent, together with the shrewd but effective policy of reconciliation and conversion towards the Danes and others settled in England pursued by kings and bishops throughout the tenth century.[101]

The single most impressive achievement by the generation of churchmen after Dunstan was the preservation of the position of the English Church within the fabric of the state during the change of dynasty by conquest in 1016. The fact that Cnut became an enthusiastic upholder of the legacy of Edgar cannot be ascribed solely to political self-interest. He inherited a venerable kingdom with an even more venerable Church, and so gained entry into the circle of Christian monarchs of northern Europe and to the orbit of Rome.[102] But his own commitment to the Christian duties of a king seem sincere, and in them he was well-instructed by his archbishops, Lyfing, Aethelnoth and, perhaps above all, by Wulfstan of York. By the time of Cnut's accession, Wulfstan had articulated the vision of Dunstan and Edgar into a full-blown Christian political ideology. It was an ideology forged upon the anvil of suffering and disappointment during the reign of Ethelred, a vision of the immediate past and a programme of intensely practical action in the present. Wulfstan of York stands as a national Church leader on a par with Dunstan, and with Oda before him. His writings, reputation and role embody the essential character, strength and limitations of the tenth-century Anglo-Saxon Church. He was in every sense the heir of Dunstan.

Wulfstan was a Fenland cleric, probably a monk, possibly from Ely.[103] He may well have been a scribe at the court of Ethelred. In 996, he became bishop of London, and he was highly regarded as a great preacher; he probably enjoyed favour at court, for London was of strategic importance to Ethelred in his wars with the Vikings. In 1002, Wulfstan succeeded Oswald's successor, Ealdwulf, as bishop of Worcester and archbishop of York. The continuation of the plurality indicates the scale of the task then before an archbishop of York in building up the Church in the north from an impoverished base among a barely Christian Danish population. It was crucial too for the English king to be able to count on the loyalty of the archbishop of York in days of invasion and uncertainty. At Worcester, Wulfstan had at hand the tools for his task in the form of a considerable library and a tradition of scholarship going back to before the time of Athelstan.[104] It was strong in Latin learning and poetry, in patristic material and in canon law; one strand of the chronicle was being compiled there in Wulfstan's day, and to it he contributed verses celebrating Edgar's reign.[105] Wulfstan continued to foster the pursuit of learning, and the scriptorium at Worcester became famous for its work in copying continental works well into the eleventh century.

Wulfstan played an active part in public affairs during the last part of Ethelred's reign, and it is his influence that may be detected behind the king's later laws. He was a close friend of Archbishop Aelfric and an executor of his will. Wulfstan in fact saw the demise of three archbishops of Canterbury, Aelfric, Alphege and Lyfing, so by the time of the appointment of Aethelnoth he had become a great figure of continuity in the English Church. He was inevitably caught up in some of the lawsuits affecting his dioceses, of which records remain, and just before he relinquished the see of Worcester in 1016 he founded a small monastery at Gloucester.[106]

The accession of Cnut found Wulfstan a senior adviser to the new king. For the rest of his life he divided his energies between the demands of the new political situation and the needs and challenges of his vast northern diocese. In this he was probably assisted by the new earl of Northumbria, Eric, and his family, who may have been Christian.[107] Wulfstan presided at the consecration of Cnut's new church at Ashingdon in 1020 and in the same year consecrated Aethelnoth as archbishop of Canterbury.[108] The correspondence remains between Wulfstan and Cnut concerning this appointment.[109] In it, Wulfstan enjoins the king and queen to respect the position of the new archbishop, 'that he may be entitled to all those things which those before him enjoyed, Dunstan the good and many others'. A writ of Cnut's in response stands, granting full temporal rights and jurisdiction to the new archbishop and his *familia* at Christ Church, Canterbury.

Wulfstan died at York in 1023, and was buried at Ely where his tomb can still be located. He was revered there and at Peterborough as a great benefactor and friend.[110]

When Danes and English met in 1018 in witan at Oxford to lay down the basis upon which the kingdom would be ruled under its new king, it was agreed that 'they would ever honour one God and steadfastly hold one Christian faith, and would love king Cnut with due loyalty, and zealously observe Edgar's laws'. The preface to this first code of Cnut's laws concluded with a little homily: 'Let us very resolutely turn from sins and eagerly atone for misdeeds, and duly love and honour one God, and steadfastly hold one Christian faith and diligently avoid every heathen practice.'[111] The hand behind this declaration was Wulfstan's and these words encapsulate the pastoral vision of his homilies and the practical attention to detailed law making that characterised his work as canonist and legislator.[112]

The codifying of law was no innovation, but at the end of Ethelred's reign and at the beginning of Cnut's it reached a new peak at Wulfstan's hands. He himself was a great collator of earlier laws, secular and ecclesiastical, and there remain several documents from the personal collection of legal material which he compiled for his own use. The most notable is a large series of extracts called the 'Excerptiones Egberti'. It is steeped in the Carolingian tradition of canon law and penitential discipline, but is broken into various chapters and groups of headings appropriate to different aspects of church life.[113] The well-being of the Church is the common thread in all the legislation that sprang from his endeavours. But the life of the Church meant the life of the whole Christian society, even the way in which its standards and laws affected parts of the pagan Danish population. Thus the homiletic flavour to his law making is integral to its force and validity. If the favour of God was indispensable to the well-being of natural life and human society, then obedience to divine law, by clergy and laity alike, was urgent and vital for the protection of society from the wrath of God, whether plague, pestilence or warfare. This preoccupation lay close to the impulse that was behind the foundation of the monasteries and the reform of the Church; for these men and women by their prayers and exemplary life won the favour of God for the society whom they represented. The traumas of Ethelred's reign served only to add even greater urgency to this vision. It fell to Wulfstan's lot to try to ensure that the life of the laity and the non-monastic clergy commended itself in like manner to that of the monks and nuns. When Wulfstan looked back to the legislation of Edgar's reign as a norm, he looked not only to its relative clarity and to the memory of the partnership between king and archbishop that was the foundation for the great reform of the monasteries and of the Church. He looked back also to the distinctly minatory tone of Edgar's fourth law: to the unequivocal connection made there between calamity and pestilence, and man's disobedience towards the king's law and the claims of the Church.[114] This is an important code for understanding the significance of Wulfstan's work, not least because it addresses the condition of the Danelaw and the claims of Christian legislation over a less than Christian population.

The first national code of law in which Wulfstan's influence may be detected is V Ethelred,[115] issued in 1008. It is similar to VI Ethelred, and both are preserved in manuscripts associated with Wulfstan. It is characterised by clemency and by condemnation of heathen practices and slavery. It emphasises the religious and secular duties of clergy and laity, and is insistent that monks, nuns and priests obey their rule and 'intercede zealously for all Christian people'. The problem of social discipline is both religious and practical: it affects the keeping of feast days, frequent confession and communion; and also the manning of ships and desertion from the king's army. 'God's law is to be eagerly loved in word and deed; then God will become gracious at once to this nation.'

In response to the invasion of 1009, VII Ethelred[116] calls for a national fast on the Monday, Tuesday and Wednesday before Michaelmas. Prayers and masses are to be said to secure divine help against pressing enemies, and all are involved, even slaves.

VIII Ethelred, published in 1014,[117] sets out the famous axiom that 'a Christian king is Christ's deputy in a Christian people, and must avenge very zealously offences against Christ'. The sanctuary of the Church is a particular concern of this code; so too is the involvement of clergy and monks in secular disputes, and their proper outcome. Anxiety is expressed at laxity in the religious life, and it is lamented that 'in the assemblies . . . since the days of Edgar, Christ's laws have waned and the king's laws dwindled'. Yet, the writer believes, 'improvement can come still', and he enjoins the vigorous prosecution of crime as a start. 'Let us take as our example what former rulers wisely decreed, Athelstan, Edmund, and Edgar who came last – how they honoured God and kept God's law and paid God's tribute as long as they lived.' The final emphasis is on loyalty to the king and to friends: a clear rebuke of the treachery that clouded the latter part of Ethelred's reign.

In the circumstances, it was a courageous piece, and it was Wulfstan's forceful courage, backed by a thorough knowledge of the traditional law, that held out hope to the English when all appeared lost. His success in commending his own highly traditional and moralistic view of royal law making to Cnut is reflected in the king's letter to the people of England,[118] written in 1019 or early in 1020, in which he alludes to papal injunctions by the hand of Archbishop Lyfing which evidently supported the position of the archbishops. The bishops emerge as mentors and judges of the people, and the king is anxious to maintain Church and secular law. The climax to Wulfstan's work came in the compendious and lengthy code of law which Cnut issued some time before Wulfstan's death in 1023. It falls into two parts, ecclesiastical and secular,[119] and is really an amalgam of earlier English laws built around the codes Wulfstan drew up under Ethelred. It is in this code that the feast of St Dunstan on 19 May is first ordered. It is a comprehensive body of law, applying with discrimination to both Danes and Englishmen, and it covers just about every area of life. It is particularly strict towards sexual and marital offences, but again there is a note of clemency where penalties in general are concerned.

Wulfstan's courage and independence of mind are reflected also in the way he challenged the corruption of the papal court in charging fees for the granting of the primatial *pallium*. After Wulfstan's death, in 1027, Cnut was able to report back from his trip to Rome, to attend the coronation of the Emperor Conrad by Pope John XIX, that:

> I complained again before the lord Pope and said that it displeased
> me greatly that my archbishops were so much oppressed by the im-
> mensity of the sums of money which were exacted from them when,
> according to custom, they came to the apostolic see to receive the
> 'pallium'. It was decided that this should not be done in future.[120]

Wulfstan's hand may also be detected in other pieces of legislation surviving from this period. Underlying Wulfstan's vision of Christian law was a hierarchy of duty towards God reflected in and confirmed by the hierarchy of social order. Each had his or her own place, and with it a clear duty towards God and neighbour; this he believed was the nexus of Christian law and the correct interpretation of English law as it had developed over the years. Traditional English law was a subtle interweaving of customary law with Christian justice; the position of the Church within society and the king as the law giver symbolised and secured that bond and relationship. From documents associated with Wulfstan come several compilations on status in Anglo-Saxon society, pertinent to the different parts of the kingdom, prepared for private use but relating to the balance of judgement required in law making.[121]

Two ecclesiastical codes remain. There is the so-called 'Peace of Edward and Guthrum', which seeks to impose ecclesiastical observances upon a semi-pagan Danish population. It is noteworthy inasmuch as it appears to countenance a refusal of episcopal sanctions and a resort to secular enforcement of law.[122] Ascribed to Wulfstan also are the so-called 'Canons of Edgar'.[123] Later tradition regarded them as belonging to the reign of Edgar, even as the work of Dunstan.[124] This error reflects perhaps the consistency of these canons with the work of the great reformers of the earlier generation, for both Dunstan and Wulfstan looked back to and built upon the traditional ecclesiastical codes of the Carolingian reform, in this case the work of Theodulf of Orleans and Amalarius of Metz. The 'Canons of Edgar' address the secular clergy principally, and Wulfstan owed much to the pastoral letters which Aelfric the Homilist wrote for him.[125] Material from these canons was later inserted into V Ethelred, the first national code in which Wulfstan's work may be detected. They were written therefore between 1005 and 1007, and are closely connected with a group of Wulfstan's homilies directed towards the secular clergy. Wulfstan draws heavily upon the collection attributed to Egbert[126] and he uses also the *homilia* of Pope Leo IV. These canons were in fact central to Wulfstan's reforming work as archbishop of York:[127]

Wulfstan was evidently active in religious reform by his own studies,
by encouragement of manuscript compilation, by the issue of a rule
of life for Canons, and a code for the priesthood in general, by the cir-
culation of pastoral letters for the clergy of his diocese, and by the
preaching of homilies to the laity.[128]

In them, Wulfstan is stern towards laxity and immorality among the clergy, and fierce in condemning paganism and commending baptism as its antidote. His prescriptions for the proper conduct of services are very precise and detailed, and indicate a high level of ignorance among some of his clergy. He emphasises the role of clergy in preaching to and teaching the laity, and outlines the basic duties of a Christian layman. It is an eclectic but coherent work, direct, forceful and clear. Some of the continuing problems of the northern Church, to which these canons were addressed, are revealed in the later 'Law of the Northumbrian priests'.[129] This was probably also written by Wulfstan, and it draws heavily on his earlier legislation. It is a brave and comprehensive attempt to sustain a coherent Christian way of life within a missionary situation.

Wulfstan's abiding monument consists of his sermons.[130] These remain as a powerful reminder of the force of his personality and the strength of his convictions. They were composed for the most part in English rather than Latin, and were carefully pitched and composed with a clear, even monotonous intention: 'to prevent apostasy among the English was the archbishop's prime care . . . he attacked with vigour all the abuses of his time'.[131] He was a great rhetorician, and by rhetoric he understood the use of eloquence for noble and moral ends – the adumbrating and chastising of wisdom itself. His sermons show a careful discipline, whether in the clarity of teaching or in the power to move different kinds of audiences. Sometimes he threw himself into impassioned diatribes and appeals, of which his famous 'Sermo lupi' of 1014 is the most striking example.[132] He used the rhythm and alliterative character of Old

English to great effect, often rendering the content of traditional homilies in this distinctive style. This was a deliberate pastoral and teaching ploy; as in the Psalms and much contemporary Old English poetry, this device stamped what was being said on the mind with more resonance and permanence. Yet his was straight preaching, with little ornament, poetry or irony. Nor did he make appeal to the lives of the saints, unlike his contemporary and mentor, Aelfric.[133] Wulfstan sought a direct moral and spiritual appeal; he was an evangelist and moralist, and there is a puritan severity about his preaching. The content of his sermons falls into two main areas. The bulk of his surviving homilies address basic aspects of the Christian faith – the creed, baptism, the gifts of the Holy Spirit and various aspects of the Christian life, both for laymen and for clergy. Some of his sermons are of a directly pastoral nature: addressed to clergy and their faults or to penitents; or episcopal sermons suitable for dedication of churches and ordination. The other main area of Wulfstan's proclamation was concern with the reality of evil and human sin and their consequences for national life, together with a lively and at times fearsome expectation of the end of the world and the return of Christ.

The unique contribution of Wulfstan, which sets him apart from his contemporary bishops on the continent, with whom he otherwise has much in common,[134] lies in his 'Institutes of polity', a work of Christian political theory.[135] The drafts that remain constitute a highly traditional work, rooted in the writings of the Carolingian era and going back before that to Isidore of Seville and, less directly, to Augustine. All the sources familiar to Wulfstan are deployed in this penetrating and comprehensive analysis of the structure and duties of a Christian Church, society and monarchy. Once again, Wulfstan reveals his debt to his older contemporary and mentor, Aelfric, and to Englishmen of a much earlier generation like Alcuin and Sedulius Scottus.

The 'Institutes of polity' are really a digest of all the principles which guided Wulfstan as he drew up laws or wrote sermons. The work follows the divinely ordained hierarchy among men through all its parts, and so outlines the duties and limitations of each. Kingship is rooted in the rule of God; the Christian king is a mirror of Christ, and may thus be regarded as the father of his people and Christ's deputy among them. This is very much the imagery of the proem to the 'Regularis concordia'. Consequently the protection of the people and the pursuit of justice and piety are royal priorities, as Dunstan had stipulated in the promise he appended to the coronation service.[136] Nonetheless, here, as in his legislation, Wulfstan recognised the two distinct spheres of power, secular and spiritual: 'if Christianity be weakened, the kingdom will soon fall'.[137] The Church may need the interposing of the secular arm to enforce religious dues, but this is within the nature of a partnership in which each plays a mutually correcting role, and both fall under the purview of the justice and rule of Christ. For the king depends on the Church to know the nature of justice and wisdom; but the Church depends on the king for the implementing of laws conducive to these ends. Eight, therefore, are the fundamental principles of Christian monarchy: truth, patience, generosity, wisdom, correction of evil, encouragement of good, light taxation and equitable judgements.[138]

The Christian kingdom rests on three pillars of society: those who pray, those who work and those who fight.[139] This image Wulfstan drew directly from Aelfric's writings. He then proceeds to examine in detail the role of each stratum of society, starting with the bishops, then dealing with the witan, to which the bishops should act as teachers and conscience, not afraid to be silent! The integrity and spiritual vigilance of bishops are crucial if they are to intercede effectively and guard against evil, and Wulfstan sets out a picture of a bishop's day work in a way which could have applied to any of the great tenth-century reforming bishops.[140] To the nobility, Wulfstan appeals for justice and respect both for the Church's property and ministers, and also for the widows and poor; reeves also are directed to be especially alert to their needs. His strictures to the clergy are direct and formidable: theirs is a pastoral and teaching task, and they are enjoined to remain celibate. Likewise, stability of life and a continual rejection of worldly concerns is the duty of those under religious vows; this applies both to monks and nuns, and to canons as well. The security of the Church, the due payment of ecclesiastical dues, observance of fasts and festivals, upholding of marriage and protection of widows are familiar themes. Throughout this work, there is a clear emphasis upon the intimate connection between private and public morality; Wulfstan's appeal is for robust Christian integrity by each and by all.

Yet Wulfstan lived with the inevitable tension between theory and reality. It took great faith and courage to proclaim this ideal and to strive to implement it by legislation and preaching. Over his life and work there loomed the shadow of violence and disorder, compounded by men's perfidy and weakness. Wulfstan saw this shadow as a sign of the times and the urgency in his writing and work is not that of an idealist. It is the prophetic clarion of a watchman for whom the end of all things was at hand, of a man who believed that the punishment of God for sin was a reality and a factor in history but at the same time a sign of hope, urging men to repent and reform. It was this belief that enabled Wulfstan fearlessly to face the problems of his day, and to counsel men in practical ways towards a surer path. His great sermon of 1014, the 'Sermo lupi', preached when all seemed lost, is the true measure of his greatness as a Christian bishop.

11

THE FLOWERING OF THE TENTH CENTURY

I – letters

*T*HE intellectual and artistic achievement of the tenth century in England mirrors the rich and varied developments in Church and society throughout the period. It is without doubt one of the finest and most original flowerings of English culture, and almost all of its many strands are influenced by the life of the Church and its teachings. The roots of this Christian culture lie in the learning and art of the Carolingian period on the continent, which was itself the heir to the inheritance of late antiquity mediated through Irish and English scholars. In the tenth century in England, however, this great tradition sprang to new and sustained life as a direct consequence of the impulse to education and learning of Alfred the Great, which reached its climax in the formation of the monasteries under Dunstan and Ethelwold.[1] The memory of the losses of the recent past, and of the precious tradition that was now at stake, was never far from the minds of the monastic scholars. In the words of Aelfric:

> Whence shall wise teachers come among God's people, unless they
> learn while they are young? And how can the faith be propagated, if
> sacred doctrine and its teachers decay? Therefore God's ministers and
> monks should take warning now, lest in our day sacred learning
> should lose its fervour and decay; as happened in England only a few
> years ago; then no English priest could compose or thoroughly inter-
> pret a letter in Latin, until Archbishop Dunstan and Bishop Ethelwold
> restored learning in the monasteries.[2]

Aelfric himself was the epitome and apogee of this development. He was regarded in his day as the most learned Englishman since Bede, whom in many ways he resembled, and it was to Aelfric that Wulfstan as a new bishop turned for practical learned help with his early homilies and canons.[3] Aelfric's pastoral letters lie behind some of Wulfstan's most important work. Aelfric was a child of the reform period, born perhaps around the year 955 and educated at Winchester under Ethelwold himself. His learning was highly traditional: scripture, theology, grammar and computation. He was not primarily an historian, but his accounts of life at Winchester, in his 'Life of St Ethelwold', and in his homily on the life and cult of St Swithun, are immediate and real.[4] Just before Dunstan's death, Aelfric was sent to the new monastery at Cerne, founded by Aethelmaer, to instruct the monks there, He may well have returned at some stage to Winchester, for he was a friend of Bishop Alphege's and a renowned master of Latin and English. In the later part of his life, his erstwhile patron, Aethelmaer, persuaded him to become abbot of his new monastery at Eynsham near Oxford. Here Aelfric remained until his death around the year 1020. He retained close ties not only with the secular clergy and the monks and bishops of the Benedictine reform, like Wulfstan and Wulfsige of Sherborne, but also with a significant circle of educated laymen (and presumably women also): Aethelmaer and his father Aethelweard; also Sigeweard and Wulfgeat, thegns of the Danelaw, for whom he composed written works. In all, Aelfric was a key link between the generation which had witnessed the reforms of Dunstan and Edgar and men like Archbishop Aethelnoth and his contemporaries who made their mark under Cnut. In the style of his work, both in Latin and in Anglo-Saxon, Aelfric represented in a living way the long continuum of monastic learning, in England and on the continent, to which Bede stood as father and guide.[5]

Aelfric was a great teacher and communicator. He never lost sight of the living and practical end of Christian learning: to build up the life of the Church. He wrote for parochial clergy, for young pupils, for hard-pressed bishops and for interested laity. He used his native language, both as an introduction to Latin learning and as a formidable and moving vehicle of expression. His was a pastoral gift in every way, to lead his hearers further along the path of truth and to make accessible for them the wealth of traditional Christian thought.

Several monuments remain to Aelfric's skill and labours as an educator. Aelfric believed that 'grammar is the key that unlocks the meaning of books',[6] and his own 'Grammar' is constructed to that end, drawing fairly freely upon the classical labours of Priscian and assuming a knowledge of Donatus. But unlike his classical mentors, Aelfric does not collate literary examples; instead:

> he was producing a working grammar, a practical grammar in the modern sense. He was also having to create an appropriate terminology in the vernacular as he proceeded. In so doing he was, as he came to see himself, also writing a grammar of current English with standardized linguistic forms.[7]

Thus Aelfric's 'Grammar' is the first of its kind in any European vernacular, a 'remarkable and original achievement'.[8] A further window is opened into Aelfric's method by the interlinear gloss in Old English which accompanies the text of his famous 'Colloquy' in one of the manuscripts; the 'Colloquy' was probably a work of collaboration between Aelfric and some of his abler pupils.[9] Aelfric's relationship with his own pupils is revealed in the 'Colloquy', which was a device for teaching schoolboys Latin in a lively and practical manner, with plenty of illustrations drawn from everyday life.[10] The aim was to enable boy oblates in the monastic school to master sufficient Latin for an understanding of the psalter and parts of the Bible, to teach them proper pronunciation and to prepare them for the study of the *trivium* – grammar, rhetoric and dialectic. Once again Aelfric breaks with tradition by encouraging the boys to do most of the talking, casting them in appropriate roles and then interrogating them! As a consequence, perhaps unwittingly, it affords a unique picture of English social and rural life in the tenth century.

On quite a different level, and one no less close to Aelfric's heart, there remains his *'De temporibus anni'*,[11] a work completed perhaps around the year 993, just after the second main cycle of homilies, to which it appears to stand as an appendix. It is derived from the works of Bede on the subject of the correct calculation of the days and seasons of the Christian year, and Aelfric follows his source, Bede's 'De temporum ratione', closely. He used too Bede's other works on the subject, 'De temporibus' and 'De natura rerum', also his commentary on Genesis and Isidore's 'De natura rerum'. Aelfric's is a concise and lucid summary of Bede's often tortuous and copious arguments; he was writing for ordinary parochial clergy and monks to whom this knowledge was indispensable for the proper understanding, calculation and use of the church year. 'In all these cases, he is dealing with living issues, questions of practical importance to the computist that were either undecided or gave trouble to the less learned. . . . Aelfric indulges nowhere in an argument purely for the sake of a scientific controversy.'[12]

Aelfric's concern for the education and welfare of the parochial clergy lay behind the three cycles of homilies which he compiled while living at Cerne. These were prompted by lay patronage from Aethelmaer and his father, Aethelweard, and at the behest of Sigeric, archbishop of Canterbury. His preface to the first cycle of homilies is very revealing:

it entered my mind by the grace of God to turn this book from the
Latin language into English, not from confidence of great learning,
but because I saw and heard much error in many English books,
which unlearned men in their simplicity accounted great wisdom. I
was sorry that they did not know or possess the evangelical teaching
among their books, except for those men alone who knew Latin, and
except from the books which King Alfred wisely translated from Latin
into English, which are still obtainable. For this reason, trusting in
God, I presumed to undertake this work, and also because men particularly require good teaching in this age which is the end of the
world.[13]

The note of urgency before the impending end of the age echoes the preaching of Wulfstan. But the style of Aelfric's English writing is very different, simple, direct and sincere, and without the heavy moralising and dire admonitions that characterise Wulfstan's work.[14] Both series of homilies for general use were written before Sigeric's death in 995, probably being completed shortly before that date.[15] There were several subsequent editions of these works. All his later homilies are written in a rhythmical prose which is the distinctive and attractive feature of his writing.[16] Before the tenth century closed, Aelfric completed another full cycle of homilies to be used on the saints' days of the monastic kalendar.[17] Such collections of sermons were not without precedent, and there exists a tenth-century collation, the 'Blicking Homilies', probably from the generation prior to Aelfric.[18] But a study of the complete corpus of Aelfric's labours reveals the care with which he ensured that virtually the whole liturgical year was covered, and as a consequence his sermons were used and reused well into the next century.[19] The manuscript traditions illustrate further the way in which these homilies were copied within Aelfric's lifetime and circulated from Winchester, Canterbury and Worcester.[20] His approach is both biblical and eclectic in that he uses traditional patristic authorities with considerable freedom.[21] His aim was quite simply to make readily accessible a carefully composed model to inform the preaching of those who would read his work. That his sermons came to be used verbatim, and lifted out of their original sequence, is the measure of Aelfric's success. If some at least of 'the secular clergy in 10th and 11th century England were more reputably learned and zealous a body of men than many of their contemporary brethren on the Continent',[22] this was in a real sense the result of the labours and example of Aelfric and Wulfstan.

Following the example of Bede, and in response to a request from Aethelweard, Aelfric began a substantial translation of parts of the Old Testament into English.[23] This turned out in the end to be a collaborative effort with some other scholars and pupils, and its main intention was to put important sections of the Bible into the hands of priests ignorant of the Latin text. However, closer examination of the way this was done, and the fact that other works of Aelfric's throughout his life turned to the proper handling and understanding of the Bible, reveal his profound interest in scripture and its theology. In this he was a close disciple of Bede, whose commentaries constituted the most important part of his legacy to later generations. Later, while abbot of Eynsham, Aelfric wrote a short treatise on the purpose and nature of the Bible, both Old and New Testaments, for a thegn called Sigeweard, who lived at Asthall in Oxfordshire.[24] It is a condensed and traditional exercise in Christian biblical interpretation, based on Augustine's 'De doctrina christiana', regarding all scripture as a pattern of revelation leading up to and foreshadowing the incarnation and the Trinity. God's purpose in history is paramount, and this has an important bearing upon the way men should live and their social order should be constructed.[25] The inner meaning of the text of scripture, with both its spiritual and moral implications, is Aelfric's goal in handling the Bible; elaborate allegorical speculations and images hold no appeal.[26]

Aelfric's grasp of orthodox Latin theology was sure, and like Bede before him, he drew heavily on such works of Augustine and Gregory as were available to him. He wrote several pieces for specific persons, spelling out the pastoral implications of classical Christian doctrine. In his pastoral letters to Wulfsige, bishop of Sherborne, and to Wulfstan, Aelfric examined closely the principles lying behind the ministry of the Church and its proper conduct; and there is a short piece on the seven-fold gifts of the Holy Spirit which Aelfric composed and which Wulfstan later adapted.[27] To his monks at Eynsham he wrote, setting out the context and content of the 'Regularis concordia'; and to the thegns, Sigeweard and Wulfgeat, he wrote on the virtues of celibacy and the doctrines of the Trinity and atonement.[28] His 'Lives of the saints' are fascinating both as homilies reworking traditional hagiography within a vernacular mode and as the fullest picture extant of the spiritual outlook and interests of the tenth-century monks. For them the saints were living contemporaries, a living past which impinged upon a present already overshadowed by divine judgement and the imminent end of the world. But it was Aelfric's genius to be able to turn this 'holy fear' to deeply human and strongly pastoral ends.

A slightly younger contemporary of Aelfric's was also engaged in the task of conveying the rudiments of Latin learning to English-speaking clerics. Byrhtferth, a monk at Ramsey, composed a 'Computistical handbook' for the use of parochial clergy and young monks.[29] In this work, as in Aelfric's 'De temporibus anni', the debt to Bede is immense. But the extent to which Byrhtferth followed his teacher, Abbo of Fleury, is clear too. Around the year 985, Abbo came from Fleury and stayed in England, mainly at Ramsey. Aelfric, in his homily upon the martyrdom of St Edmund, makes explicit and precise mention of this visit and of the way Abbo received the story from Dunstan himself.[30] Shortly after his return to Fleury, Abbo became abbot of that monastery in 988, and before his untimely death in 1004 he had established a reputation as a rhetorician and computist.[31] He left behind him at Ramsey a grammatical treatise for the benefit of his pupils there. Abbo was an old friend of Oswald and a great admirer of Dunstan, to whom he dedicated two curious acrostic poems.[32] His works on astronomy and mathematics were known to Byrhtfeth, as was Aelfric's own essay into the subject; the 'Computistical handbook' was in fact composed after Abbo's death, for Byrhtferth alludes to it and describes Abbo as 'experienced in doctrinal knowledge and perfect in philosophy', deeply committed to understanding the Christian faith.[33] In his 'Computistical handbook' Byrhtferth attempted to bridge the gap between the work of Bede and Abbo in Latin and the clergy competent only in English or the elements of basic Latin. 'It is not clear how far Byrhtferth had to create new words for this purpose (he had been partly anticipated in this by Aelfric): but the range of ideas, often of considerable complexity, of which the English language was a medium was now greatly extended.'[43]

Byrhtferth, however, was not otherwise strongly committed to education in the vernacular, and all the remaining works associated with him are in Latin. His interest in the speculative dimension of scientific thought was deep and real, as his preface to Bede's 'De temporibus' reveals,[35] and his view of learning and the role of the human mind was sustained by a profound belief in the Holy Spirit as the guide 'into all truth'.[36] Thus the ordered composition of reality, visible and invisible, and its rational apprehension by number, calculation and speculation, testified to the mystery of divine creation and was a mirror of the divine nature.[37] The purpose of learning was 'so that we may be strong to the end, to behold with pure eyes the fountain of pure light, which is God'.[38]

Byrhtferth inherited too from Bede a keen interest in the history of his own age. He was almost certainly the author of the first biography of Oswald, whose pupil and profound admirer he was.[39] It is cast very much in the convoluted style of the 'Computistical handbook'. It bears too the influence of the connection with Fleury which was the salient feature of monastic life at Ramsey, about which foundation the author is evidently very well informed. It is not altogether an accurate work, and at times some sensitive areas like the murder of Edward at Corfe are glossed over, perhaps deliberately. Nonetheless it is close to the tradition which produced the first biography of Dunstan, the reliability of which Byrhtferth corroborates.[40] There are prayers to Dunstan embedded in his writing and his veneration for the saint is clearly evident from the way he refers to him in his 'Life of Oswald'. Byrhtferth would have been well-placed for access to sources at Worcester and York, and he may have conducted some of his researches under the patronage of Wulfstan. It would appear that his work lies behind some of the earliest annals attributed to Symeon of Durham, and his influence has also been detected in the compilation of the Ramsey annals.[41] He probably wrote the tenth-century 'Life of St Egwin'; Egwin was an early bishop of Worcester, the purported founder of Evesham and a friend of Aldhelm's.[42]

'A man of wide reading, in width of knowledge and scientific temper of mind he is probably the greatest of English monastic scholars.' His was 'the most important scientific treatise in England since the time of Bede'.[43] But this work reflects too the very real intellectual and scholarly limitations that surrounded an English monastic scholar of the tenth century: florid and recondite use of language, a highly traditional and tradition-bound way of handling scripture and a haphazard inheritance from late antiquity and the fathers. All these features handicapped a speculative mind and rendered the learning of this period out of date within a hundred years. But men like Aelfric and Byrhtferth were restorers first, and layers of foundations also. Their sense of the precariousness of learning and the value of transmission of scholarship, are a salutary reminder of the battle that was fought hard and won in the tenth century to lay the permanent basis for medieval Christian thought as it emerged on the continent and in England over the next 200 years.

The work of Aelfric and Byrhtferth sheds much light upon the range of sources available to monastic scholars by the end of the tenth century. The homilies of Aelfric in particular show the degree to which the reception of classical patristic teaching depended upon the commentaries and homiliaries composed during the Carolingian revival of learning in the first half of the ninth century.[44] The great Latin fathers, Jerome, Augustine and Gregory the Great, are the principal authorities; and the thought of Augustine is dominant, although incompletely represented. But it cannot be assumed that all the works of these fathers could actually be consulted in England at this time, and Aelfric's work rests heavily upon two important homiliaries of the Carolingian era: the one produced for Charlemagne by Paul the Deacon, and the one of Haymo of Auxerre.[45] Aelfric's work on the lives of saints draws on traditional hagiography such as the life of St Benedict in the *Dialogues* of Gregory the Great, and Sulpitius Severus' 'Life of St Martin of Tours'.

Standing behind the Carolingian sources were the three great English scholars of an earlier era, Alcuin, Bede and Aldhelm. For Aelfric, Bede was by far the most important. But for other scholars, like Byrhtferth, the influence of Aldhelm was profound. His 'On virginity' was probably one of the books most studied in the tenth century, and all the surviving manuscripts from the tenth and eleventh centuries are heavily glossed, both in English and in Latin.[46] The likely author of the first life of Dunstan, for example, was on his way to Winchester to read this very work when he composed his lengthy letter of introduction to Archbishop Aethelgar,[47] and it was in many ways the manifesto of the tenth-century monastic reform. Aldhelm exerted a profound and wide influence also on the way almost all scholars in England wrote Latin; Aelfric was the notable exception, being a strict follower of Bede. This so-called 'hermeneutic style'[48] was much in vogue in tenth-century monastic circles, and was perhaps 'cultivated energetically in England in an attempt to show that English learning was as profound, and English writing as sophisticated as anything produced on the Continent'.[49] The first life of Dunstan, and Byrhtferth's 'Life of Oswald' and 'Computistical handbook', are all written in this manner, though from the time of William of Malmesbury their style was regarded as an impediment to their content.

A brief survey of the wider sources alluded to by monastic scholars indicates two main groups of authorities. Quite a substantial body of eighth- and ninth-century continental learning became available as the libraries of the monasteries in England were built up: Hrabanus Maur, Smaragdus of Rheims and Heiric of Auxerre are leading examples.[50] Wulfstan was able to draw on the works of scholars and canonists like Adso, Theodulf of Orleans, Sedulius and Amalarius of Metz; and monastic scholars copied classic works like the Rules of St Benedict, Chrodegang of Metz and Benedict of Aniane in Latin, and also made translations into English.[51] The second main group consists of Christian writers of late antiquity together with fragments of ancient classical learning passed down by earlier Christian scholars; notably Prudentius, Macrobius, Arator,

Martianus Capella, Martin of Braga, Julian of Toledo, Isidore of Seville, Cassiodorus, Ambrose, Rufinus, Origen, Virgil, Cicero, Donatus and Priscian and, perhaps most important and influential of all, Boethius.[52] This reflects a highly traditional monastic library, similar in range and content to that enjoyed by Alcuin at York in the eighth century or used by Bede somewhat earlier.[53] All such learning revolved around the study of the Bible in Latin, meditation upon the lives of the saints and the daily recitation of the divine office, which was largely comprised of the psalter. From this common core interests in canon or secular law and science in the form of astronomy and computation sprang. The aim was to understand fully and to pass on accurately the rich inheritance of the Christian past, and to devote learning and its artefacts to the glory of God and the well-being of his Church.[54]

The consequence of this intensive labour was the burgeoning of a distinctively monastic and clerical culture in England. A complete circle of monastic scholars may be readily identified by the beginning of the eleventh century. The most immediate examples include Aelfric 'Bata', a pupil of Aelfric's; another Aelfric, of Bath, who was translating the gospels into English; also Wulstan, the cantor of Winchester Cathedral, who rewrote Aelfric's 'Life of Ethelwold' and appended a long poem on the cult and translation of St Swithun.[55] At Winchester for a time there lived Lantfrith, probably a foreigner, whom the monks pressed to compile a record of the miracles of Swithun.[56] Elfweard, abbot of Glastonbury, has already been noted as a figure of some importance;[57] the unknown compilers of the monastic editions of the chronicle at Winchester, Abingdon and Worcester; the anonymous writer of the 'Life of St Grimbald';[58] and the shadowy mentors of Osbern at Canterbury – all these and others now forgotten testify to a lively religious and learned culture.[59]

Study of the books which they relied upon, and especially their liturgical material, confirms the pattern. Gradually the Gallican usage of the psalms replaced the older Roman version in all the monasteries except Christ Church, Canterbury;[60] and the new hymns and antiphons of Carolingian monasticism spread in a similar manner. Winchester became the centre of English monastic culture, and its influence came to be felt in the dissemination of kalendars as well as of illuminated manuscripts.[61] It had become also, under Aelfric, the principal centre of monastic education, though this in no way eclipsed the continuing importance of the monastic schools at Glastonbury, Abingdon, Canterbury and Worcester; also Ramsey and possibly Ely as well. The best evidence for the relative wealth, diversity and limitations of this tradition may be found in the psalters still remaining from this late Anglo-Saxon period.

> The psalter was the commonest book in Anglo-Saxon times. Many of the devout read it privately; every priest who served a church or chapel must have it; and in the great churches or monasteries several copies were needed. Of some twenty-five extant psalters produced in England in Anglo-Saxon times, the psalms were wholly or partly glossed (into English) in fifteen. . . . If this is anything like the proportion in contemporary use, we must reckon the English glossed psalters of the tenth and eleventh centuries in hundreds.[62]

Glossed psalters are a unique memorial to the way in which biblical study bridged the gap between Latin and English, for a glossed book was intended for study; it was no longer purely a service book.[63]

The so-called 'hermeneutic style' is further and ubiquitous evidence of a distinctly monastic culture.[64] So too is the gradual standardisation of Old

English, which emanated from Winchester: 'the Benedictine reform paved the way for the process of language unification'.[65] The emergence of drama at Winchester, testified to in the *'Regularis concordia'*, is a striking and unique development of the period, imported almost certainly from Fleury and associated with the Easter ceremonies. The two surviving Winchester Tropers contain the music of the special chants for this occasion, and this marks the beginning of formal drama in England.[66]

It is impossible to assess the literacy and culture of the clergy outside the monasteries during this period. The demand for service books and homilies, and the property which some clergy were able to dispose of in their wills, including books and precious objects like vestments and chalices, reflect the sophistication and devotion of some. The strictures of Wulfstan and the more oblique remonstrances of Aelfric reflect the perennial problem that the learning and vocation of the clergy could never be taken for granted.[67] Yet the beginning of the eleventh-century campaign for clerical celibacy, to which Wulfstan was particularly attached, reflects the basic strength of the position of the clergy, both senior and monastic. This cut against the grain of Anglo-Saxon society, within which the priest for generations had been married and perhaps too much a part of normal lay life for his own good. The advocacy of celibacy was perhaps a natural outcome of the pre-eminence of the monasteries. The success of this movement, however, fathered quite unfairly by posterity upon Dunstan himself, was probably very restricted; but by declaring and popularising the idea, Wulfstan and his fellow bishops were very much in step with developments on the continent.[68]

Three further areas of cultural development directly stimulated by this monastic culture remain to be examined: the state of medicine and the care of the poor; the remarkable foundation at Durham; and the circle of lay literacy and culture which developed in response to the vitality and example of the Church.

The documentary evidence remaining for monastic interest in medicine at this time is not great. There is a fine herbal in the British Museum from the middle of the eleventh century which is a copy of an English translation of works by Apuleius and Sextus Placidus. It is one of the earliest examples of a medical text translated into a vernacular, and the finished work was probably executed at Winchester. The medical properties of both plants and animals are its concern, and it is beautifully illuminated. Another book from the late tenth century in the British Museum is a miscellany of herb recipes and charms, classical, pagan and Christian, such as were very common at the time. Examples abound in many other manuscripts and illustrate the way in which magic, medicine and religion mingled together.[69] The Hyde *'Liber vitae'*, for example, contains a recipe for the cure of boils, and the *'Nunnaminster Codex'* is replete with prayers and charms of diverse provenance.[70] The writings of Byrhtferth allude to such scientific background to medical complaints as was then available.[71] The line between science and sorcery was as confused as that between magic and medicine, and Aelfric composed a homily cautioning people against the use of auguries.[72] Wulfstan had to battle against a real recrudescence of paganism and its remedies, and not just in the north.

Care of the poor was a constant theme of Church pronouncements in the tenth century. Oda, in his canons, enjoins the keeping of Lent as a season of fasting and almsgiving.[73] Oswald died washing the feet of the poor, and Ethelwold and Dunstan were remembered for their care of widows and orphans.

Osbern records how it was three pensioners of the late archbishop who were cured of blindness at his tomb.[74] The *'Regularis concordia'* was particularly emphatic about the monks' duties to Christ's poor, and in the 'Life of Edith' it is told how a hostelry for thirteen paupers was set up at the gate of Wilton nunnery and endowed in Edith's memory.[75] Sundry wills of the period reflect the impact this Christian teaching had on people outside the monasteries. The will of Eadred provided for the relief of hardship in the shires; those of Bishop Theodred of London and the noblewoman, Wulfwaru, testify to the importance of the manumission of slaves.[76] The will of Athelstan the *aetheling* (c. 1014) orders:

one day's food-rent . . . to the community at Ely on the festival of St Etheldreda; and that 100 pence shall be given to that monastery, and 100 poor people fed there on that day; and may this charitable bequest be for ever performed yearly, whoever shall hold these estates, as long as Christianity shall last. And if they who have the estates will not discharge these charities, the property shall revert to St Etheldreda's.[77]

The story of Durham may be readily told. The memory of St Cuthbert was ever strong in the north, where the community descended from the episcopal monastery at Lindisfarne wandered hither and thither during the Viking raids until it came to rest at Chester-le-Street. There Athelstan paid homage to the saint on at least one visit, leaving superb gifts devoted to the cult of the saint who, it was believed, had assisted his grandfather, Alfred, at his darkest hour.[78] Later in the tenth century, Dunstan himself visited the tomb and found the body of Cuthbert incorrupt, and the cult of the northern hero was strong in Wessex throughout the reform period.[79] In 995 or thereabouts, Ealdhun, the bishop at Chester-le-Street, began to build the first cathedral at Durham on the narrow isthmus above the River Wear. Around this new shrine, which swiftly gathered to itself all the devotion and wealth given to the saint, there coalesced a body of lands privileged with certain liberties and called 'St Cuthbertsland'.[80] According to Symeon of Durham, Ealdhun was a learned monk, yet his foundation did not remain monastic for long. But as a wealthy body of clerics with a long tradition, it enjoyed relative independence in the days of Cnut and fostered learning and art and a sense of the past.[81]

It is hard to assess how many lay people were caught up in the education and culture of the Church. There may well have been lay oblates at Glastonbury and Abingdon from the earliest period of the Benedictine reform, though this is unclear. Certainly the strong bonds of friendship between the leaders of the reform and members of noble families like that of Athelstan probably rested in part on a common interest in Christian culture and learning, and the royal princes like Edgar and, later, Edward were educated at the hands of monks.[82] The most striking single example of lay literacy was the ealdorman Aethelweard, who produced a Latin version of the *Anglo-Saxon Chronicle* for his kinswoman, Matilda. She was abbess of Essen in Germany and a granddaughter of the English queen of Otto I.[83] This work is another example of the continuing contact maintained between England and Germany throughout the tenth century. It reflects too the real interest in national history that lay behind the compilation of the chronicles during this period, a tradition deeply embedded in the outlook of the royal house of Wessex. Aethelweard's style is that of the monks, the so-called 'hermeneutic' style, and that is a good clue to the source of his education. His son, Aethelmaer, shared his father's interest in learning, and both of them were active patrons and interlocutors of Aelfric's. Aethelweard was familiar with extracts from Isidore of Seville, and he used Bede, as well as a version of the chronicle now lost. For part of the reign of Alfred, and for most of the first half of the tenth century, he is able to draw on material otherwise unknown; the work closes with the death of Edgar in 975. It is, for instance, to him that knowledge of the family ties between the house of Wessex and the German royal family is owed. Aldhelm is mentioned with praise, and he responds warmly to Alfred's own translation of Boethius.[84] He seems also to have used the Old English version of Bede's *Ecclesiastical History*, another of Alfred's commissions. It is in all a remarkable work, unique for this period, and perhaps an indication, albeit fragmentary, of a wider circle of lay literacy and culture in late tenth-century England.[85]

Almost all the collections of Anglo-Saxon poetry that now remain date from the turn of the tenth century. Dunstan himself in his youth had a love of ancient songs, and there seems to have been a conscious if Christian interest in the past, both ecclesiastical and archaic. The example and interest of Alfred the Great helped to rekindle that Anglo-Saxon sense of their past which was earlier well-established by the time the great poem *Beowulf* was finished, probably in the eighth century. The text in which this epic is preserved dates from the tenth century.[86] Taste in these matters is reflected in the poem 'The Battle of Maldon', which is the last known epic in the vernacular, composed after the heroic defeat of Bryhtnoth at Maldon in 991.[87] Of comparable vintage is the famous 'Exeter book', and a little later the Caedmon manuscript, which probably originated from Canterbury.[88] These, together with the *'Vercelli Codex'* 'may be seen as representing a conscious attempt to gather together and preserve the vernacular literature of an earlier age'.[89] They reflect too the great common ground of taste and interest between laymen and clergy.[90] Perhaps they reflect too the desire to treasure and restate common values and hopes in a time of resurgent violence and upheaval.[91]

Loyalty, courage and revenge of kinsmen were the proper concern of lay lords and bishops alike, and always had been in early English society. Christianity fashioned and moderated those deep impulses, which were vital to the survival of society. Men were still anxious about the fate of their pagan ancestors, and regarded their obligation to their lord as their ultimate earthly duty. Edgar had to stipulate formally and categorically that abbots and abbesses were to be freed from the heriot, the payment in arms and kind to the king on the occasion of death; but there is little evidence that this ancient custom was ever completely set aside by all senior clergy.[92] Indeed, the figure of the bishop militant and armed remained prominent throughout the Anglo-Saxon period, as wills and battlefield obituaries testify.

Bishops like Wulfstan wove Christian values into the heart of Anglo-Saxon society in order the better to reinforce the basic duties of Christian men. No one could be fiercer in condemning treachery and wanton violence. But over and against loyalty there stood justice, and where necessary clemency, and these too were held out as signs of the ultimate Christian vocation. That the Church in some measure succeeded in creating a lay Christian ethic may be seen in the attempts to moderate the severity of the law and to regulate trade and false coin; also the whole edifice of justice, a partnership between lay lord and bishop under the patronage of the king, represents a marriage between Christian values and the ancient customs of English society. On a different plane altogether, the alms of the laity towards the Church, and perhaps especially towards the poor, reflect a genuine commitment, not solely made out of fear or spiritual self-interest. The

Hyde 'Liber vitae' stands as a memorial to the reality and scope of lay confraternity, the involvement in prayer shared by the monks and their lay benefactors.[93] Moreover, the quality and style of the many gifts of the period to churches, both those extant and those mentioned in wills, reflect the extent to which the styles and tastes of contemporary Christian culture embraced noble and educated men and women, clergy, religious and lay.

This phenomenon must not be idealised as an achievement, for much remained that was cruel and barbarous in English society, especially in Ethelred's reign. Aelfric and Wulfstan are frank and fearlessly outspoken about the shortcomings of their fellow countrymen and the acute moral crisis of their times. But people still turned to the Church, its life and its values, as a source of light and hope in a darkling world, and from it imbibed a love of learning and a love of liberty which was never overwhelmed.

II – the arts

The wealth and beauty of such Anglo-Saxon art as now remains from this period is hard to convey in mere prose. The second half of the tenth century and the first third of the eleventh saw the peak of a movement whose roots lay in the earlier part of the tenth century and in the Carolingian traditions on the continent before that. The vitality of Anglo-Saxon art continued to flourish for almost a full century after the Norman Conquest, leaving some of its finest expressions in, for example, the carvings in Ely Cathedral, which were executed in the early twelfth century.[94] Without doubt, the exhibition publication from the British Museum, *The Golden Age of Anglo-Saxon Art* (1984), is the most comprehensive and invaluable guide to this aspect of Anglo-Saxon history and culture. Detailed descriptions of the works referred to in this chapter can be found in this volume.

The most striking monuments of the art of the tenth-century reform are the fine series of illuminated manuscripts which emanated principally from Winchester and from Canterbury. Dunstan and Ethelwold were themselves master craftsman in the practical arts, and proved to be important patrons of manuscript illumination. The Bosworth Psalter[95] with its noble lines and elaborate coloured initials was almost certainly commissioned by Dunstan for his own use at Canterbury, and it accords to the demands of the Benedictine office. From Winchester came the beautiful Ramsey Psalter, probably commissioned by Oswald for use at Ramsey; the artist who produced the remarkable initials in gold and colour and the imposing line drawing of the crucifixion also worked for a while at Fleury. So dominant was the style of the Winchester artists that it has rightly been designated a school. Its vitality, richness and strength reflect the formidable patronage of Ethelwold himself. The first example of this is the New Minster Charter of 966; it is written in gold, with a famous picture of Edgar, supported by the Virgin and St Peter, offering the reformed monastery in the form of the charter itself to Christ. Both art and contents were powerful propaganda for the new monasticism. The most striking single example of the art of Winchester under Ethelwold is the Benedictional of St Ethelwold and executed by his chaplain, the monk Godemann, who later became abbot of Thorney in 972. It is prefaced by a poem in which Godemann recounts how Ethelwold 'commanded to be made in this book many frames well-adorned and filled with various figures decorated with numerous beautiful colours and with gold'. Prominent among these were miniatures of Etheldreda and Swithun, two of Ethelwold's favourite saints. Of comparable quality is the so-called 'Benedictional of Archbishop Robert', more strictly a pontifical, and probably produced for Aethelgar, abbot of New Minster, then bishop of Selsey and finally Dunstan's successor at Canterbury. Of a later period and less ornate are the Prayerbook of Aelfwine and the New Minster *'Liber vitae'*, written around 1030 by the monk Aelfsin with miniatures in line and colour, one of which portrays Cnut and his queen, Emma, presenting a cross to New Minster. Both the Tiberius and Arundel Psalter and the Winchester Troper remain from slightly later still, full of brilliant line drawings, tinted but not illuminated, of remarkable vigour, poise and execution.

From the two Canterbury houses of Christ Church and St Augustine's there issued a stream of books which has its beginning in the closing years of Dunstan's archiepiscopate.[96] The most notable examples are all books typical of a monastic library: a fine copy of the 'Rule of St Benedict' written and illuminated at St Augustine's around 1000 with intricately decorated initials; and the copy of the *'Regularis concordia'* (probably from Christ Church) which contains the famous picture of Dunstan and Ethelwold either side of King Edgar, who is issuing the decree by which the monks are to be bound. From St Augustine's there remains a copy of Aldhelm's 'On virginity', a favourite tenth-century text, with a fascinating miniature depicting Aldhelm presenting a copy of his work to the abbess and nuns of Barking for whom he wrote it. Probably from St Augustine's also, before the close of the tenth century, comes an edition of Gregory the Great's 'Pastoral care', into which is bound an imposing line drawing of Christ from earlier in the century, comparable with the famous picture in *St Dunstan's Classbook*. This taste in monumental line drawing was not dead, for there is a remarkable figure of 'philosophy' as frontispiece to a copy of Boethius' *Consolation of Philosophy*, also made at St Augustine's at this time. One of several remaining copies from this period of Prudentius' 'Psychomachia' comes from Canterbury, probably Christ Church, and is superbly illustrated with vigour and humour. It is an allegory of the battle between Christian virtues and pagan vices, a perennial and popular theme! From Canterbury too may have come the beautiful Arenberg Gospels, and perhaps the York Gospels as well.

The most notable artist of Canterbury was Eadwy Basan, who flourished at Christ Church in the early eleventh century. A scribe of known firmness of hand and clarity of style, he produced the outstanding Grimbald Gospels for New Minster at Winchester. He illustrated these with portraits of the evangelists, executed by careful line drawing and heavy use of silver and surrounded by superb miniatures and intricate decoration. Closely comparable with this work is the Eadwy Gospels, a book which was exported to Germany before the end of the eleventh century. From his hand also was the Eadwy Psalter, which has a Christ Church kalendar with one of the earliest commemorations of the martyrdom of St Alphege in 1012. The only full-page miniature in this work is of St Benedict and some monks; at the foot of the saint lies Eadwy himself, prostrate in humility. It has been described as the best extant example of the integration of line drawing and fully coloured painting.

Eadwy also had a hand in one of the most remarkable books to have emerged from Christ Church, Canterbury, in the early eleventh century. Over a period of perhaps two decades, and at the likely behest of Archbishop Aethelnoth himself, scribes and artists at Canterbury laboured to produce an elaborate copy of the

Utrecht Psalter. The Utrecht Psalter was an imported copy of the psalms made in Rheims in the early ninth century, illustrated throughout by intricate and lively line drawings conveying the contents of each psalm. This proved a work of great educational value and wide artistic influence, stimulating the strong native tradition of line drawing with colour to new, more vigorous and scintillating heights.

The wealth of illumination and artistic skill in English monastic houses at this time was by no means confined to Winchester and Canterbury. Interesting and attractive works remain from houses as diverse as Winchcombe and, possibly, Crowland and Bury. There is a fine pontifical from Sherborne, probably commissioned by Wulfsige, the first monastic bishop of that see. The Salisbury Psalter contains remarkable illustrated initials, and may have been produced at the nunnery at Shaftesbury. From an unknown genius of the Winchester school comes the outstanding Missal of Robert of Jumièges, a sacramentary drawn from a Peterborough model and replete with colourful and expressive line drawings and miniatures. It is a rare and wonderful book whose scribe was responsible also for the Trinity Gospels, the Kederminster Gospels, most of another set of gospels which came to rest for a time at Canterbury and the remarkable Copenhagen Gospels. All these carry outstanding illuminations, and the last example bears affinities to the Lindisfarne Gospels of an earlier period, then at Durham.

This profusion of artistic prowess expressed itself also in the skill and intricacy of metalwork, ivory carving, glass, jewellery and ceramics for which the Anglo-Saxons were justly famous throughout Europe.[97] Dunstan and Ethelwold were remembered for the works of craftsmanship of their own making which they donated to the several religious houses of their foundation, and the impetus for monks and clergy to be skilled craftsmen following their example found formal expression in the 'Canons of Edgar' issued by Wulfstan.[98] Such examples as now remain are fragmentary and often uprooted from their original setting. Some, like textiles, embroidery and precious jewellery have perforce perished. What remains, mainly fragments of metalwork and carving in ivory, stone and wood, reflect vividly the power of the prevailing styles of the tenth-century reform. Most of these remnants were designed for ecclesiastical or religious purposes. There is a spouted jug, possibly from Winchester, and probably part of a cruet for liturgical use. A censer cover from London Bridge is so close in design to the famous one from Canterbury as to indicate a workshop producing such objects there. All these are worked with designs closely allied to those used in the production of manuscripts at both centres. The Pershore censer cover is of similar architectural design, but more elaborate in its decoration and bearing the name of its maker, Godric, probably a craftsman and perhaps a monk of the monastery there. A portable altar of porphyry set in silver is inscribed with delicate and expressive figures of saints and angels, reminiscent of the drawings in the Hyde 'Liber vitae', a work of comparable date. Finally, a little silver sundial, found at Canterbury, embodies precisely principles laid down by Byrhtferth for such a device in his 'Manual'.

The finest examples of such Anglo-Saxon craftsmanship are perhaps the remaining carved ivories. This was an art form which probably began in England during the reign of Alfred,[99] and which reached its peak at Winchester during the reform period. There remain a triangular panel bearing winged angels and a panel portraying the nativity; both reflect the fusion of Carolingian influences with native English love of pattern and intricacy. An oval box, carved out of ivory, tells a story of a miraculous recovery of a chalice to a monastery for celebration of the mass; carved in the universal Winchester style, it conveys a tale very similar in essence to that experienced by one of Ethelwold's clergy in Aelfric's 'Life of Ethelwold'. Fine free-standing figures of the Virgin and St John, now at St Omer, intended for a crucifixion scene, express the profound emotional intensity of many comparable manuscript portraits. They are closely associated with famous productions of the Winchester school like the Benedictional of St Ethelwold, and they epitomise the genius and beauty of that artistic centre. Most of the other examples are crosses, either pectoral, processional or devotional, reflecting the popularity of that subject in Anglo-Saxon life and religion, and demonstrating the complete range of tastes and technical skills of the period. Powerful demonstrations of Anglo-Saxon skill at carving exist in the form of caskets in wood and ivory and some individual panels; also in the few remaining examples of stone carving, notably the flying angels at the Saxon church at Bradford-on-Avon, the cross-head at Durham Cathedral decorated with the Lamb of God and a piece of narrative frieze depicting a pagan theme, found recently at Winchester. Small fragments of Anglo-Saxon glass, together with ceramic tiles and pieces of bell moulds, from the site of the Old Minster, have also been found at Winchester; they are small tokens of the great industry of the tenth-century monks as related in the documentary sources.[100]

The tenth century witnessed major developments in church music in England and on the continent. A copy of the Winchester Cantatorium remains from the eleventh century, and is itself a copy of a text produced between 978 and 984. It contains music for liturgical drama similar to that prescribed in the *'Regularis concordia'* for Easter; also tropes or musical additions to the basic plainsong of the chant.[101] Three musical texts survive from Worcester which display the debt owed by pre-conquest church music in England to the exemplar from Corbie which Ethelwold imported to regularise the chant of the monks at the beginning of the reform.[102] Music in the monasteries of England swiftly took root and developed in distinctive ways; the steady elaboration of the chant for the offices and the mass mirrored developments on the continent, with extensions in the forms of tropes which were sometimes quasi-poetical settings of saints' lives.[103] In this period, the beginnings of polyphony may be detected; in the Winchester Troper, for example, primitive harmony is prescribed in pieces called *organa*, and in the first life of Oswald there is an impressive description of the richness of monastic singing at the dedication of Ramsey in 991:

> The monastic rank began devoutly to sing to God, the precentor hold-
> ing forth with three choirs. Having finished the solemn response of
> jubilation, the hymns of praise continued. . . . For the master of the
> organs ascended with his band into the highest seats above the
> people [i.e. a westwork?], where he aroused by his full-toned sound
> the minds of the faithful. . . . Then the choir . . . sought to sing
> sweetly alternating praises: when the right-hand part sounded forth
> with holy voices a sound of melody, the left then replied in polyphony
> with a joyful noise of praise.[104]

Dunstan and Ethelwold played a leading role in the revival of music in the monasteries and cathedrals of England. Ethelwold, for example, constructed an organ for Abingdon and Dunstan constructed one for Malmesbury.[105] The instrument at Winchester in the cathedral required seventy men to pump it, and it emitted a correspondingly magnificent blast, according to Wulstan![106] Oswald was remembered by his monks for his lovely singing voice.[107]

Dunstan's own contemplative spirituality was permeated by a musical dimension which left a tangible mark on the monastic tradition in England. According to the first life of Oswald, monks were singing a version of the *Kyries* which they believed Dunstan had received in a heavenly vision.[108] This was the *'Kyrie rex splendens'*, a chant widely popular in England in the generations following. It was Eadmer who directly associated it with Dunstan,[109] but it rests on older traditions about Dunstan's musical genius. In the first life, it is recorded that at a young age Dunstan heard the harp on the wall play the antiphon, *'Gaudent in coelis'*;[110] during the heavenly vision of his mother, Dunstan was taught a new tone for the antiphon, *'O rex gentium'*, which he commanded in the morning to be written down and learned by his monks.[111] Towards the end of his life, he enjoyed a vision of heavenly virgins singing the hymn of Sedulius, *'Cantemus socii Domino'*, in the ancient shrine of the Virgin at the back of St Augustine's, Canterbury.[112] According to this biographer, 'Dunstan often learnt by spiritual vigilance and divine intuition the melodies of sacred songs and other fitting praises of God, even while asleep',[113] and it was to sing the *'Sanctus'* in Rome before the pope in the company of the heavenly throng that Dunstan was summoned on the eve of his death in 988.[114] In this way, Dunstan's own reputation as a creative musician is recorded; so too is the intimate connection at this time between the generation of a rich monastic chant and a deeply contemplative and at times charismatic spirituality.[115]

Throughout the heyday of the flowering of the tenth century, English contacts with the continent remained strong, and influences were exerted in both directions. The impact of Carolingian art forms and ideas was fundamental to the whole revival of Christian culture in the tenth century, on both sides of the Channel. In the field of art this is evident in the way in which English sculpture, and especially the use of ivory, reflect the influence of the early tenth-century Metz school; the rich Lotharingian tradition which determined, for example, the pose of the figures in the nativity panel from Winchester.[116] Another line of influence was through the Utrecht Psalter, the most notable example of direct continental influence upon English style; the Leofric Missal and the Harley Psalter are two of the most prominent consequences.[117] In the Benedictional of St Ethelwold both style and iconography reflect the way in which classical ninth-century models had been thoroughly absorbed by an Anglo-Saxon artist of the first order who revitalised them with a superb use of colour which was quite unprecedented.[118] Edith, Edgar's daughter, was instructed by two foreign clergy, Radbod of Rheims and Benno of Trier, who was also the artist who decorated the royal nun's chapel of St Denis at Wilton.[119] Benno is an interesting example of a craftsman at work both in his home city and in England, a tangible link between two important schools of art at the time, perhaps.

The friendship which existed between prominent religious houses on both sides of the Channel was demonstrated in the exchange of books and artefacts and also of craftsmen. The Boulogne Gospels are an example; they were written at St Bertin but illuminated by the artist who decorated the Ramsey Psalter. There is here a direct link too with Odbert, abbot of St Bertin's, whose correspondence with the two archbishops after Dunstan still remains.[120] Similarly, a copy of the 'Phenomena' of Aratus, an important astronomical text, which survives in the company of two treatises by Abbo of Fleury, was written at Fleury but illustrated by the same Ramsey artist. Ramsey sent lavish gifts to Gauzlin, abbot of Fleury (1004–29), in the period after Oswald's death, and a number of prominent works of English art ended up in continental monasteries at this time; the Eadwy Gospels are a case in point. Anglo-Saxon craftsmen also worked abroad, for example in Scandinavia, Germany and Ireland. Sometimes the donors were kings: a Lobbes Gospel of the ninth century, now in the British Museum, was the gift of Otto I to Edgar, and it is quite likely that the Arenberg Gospels were part of Cnut's gifts to the church at Cologne.[121] Links with Germany remained strong as Aethelweard's dedication to his kinswoman, the abbess of Essen, shows; also there was an Irish house in Cologne, and Gregory, abbot of Einsiedeln (964–96), was an Anglo-Saxon of royal descent.[122] The correspondence associated with Dunstan and his immediate successors testifies to the relative ease with which communications across the Channel could be maintained, and the importance which leading churchmen attached to them.[123]

This interaction of continental and English idioms occurred within the wider unity of a revived Christendom whose fundamental imagery and symbolism were being used to reinterpret traditional Christian values in the light of the new political developments on the one hand, and the resurgence of organised monasticism on the other.

The striking feature of tenth-century art is that it is predominantly Christ-centred. For example, in the Tiberius Psalter, the psalms are illuminated by reference to the life of King David and to the life of Christ himself, the ancestor interpreting the descendant. There is a marvellous box-wood casket of the mid-eleventh century on which the principal moments of Christ's life and death are carved, surrounded by angels and elaborate carved relief. The association of the cross, the eucharist and the doomsday forms another common theme, for example in an early eleventh-century reliquary cross with an inscribed allusion to the poem 'The dream of the rood'. The Anglo-Saxon love of intricate intertwining of plants, with animal forms moving within, finds supreme expression in a pierced panel, carved out of ivory, displaying an inhabited vine, the symbol of Christ, the true vine (cf. John 15) – a symbol capable of conveying the dependence both of creation upon the creative word and of the Church upon its Lord.

This Christological emphasis spoke directly to the Church's articulation of the role of Christian monarchy. The English coronation order appealed both to the Old Testament history of monarchy and to the example of Christ, both as servant and Lord, in order to establish the duties of the new king and to assert the sacral aura which now surrounded 'the Lord's Anointed'.[124] In the iconography of this time, and originating in England, Christ appears as a crowned figure, to whom also crowned magi offer gifts.[125] The first known example of this is found in the Benedictional of St Ethelwold, but the example was soon followed in Germany, at Trier, Reichenau, Regensburg and Hildesheim. This was without precedent in either Byzantine or Carolingian art, although the latter had occasionally portrayed Christ bearing the victor's wreath. The tenth century switched the emphasis away from victory to kingship as such; Christ the King becomes the over-arching motif. The kingship of the magi was deduced from the prophetic language of Psalm 71. 10 and was hinted at, for example, in the appropriate illumination in the Utrecht Psalter. But in the Benedictional of St Ethelwold, the leading royal figure appears to offer his crown – in fact three overlapping gold diadems – to the infant Christ. The imperial overtones are clear: Christ the King is king of kings. Thus the theological and cosmological justification is declared for a Christian view of kingship as a 'type' of Christ, to whom other lesser kings might make obeisance for the better ordering of a Christian *imperium*. The royalty of earthly monarchs is derived only and directly from Christ himself: an essentially subordinate but very real and potent authority. Both in Ottonian Germany and in England under Edgar, this mystical bond between the ruler and his *imperium* and the rule of Christ is developed and enshrined, not least in the Coronation *'Ordo'*. The Christian ruler was called therefore to a peculiar and unique form of *imitatio Christi*, and it is not hard to account for cross-fertilisation between the imperial court and the English Church and royal family. The timing of the production of the Benedictional of St Ethelwold is crucial to this iconographic development: it cannot have been produced before 971 and is unlikely to have been completed much after the date of Edgar's death in 975; it is therefore very close to the 'imperial' coronation of Edgar at Bath in 973. It is perhaps striking that the benedictional contains 'an unprecedented representation of the Coronation of the Virgin', one of the many regal motifs in this cycle of illumination,[126] exemplifying and reinforcing the sacred vocations of both kings and queens. It is not hard to detect the political vision and determination of Ethelwold and Dunstan behind this remarkable and influential development. The speed with which the German artists took it up is testimony to its potency and appeal there. It illuminates perfectly that 'complex political & artistic dialogue then existing between the two countries'.[127]

By the time Cnut ascended the English throne in 1016, England possessed a Christian culture which was richly developed and mature in its artistic expression. At the heart of this phenomenon lay the monasteries which had become the centres of culture and learning and artistic skill. The art and learning of the period interpreted and furthered the reform and renewal in both Church and society which by now had been underway for over a hundred years. The vision and plans of Alfred the Great and his successors had borne fruit in a remarkable and lasting way. At the same time, English monastic culture was never far removed from developments on the continent, and lines of communication and influence ran both ways throughout the whole period.

In no way was the life of the monasteries cut off from the wider life of Church and society. Rather the monastic life and culture served the needs of both clerical and lay taste and belief. The monasteries were the focus of that balance between Church and society which is the salient feature of England in the tenth century. It is possible to discern the ways in which secular and religious life permeated each other, sometimes blurring the distinctly spiritual vocation of the clergy and monks, but more often reinterpreting social values within the light of Christian vocation and principles.

The monastic reformers would have regarded the stability and spirituality of the monasteries as the essential preconditions for that profound artistic flowering which is the glory of the tenth century. The necessary stability of life inevitably embroiled the monks in the ways of the world: monasteries needed endowment and protection and artists needed patronage and wealth. Yet the brilliance of the age from the artistic point of view, and the diligent pursuit of a learning that was not exclusively clerical, imparted a strength and a splendour to English Christian society at the time which the vicissitudes of politics in no way tarnished or undermined.

12

ST DUNSTAN

*I*T has been well said that if the tenth century gave shape to English history, Dunstan gave shape to the tenth century.'[1] The fact that he lived to the great age of almost 80 (909–88), and presided at Canterbury for a full twenty-eight of those years (one of the longest primacies in English history), made him a legend in his own lifetime. Throughout the reigns of Eadred and Edgar, he had exercised a unique influence at the heart of ecclesiastical and political affairs, and if his political role under Ethelred was less active, his reputation was in no way diminished. His own example both as an abbot and a bishop undergirded his influence; in words used to describe an earlier monastic bishop, Martin of Tours, 'Full alike of dignity and courtesy, he kept up the position of a bishop properly, yet in such a way as not to lay aside the objects and virtues of a monk'.[2] The friendship of his fellow bishops, the devotion of former pupils and the affectionate esteem shown him by foreign churchmen testify to his warmth and standing as a person. He was regarded both by Abbo of Fleury and by his first biographer as a scholar of ability and dedication, and he was remembered at Glastonbury and elsewhere both as an educator and a master craftsman. At Canterbury itself, it was his memory as a formidable archbishop and yet a sensitive, contemplative and gifted musician which lingered into the eleventh century. When men looked back to the 'golden age' of Edgar, it was the outstanding character of Dunstan, and also of Ethelwold and Oswald, which they identified as the determining factor. Discretion and constancy are mentioned both by the first biographer and by Aelfric in his 'Life of Swithun' as the hallmark of Dunstan's character.[3] His friends have left on record something of their feeling towards him, the affection and veneration which help us to understand how truly Dunstan was the grand figure of his day. To them he is the 'immoveable mountain', the 'pillar of God' (Adelard); 'unshakeable bulwark', 'magnificent figure' (writer of 'Life of Ethelwold'); 'the glory of his native land' (writer of 'Life of Oswald'); and 'Dunstan the well-loved', 'outstanding priest' (Abbo of Fleury); he is addressed by others as 'beloved Dunstan', 'our Dunstan', and, in the words of the *Liber Eliensis*, 'the jewel of the English'.[4] The 'Life of Oswald' especially emphasises his spiritual stature: 'a glorious father-in-God', 'a man of Apostolic character', 'a faithful bishop and oak-like in hope'.[5] Both this writer and Wulstan, the cantor at Winchester, regarded Dunstan as a saint in his own lifetime: 'this blessed man';[6] and Wulstan describes his countenance as 'angelic' more than once. The correspondence associated with Dunstan from friends at home and abroad echoes this reverence and esteem.[7]

The cult of Dunstan as a saint sprang up almost immediately after his death in 988. Within ten years, Ethelred confirmed the will of Aethelric of Bocking, a man he had suspected of complicity towards Swein's invasion plans. This granted land at Bocking to Christ Church, Canterbury, and, at the archbishop's intercession, the king relented 'for the sake of Christ Church and of St Mary and of St Dunstan and of all the saints who rest at Canterbury'.[8] Shortly after, around the year 1000, Wulfric, abbot of St Augustine's, Canterbury, wrote to Abbo of Fleury asking him to turn the first life of Dunstan into verse 'for the love of that magnificent man, St Dunstan'.[9] The influence of Wulfstan of York ensured that in the general legislation issued by Cnut shortly after his accession, in which the broad pattern of Anglo-Saxon laws was confirmed, the feast of St Dunstan on 19 May was for the first time formally enjoined.[10] It is also from this early part of the eleventh century that the two earliest prayers to St Dunstan date: the first anonymous, the second inscribed in Byrhtferth's 'Manual'; there is a hymn of similar date imploring Dunstan's heavenly assistance against the marauding Danes.[11]

The cult of St Dunstan was fostered not only by the recent memory of his goodness and greatness. It rested also upon the belief that miracles were wrought by him at his shrine in the cathedral at Canterbury. In his 'Life of Swithun', Aelfric recalls the role of Dunstan and Ethelwold in establishing the peace and prosperity of Edgar's reign, and asserts that divine approval of their labours is confirmed by 'the miracles which God works through them'.[12] The second life of Dunstan was written to enable monks to commemorate his memory at the night office in a series of 'lections', and the last of these demonstrates clearly why men numbered Dunstan among the saints in heaven. In the list of saints' resting-places in the Hyde *'Liber vitae'*, St Dunstan alone represents the saints found at Christ Church, Canterbury.[13] Some of the kalendars of this period begin to record the commemoration of his feast on 19 May, and also the ordination feast at Canterbury on 21 October.[14] It is probably to this period that the first dedications of churches to St Dunstan date: in Canterbury itself; in rural parts associated with his memory, notably Mayfield in East Sussex and Baltonsborough, his birthplace; also Sapperton in Gloucestershire in connection with a miracle; and two parishes on the eastern and western fringes of Anglo-Saxon London.[15]

The miraculous in the life of Dunstan, and the miracles he was believed to have wrought after his death, prompted the writing of the earliest lives. The whole cycle of the five lives of Dunstan, and the accounts of the miracles appended to two of them, afford a fascinating picture of the way hagiography tended to develop during this period, and of the way miracles were regarded and recorded.[16] Both Ethelwold and Oswald were also venerated as saints who worked miracles, and taken together with the reputation of Edith, Edward the martyr and Alphege, they demonstrate a notable revival of Christian thaumaturgy in late Anglo-Saxon Church and society. In the minds of contemporaries the greatest achievement was to have produced saints who, like Swithun, Etheldreda and Cuthbert before them, could ensure the intervention of heaven itself, and at whose intercession the relentless course of nature and suffering might be averted.[17]

Full justice can hardly be done to the life and memory of Dunstan without careful assessment of his reputation as a miracle worker. It is, however, possible to discriminate between the various miracles with which he was involved. The first main group of miracles actually occurred during his own lifetime, and were on the whole concerned with his own spiritual development. The miracles are mainly recorded by the first biographer, who received them either at first hand from Dunstan when an old man or from members of his *familia* and friends at Canterbury. They are almost without exception strictly autobiographical reminiscences: his childhood visions at Glastonbury, the crisis over marriage and his deliverance from illness, his narrow escape at Winchester in the company of Bishop Alphege the monk and his vision of his dead friend, Wulfred. Some of his divine intimations occurred at critical turning-points in his life: the miraculous escape of Edmund hunting reverses his estimate of Dunstan and opens the door to the abbacy of Glastonbury; Dunstan's reprimand by the apostles occurs after his refusal of a bishopric, a decision he lived perhaps to regret. Some are of a more psychological nature, like the vision he received while in exile of the riven community at Glastonbury, where cabal and intrigue had hastened his departure. Likewise his premonitions of the murder of Edmund, the demise of Eadred and the likely difficulties of Edwy's reign reflect the depth of his involvement in political affairs. Other premonitions, for example of the child's death at Glastonbury and of the bursar's impending end, also at Glastonbury, are more pastoral in nature. His confidence that God would provide all things necessary for the journey to Rome, despite the panic of his steward, is testimony to the basic faith of a prayerful man. The remaining lifetime 'miracles' are signs of a holy life and the spiritual conflict it entails; they are all of a contemplative nature, and some reflect the way Dunstan's musical sense deepened this spiritual apprehension. The story of the harp on the wall which played unaided a particular antiphon associated with martyrdom is the epitome of this process. Some of Dunstan's visions brought him face to face with evil and the way in which that evil was ever working to undermine his labours at Glastonbury in particular; on one occasion at least, Dunstan was frank enough to intimate that this sometimes occurred at the threshold of sleep during a vigil. Other visions were directly heavenly and spiritual. The descent of the Holy Spirit in the form of a dove upon his old friend, the godly widow Aethelfleda at Glastonbury; the marriage in heaven of his own mother; and the singing chorus of virgins at Canterbury; all these clearly touch deeply the heart of his own spiritual life, of which the musical outpouring was but a tangible sign. Similarly his gift of tears and ecstasy during the eucharist reflected the deeply charismatic character of his spirituality, a sign of sanctity which his first biographer compares with the example of Martin of Tours. It is notable and interesting that it is these spiritual 'miracles' of Dunstan that are recounted in the first life of Oswald, and which the writer associates with the saint's posthumous miracles of his own day.[18]

The second life, written by the monk Adelard, marks a transition point between personal spiritual reminiscence, albeit framed in miraculous language, and more formal hagiography supported by 'typical' miraculous happenings. On the one hand, Adelard taps traditions unknown to the first biographer which confirm the strong personal ties between Dunstan and his uncle Athelm, archbishop of Canterbury; also those with the family of Edgar, whose birth Dunstan presages; with Oda, the archbishop who prophetically consecrated Dunstan to Canterbury; with Alphege, whom Dunstan sent to Winchester by divine command; and with Aelfgar, his chaplain, later bishop of Elmham, who had a vision of Dunstan's impending death. In addition, he intrudes two stories which are strictly typical of hagiography: the legend of the miraculous kindling of Dunstan's mother's candle at Candlemas in Glastonbury while the child was still in the womb; and an account of how Dunstan managed to stay the fall of a beam of wood during building operations in the church at Glastonbury.[19] Both these stories have close parallels in Aelfric's 'Life of Ethelwold'. Further comparison with this work is, however, instructive, for all the miraculous happenings in Ethelwold's life bear by contrast the stamp of his temperament as a monastic disciplinarian, an abbot among his monks and a bishop amidst his clergy. In neither of the early lives of Dunstan or Ethelwold are there any accounts either of healing miracles or of exorcisms, which is intriguing in the light of their posthumous reputations. Nor for that matter are there any in the first life of Oswald, although Oda the archbishop is credited with one during his youth.[20]

The later biographers of both Dunstan and Oswald, Osbern and Eadmer of Canterbury, append several more 'typical' miracles condign to their subject's more distant reputation. Osbern tells how Dunstan interceded for the soul of Edwy and how he called forth a spring of water while dedicating a church when he was archbishop. He introduces the story of the speaking crucifix at a synod at Winchester, and includes the tale from the chronicle of Dunstan's miraculous preservation when the house collapsed during the synod at Calne. He makes great play, as well he might after the debacle of 1066, with Dunstan's purported prophesies against Ethelred, and concludes with the strange story, which can now be found appended to one of the manuscripts of the first life of Dunstan, about the way Dunstan's death bed was elevated into the air just prior to his demise. With Eadmer the lifetime tradition grows more remote and legendary: he gives the notorious stories of how Dunstan tweaked the devil's nose with his tongs at Glastonbury, how he hung his chasuble on a sunbeam and how he corrected the alignment of the wooden church at Mayfield by leaning on it;[21] all strange stories which have served the reputation of Dunstan ill.

William of Malmesbury is more judicious: he refers to Dunstan's vision about Ethelwold's role in the development of monasticism in England, which happened while they were both at Glastonbury, and this he derives from Wulstan's 'Life of Ethelwold'. From the 'Life of Edith' he includes Dunstan's prophecies about the sanctity of that virgin before and after death. These, together with the delightful story in Osbern about how Dunstan predicted the imminent deaths of his friends Ethelwold and the bishop of Rochester at their last meeting, illustrate the way in which some of these miracles sprang out of the close web of relationships which existed in Dunstan's generation.[22] Even the proverbial tale about Dunstan's condemnation of the claims of the renegade monk Alwold against Glastonbury has a root in the turbulent upheavals of Ethelred's reign.[23] What is striking is that more of a legendary character has not insinuated itself into the later hagiography of Dunstan.

Behind the way these early saints' lives were written stands the potent tradition of Christian hagiography which formed the staple diet of monastic culture. The fascination with the examples and reputations of earlier English saints like Cuthbert and Etheldreda and more recent if obscure characters like Swithun and Grimbald permeated the thinking of tenth-century English Christians.[24] The way a monastic saint's life was told was influenced particularly by the three great and classic lives – of Anthony by Athanasius, of Martin of Tours by Sulpitius Severus and of Benedict by Gregory the Great.[25]

Many of the details of the miraculous in the life of Dunstan or of Ethelwold find their precedent in, for example, the 'Life of Benedict': childhood precosity of religious experience; a contemplative beginning as a virtual hermit; an attempt on the saint's life and instances of deep and jealous opposition from demons and men; also the capacity to open the spiritual eyes of others to the reality of evil, to produce water out of a rock, to preserve the lives of those at risk while at a distance and to intervene successfully in difficult building operations; finally a simple trust in providence and a running warfare with the devil. The first life of Oswald demonstrates on numerous occasions the devotion of the tenth-century monks to the cult of Benedict, a cult much revivified by the monastery at Fleury which claimed his remains. It would be surprising if the famous life of that saint did not fashion profoundly the way in which they regarded their own monastic 'fathers', Dunstan, Ethelwold and Oswald. But compared with the 'Life of Benedict' by Gregory, the fantastic is conspicuous by its relative absence both from the earliest lives and from the post-conquest hagiography of these English saints. At all points the respective characters of each figure can be recovered through the miraculous reputation, and the extent to which any one miraculous happening accords with an earlier 'model' reflects the current of spiritual comprehension at the time which identified such events as genuine milestones in a saint's spiritual pilgrimage. The pattern of earlier saints' lives, and of the Bible itself, is the norm by which such spiritual moments are judged because this is the way, broadly, that true Christian spiritual growth unfolds. The first life of Dunstan, for example, leans heavily upon the 'Life of Benedict' in the way the story of a man's inner spiritual pilgrimage and its interaction upon external events is told; but the fact that much which apparently happened in the life of Benedict did not happen to Dunstan or Ethelwold confirms that the detail given about them is firmly rooted in what was actually remembered about them. This understatement, whether by the subject or by his biographer, is significant as a preventative to mere hagiography.

With the miracles accomplished after a saint's death, different criteria apply, and the historical reputation of a particular saint is only enhanced by an indirect apprehension. What emerges is why men continued to regard him as a saint, and here contemporary experience and expectation tended to supersede the historical memory in the minds of all but a few.

The cult of saints in Christianity has its roots in the devotions paid at the tombs of martyrs in fourth-century Roman society and, slightly later, in the memory of ascetics, holy men and women and notable bishops.[26] Two things predominate: the importance of the place, either where the person lived and worked or, more usually, his or her burial site; and the essentially popular character of the devotion, fortified by a well-defined pattern of miracles, which the authorities of the Church in due course confirmed and at times exploited. The miracles of Dunstan are no exception to this general pattern: they are carefully recorded by one of the monks of Christ Church, Canterbury, Osbern, who wrote just after the Norman Conquest. He was himself a child educated by men who remembered the latter days of Dunstan and the beginnings of his cult, and he claims to have been an eye witness to miracles on more than one occasion.[27] His successor, Eadmer, also a monk of Christ Church, adds little of note to this cycle. The miracles ascribed to Dunstan fall into several groups, and parallels can be drawn with the miracles attributed to both Oswald and Ethelwold, and also those of Swithun as recorded by Aelfric.[28]

The majority of the miracles occur in proximity to Dunstan's shrine at

Canterbury Cathedral, which in the days before the great fire of 1067 was before the high altar. Lanfranc in the course of his rebuilding translated the relics, and Anselm placed them and those of Alphege on either side of the new high altar.[29] There are healing miracles and exorcisms, also miracles of liberation from penance or prison. Another group entails actual visions of Dunstan himself, either in the cathedral or in the vicinity of Canterbury, often with warnings or messages being entrusted to the recipient. Lanfranc himself was apparently the beneficiary of Dunstan's heavenly assistance in his role both as archbishop and as head of the monastic community at Canterbury, and on occasion the saint was believed to have intervened in disputes in favour of Christ Church. Anselm also was vouchsafed by Dunstan a premonition of his own impending death.[30] Some of the miracles are directly monastic, affecting the discipline and morale of individual monks as well as of the whole community; Osbern himself claims personal experience of the saint's help, and his own deep devotion to his memory is but thinly veiled throughout. What is lacking from this cycle, at least at Osbern's hands, is more standard miracles of the almost magical kind. For example, Eadmer in his 'Miracles of St Oswald' records, in addition to a few miracles at the shrine and on the occasion of the translation of the relics at Worcester, stories of how contact with Oswald's drinking cup cured a monk at Ramsey, how the staff of Oswald cured a dumb man and how the portable shrine of the saint warded off both fire and pestilence on several occasions. It is interesting that it is this kind of secondary miracle that Eadmer sees fit to intrude also into Osbern's cycle of miracles attributed to Dunstan, miracles of which Osbern himself was expressly wary.[31] Healings at the shrine are common to the earliest traditions of Dunstan, Ethelwold and Oswald, and this is the proper starting-point for any critical enquiry.[32]

Osbern's cycle of Dunstan miracles repays close scrutiny from several angles. As with all bodies of miracle stories drawn from a particular place and spanning a limited period, much may be learnt incidentally from the details of the separate stories about the beliefs, conditions and customs of the time, in this case the Church and community at Canterbury before and after the Norman Conquest. The reason why the stories came to be written down is always revealing. Osbern recorded these acts of Dunstan in order that his cult should not be set aside by the new Norman regime; he is careful to emphasise the impact the memory of the saint made upon Lanfranc himself, but this is against a background, not admitted, of Dunstan's temporary eclipse from the liturgical life at Canterbury. Both the 'Constitutions of Lanfranc' and the contemporary kalendars show that the feast of Dunstan was dropped altogether for a while, probably for political reasons, after the conquest. It was Anselm who was responsible for Dunstan's formal rehabilitation.[33] Osbern's work is on a par with Aelfric's account of the burgeoning cult of St Swithun at Winchester during the time of Ethelwold; both blend the immediacy of personal experience and enquiry with a sober judgement which in both cases is well-rooted in Christian theology.[34]

Osbern's preface and conclusion are notable for their frankness and rationality:

> For this reason, all that has been deemed worthy to be read here we
> invite you to believe; for if people wish themselves or what they write
> about their own times to be believed, then let them believe us when
> they hear those things related which we have been able to see for
> ourselves. For if they wish to have a right estimation of themselves by
> those who follow them, then they ought to concede the same and

rightly to those who went before them. For if what had to be written down does not suit their own times, let them not immediately accuse us of falsity, as if because in one age the providence of God was not hidden, it should not still be possible to correct the corruptions of men in another age, when the grace of miracles always has an opportunity in all manner of times and places.

By reference both to the Bible and to normal human analogies, Osbern dispenses with the fallacious argument, common to all ages, that just because something does not seem possible or probable it cannot therefore happen. At the end of his labours, Osbern alludes to some of the miracles which Eadmer would later see fit to record, and with critical irony refuses to trade upon the patience of his hearers.

Whatever I have recalled, I do not doubt must seem incredible but for the fact that nothing is so if Christ be the author of the work. So let us magnify God and so exalt with confidence the name of Dunstan, for we should reverence him in God.[35]

Osbern's 'Miracles of Dunstan' in fact reflects his abilities more surely than does his 'Life of Dunstan', though both proved of lasting popularity throughout the Middle Ages. They comprise a shrewd and careful case-study of a powerful cult at different stages of its local development, and there is little that is really fantastic or sentimental.

Osbern's 'Miracles of Dunstan' falls into four main parts. He begins with a simple account of the earliest local miracles at Dunstan's shrine: a blind man cured; three former pensioners of Dunstan's also cured of blindness; and a cautionary tale of a noble priest from Folkestone, cured *in extremis* but still too proud for his own good. These signal events precipitated the popular cult and people began to come from far and wide: a crippled youth was restored; a blind child, whom the clergy tested by rolling apples along the church floor, was cured; and a simple tale is told of an old woman, blind, who left the shrine disappointed but who was healed crossing the bridge in the moment of shock when she lost contact with her guide. Two curious figures are outlined: a tailed German priest exorcised at the tomb and a giant of a man paralysed but now cured and able to offer his musical talents in the praise of Dunstan. Another cripple met Dunstan in a vision on his way back from many futile hours of prayer at the cathedral and was duly promised a complete cure on a certain day. The reason for the delay? Dunstan had been involved in defending the interests of Christ Church against the predatory claims of one Aelfric 'Bata'. This last story reflects obliquely upon the tensions within the monastic community at Canterbury in the years leading up to the conquest.

The next sequence of miracles are those drawn from the childhood memory of Osbern himself and from the pre-conquest traditions of his community. A nun, devout yet blind from birth, was healed during the feast of St Bartholomew and St Ouen: 'we boys turned our faces towards her, peeping with our eyes & nodding to and fro!' But the boys remembered also how the dean, Godric, had intervened to spare them a beating from their schoolmasters, furious at this marring of such a celebration. There follows a most vivid account of how Osbern, while serving at the eucharist, guided a little old woman with a hopelessly deformed daughter to the tomb of Dunstan. It is a harrowing picture, but has a joyful ending. This was but one of several healings of cripples. A boyish tale of how the saint intervened again to spare the boys a beating from their educators is overshadowed by a warning to the community over the body of an unbaptised infant son of Earl Harold of Wessex. But this event is symptomatic of a crisis within the community, and was regarded by many as presaging the destruction of the old church and monastery by fire in 1067, an event which in more ways than one marked the end of an era.

The most striking part of Osbern's work concerns the miracles that happened during the primacy of Lanfranc and the impact they made on the life of the community at Christ Church which he was seeking to reform. When Lanfranc was translating Dunstan's remains prior to rebuilding the cathedral, two knights hung on to the coffin for sanctuary from Scoland, abbot of St Augustine's. While this embarrassing impasse was still underway, the chastened abbot burst in to make his peace, terrified by a vision of Dunstan in his wrath! Lanfranc himself became embroiled in the cult of Dunstan in a dispute with Oda of Bayeux over lands purloined from Christ Church; the saint ensured a painless victory. The most fascinating story takes on a decidedly psychological hue. It concerns a young monk called Ethelward who became mentally unbalanced and possessed, as a consequence of what appears to have been a homosexual liaison with a fellow monk and protégé of Lanfranc's. His deliverance was protracted and traumatic for all concerned and his plight evidently pointed a dagger at the heart of the community's life. Lanfranc's own charisma proved powerless despite repeated attempts to exorcise and counsel him. Finally they left him in the relic house with the body of Dunstan: 'only a certain monk remained who had a special and close affection for the lord Dunstan, and who carried on his memory as much as he could in many ways'.[36] Using Dunstan's own processional cross, this monk implored the saint's help, and the young man was calmly and completely delivered. It is a sharp insight into the intense life of a monastery and the cross-current of pastoral, psychological, personal and spiritual forces at work. The section concerning Lanfranc concludes with Dunstan delivering Lanfranc from a fatal illness, and also his chaplain from a severe fever. Osbern cites two notorious instances of the saint's intervention: to liberate a victim of the monks' *bête noir*, Oda of Bayeux; and turning back a cruel pirate to his just fate by preventing his approach as a fugitive to Canterbury. These happenings Lanfranc declared authentic, and Osbern was commissioned to publicise them. The closing story is of Edward, archdeacon of London, who became a monk at Canterbury but found himself hankering for his old style of life and tried to leave; he was prevented by visions of Dunstan and died a penitent, a story illuminating the perennial tension between clerical and monastic life, a tension peculiarly threatening to the community at Canterbury.

Osbern closes his cycle of miracles with some personal experiences and reminiscences. He relates a conversation with an old friend, a soldier in Thanet, concerning a dispute with Scoland, abbot of St Augustine's, in which they had both been involved, and which the soldier claimed was resolved by the aid of St Dunstan. The last episode is Osbern's own testimony to the saint's assistance when he was being assailed by calumny and felt the disfavour of his superiors. A heavenly vision of Dunstan and his clergy and a word from the gospel dispel Osbern's fears. The outcome vindicated his integrity completely, and the note of personal relief concludes his account.

Osbern appears to have composed a service in honour of Dunstan at the eucharist in which the glory of his visions and miracles in life and after were extolled.[37] Eadmer too composed a hymn in similar vein, no doubt to furnish the revival of the cult under Anselm.[38] To Anselm there came to be attributed, erroneously, a lengthy prayer to St Dunstan, recalling his miracles,[39] and there remains an anonymous sermon, drawing heavily upon the last of Adelard's 'lections', and regaling the sanctity of Dunstan by comparison to each rank of the heavenly host.[40]

The dramatic martyrdom of Thomas Becket in 1170 and the cult which swiftly grew up in its wake came to overshadow and somewhat eclipse the cults of Alphege and to a lesser extent of Dunstan at Canterbury. Nonetheless the relics of Dunstan remained the focus of an unseemly quarrel between Canterbury and Glastonbury which lasted from the time of Eadmer until the eve of the Reformation. Around the year 1120, the hard-pressed monks at Glastonbury began to assert that they possessed the remains of Dunstan which had been spirited away from Canterbury when the cathedral was sacked by the Danes and Alphege captured! To rebut this nonsense, Eadmer wrote a lengthy and well-researched piece which is still extant.[41] He claims himself as a boy to have seen the body of the saint when it was raised by Lanfranc in the presence of Scoland of St Augustine's and Gundulf of Rochester. The body was fully dressed in episcopal robes and *pallium*. He disputes the ravaged and exposed state of the cathedral after the capture of Alphege in 1011, and denounces the Glastonbury claim as an unworthy deceit, unlikely to have been perpetrated by any monks there from pre-conquest days: 'If they had known that they had the body of St Dunstan at Glastonbury, why would they have made the annual pilgrimage to Canterbury to celebrate his feast?'[42] It is very interesting that William of Malmesbury steered clear of this issue although he was writing for the Glastonbury monks when composing his 'Life of Dunstan'. He treats of no posthumous miracles at all.[43]

The controversy rumbled on, and almost 400 years later Archbishop Warham of Canterbury commissioned a formal enquiry to settle the matter in 1508.[44] The monks at Glastonbury had set up a new and conspicuous shrine purporting to contain the relics of Dunstan. The commission reports the finding of Dunstan's coffin at Canterbury, identified by a tablet of lead duly inscribed; the event was solemnly witnessed by, among others, Tunstall, later bishop of London and of Durham. The archbishop confirmed the claim of Canterbury, and sought to curb the pretensions of Glastonbury, summoning the abbot to bring his relics to the archbishop himself at Canterbury. To this the abbot of Glastonbury made specious excuses and refused a visit on the grounds of health. Warham's reply is trenchant and devastating. He condemns the false relics and orders compliance to his command, but whether he got it is unknown. Within a few years both sets of relics, the true and the false, were swept away in the maelstrom of the Reformation.

It was at Canterbury that the memory of Dunstan was kept alive throughout the eleventh century. Plummer identified the hand of a Canterbury scribe at the close of that century who interpolated entries for the tenth century into the chronicle at several points, highlighting the connection with the life of Dunstan.[45] Both Osbern and Eadmer were able to draw on personal sources of information like Nicholas of Worcester; Ethelred, precentor at Canterbury; Ethelric, bishop of Selsey; and the unnamed monk in the miracle of the great exorcism.[46] Osbern also refers to lost volumes containing miracles of Dunstan from which his selection is drawn.[47]

There is a distinct break in the two main strands of historiography concerning Dunstan. The first life, and the 'lections' by Adelard, were composed within living memory of the saint. But Osbern, followed by Eadmer, wrote after the

Norman Conquest in an attempt to salvage and preserve such memories of the old order as still remained. William of Malmesbury's two-volume 'Life of Dunstan' is, however, closely connected with his other historical writing, notably his book on the antiquities of Glastonbury; both works were compiled at the behest of the monastery at Glastonbury and reflect the interests and traditions of that house.

The writer of the first life of Dunstan is something of a mystery. Identifying himself with the initial 'B', he dedicated his work to Archbishop Aelfric of Canterbury, who reigned from 996 to 1006. He was therefore writing within a decade of Dunstan's death, and the writer of the first life of Oswald, probably Byrhtferth, testifies to the existence of this work, and to its value.[48] The writer was probably a cleric rather than a monk and he does not dwell on the monastic side of Dunstan's career except in the most general terms. He is not privy to its political side either. Rather he tries to collate the personal reminiscences of the great man, appealing to the memory of his friends for verification and occasionally to his own personal experience of Dunstan.[49] Stubbs was of the view that he was probably a foreigner, possibly from Liège, who joined the *familia* of Dunstan at the very end of his time as archbishop. Certain letters associated with Dunstan and his successors remain which seem to provide a context for this unknown biographer. A letter to Aethelgar, Dunstan's immediate successor, is close in style to the prologue of the first life. It discloses a wandering scholar, a protégé of Ebracher, the great reforming bishop of Liège (959–71), who now craves the archbishop's patronage. He is on his way to the New Minster at Winchester to read Aldhelm's work 'On virginity'.[50] An earlier and similarly plaintive letter to Dunstan himself seems to indicate that he was a political exile who needed the archbishop's protection and mediation; and the last possible glimpse of him is penniless and lost upon the continent, in another fragmentary epistle.[51] Nonetheless, he has provided a sensitive picture of Dunstan, deeply personal and unassuming, a true impression of his character and inner spiritual motivation. Its relationship with the historical developments in the Church and state at the time can now be confirmed at every point, and it benefits from the slight detachment brought to it by a newly arrived foreigner.

The first life is preserved in three manuscripts, each with a fascinating history.[52] The first text, now at Arras, is a close copy of the original version; the amazing Latin and convoluted style stands undiluted and makes hard reading. The second text, now at St Gall, represents a rewriting of the original in the interests of clarity, probably at St Augustine's. From there it was sent by Abbot Wulfric to Abbo of Fleury before his death in 1004 to be turned into verse. It ended up at Squirs in Gascony, where Abbo met a violent death at the hands of a mob while trying to reform the monastery there. The third text, now in the British Museum, is a further revision made at St Augustine's into clearer prose and it remained at Canterbury throughout the Middle Ages.

The second life is a very different endeavour. It is dedicated to Archbishop Alphege and was composed by a monk, Adelard, of the very house at Ghent where Dunstan had resided in exile.[53] It is essentially a summary, cast in the form of twelve 'lections' for use in the monastic office on St Dunstan's Day. The writer refers to the first life, which may have been entrusted to him also for versification. He introduces other traditions, and the work reflects the incipient hagiography associated with the cult. It became the basis of all the monastic liturgical texts, and it lay behind the Icelandic 'Dunstan saga' of the thirteenth century.[54]

Osbern wrote from a very different standpoint. In his day, c. 1080, the thread of living continuity ran through the steady pattern of miracles at the shrine of Dunstan and the fading memories of older monks who remembered the pre-conquest regime. Moreover, the time of Dunstan and of Edgar was now regarded by Englishmen of learning as a veritable golden age from which they were sundered by the ignominy of Ethelred's time, the quarrels and uncertainties of the Danish kings and the tide of Norman domination. This nostalgia generated a need for and a new regard for Anglo-Saxon history which found its fullest flowering in the work of William of Malmesbury and the first school of English history in the early twelfth century.[55] More urgent ecclesiastical needs also prompted research into recent history. Title deeds to lands needed verification and if need be spiritual support in the face of forceful claims by the new Norman lords. A catastrophe like the burning of Christ Church and its library underlined the urgent need to establish the past. To this challenge Osbern responded with considerable skill and determination, and produced at the same time a highly popular work which ensured that the memory of Dunstan and what he stood for would not be forgotten. His 'Life of Dunstan' is a subtle and successful blend of the two earlier lives, and achieves dubious dramatic effect by the placing of fictitious speeches in the mouths of principal figures, thus giving life to old issues and colouring them on occasion by the preoccupations of a very different period. His approach is not dissimilar to that of Sulcard of Westminster,[56] and he interweaves certain independent traditions with material drawn from the chronicle. His work has none of the immediacy of the 'Miracles of Dunstan', but it is an intelligent reordering of the earlier material in a way which would appeal to his contemporaries.

Appeal it did, for both Eadmer and William of Malmesbury tried to revise and correct Osbern's work, though with nothing like the same lasting popularity. Eadmer knew Osbern, and perhaps his own keen interest in history was nurtured by Osbern's example. Eadmer's revision adds little of value, apart from clarifying certain points of detail, historical and stylistic. As an early example of Eadmer's history writing it is of significance, not otherwise.[57] It is rare in manuscripts, unlike Osbern's life, of which many copies still remain.

Only one manuscript remains of William of Malmesbury's 'Life of Dunstan', and that is a late copy. It was written for the monks of Glastonbury as a thorough revision of Osbern's work,[58] and it does not appear that William knew of Eadmer's version. He wrote his 'Antiquities of Glastonbury' in the same connection, and for both tasks he enjoyed full access to the monastic archives there. The precise interrelationship between these texts is still unclear, however; the interpolations in the 'Antiquities of Glastonbury', made by monks at Glastonbury shortly afterwards to establish their own interests, make the connection particularly difficult to establish. It may be that William's caution as an historian prevented him from supporting their many pretensions, for example to the relics of Dunstan, and his finished work laid itself open to subsequent doctoring.

The 'Life of Dunstan' is nonetheless a creditable example of William's skill as an historian. He was able to use the earliest two lives of Dunstan as well as Osbern's work, and he is scathing towards several blemishes, historical and theological, in the work of the Canterbury monk. He includes too material from the lives of Oda, Oswald, Ethelwold and Edith, and like Osbern he seeks to create a synopsis of a systematic kind of the earliest lives of Dunstan. The importance of Glastonbury receives attention, rightly, and he follows closely the earliest life.

He draws on his own earlier researches for the *'Gesta regum'* and the *'Gesta pontificum'*, using documents like the English commentary upon the *'Regularis concordia'* and the letter from Pope John XII to Dunstan.[59] Like Osbern and Eadmer, William tended to regard Dunstan both as a hero from a lost golden age and as a prophet of the impending calamities of the English, a judgement, it was believed, from God upon their perfidy. With them too he shared a profound veneration for all things English and on occasion could express his dismay at the Norman inheritance.[60]

In general the medieval historians added little of value to the memory of Dunstan. Florence of Worcester wove together details from the first two lives and from the chronicle, but Henry of Huntingdon and Orderic Vitalis made no use of the lives,[61] and the later historians culled from the Canterbury writers or from William of Malmesbury. Stubbs printed Capgrave's summary in the *'Memorials of St Dunstan'* as an example of this kind of writing,[62] composed in the middle of the fifteenth century. The exception to this tendency was John of Wallingford, a monk of St Albans, who lived in the thirteenth century and was a contemporary of Matthew Paris and Roger of Wendover. He used the first life of Dunstan quite closely, and from it deduced an alternative and more accurate view of the likely date of Dunstan's birth. His writing demonstrates access to some other traditions concerning Dunstan's life and work, mainly drawn from the vicinity of Glastonbury, including closer cognisance of the political circumstances surrounding the accession of Edwy, the consequences of Dunstan's exile and the disputed succession after the death of Edgar.[63]

After the Reformation, the texts by which the memory of Dunstan was preserved owed much to Parker and Ussher for their preservation, and to Mabillon and the Bollandists for their dissemination.[64] But the text of Adelard and the text of William of Malmesbury's life were only published for the first time by Bishop Stubbs in 1874 in the *Memorials of St Dunstan*, part of the Rolls Series. This indispensable volume rescued Dunstan from virtual oblivion and occasional misinterpretation as a clerical fanatic.[65] Stubbs was anticipated in his view by J.R. Green in 1863, who hailed Dunstan as a 'great ecclesiastical statesman', a verdict reinforced by E.W. Robertson in his *Historical Essays* (1872).[66] But it was Stubbs' scholarship and sympathy, expressed in his masterly introduction to the *'Memorials of St Dunstan'*, which laid the basis for all future Dunstan studies, the first-fruits of which are to be found in the appropriate entry in the *Dictionary of National Biography*.

But Stubbs was no sympathiser with monasticism,[67] and it was Edmund Bishop and J. Armitage Robinson who established again Dunstan's reputation as a religious reformer and spiritual figure in his own right.[68] Dom David Knowles and Dom Symons in their work on the origins of English Benedictinism redressed the balance of scholarship and placed Dunstan and his friends firmly within the tradition of monastic episcopacy and reform prevalent throughout Europe at their time.[69] Stenton and Whitelock have amplified the significance of Dunstan within the wider context of English Church and society under the later Anglo-Saxons.[70] From this basis, there has been a steady advance in all aspects of tenth-century English studies, and it is now possible to do full justice to Dunstan and his colleagues as reformers, statesmen and spiritual leaders of the first rank within the long tradition of English history.

NOTES

Chapter 1: The legacy of Alfred the Great

1 The reign of Alfred the Great is best approached using F.M. Stenton's *Anglo-Saxon England* (Oxford History of England, 3rd edition, 1971); and the introduction to the Penguin translation of Asser's 'Life of Alfred' and other documents: *Alfred the Great*, ed. S. Keynes and M. Lapidge (1983).

2 *Asser's 'Life of Alfred'*, ed. W.H. Stevenson (Oxford, 1959 edition), chapters 56 and 94; cf. note on p.334 for the subsequent implications of this policy.

3 See D. Whitelock, 'The conversion of the eastern Danelaw' (*Saga-book of the Viking Society*, XII, 1941); also 'Fact and fiction in the legend of St Edmund', in *Proceedings of the Suffolk Institute of Archaeology*, 1969. In the same volume of proceedings is 'The St Edmund memorial coinage' by C.E. Blunt; cf. ASC ii 86 for discussion of the cult.

4 Asser, chapters 102 and 74; cf. Stevenson's note on p.307f. for Alfred's reputation on the continent; cf. also 'A king across the sea: Alfred in a continental perspective', J.L. Nelson (TRHS XXXVI, 1986).

5 ASC 883, 887, 888, 890 (EHD 1); Asser, chapter 71, cf. note on p.243f. for Rome. For the marriage to Baldwin II, see *Chronicle of Aethelweard*, ed. A. Campbell (Nelson, 1962), p.2; cf. 'Relations between England and Flanders before the Norman Conquest', P. Grierson (TRHS, 1941).

6 *Chronicle of Aethelweard*, ibid.; cf. 'A tale of two kings: Alfred and Ethelred the Unready', S. Keynes (TRHS XXXVI, 1986).

7 Alfred's preface to his translation of Gregory the Great's 'Pastoral rule' (ed. Keynes and Lapidge, op. cit. p.124f.); also EHD 226.

8 ASE p.234 n.2; cf. H&S III 617–20; and S 286. Also ASC i 283–4 (s.a. 870 F).

9 There is some uncertainty over the date of Plegmund's death; Plummer (ASC ii 103) supports 914, but Robinson (JAR p.25) asserts 923 on the authority of the later Canterbury insertion in the chronicle (EHD p.217 n.3). For Asser's verdict on Plegmund, see chapter 77.

10 See Dunstan's letter to Ethelred (EHD 229); cf. 'Sherborne, Glastonbury, and the expansion of Wessex', by H.P.R. Finberg (TRHS, 1953), and Ad III p.55 for the tradition that Athelm of Wells (and Canterbury) was Dunstan's uncle.

11 Asser, chapters 92–7; cf. notes in Keynes and Lapidge, op. cit. p. 271f.

12 Asser, chapter 98 (cf. also 75 where Aethelgifu is described as *'monasticae vitae regulis . . . consecrata'*); cf. Keynes and Lapidge, n.237.

13 The problem of 'lay dominion' of monasteries persisted throughout the Anglo-Saxon period; see Bede's letter to Archbishop Egbert (EHD 170 p.804–5), and Ethelwold's reflection on the renewal of the monasteries (EHD 238); cf. also Knowles MO appendix I; also Asser, chapter 93 for the wealth of English clergy and laity as an impediment to monastic devotion.

14 For Edward's daughters, see the introduction to the *Nunnaminster Codex*, ed. W. de Gray Birch (HRS, 1889); and *Liber de Hyde*, ed. E. Edwards (RS, 1866), p.112; cf. ASE p.445.

15 LVH pp.3–7; a similar clerical foundation was made at Gloucester in 909 by Aethelflaed, lady of the Mercians, and her husband Ethelred (ASC ii 118).

16 Asser, chapters 22–4.
17 ibid. chapters 76–7; cf. Keynes and Lapidge, op. cit. n.162–7.
18 ibid. chapter 78; cf. 'Grimbald of St Bertin's', P. Grierson (EHR, 1940), and 'Grimbald of St Bertin's', J. Batey (*Medium Aevum*, 35, 1966).
19 LVH p.5.
20 Keynes and Lapidge, op. cit. p.29f. for a lucid survey of this revived learning.
21 ibid. p.34.
22 See 'The educational tradition in England from Alfred to Aelfric: teaching "utriusque linguae"', D.A. Bullough (*Settimane di studio del Centro italiano di studi sull'alto medioevo*, Spoleto, 1972).
23 This is qualified by Keynes and Lapidge, op. cit., in their introduction p.40 and n.62.
24 GA p.18f.; cf. 'The Winchester school before St Ethelwold', F. Wormald, *England before the Conquest*, ed. P. Clemoes and K. Hughes (CUP, 1971), p.313.

Chapter 2: Oritur puer strenuus

1   e.g. O p.71; cf. the Canterbury tradition in the ASC (F) for 925, and Plummer's note, vol. ii p.134; both he and Stubbs regarded this as the correct date (MD p.lxxiii).
2   JW p.40 and n.1; cf. J.A. Robinson, 'Times of St Dunstan' (JAR) p.92f.
3   See the appendix by L.A.StA. Toke in *The Bosworth Psalter*, ed. F.A. Gasquet and E. Bishop (1908), pp.131–43; this verdict was accepted by Stenton (ASE 446) and also Knowles (MO 37 n.3); see also J.A. Robinson, *The Saxon Bishops of Wells* (British Academy, 1918), p.28f.
4   MD p.lxxivf.; B p.6.
5   Athelm – Ad p.55; Alphege – B p.3; Kinsige – ibid. p.32; kinsmen – ibid. p.11.
6   JW p.53; cf. J.A. Robinson, 'Memories of St Dunstan in Somerset' (Somerset Archaeological & Natural History Society Proceedings, 1916, vol.LXII), pp.xxvii–xxxvii and 1–25.
7   Letter of 6 February 1914; quoted in JAR p.94.
8   Ad p.54; this is not an unusual detail of hagiography – cf. Aelfric's 'Life of Ethelwold' (VE), chapters 2 and 3 (EHD 235 p.904).
9   B p.7; was the 'old man' in the dream St Benedict? cf. VO p.422.
10 B pp.6–7; cf. WMDA p. 47 from which this translation is drawn with William's interpolations marked in round brackets which elucidate the sense; this is the occasion when William directly refers to the existence of life B.
11 This was probably Ine's foundation; cf. Plummer, ASC ii 32–3 and H&S III 164 for discussion of the pre-Saxon origins; cf. H&S I 38.
12 See entry in *The Archaeology of Anglo-Saxon England*, ed. D.M. Wilson (Cambridge, 1976), pp.241f.
13 There is a full discussion by John Scott in WMDA.
14 cf. MD p.lxxxii; see H&S III 284.
15 WMDA p.6f.
16 *Chronicle of Aethelweard*, ed. A. Campbell (London, 1962), p.36.
17 ASC 883 and 885; cf. Asser, chapter 71 and WMDA p.113.
18 B pp.7 and 17f.
19 cf. *The Pre-Conquest Church in England*, M. Deanesley (London, 2nd edition; 1963), p.13f.
20 On this obscure topic, see JAR p.100f. and more recent discussion in, for example, *St Patrick, his Origins and Career*, R.P.C. Hanson (Oxford, 1968); 'St Patrick at Glastonbury' and 'The cult of St Indracht at Glastonbury', M. Lapidge, in *Ireland in Medieval Europe: Studies in Memory of Kathleen Hughes*, ed. D. Whitelock and others (Cambridge, 1981).
21 'Glastonbury Abbey and the fusing of English literary culture', C.H. Slover, *Speculum*, X, 1935, pp.147–60.
22 WMDA, p. 93; but see Scott's discussion of this difficult text, p.198.
23 ibid. pp.67–8.
24 B p.10.
25 MD p.cxii.
26 ibid. pp.cx–cxi; cf. *St Dunstan's Classbook*, facsimile edition by R.W. Hunt (Amsterdam, 1961); the list of biblical texts is to be found in H&S I 192f.
27 From 'St Patrick at Glastonbury', Finberg, art. cit. p.86.
28 Note the terms on which Dunstan was eventually offered the abbacy of Glastonbury: B p.25; both Abingdon and Ely were at this time in the royal gift: cf. VE cap.7 (EHD 235 p.905) and LE 73 n.4, and discussion in JAR 118f. (cf. S 646) and VE cap. 17.
29 See 'Saxon abbots of Glastonbury', J.A. Robinson, in *Somerset Historical Essays* (1921), for the view that these 'abbots' were thegns.
30 O pp.74–5; cf. B pp.10–11 and WMGP 196; see MO p.37 n.4.

31 *The Saxon Bishops of Wells*, J.A. Robinson (1919); cf. WMDA 137 and 113.
32 ibid. p.67; 'by the old church' was a hallowed oath in William's day.
33 B p.7.
34 Ad p.55.
35 B p.10 – 'disciplinis innexus Deificis'.
36 ibid.
37 ibid.; cf. Stevenson's note in Asser, pp. 302–3, on the popularity of this particular metaphor.
38 Finberg in 'St Patrick at Glastonbury' refers to L. Gougaud's observation in his *Christianity in Celtic Lands* (London, 1932) that the word 'peregrini' does not only refer to pilgrims; it is a common way of describing a school of Irish scholars abroad.
39 B pp.10–11; there is a translation of this chapter in EHD 234 pp.897–8 from which this excerpt is taken.
40 B pp.20–1 and 49.
41 ibid. pp.11 and 20; many of Dunstan's visions during sleep had a strong musical dimension; e.g. pp.21, 43 and 48.
42 ibid. pp. 7–8; 'exsurgat patiens humilis ruat atque superbus'.
43 ibid. p.10.
44 ibid. pp. 10–11; from translation in EHD 234 p.898.

Chapter 3: At the court of Athelstan

1 For what follows, see especially ASE 339f.; Dumville, op. cit.; 'The making of King Athelstan's empire: an English Charlemagne?', by Michael Wood, in *Ideal and Reality* (*Festschrift for Wallace-Hadrill*) (Blackwell, 1984); S 394, a coronation charter for St Augustine's, Canterbury; and Asser p.184, for Alfred's fondness for Athelstan – cf. EHD 8 for the lost sources behind William of Malmesbury's account of his reign.
2 Oda, bishop of Ramsbury, was a Dane (VO 404) and there were Danes at Athelstan's court (cf. ASE 351); cf. also JW 42 for evidence of the king's personal friendships with Danes.
3 ASE 343; cf. EHD 8 and ASC 937; there is a prayer of Athelstan's in the *Nunnaminster Codex*, ed. Birch (HRS, 1889), p.116 n.1; cf. JAR p.68.
4 ASE 340f.; also H&S I 208f.; see D. Binchy, *Celtic and Anglo-Saxon Kingship* (Oxford, 1970) p.29f.; and H.R. Loyn, 'Wales and England in the tenth century and the context of the Athelstan charters', in *Welsh Historical Review*, vol.X, p.283f. For Cornwall see H.P.R. Finberg, 'Sherborne, Glastonbury and the expansion of Wessex' (TRHS, 1953).
5 ASE 356.
6 ibid. 353; cf. EHD 1 (ASC) p.219 and 8 p.306
7 ASE 353–5.
8 ibid. 344 n.1; cf. *Chronicle of Aethelweard*, ed. Campbell, p.2.
9 ASE 344–9; cf. Wood, art. cit. p.269 n.90 for Breton influences in England.
10 EHD 228, cf. discussion in C&S 9; cf. MD p.382 for an example of a Breton hermit in the west country at this time, and H&S II p.85 for a Breton litany from this period mentioning the English royal house.
11 ASE 443f.; cf. Wood, art. cit. p.261 for a valuable discussion of this matter, and for a Frankish manuscript of Aldhelm's 'On virginity' which came to England at this time and was probably handled by Dunstan.
12 EHD 26 'Annals of St Bertin'; Count Adelolf of Boulogne, a kinsman of Athelstan, became a crucial diplomatic link between England and the continent.
13 MD p.lxxv; cf. E. Bishop, *Liturgica Historica* (Oxford, 1918), in the chapter 'Some ancient Benedictine confraternity books'; whether Dunstan's mother, Cynethrith, was amongst them is discussed in C&S 10; see also J.A. Robinson 'The Saxon Bishops of Wells' (1919).
14 JAR p.67; also p.154; see Wood, op. cit. p.261 n.53; about this time Wulfhelm became the first known archbishop of Canterbury to travel to Rome to collect his *pallium* (ASC 927) (see W. Levison, *England and the Continent in the Eighth Century* (Oxford, 1946), chapter 1, especially p.21 for the background to this practice).
15 Finberg, art. cit. p.115; see H&S I 676f. and S 450; also Dunstan's own letter concerning the Cornish see: EHD 228 (C&S 35, where there is a full discussion of the background).
16 'The conversion of the eastern Danelaw', D. Whitelock (*Saga-book of the Viking Society*, vol.XII, 1941), p.176.
17 S 405, 407, 419, 421, 422, 424, 444; WMDA p.115; B p.17f. tells of a visit to Glastonbury by Athelstan and his retainers.
18 JAR 51–5; there is a full discussion in Wood, op. cit. p.255.

19 JAR 56f.; cf. Wood, op. cit. p.252 for a valuable analysis of the background to these manuscripts; cf. 'King Athelstan's books', S. Keynes, in *Learning and Literature in Anglo-Saxon England*, ed. M. Lapidge and H. Gneuss (CUP, 1985).

20 JAR 72f.

21 EHD 8 p.308; cf. 'The holy relics of Charlemagne and King Athelstan: the lances of Longinus and St Mauricius', L.H. Loomis, *Speculum*, XXV, 1950); see discussion of the parallel made between Charlemagne and Athelstan in Wood, op. cit. p.267f.; see also 'Relic cults as an instrument of royal policy between 900 and 1050', D.W. Rollason, A/S xv, 1986.

22 Wood's article is invaluable for what follows; cf. Asser, chapters 75 and 76.

23 Wood, art. cit. p.255.

24 GA pp.18–19f.

25 JAR p.70f. (cf. appendix D 172f.); Wood, art. cit. p.269.

26 S 394; cf. J.A. Robinson, *'The Saxon Bishops of Wells'* (1919) which establishes the likely dates of Athelm's primacy.

27 Ad 55–6.

28 ASE 349; cf. article on the archaeological excavations at Cheddar by P. Rahtz in *The Archaeology of Anglo-Saxon England*, ed. D.M. Wilson (Cambridge, 1981), p.65f. with bibliography.

29 MD 378f.; also in M. Winterbottom, *Three Lives of English Saints* (Toronto, 1972); it is translated in *St Dunstan of Canterbury*, E. Duckett (London, 1955), pp.204–5.

30 B p.11f.; cf. Wood, op. cit. p.264 n.71; was Athelstan encouraging the collection of ancient poetry and traditions?

31 B p.12f.

32 MD p.354, where Dunstan describes Wulfhelm as *'pastor apostolicus'*; from around this period, the bishop of Winchester heads the witness lists to charters after the archbishop of Canterbury; Wood, op. cit. p.257.

33 MD p.lxxv.

34 B pp.12–13.

35 JW p.42f.; cf. 'English monastic reform in the tenth century', Dom Symons (DR 41, 1942); which is a crucial article for establishing the early biography of Dunstan.

36 cf. ASC ii 136–7 for the episcopal succession at Winchester.

37 B p.13.

38 ibid., cf. Alfred's similar (psychosomatic?) illness: Asser, chapter 74; JW asserts on p.43 that Dunstan thought he had contracted leprosy.

39 VE chapter 5 (EHD 235).

40 B p.14.

41 This is an important early reference to the monastic custom of the formal double confession in England; the church of St Gregory is mentioned in S 1443.

42 *Archaeology of Anglo-Saxon England*, D.M. Wilson (Cambridge, 1981), p.101f. and bibliography, see article on towns by Martin Biddle.

43 For the origins of the New Minster see LVH 3f., and for the origins of the Nunnaminster see Birch's introduction to the *Nunnaminster Codex* (HRS, 1889); see also Wood, op. cit. p.253f., for the significance of the Winchester manuscripts as evidence of the cultural vitality there at this time.

44 VO p.410f.

45 WMGP ii p.163.

46 Aelfric's homily on Ash Wednesday in *Lives of the Saints*, Skeat (EETS), vol. 1, p.266f.

47 Wulstan's 'Life of Ethelwold', ed. M. Winterbottom, *Three Lives of English Saints* (1972).

48 For the possibility that *'calvus'* (bald) signified a monastic tonsure, see JAR 83 n.1, also O p.85; for Cenwald of Worcester, see JAR 39: FW describes him (s.a. 957) as a man of 'great humility and monastic profession'. Dunstan succeeded him as bishop of Worcester.

49 Symons, art. cit. p.200f., where the reality of Dunstan's monastic profession is emphasised and clarified.

50 There was a Benedict at the New Minster, and a grant to the church at Bath describes it as dedicated to St Benedict (cf. JAR 53 and 61f.); for the wealth of contact between the Churches of Germany and England, see Wood, art. cit., notably the story of Ursula and her companions which reached Cologne from England at this time (p.259f.). In this connection see also the article by Mrs J. Tout in *Historical Essays*, ed. Tout and Tait (Manchester, 1907), pp. 17–56.

51 B p.13f.

52 VE chapter 5 (EHD 235).

53 VO p.413; cf. MO p.35 n.4; Oda's foreign travels may have brought him into contact with Fleury before 940. Fleury was reformed c.930.

54 See especially the *Letters of Alcuin*, ed. Alott (1974), and the work of Benedict of Aniane (MO chapter 1).

55 The ambivalent position of bishops who were royal nominees is confirmed by Barlow in *The English Church: 1000–1066* (London, 1979); i.e. in the period after the reform period in the tenth century.
56 Knowles is less certain: MO 35–6; but see ASE 445.
57 Mark 4: 30f.
58 ASE 445; in 932 (S 419) Athelstan endowed Shaftesbury nunnery: *'fidelissime familie monialium qua sub regulari devote exercitationis vita in monasterio'* (cf. Asser, chapter 98).
59 JAR p.83; B p.15f.
60 ibid. pp. 17–20; MD p.lxxvii.
61 The story of the mead that did not fail (B ibid.) may be compared with a similar tale in VE chapter 8, concerning Ethelwold at Abingdon.
62 B p.18 refers to Dunstan's coteries of 'scholars'.
63 B p.19.
64 cf. Luke 3:22; appearances of the heavenly dove occur in association with the lives of Oda and of Oswald also; Ad p.62; O p.109; VO p.472.
65 O p.89.
66 B p.20; the embroidery found in the tomb of Cuthbert is the sole relic of this skill remaining from the tenth century in England.
67 O p.80 – *'domum religiosae'.*
68 B. p.21; cf. EHD 234, p.898 n.2, where this passage is translated.
69 Revelation 14: 1–5; Matthew 19: 10–12; I Corinthians 7.
70 O p.84.
71 See *The Coming of Christianity to Anglo-Saxon England,* H. Mayr-Harting (London, 1972), pp. 172, 193–4; cf. Wood, op. cit. p.261f. for the reintroduction of Aldhelm's 'On virginity' into England at this time.
72 S 448 and 449; cf. Edmund's grants, S 464, 465, 474, 482, 485, 487, 493.
73 ASE 445; Eadred's will is in EHD 107 (text in *Liber de Hyde,* ed. Edwards (RS, 1866), p.153f.).
74 ibid. p.112f.; see Birch's introduction to the *Nunnaminster Codex* (HRS, 1889).
75 cf. Roger of Wendover, s.a. 925 (EHD 4 p.283) for the piety of Athelstan's sister, Edith (of Polesworth).
76 *An Ancient Manuscript,* ed. W. de Gray Birch (HRS, 1889).
77 This is fully discussed in Birch, op. cit.; cf. H&S II 320.
78 ODS p.118 comments on the later cult of Edburga among the reformed monasteries of the 'Ethelwold connection'.

Chapter 4: Abbot of Glastonbury

1 B p.21.
2 ibid. (this passage is translated in EHD 234, from which the rest is also taken).
3 ibid. p.25.
4 S 466: lands at Christian Malford, Wiltshire; cf. ASE 446 n.2.
5 EHD 26: from *'Folcwini Gesta Abbatum S. Bertini'.* MGH SS XIII (1881); cf. JAR p.62.
6 cf. ASC ii 144–5 and MD p.lxxix; cf. also O p.92f.
7 e.g. S 509: *'Ego Dunstanus abbas nolens sed regalibus obediens verbis hanc cartulam scribere iussi.'*
8 B pp. 44–5.
9 WMDA talks about lands at Wrington, Somerset, being restored to Dunstan (p.115).
10 See ASE 357; cf. Roger of Wendover s.a. 940 (EHD 4).
11 B ibid; cf. 'Flodoard's annals', EHD 24 (s.a. 946).
12 ASC ii 146.
13 *Chronicle of Aethelweard,* ed. Campbell, p.54. Aelfgifu was venerated at Shaftesbury; ASC (D) s.a. 943 – Edmund besieged Wulfstan at Leicester.
14 *Liber de Hyde,* ed. Edwards (RS), p.138.
15 WMDA p.117; cf. H&S I 677 for two of Edmund's manumissions at Bodmin (EHD 141).
16 VO, beginning, concerns the life of Oda (cf. Eadmer's later life of Oda, discussion in *'St Anselm and his Biographer',* R.W. Southern (Cambridge, 1963) p.279f.); for the general background, see *The Early History of the Church at Canterbury,* N. Brooks (Leicester, 1984), chapter 10, especially p.222f.
17 Asser, chapter 94; see Stevenson's comment on p.334.
18 ibid.; cf. ASC s.a. 971; also VO p.420.
19 Stubbs, *Constitutional History,* vol.I, p.241 n.1 and p.258 n.9 for Ramsbury.
20 cf. N. Brooks, op.cit. p.371 n.47, where the authorities are adduced.
21 See MO chapter 2 for the Cluniac reforms; cf. VO 413 for Oda's profession.

22 VO p.401.
23 See N. Brooks, op.cit. chapter 9.
24 ibid., chapter 10 – beginning.
25 I and II Edmund (C&S 17 and 18); for ecclesiastical sections cf. EHD 38 also.
26 C&S 19 and 20; cf. G. Schoebe, 'The chapters of archbishop Oda and the canons of the legatine councils of 786', in *Bulletin of the Institute of Historical Research*, XXXV (1962), pp. 75–83; cf. N. Brooks, op. cit. p.223.
27 EHD 106.
28 C&S 22, where there is a full discussion of this curious document.
29 LE p.73 n.4; cf. p.106 n.5; cf. JAR pp.118–120.
30 VO p.407.
31 See N. Brooks, op. cit. p.228f.
32 ibid.
33 See Symons' verdict in *'Regularis concordia'* (London, 1953), p.xix n.1; JAR 116.
34 VO p.413. cf. note 114 below for the character of Abbot Wulflad.
35 C&S 20 (p.72 and n.4).
36 VO p.408: 'This most brilliant light of the city of Canterbury.'
37 E p.203; cf. ASC (F) 961 and Eadmer's 'Life of Oda', Southern, op. cit. p.280.
38 WMDA p.115f.; see Scott's notes 112 and 113 for a full discussion of these grants. cf. also 'Monastic lands and England's defence in the Viking Age', R. Fleming (EHR, April 1985).
39 WMDA p.117f.
40 MO Appendix VI for Glastonbury's vast wealth in 1066: £827 p.a.
41 cf. Theodred's benefaction: EHD 106.
42 WMDA p.117.
43 See 'Athelstan "Half-king" and his family', C. Hart (A/S 2, 1973) and 'Danelaw charters and the Glastonbury Scriptorium', by the same author, in DR, 1972.
44 Ad p.56; cf. Prologue to the *Rule of St Benedict*.
45 B p.25f. (another translation of this passage is in EHD 234).
46 ibid. p.28; cf. RSB chapter 66.
47 RC p.xvi and also 'English monastic reform in the tenth century' T. Symons (DR 41, 1942), an article of crucial importance.
48 *Archaeology of Anglo-Saxon England* (ed. D.M. Wilson), article by R.J. Cramp, 'Monastic sites', p.241f. and bibliography.
49 WMVD p.271f.
50 B p.48.
51 Ad p.59 (cf. VE chapter 11 for a similar incident in the tradition about Ethelwold, and VO p.407 for one in the life of Oda).
52 cf. Somerset Archaeological Society's Report for 1928.
53 WMDA p.137.
54 ibid. pp. 115 and 119 for St Dunstan's Gospel Book.
55 RC p.xxxi.
56 Aelfric's 'Grammar', ed. Stevenson (1929); quoted by Cramp, art. cit. p.208.
57 *Archaeology of Anglo-Saxon England*, ed. Wilson, pp.244–6.
58 S 589; cf. B p.25.
59 ibid. p.28; cf. also pp.46–7 for a similar story; see MD p.lxxxv.
60 MS Trinity College 0.1.18 (1042) 112v–113r; discussed in M. Lapidge, 'St Dunstan's Latin poetry' (*Anglia*, 1980), XCVIII, pp.101–6).
61 *St Dunstan's Classbook*, ed. R.W. Hunt (Amsterdam, 1961).
62 cf. MD p.378 for Abbo's letter to Dunstan; also p.410 for acrostic poems to Dunstan, found in VO p.460f.; cf. M. Lapidge 'Latin poems' (A/S 9, 1980).
63 VE chapter 6 (EHD 235 p.905 from which this translation is taken).
64 See 'An early example of insular Caroline script', T.A.M. Bishop, *Transactions of the Cambridge Bibliographical Society*, IV (1968), p. 396f.
65 Hatton MS 30; cf. MD p.cxii; also reference in *St Dunstan's Classbook*, ed. Hunt.
66 T.A.M. Bishop, op. cit.; cf. entry in *'Manuscripts at Oxford: R.W. Hunt, Memorial Exhibition'*, ed. A.C. de la Mare and B.C. Barker-Benfield (1980), p.12; also *'English Caroline Minuscule'*, T.A.M. Bishop (Oxford, 1971); there is evidence too of Dunstan's work in a manuscript of Boethius: see 'A fragment of an early tenth-century Anglo-Saxon MS', M.B. Parker (A/S 12, 1983).
67 From 'The hermeneutic style in tenth-century Anglo-Latin literature', M. Lapidge (A/S 4, 1975), p.73.
68 'On virginity' may be consulted in *Aldhelm: the Prose Works*, ed. M. Lapidge and M. Herren (Ipswich, 1979).

69 B pp.26–8.
70 Hunt's facsimile edition (1961) is indispensable; see also MD p.cxi; also 'Glastonbury and the fusing of English literary culture', C.H. Slover, (*Speculum*, X, 1935).
71 Hunt's, *St Dunstan's Classbook*, p.xiv.
72 cf. 'Hermeneutic style', M. Lapidge, art. cit. p.96 for a similar poem.
73 'Dunstanus und Hrabanus Maurus', H. Gneuss (*Anglia*, 96, 1978), p. 136f.
74 Hunt, *St Dunstan's Classbook*, p.xii.
75 cf. H&S I 192f. and note.
76 MD p.cxi.
77 cf. Hunt, *St Dunstan's Classbook*, introduction; also MD p.cxii: Stubbs conjectures that the head of 'Wulfric child', drawn in the margin, may be a portrait of Dunstan's own brother (cf. p.lxxvii).
78 Hunt, op. cit., his conclusion to the introduction; cf. B p.26 for the emphasis on training in the administration of justice.
79 See 'St Dunstan's Latin poetry', M. Lapidge (*Anglia*, 98, 1980), p.101f.; some of the relevant texts are in WMDA p.137 and WMVD p.301f.
80 'A note on MS Vatican Bibl. Apost. Lat. 3363', M.B. Parkes; in *'Boethius – His Life, Thought and Influence'*, ed. M. Gibson (Blackwell: Oxford, 1981).
81 See the important article by J. Higgett, 'Glastonbury, Dunstan, monasticism and manuscripts' in *Art History*, 2 iii, 1979, p.275f.
82 *'The Bosworth Psalter'*, ed. F.A. Gasquet and E. Bishop (London, 1908).
83 JAR 98f.; cf. *'English kalendars before 1100'*, F. Wormald (HBS, 1934) for a full and detailed discussion.
84 See MO appendix IV; also HRH; also MWDA p.137f.
85 B pp.26–8 for evidence of continuing spiritual conflict.
86 Ad p.56.
87 B p.31.
88 See ASE 360f.; also 'The end of the Kingdom of Northumbria', A. Campbell (EHR lvii, 1942).
89 ASC (D) 952; cf. ASE 361 n.1; (also ASC ii p.ix for its ecclesiastical bearing upon the see of York).
90 ASC (A) 955; cf. MD p.lxxxviii.
91 B p.29 (EHD 234 p.900 for another translation of this passage); cf. Ad p.56f.
92 O p.95.
93 Stubbs' view: MD p.lxxxvi.
94 EHD 107.
95 B p.31; cf. *Liber de Hyde*, ed. Edwards (RS), p.152.
96 In 952 (ASC (D)), Eadred punished the people of Thetford for the murder of Abbot Eadhelm (of St Augustine's Canterbury? – see EHD 1 p.223 n.4).
97 Ad p.56; cf. *Chronicle of Aethelweard*, ed. Campbell, p.54.
98 VO p.428, where there is an illuminating comment on the influence of her husband, Athelstan the half-king, also.
99 B p.29f.; there was a community at Crediton (Athelstan's grant, S 405): the see of Crediton supervised and supported the bishop in Cornwall, EHD 229.
100 Ad p.56f.
101 Abbo mentions this in his letter to Dunstan: MD p.379.
102 S 568.
103 See full discussion in ASC ii p.ix; VO p.419f.; also LE pp.96 and 106 and n.6 and 5 respectively for evidence that Oskytel probably held the sees of York and Dorchester in plurality.
104 VE chapters 7 and 8 (EHD 235, from which this translation is largely drawn).
105 See *The Early History of Abingdon*, F.M. Stenton (Oxford, 1913).
106 cf. *Archaeology of Anglo-Saxon England*, ed. Wilson (1976), p.215f.
107 JAR p.110.
108 RC – proem 1; cf. EHD 238.
109 Wulstan's *Life of Ethelwold*, ed. M. Winterbottom (1972), chapter xxxviii f., cf. William of Malmesbury's comment in his 'Life of Dunstan', p.273 on the close rapport between Dunstan and Ethelwold: *'Gloria patris filius sapiens.'*
110 This relationship persisted until the end: cf. VE chapter 20 and O p.115f.
111 VE chapter 10 (EHD 235).
112 JAR p.111 n.2: from the Lambeth MS of Florence of Worcester: *'Viros monastica disciplina exquisite callentes, ex Corbeiensi Gallia coenobio.'*
113 *Early History of Abingdon*, Stenton (1913), p. 6.
114 VO p.419; Wulflad, abbot of Fleury, was remembered as a *'vir strenuus et sapientissimus'* (Hugh of Fleury, MGH SS IX p.384).

115 cf. Eadmer's 'Life of Oda', chapter 9, PL cxxxiii p.931f.; the restricted value of this work is discussed in *St Anselm and his Biographer*, R.W. Southern (Cambridge, 1963), p.279f.

Chapter 5: Exile and return

1 *Chronicle of Aethelweard*, ed. Campbell, p.55.
2 LVH p.7.
3 ASE 436; cf. EHD 108; see 'The founding of Southwell Minster', F.M. Stenton, in *Collected Papers* (Oxford, 1970).
4 ASE 364–6.
5 e.g. S 614–15 for Byrhthelm's kinship with the king.
6 S 646; cf. JAR p.119f. and LE p.73 n.4.
7 S 605: *'beato Benedicto praeclarissimo monachorum patrono'*.
8 ASC ii p.150; cf. *Orbis Britanniae*, E. John (Leicester, 1966), p.158f.
9 B p.32f. (EHD 234 gives another translation of this passage).
10 B p.33.
11 LVH p.57; cf. S 1292 with detailed discussion of its significance in MD p.xcii n.1.
12 S 1211.
13 JW p.50.
14 B p.45: this intimation occurred before the death of Edmund.
15 WMVD p.281f. (cf. Ad p.58).
16 Ad p.59.
17 ibid. (cf. B p.28).
18 B p.33f.
19 From 'The authorship of the Old English account of King Edgar's establishment of the monasteries', D. Whitelock, in *Philological Essays . . . in Honour of H.D. Meritt*, ed. J.L. Rosier, (1970), p.136.
20 WMDA p.121; but see note 119 and HRH p.50f.; Aelsige may have been an interpolated name in S 625 (cf. S 626 where the name is omitted).
21 B p.34.
22 Ad p.59f.; for the saints mentioned here and their subsequent cults in England, cf. the respective entries in ODS.
23 cf. *Chronicle of Aethelweard*, ed. Campbell, p.2; ASC ii 137 and addenda p.viii.
24 For what follows, the best survey is in MO, chapters 1 and 2.
25 The life of John of Gorze is in MGH SS IV p.335f.; that of Gerard of Brogne is in MGH SS XV (2) p.654f.
26 See 'The continental background of the reform', D.A. Bullough, in *Tenth Century Studies*, ed. D. Parsons (1975).
27 MO p.26f.; there is a convenient translation of the 'Rule of St Benedict' by Dom Bernard Basil Bolton, OSB (Ealing Abbey, 1970); for what follows see also *The Frankish Kingdoms under the Carolingians*, R. McKitterick (London, 1983), chapter 11.
28 EHD 170.
29 EHD 238.
30 *From Pachomius to St Ignatius*, D. Knowles (Oxford, 1966), p. 7 and note.
31 See *A Short History of the Papacy in the Middle Ages*, W. Ullmann (London, 1972), pp.113–15.
32 Cited by D.A. Bullough, art. cit. p.21.
33 Hugh of Fleury describes Wulflad as *'vir strenuus et sapientissimus'* (MGH SS IX p.384).
34 For what follows see 'Folcwini Gesta Abbatum S. Bertini' (MGH SS XIII pp.600–35), of which there is a brief extract in EHD 26.
35 ASC ii 137 and addenda p.vii; cf. EHD 8 p.308.
36 EHD 26.
37 S 610.
38 MGH SS V p.25f.; O p.101 mentions the wealth and prestige of Blandinium.
39 See 'Relations between England and Flanders before the Norman Conquest', P. Grierson (TRHS, 1941).
40 B p.35.
41 Job 6: 25f. According to the first biographer, this antiphon was being sung to the Magnificat (i.e. at vespers).
42 Ad p.60.
43 WMVD p.285.
44 S 728: the matter is mentioned in Grierson, art. cit. p.90, and is fully discussed in *'La donation d'Elftrude à St-Pierre de Gand'*, J. Dhondt (Académie Royale de Belgique: *Bulletin de la Commission*

Royale d'Histoire, CV (1940), p.117–64), where he asks the crucial question, 'N'a-t-il pu excercer sous Womar les fonctions de *prieur*?' (i.e. of Dunstan in exile).

45 MD p.359 and notes (see C&S 26 for the difficulty of dating the letter): Arnulf's circumspect approach is interesting.
46 e.g. correspondence in MD pp. 361 and 380.
47 LVH p.24. c.f. ASC ii 169.
48 B p.35f. (this translation is from EHD 234, p.901); cf. ASE 366f.
49 VE chapter 9 (EHD 235).
50 EHD 238; cf. Eric John, op. cit. pp.157–9.
51 O p.102 (cf. E p.194).
52 B p.36.
53 WMVD p.291.
54 B p.36.
55 JW (p.53) says that Edgar 'reassembled the faithful retainers of his predecessors'.
56 Stenton, art. cit.; Edgar, while only king of Mercia, also granted land to Oskytel (S 679).
57 cf. MD p.xc and ASC ii p.150f.; the charter here referred to is S 1447, printed by Tapp (1951).
58 ASC (D) 958; cf. VO pp. 402–3; discussion in MD p.xcii and ASC ii p.151.
59 cf. *Early History of the Church at Canterbury*, N. Brooks, p.224f.
60 B p.36 (EHD 234 from which this translation is largely taken).
61 Ad. p.60.
62 B p.36; note JW p.53, who stresses the close family ties between Dunstan and Edgar.
63 B p.36 (EHD 234 from which this translation is taken).
64 MD p.xci (but see note 81 below).
65 Ad p.60.
66 VO p.420.
67 ibid.
68 Eadmer's 'Life of Oswald', p.14; Levison in *England and the Continent in the Eighth Century* (Oxford, 1946) does not think that any archbishop of York went to Rome for the *pallium* before Aelfric in 1026 (appendix III); but VO p.435 mentions a visit by Oswald when he became primate in 972, so it may be that the custom goes back well into the tenth century; cf. C&S 61.
69 B p.37; see MD p.xc n.1 for charters in which Dunstan signs as either bishop of Worcester or of London (S 674 etc.).
70 See ASC 1001; cf. Plummer's note, ASC ii p.181.
71 VO p.408.
72 WMGP p.25f. (he wrongly makes Edgar the instigating monarch!).
73 B p.38; cf. WMGP ibid.; see MD p.xciii and ASC ii pp.153–4; the matter is fully discussed by Brooks, op. cit. p.237f.
74 MD ibid.; cf. 'The appointment of Dunstan as archbishop of Canterbury', D. Whitelock, in *Otium & Negotium: Studies presented to O. von Feilitzen*, ed. F. Sangren (Stockholm, 1973), pp. 232–47.
75 S 660 (printed in *Liber de Hyde*, ed. Edwards (RS), p.174f.); this charter is discussed in conjunction with S 652 by Stenton in *The Latin Charters of the Anglo-Saxon Period* (Oxford, 1955), p.22.
76 cf. S 683: Byrhthelm, if a kinsman of Edgar, was a kinsman of Edwy too, and his appointment to Winchester would have antedated Edgar's accession.
77 O p.104.
78 B p.36 (another translation is in EHD 234); cf. S 1211 for restoration to the queen mother, Eadgifu (see note 12 above); S 687 is another charter of restoration to a thegn, Wulfric, of lands held in the southern part of the kingdom.
79 B p.38; a similar overruling occurred in the succession to Oskytel at York, when a certain Ethelwold resigned 'because he wanted a quieter life', but probably to make way for Oswald – see ASC ii p.ix (addenda), and Whitelock, art. cit.
80 B ibid.
81 See note 64 above; cf. MD p.xcvi; see also Brooks, op. cit. p.244 and n.117; and *English Kalendars before 1100*, F. Wormald (1933), pp.193 and 221.

Chapter 6: Archbishop of Canterbury

1 B p.38; cf. FW p.139: '*per pacis itinera ad patriam remeavit*'; for the hazards of the journey, see a description in the Ramsey Chronicle and cited by D. Whitelock, art. cit: '*maris injurias, intemperiem aeris, praedonis insidias, et totius itineris suscepta pericula*'; cf. C&S 61 for another reference to the difficult journey.

2 MD pp.391–5 where Stubbs has identified the stages of the route; see 'L'itinerario romano di Segerico, arcivescovo di Canterbury e la lista dei papa da lui portata in Inghilterra', B. Pesci, in *Rivista di archaeologica cristiana*, XIII, (1936), pp.43–60 (map in Barlow, op. cit. p.12).

3 ASC ii p.154 (ex. MGH SS XXV p.777); cf. MD p.388.

4 B p.39.

5 The matter is fully discussed in Levison, op. cit. chapter 2 and appendix III.

6 cf. Brooks, op. cit. p.244 and notes 119 and 120; cf. also D. Whitelock, art. cit. and Levison, op. cit. p.201, n.4; the text is printed in MD p.296f. with its later interpolations duly noted in the footnotes; cf. C&S 25.

7 e.g. B p.41f. and 48f.; cf. also p.10.

8 For the full story, see Ullmann, op. cit. chapter 6, p.116f.

9 From *Early Christian Creeds*, J.N.D. Kelly (London, 1972, 3rd edition), p.432f., citing Th. Klauser in 'Hist. Jahrbuch', liii (1933), p.189.

10 See Ullmann, op. cit. p.124.

11 B p.40.

12 cf. Asser, p.243.

13 cf. F. Wormald, *English Kalendars before 1100*, op. cit. passim; see respective entries in ODS, and also Levison, op. cit. chapter 2.

14 *Blickling Homilies*, ed. R. Morris (EETS, OS 58/63/73, reprint 1967).

15 See ASC ii p.163 (there is a letter of commendation for a pilgrim in MD p.381f.); cf. EHD 137 for provision for pilgrimages to Rome in the Exeter Guild statutes.

16 VO p.435.

17 'Homily on St Swithun, bishop', in Aelfric's *Lives of the Saints*, ed. W. Skeat (EETS, OS 76/82/94/114, reprint 1966), vol.I, p.441f.

18 B p.30f. and Ad p.64f.

19 EHD 40; cf. C&S 27; cf. Asser, pp.211 and 244 on the origins of this tax.

20 Ad p.67; this is a striking reflection on the corruption of the Roman curia!

21 cf. ASC ii p.157.

22 MD p.364f.; cf. C&S 29; Levison, op. cit. p.196f.; the pope was John XII.

23 See note 44 of chapter 7.

24 MD ibid. n.1: cf. RC proem 9 and MO p.45.

25 WMDA p.129 and Scott's n.124; the pope in question was probably John XII.

26 Ullmann, op. cit. p.126; cf. Levison, op. cit. p.22f.; see note 32 of chapter 5.

27 MD p.396 (EHD 231 and C&S 36).

28 MD p.397f. (EHD 230 and C&S 38).

29 e.g. MD p.370f.

30 O p.109 (cf. Ad p.62); ASC (F) 961 also describes Oda as 'the Good'.

31 See the episcopal lists based on Stubbs in *Handbook of British Chronology*.

32 cf. Brooks, op.cit. p.238f. for the problems of disentangling the different bishops called Byrhthelm.

33 EHD 229, from which this translation is taken (C&S 35).

34 VO p.420.

35 ibid. p.424.

36 ASC 963 (cf. VE chapter 11, EHD 235 p.907).

37 cf. EHD 238.

38 O p.115, but note Stubb's caveat (n.3); cf. Abbo's letter, MD p.378.

39 From *Ecclesiastical Reform in the Late Old English Period*, R.R. Darlington (EHR LI, 1936), p.387.

40 B p.26 (see note 84 of chapter 4).

41 Ad p.61.

42 See MO appendix IV for this, and for what follows.

43 cf. ASC ii p.ix (addenda) for evidence that Oswald's appointment overrode that of a more timorous successor to Oskytel (see note 79 of chapter 5).

44 RC proem 9.

45 B prologue, p.3f. – dedicated to Archbishop Aelfric of Canterbury; Ad p.53 – writing to Aelfric's successor, Archbishop Alphege.

46 VE chapter 20 (EHD 235 p.909); cf. VO p.420 for Oswald's appointment.

47 Ad p.64; cf. B p.28 for another episcopal reminiscence.

48 Ad p.61f.

49 VE chapter 10 (EHD 235 p.906); Wulstan mentions the future see.

50 VE chapter 16 (EHD 235 p.908).

51 ASC (E) 992; cf. ASC ii pp.176–7.

52 VO p.463.

53 See ASC, ibid.

54 MD 400f.
55 Wulstan, VE chapter 40 (ed. Winterbottom).
56 LVH p.23.
57 This may have been the purpose of S 287 (cf. S 1642); see 'The archdeacons of Canterbury under Archbishop Ceolnoth', M. Deanesly (EHR XLII, 1927).
58 cf. *St Anselm and his Biographer*, R.W. Southern (Cambridge, 1963), chapter 7; also 'Religious sentiment and church design', C. Brooke, in *Medieval Church and Society* (London, 1971), p.169f.; also N. Brooks, op. cit. p.38f.
59 MO appendix III.
60 B p.49 (EHD 234 p.902); for Frithegod, see note 31 of chapter 4.
61 Ad p.64.
62 B p.41; note that it was a monk who was at hand in Dunstan's cell to take the dictation.
63 cf. Abbo of Fleury's letter, MD p.378f.
64 e.g. the *Bosworth Psalter*, ed. Gasquet and Bishop (1908), which was almost certainly composed for Dunstan's use at Canterbury.
65 B p.52.
66 cf. Brooks, op.cit. p.250f.; S 1211 and 1212.
67 ibid. S 1511.
68 See *Archaeology of Anglo-Saxon England*, ed. Wilson (1971); p.175 and note; there is considerable dispute over the dating of the crypt but it is Eadmer who draws the comparison with St Peter's, Rome, and intimates that Dunstan prepared his own tomb under the matutinal altar: see Southern, op. cit. p.262f.; E p.221; O p.126f.
69 Southern, op. cit. p.242f.; see also Brooks, op. cit. p.266f.
70 cf. *Bede: His Life, Times and Writings*, A. Hamilton Thompson (Oxford, 1935), chapter 9, 'The library of the venerable Bede', M.L.W. Laistner; and Alcuin's description of the library at York, translated in *Alcuin of York*, S. Alott (York, 1974), p.165.
71 B p.49; cf. VE chapter 24 for Ethelwold's reading habits (EHD 235 p.910); for the work of the scriptorium, see Brooks, op. cit. chapter 11.
72 EHD 121.
73 RC p.xix n.1 (S 1506).
74 HRH p.34f.; cf. MD p.xxvii f.
75 B p.48f.; cf. VO p.458.
76 See *Archaeology of Anglo-Saxon England*, ed. Wilson (1971), p. 165 for a plan of St Augustine's, and p.248 for a review of the archaeological evidence.
77 See *St Dunstan of Canterbury*, E.S. Duckett (London, 1955), p. 195; William of Thorne's 'Chronicle of St Augustine's Abbey' (fourteenth century) was translated by A.H. Davis in 1934 (Oxford).
78 *English Caroline Minuscule*, T.A.M. Bishop (Oxford, 1971), p.xx.
79 MD p.xxviii f.
80 'The early community at Rochester', R.A.L. Smith (EHR, 1945).
81 Abbo's letter in MD p.378f. and the story in O p.115 (but there may be a confusion of Elfstans here – see Stubbs' note).
82 Ad p.61.
83 O p.117; cf. ASC (E) 986; this is corroborated by Sulcard of Westminster (quoted in *The Diplomas of King Aethelred the 'Unready': 978–1016*, S. Keynes (Cambridge, 1980), pp.178–80.
84 S 1457 and 1458; see Southern, op. cit. p.263 and n.3 for the tradition of pleas being heard and settled, as if before a supreme court, at the south porch of the old cathedral in Canterbury.
85 B p.40.
86 E p.204.
87 EHD 40 (C&S 27); cf. *The Beginning of the Parochial System*, G.W.O. Addleshaw (St Anthony's Hall Publication, 3: York, 1959).
88 S 287; cf. Brooks, op. cit. p.251.
89 Wulstan, VE chapter 14 (ed. Winterbottom).
90 VO p.457.
91 Translated from Wulfstan's 'Institutes of polity' by H.R. Loyn in 'Church and state in England in the tenth and eleventh centuries', p.101, in *Tenth Century Studies*, ed. D. Parsons (1975); cf. C&S 56.
92 B p.49 (cf. EHD 234 p.902f. for another translation); this is an excerpt.

Chapter 7: The monasteries

1 cf. T. Symons, 'The monastic reforms of King Edgar' (DR, 1921), p.45.
2 WMVD p.301 (cf. O p.89); William's interest, of course, is in Malmesbury; Osbern stresses Dunstan's personal endowments and liberality.

3 HRH p.215–16; cf. MD p.156f. for St Augustine's, Canterbury, in a law suit with a thegn in Thanet.
4 ASC 969; cf. Roger of Wendover's account, s.a. 974 (EHD 1 and 4).
5 WMDA p.121; see HRH p.50 for the complications and obscurities surrounding the succession of abbots at Glastonbury.
6 VE chapter 10 (EHD 235, p.906) and LVH p.23; cf. FW s.a. 970.
7 J.A. Robinson, *Somerset Historical Essays* (1921); cf. MD p.400 and n.1.
8 B p.46f.
9 ibid. p.47f.
10 ibid. and WMDA p.137: 'Archbishop Dunstan ordered this stoup to be cast. May the Almighty grant him eternal salvation.'
11 ibid. p.121f.; for his burial, see LVH p.9.
12 MD p.396 (EHD 231 and C&S 36); see also WMVD p.313 for the story of Alwold and the foxes.
13 B p.46; cf. Symons, RC p.xx.
14 cf. Osbern's *Life of St Alphege*, chapter 1; there is considerable uncertainty over the reported abbacy of Aescwy, as discussed in HRH p.27f.; cf. JAR p.61f.
15 See *The Cartulary Rolls of Muchelney and Athelney Abbeys*, E.H. Bates (Somerset Record Society, 1899), p.151.
16 MO p.49; cf. ASC 964 and FW s.a. 968 (p.141).
17 WMGP p.178; cf. MO ibid. n.2.
18 S 670: J.A. Robinson thought this the likely date; see John Flete's *History of Westminster* (Cambridge, 1909), p.12.
19 WMVD p.304; cf. some correspondence associated with him in MD p.406f. (C&S 41 and 42).
20 ODS p.415, under 'Wulsin'; cf. 'The life of St Wulsin of Sherborne by Goscelin', C.H. Talbot (*Revue Bénédictine*, LXIX, 1951), p.68f.
21 See J.A. Robinson op. cit. (1909); also 'Sulcard of Westminster', B.W. Scholz (*Traditio*, XX, 1964); cf. story in E p.246.
22 WMGP 407f. and WMVD p.301f.
23 MD p.378 and n.6, where Stubbs raises doubts; but see J.A. Robinson, *The Saxon Bishops of Wells* (1919) and the verdict of HRH p.54.
24 WMVD p.302f.; also for what follows.
25 ibid. p.301.
26 ASC ii p.158 (ASC 964).
27 WMDA p.131; this translation is from Scott's edition.
28 ibid. p.123 (S 783: this privilege is almost certainly spurious, but cf. C&S 39 for a comparable and apparently genuine grant by Ethelred).
29 JAR p.75f.
30 WMDA p.115.
31 JAR pp.63 and 76.
32 VE chapters 9 and 10 (EHD 235 p.906).
33 JAR p.111 n.2.
34 EHD 238 and RC proem 11; cf. LVH p.7 for Edgar as *'vir strenuissimus'*.
35 VE chapter 12 (EHD 235 p.907).
36 VO p.410f.; reference in LVH to *'inertem nobilium clericorum turbam'* (p.7).
37 See notes 70–2 of chapter 5.
38 VE chapters 12–14 (cf. ASC 964).
39 VE chapter 17; Wulstan, VE chapter 23 (cf. LE p.74).
40 VE chapter 15 (cf. Mark 16: 18).
41 ibid. chapter 16 (this translation is from EHD 235 p.908).
42 ASC 964 (EHD 1 p.226); cf. ASC ii p.157f.
43 cf. VE chapter 7.
44 See note 22 of chapter 6.
45 *Liber de Hyde*, ed. Edwards (RS), p.18f. where there is evident confusion with accounts of the later synods at Calne and Kirtlington; cf. *Orbis Britanniae*, E. John (Leicester, 1966), p.249f. – 'The beginning of the Benedictine reform in England' – where the likelihood and significance of this council are fully discussed.
46 VO pp.424–7, where the tone is almost one of monastic propaganda.
47 S 818 (there are strong similarities in style to the proem of the RC).
48 Printed by Birch Carticularum Saxonicum (1276) but not listed by Sawyer.
49 S 745; the text is printed in LVH p.232f. (incompletely also in *Liber de Hyde*, p.192f.); cf. E. John, op. cit. p.271f.
50 Quoted by E. John, op. cit. p.272, from Wormald, *Studies in Western Art: I, Romanesque and Gothic Art* (Princeton, 1963), p.25.

51 The debate over the authorship of the two lives of Ethelwold and their respective dates may be traced in JAR p.168f. (cf. p.106f. also) and in the article by D.J.V. Fisher ('The early biographers of St Ethelwold') in EHR, lxvii, p.381f.; cf. discussion by Whitelock in EHD 235 (p.903) and Winterbottom's introduction to his edition of the two lives (Toronto, 1972).

52 VE chapter 18.

53 Wulstan VE chapter 28 (ed. Winterbottom).

54 VE chapter 20.

55 LVH p.22f.

56 ibid. p.98; this is a fascinating tradition from the middle of the next century but resting on authentic memory and personal testimony.

57 See *Nunnaminster Codex*, ed. Birch (HRS, 1889), appendix D (Birch cf; n.48 1168); this document is not however listed in Sawyer; cf. LVH p.xii f. (cf. S 807) for evidence that secular dwellings were destroyed to establish the complete enclosure of the three monasteries.

58 Wulstan, VE chapters 2 and 22; this Aethelthryth may well be the lady in whose presence the document mentioned above was signed: Edgar seems to have intruded his own daughter as abbess (see note 141 below).

59 See summary of findings in *Archaeology of Anglo-Saxon England*, ed. D. Wilson (Cambridge, 1976), pp.246–7 and bibliography.

60 LVH pp.8–11.

61 VE chapter 23, where it tells how the monks worked alongside the workmen.

62 ed. D. Wilson, op. cit. p.186; see the bibliography for the full list of articles by M. Biddle unfolding the archaeological discoveries, also Biddle's review of the known situation in his article, *'Felix Urbs Winthonia'* (in *Tenth Century Studies*, ed. D. Parsons, 1975).

63 Wulstan, VE chapter 40; cf. R. Quirk, 'Winchester Cathedral in the tenth century' (*Archaeological Journal*, CXIV, 1959, p.26f.).

64 ibid.; cf. 'The dedication of Old Minster in 980', D. Sheerin (*Revue Bénédictine*, 1978).

65 Wulstan's metrical 'Life of St Swithun', ed. A. Campbell (Turin, 1950).

66 ed. Wilson, op. cit. ibid.; cf. LVH ibid.

67 Biddle's view in his art. cit. in *Tenth Century Studies*, ed. Parsons (1975); the Nunnaminster had a fine tower dating from the beginning of the tenth century – cf. *Chronicle of Aethelweard*, ed. Campbell (1962), p.52.

68 VE chapter 18; cf. Farmer's entry and bibliography for Swithun in ODS; also ASC ii p.83.

69 See Wulstan's metrical 'Life', ed. A. Campbell (1950); Aelfric's homily in Aelfric's *Lives of the Saints*, ed. W. Skeat (EETS, 1881), i p.440f.; Lantfrith's letter of dedication to the monks of Old Minster is in MD p.369 (there is an extract in *Liber de Hyde*, ed. Edwards, p.23f.).

70 From 'Aelfric's homily' (ed. Skeat), lines 83–90; Fadsige is one of the three clerics of Old Minster who are named as becoming monks in Aelfric's VE chapter 14.

71 MD p.369.

72 cf. Farmer's entry, 'Swithun' in ODS.

73 'Aelfric's homily', lines 431–4.

74 ibid. lines 444–end (EHD 239 (g)).

75 cf. D. Sheerin, art. cit. p.269.

76 cf. Farmer, art. cit. in ODS; ASC ii 183.

77 LVH p.18.

78 ASC ii 158; cf. HRH entries for Chertsey and Milton; also Plummer's Bede ii 217f.

79 VE chapter 17 (EHD 235, p.908 for this translation); cf. JAR p.116f.

80 LVH p.24; cf. also p.49 where there is an extensive note on confraternities.

81 HRH p.64f.; cf. VO p.427 where Edgar first offered St Albans to Oswald.

82 JAR p.117f.; cf. Peterborough Chronicle in ASC (E) 963 (ASC ii p.155); the charter which lists Ethelwold's gifts of books is S 1448.

83 VO p.428; cf. the important article by C. Hart, 'Athelstan "Half-king" and his family', in *The Anglo-Saxons*, ed. P. Clemoes (II, 1973).

84 LE p.96 n.6 and p.105; cf. HRH entries for Bedford and Crowland.

85 LE p.74.

86 ibid. introduction by E.O. Blake (with valuable foreword by D. Whitelock); see also *The Abbey and Bishopric of Ely*, E. Miller (Cambridge, 1951).

87 VO p.427.

88 LE p.73f.

89 ibid. p.126.

90 JAR p.120.

91 See the illustration in GA (British Museum, 1985), plate vi.

92 LE p.123; cf. Blake's introduction p.lii where a comparison is drawn with the Peterborough list of lands and acquisitions.

93 LE p.74f.
94 S 779, but regarded as spurious In its present form.
95 LE p.78f.
96 ibid. p.117; for the comprehensive lists see p.290.
97 ibid. p.120f.; see Farmer's entries for these saints in ODS.
98 See *The Early Sculpture of Ely Cathedral*, G. Zarnecki (London, 1958); but Zarnecki makes no conclusive identification.
99 ASC ii p.160 and addenda p.ix.
100 VO p.455.
101 ibid. p.420ff.
102 Most English monasteries of the tenth century were dedicated either to Mary or to St Peter, often with appropriate local dedications conjoined (cf. entries in HRH). In VO there are frequent references to Benedict: notably p.442, 'Benedict our ruler'; also pp.447, 464 and 467.
103 VO p.463.
104 ibid. p.431 where a poem of Abbo's is quoted in praise of Ramsey.
105 For Byrhtferth, see chapter 11.
106 VO p.439.
107 MO p.51f.; cf. VO ibid. for the seven monasteries of western Mercia.
108 See note 18 of chapter 9; cf. VO p.443f. (EHD 236).
109 This is the view of J.A. Robinson, 'St Oswald and the church of Worcester' (*British Academy Supplementary Papers*, V, 1919) and also of Sir Ivor Atkins, 'The church of Worcester from the eighth to the twelfth century' (*Antiquaries' Journal*, XVII, 4, October 1937, pp.371–91). For a contrary view see E. John, op. cit. p.234f. (see FW s.a. 969).
110 See E. John, op. cit. p.236f. for some of the evidence from the charters.
111 From VO p.462: cf. discussion in A. Hamilton-Thompson, *Bede – His Life, Times and Writings* (Oxford, 1935), p.98, n.2.
112 See J.A. Robinson, art. cit. pp.1–6: it was apparently a *basilica* like the church built by Ethelwold at Peterborough; cf. S 1345.
113 See F.W. Maitland, *Domesday Book and Beyond* (1897, Fontana edition, 1969), p.357f.; also E. John, op. cit. passim.
114 JAR p.131; the appropriate charters are listed in Sawyer, S 1297–1374.
115 See the full discussion in E. John, op. cit. p.228f.; also in *Land Tenure in Early England* (Leicester, 1964), p.80f.
116 cf. Bede's famous letter to Archbishop Egbert of York (EHD 170) and Ethelwold's observations on *secularium prioratum* in EHD 238; cf. also E. John, *Orbis Britanniae*, p.154f.
117 ibid. p.179 n.1; the charters in question are S 1370, 1315, 1326, 1340, 1309, 1345, 1348, 1361 and 1310.
118 cf. MO p.721 for a helpful diagram; also VO p.434.
119 VO p.424f. and RC proem.
120 WMDA p.129f.
121 LVH pp.21 and 57f.
122 See 'The family of Athelstan "Half-king"', C. Hart (A/S II, 1973); also H.P.R. Finberg, 'The House of Ordgar and the foundation of Tavistock Abbey (EHR LVIII, 1943), p.190f.
123 See introduction to *Chronicle of Aethelweard*, ed. A. Campbell (London, 1962).
124 cf. *Anglo-Saxon Wills*, D. Whitelock (Cambridge, 1930).
125 JW p.53; Adelard VD p.56; EHD 238; VO p.426.
126 II Kings 21.
127 MD p.363 and 366f.; also S 728 (see note 44 of chapter 5).
128 MD p.364f. (C&S 29).
129 See note 40 of chapter 9.
130 JAR p.121; cf. LE p.111 and n.7; cf. RC introduction p.xxiii n.2.
131 See EHD 238 and RC proem chapter 3.
132 cf. D.A. Bullough's article in *Tenth Century Studies*, ed. D. Parsons (1975), p.35 n.50 and 51.
133 Asser, chapter 98 and *Chronicle of Aethelweard*, ed. A. Campbell, p.54.
134 See Birch's introduction to the *Nunnaminster Codex* (HRS, 1889); also *Liber de Hyde*, ed. Edwards (RS, 1866), p.112f.
135 ASE p.445 (see notes 72f. of chapter 3); the appropriate entries are in HRH.
136 See note 58 above.
137 See the appropriate entries in HRH.
138 LVH pp. 57f. and 62.
139 See *The Salisbury Psalter*, ed. C. and K. Sisam (EETS, 1959).
140 RC proem chapter 7.

141 See appendix D of *Nunnaminster Codex*, ed. Birch (HRS, 1889), and the careful discussion in HRH p.223.
142 See H. Farmer's appendix II to the first published report, 'Regularis Concordia – Millenium Conference', ed. A. Stacpoole (Leicester, 1971).
143 O p.111f.; cf. Stubbs' discussion of this in MD p.xcix f.
144 cf. Goscelin's 'Life of St Edith' (*Acta Sanctorum Bollandiana* Sept V (1755) p.364f.) and Farmer's entry in ODS.
145 The life alludes to the shadowy influence of a saintly aunt, a sister of Athelstan's, also called Edith, who lived as a nun at Polesworth; cf. Roger of Wendover, s.a. 925, EHD 4 p.283.
146 See Athelstan's *Liturgica Historica*, E. Bishop (Oxford, 1918), p. 241.
147 Ed. Symons (London, 1953), to which all references in this section are made.
148 MO p.25f. is the best overall introduction to this period.
149 RC proem chapter 5; see Symon's article in *Tenth Century Studies*, ed. Parsons (1975).
150 EHD 238; cf. RC introduction p.xxiii n.2; cf. M. Bateson, 'Rules for monks and canons after the revival under King Edgar' (EHR IX, 1894), p.690f.
151 Ed. M. Bateson in *The Obedientiary Rolls of St Swithun's*, ed. Kitchin (HRS, 1892); cf. RC introduction p.li and note.
152 cf. JAR p.155; also Stubbs' verdict in MD p.xcviii; this was also the view of St Anselm (see note 178 below).
153 See C&S 32.
154 See proem chapter 7 n.1 for the material drawn from the second council of Seville.
155 MO p.45f.
156 ibid.; cf. RC proem chapter 9 n.4 where once again precedent can be drawn from earlier English tradition – this time the legatine synod of 787: H&S III 450f.
157 RC proem chapter 9.
158 ibid. proem chapter 10; cf. EHD 238.
159 See notes 50–1 above; the text is in C&S 31.
160 cf. RC epilogue chapter 69.
161 cf. Dunstan's own customs in B p.39.
162 RC proem chapter 11; the necessity for such provision is shown in one of the stories from Christ Church, Canterbury, recounted by Osbern in his 'Miracles of St Dunstan', MD p.144f. (see note 37 of chapter 12).
163 Dunstan appointed his own brother, Wulfric, as agent of the business of the monastery at Glastonbury: B p.28 (see note 46 of chapter 4).
164 RC proem chapter 11; cf. similar stipulations in the New Minster Charter (C&S 31).
165 RC proem chapter 12.
166 RC introduction p.xlvii.
167 cf. note 155 above; see the bibliography for the many articles by Dom Symons, mainly in the *Downside Review*, in which he has pieced together a thorough and comprehensive review of the sources, composition and significance of the RC.
168 See the table of the monastic day prescribed by the RC for summer and winter in MO p.714f.; it is printed also in RC introduction xliii f.
169 RC proem chapter 5, where Fleury and Ghent are mentioned by name; whether Abbo of Fleury was actually present is uncertain: cf. MO p.46 n.3.
170 cf. JAR p.154; Gregory was a contemporary of Dunstan's and Ethelwold's, and was abbot from 964 to 996 (see 'A note on MS Vatican Bibl. Apost. Lat. 3363', by M.B. Parkes, in *Boethius – His Life, Thought and Influence*, ed. M. Gibson (Blackwell: Oxford 1981), for evidence of documentary links between Einsiedeln and south-western England (probably Glastonbury) at this time).
171 cf. Symons' introduction to RC section III (p.xlv f.); also his article 'Sources for the Regularis Concordia', in DR, 1941.
172 Symons, art. cit. (1941) p.15 n.1.
173 Symons, RC introduction p.li; but cf. also a letter from Fleury to Dunstan (MD p.376) and note also the importance of the personal friendship between Abbo of Fleury and Dunstan (letter in MD p.378f.).
174 Symons, art. cit. (1941), p.147.
175 RC chapter 32.
176 RC chapter 23: this is actually from St Ambrose, *De Sacramentis*, V, iv, 25, ed. H. Chadwick (Mowbray: London, 1960).
177 Symons, art. cit. (1941); Bede's letter, EHD 170; cf. H&S III 370f. for the important provisions of the synod of Cloveshoe in 747 on this very point.
178 cf. RC introduction p.lii: Anselm's letter is in PL clviii p.1104, and is no.39 in the edition by Schmitt (vol.iii, p.151); cf. Southern, *St Anselm and his Biographer* (Cambridge, 1966), p.248.

Chapter 8: The statesman

1 cf. *Chronicle of Aethelweard*, ed. Campbell (1962), p.54.
2 EHD 238 and RC proem chapter 11.
3 See notes 58f. of chapter 5; also J.L. Nelson, 'Inauguration rituals', in *Early Medieval Kingship*, ed. Sawyer and Wood (Leeds, 1977), p.65f.
4 cf. Eadmer VD (MD) p.214 and Nicholas of Worcester's letter, MD p.422f., where it is alleged that the later objections to the succession of Edward in 975 rested on the fact that he had been conceived before Edgar's formal consecration as king (cf. Nelson, art. cit. p.67 n.101).
5 cf. Nicholas of Worcester's letter, ibid. p.423; also ASC ii 158f.
6 See the subscription list of the New Minster Charter (S 745) printed in LVH p.244f.; there is a full discussion in E. John, op. cit. p.275.
7 Ad p.56 and JW p.53.
8 LVH p.23; ASC 977 for his death (cf. ASC ii p.165); also VO p.449.
9 ASE p.367f.
10 ASC 966: discussion in ASC ii p.159f.
11 ASC 969; cf. Roger of Wendover s.a. 974 (EHD 4 p.284).
12 VO p.454.
13 e.g. FW p.139.
14 ASC 959 (D) (EHD 1 p.225).
15 For Wulfstan, see note 103 of chapter 10. David's adultery and Solomon's introduction of pagan worship to please his wives may even be alluded to in this encomium: cf. II Samuel 11 and I Kings 11.
16 ASE p.346; cf. ASC 982 (E) and E. John, op. cit. p.57.
17 FW p.139 and VO p.435.
18 VO ibid.
19 MD p.359 (C&S 26, where the problems of dating are discussed); see notes 45f. of chapter 5.
20 MD p.364f. (C&S 29).
21 VO p.435.
22 MD pp.363 and 366f.
23 B p.37; cf. ASC ii 73 and 113; discussion in E. John, op. cit. p.56f.
24 See ASC ii p.158; cf. D.A. Binchy, *Celtic and Anglo-Saxon Kingship* (Oxford, 1970), p.27f. Hwyl Dda's laws are printed in H&S I 209f.
25 ASC ii p.162.
26 See EHD 4 p.284 and n.6.
27 Aelfric's *Lives of the Saints*, ed. Skeat (EETS, 1966 reprint), i p.469 (EHD 239 p.927 (g)).
28 EHD 1 p.228 and n.1 (ASC 975); note ASC 962 (EHD 1 p.226 n.3) for mention of a sub-king called Sigeferth at Edgar's court, who killed himself.
29 ASE p.369.
30 S 745 (cf. LVH p.237); cf. also VO p.425f. and p.436.
31 See H&S I pp.284–7.
32 ibid.; cf. also pp.208–9: Asser, chapter 79.
33 ibid. p.286 and n.a.
34 O p.113; the bishop's name was Beornhelm, presumably he was a Saxon.
35 See Dunstan's own letter to Ethelred: EHD 229.
36 H&S I p.682f. (EHD 144, 145, 146); cf. note on p.698 also.
37 cf. H. Farmer's entry in ODS, and Stevenson's discussion in Asser p.297.
38 H&S II p.85 and note.
39 See Whitelock's introduction to the extracts from the laws in EHD p.357f.; and 'Canons of Edgar', ed. R. Fowler (EETS, 1972), where there is a full discussion of their provenance and significance (see notes 125f. of chapter 10).
40 Alfred's laws are EHD 33; cf. discussion of Alfred's role as law giver in *Early Germanic Kingship*, J.M. Wallace-Hadrill (Oxford, 1971), p.124f.
41 e.g. Oda's canons (see note 26 of chapter 4); also Dunstan's own example (see notes 85f. of chapter 6).
42 cf. Deanesly, op.cit. p.309f.; for a general review see Stubbs, *Constitutional History* (Oxford, 1891), chapters vi–viii; also ASE p.371f.
43 See note 26 of chapter 4.
44 EHD 40 (cf. C&S 27).
45 MD p.355 and VO p.437.

46 cf. W. Ullmann, op. cit. chapter 6.
47 MD p.355 (for this translation) (cf. Latin text in VO p.437).
48 ibid.; for IV Edgar see EHD 41 (also C&S 28); cf. Nelson, art. cit. p.69 n.119 and 120.
49 See *The Frankish Kingdoms under the Carolingians*, R. McKitterick (London, 1983), chapters 5 and 7.
50 EHD 41 clause 1.
51 See Whitelock's note (p.435 n.3 EHD) on this clause, and Stubbs' discussion of the issue in MD p.cxix (cf. H&S I p.286).
52 e.g. EHD 38 (II Edmund); see C&S 19 and 20 for the 'Canons of Oda' (see notes 26f. of chapter 4).
53 Deanesly, op.cit. p.311; see also *The Beginning of the Parochial System*, G.W.O. Addleshaw (York, 1959), and 'Ecclesiastical reform in the late Old English period', R.R. Darlington (EHR LI, 1936).
54 B p.49 and Ad p.67; for Oda and Edwy, see note 58 of chapter 5.
55 B p.26 (EHD 234, p.900).
56 B p.49.
57 On Hincmar of Rheims, see R. McKitterick, op. cit. chapter 7; also J.M. Wallace-Hadrill, op. cit. passim.
58 Psalm 34: 11 and Psalm 45: 7; cf. R.W. Hunt, *St Dunstan's Classbook* (Amsterdam, 1961).
59 RC proem 3.
60 FW p.144.
61 'The conversion of the eastern Danelaw', D. Whitelock (*Saga-book of the Viking Society* XII, 1941); cf. introductions to LE (ed. Blake).
62 IV Edgar, EHD 41; cf. ASE p.371; see also N. Lund, 'King Edgar and the Danelaw', *Medieval Scandinavia*, 1976).
63 cf. Stubbs, *Constitutional History*, p.261.
64 ASC 959 encomium (EHD 1 p.225).
65 On the mission to Scandinavia, see note 87f. of chapter 10.
66 EHD 4 p.284.
67 See *Archaeology of Anglo-Saxon England*, ed. D. Wilson (Cambridge, 1976); article by M. Dolley, p.358f. and copious bibliography; see too GA p.170f. for illustrations.
68 EHD 35 p.420.
69 O p.106 and E p.202 where the tale is suitably expanded into a homily by Dunstan.
70 VO p.436; cf. ASC s.a. 973.
71 MD p.ci and n.2; cf. E. John, op. cit. p.56f., and Nelson, art. cit. also.
72 Nelson, art. cit. p.68 and n.107 on reference to Bath in the poem 'The ruin'; see 'Bath: Mercian and West Saxon', C.S. Taylor (*Transactions of the Bristol & Gloucester Archaeological Society*, 1908) for the importance of Bath
73 ASC 972 (D) (EHD 1 p.227); VO p.436f. and *Chronicle of Aethelweard*, ed. Campbell (1962), p.55, emphasise this dimension: 'a troop shaven upon their heads with steel'.
74 Nelson, art. cit. p.69 and n.117.
75 ASC 972 (D); cf. Aelfric, *Life of Swithun*, ed. Skeat (1966), I p.468 (EHD 239 (g) p.927).
76 The background to this coronation and the liturgical texts remaining are discussed in 'The earliest surviving royal "ordo": some liturgical and historical aspects', J.L. Nelson, in *Authority and Power*, ed. B. Tierney and P. Linehan (Cambridge, 1980), and the implications of the Bath event of 973 are further unfolded in the same author's study, already mentioned: 'Inauguration rituals' (1977).
77 Nelson, 'Inauguration rituals', p.70 and n.127.
78 VIII Ethelred (EHD 47); cf. RC proem and Deshman, '"Christus rex et magi regnes": kingship and Christology in Ottonian and Anglo-Saxon art', (*Frühmittelalter liche Studien*, Münster: Berlin, 1976), p.393f.
79 RC proem: opening lines.
80 The text is edited in full by P.L. Ward, 'An early version of the Anglo-Saxon coronation ceremony'. (EHR 1942), p.346f.
81 cf. 'The earliest surviving royal "ordo"', J.L. Nelson.
82 ibid. p. 48.
83 VO p.437f. and MD p.355 for the text of the royal three-fold promise: in the extant Ratoldus 'Ordo' the text is inserted at the end of the rite, but there is a rubric prescribing a royal promise at the beginning; P. Stafford has demonstrated that Dunstan was responsible for making the royal promises a precondition for the solemn anointing ('The laws of Cnut and the history of Anglo-Saxon promises' A/S 10, 1982); by the time of Ethelred, these promises were recited in the vernacular as well as in Latin, and the English text is what is recorded in MD p.355f.
84 I Kings 1: 39f.
85 VO pp.437–8.

86 This is provided for in the Ratoldus *'Ordo'*; it is only implied in VO.
87 VO p.438; at the banquet afterwards for the bishops and the nobility, the two archbishops, Dunstan and Oswald, were elevated alongside the king; the queen entertained the abbots and abbesses separately.
88 See 'A re-examination of the "coronation" of Symeon of Bulgaria', A. Louth (JTS XXIX/1, 1978), p.117.
89 VO p.425f.
90 cf. Athelstan's prayer in *Nunnaminster Codex*, ed. Birch (HRS, 1889), p.116.
91 For precedents, cf. Nelson, 'Inauguration rites', p.70.
92 cf. New Minster Charter (S 745) in LVH p.241F.
93 J.A. Robinson, art. cit. (JTS, 1917).
94 RC p.13 and n.10.
95 'Ratoldus Ordo' (Ward, art. cit., EHR, 1942), p.360.
96 E. John, *Orbis Britanniae* (1966), p.61f.

Chapter 9: Two kings

1 *Chronicle of Aethelweard*, ed. Campbell (1962), p. 56.
2 FW p.143; cf. ASC 975 (EHD 1 p.228).
3 LVH p.9.
4 WMDA pp.131 and 135.
5 ibid. p.131.
6 ibid. p.135.
7 See note 5f. of chapter 8, S 745; cf. E. John, op. cit. p.274f.; and Nelson, art. cit. p.67.
8 ASE p.372f.
9 O p.114.
10 EHD 123 (S 937).
11 cf. ASC ii p.163; cf. LVH p.9 – 'gubernacula *decenter* suscepit'.
12 FW p.145.
13 VO p.448 (EHD 236 p.914).
14 JW p.56.
15 VO ibid.; cf. p.443f. also.
16 ASC (C) 975 (EHD 1 p.229).
17 EHD 114.
18 VO p.443f.; cf. *'Princeps Merciorum Gentis'*, A. Williams (A/S X, 1982).
19 ASC 975; cf. ASC ii p.164, and WMVD p.307.
20 JW ibid.; charters S 828–32.
21 EHD 115.
22 ASC (D) 975 (probably from the pen of Archbishop Wulfstan of York).
23 VO ibid. (translation is from EHD 236 p.913).
24 EHD 123.
25 Williams, art. cit.; also 'The anti-monastic reaction in the reign of Edward the Martyr', D.J.V. Fisher (*Cambridge Historical Journal* X, 1952), which is of fundamental importance for understanding this episode.
26 LE pp.126–7.
27 VO ibid.
28 e.g. Aelfric, *Life of St Swithun*, ed. Skeat (EETS, 1966).
29 O p.113.
30 ibid.; cf. ASC (E) 977 (EHD 1 p.230).
31 ASC ibid.; also (C); according to FW (p.145) there was also a third synod at Amesbury in this year (cf. C&S 34).
32 VO p.444 (EHD 236 p.914).
33 ibid. p.448f.
34 ASC 978 (D) (EHD 1 p.230).
35 cf. D. Bethurum, *Homilies of Wulfstan* (Oxford, 1971 edition), XX and p.361f., translated in EHD 240; note 3 (p.931) underlines the unique significance of Wulfstan's assertion that the body of Edward was burnt. If this is true, then the translation of his remains in 980 may not have been quite as the biographer of Oswald describes (but see below: note 40f). EHD 236 p.915: cremation of a king's body was tantamount to sacrilege.
36 VO ibid.
37 O p.114; cf. LE p.128 and n.4, and 127 n.4 also, where attention is rightly drawn to the treatment of this tale in the telling by C.E. Wright in *The Cultivation of Saga in Anglo-Saxon England* (Edinburgh, 1939).

38 cf. ASC ii 166f.; see *Dunstanus Saga*, C.E. Fell (Copenhagen, 1963) for the text of the Icelandic saga and its development and provenance, also her edition of the 'Passion of St Edward the Martyr' in *Edward, King and Martyr* (Leeds, 1971) where the text may usefully be consulted in appendix II.
39 JW p.57.
40 ASC (E) 980; see Plummer's discussion in ASC ii pp.166–7f.
41 Plummer ibid. p.168 for chronicler 'F': he regards this as a later and perhaps speculative assertion (but cf. MD p.cii f.).
42 VO p.450 (EHD 236 p.915).
43 VO p.452; cf. LVH p.93 also.
44 S 899: see ASE p.374 n.1.
45 V Ethelred 16 (EHD 44 p.444); cf. Hugh Farmer's entry in ODS.
46 cf. *The Diplomas of Ethelred the Unready*, S. Keynes (Cambridge, 1980), p. 166f. (see also H&S III p.453f. and 'Ratoldus Ordo' in Ward, art. cit. (EHR, 1942)).
47 MD p.378f.; cf. discussion in 'The cults of murdered royal saints in Anglo-Saxon England', D.W. Rollason (A/S 11, 1983), p.18f.
48 There are two dates recorded in the chronicle: cf. ASC ii p.166.
49 ASC (D) 978.
50 VO p.455.
51 MD p.355f.
52 O p.115.
53 Wulstan's 'Life of Ethelwold', chapter 40.
54 See 'The dedication of the Old Minster in 980', D. Sheerin (*Revue Bénédictine*, 1978).
55 Keynes, op. cit. is indispensable for the study of this reign, and is fundamental to the assumptions about the political situation made here.
56 ibid. p.175.
57 ASC (C) 979; cf. ASC ii p.167.
58 cf. *Archaeology of Anglo-Saxon England*, ed. D. Wilson (Cambridge, 1976), index references for the important discoveries from this period made at Southampton.
59 ASC (C) 980; 981; and 982.
60 ASE p.375; and ASC ibid.: Otto II died in 982.
61 cf. Wilson, op. cit. p.358 for evidence of some decentralisation of the production of the coinage during these years.
62 S 835–7; also 841–3; 845 and 850.
63 EHD 229, where there are some interesting errors evident in the way such relatively recent history was remembered.
64 ASC 984.
65 O p.115.
66 Ad p.61f.
67 ASC s.a. 985.
68 See Keynes, op. cit. for what follows.
69 cf. S 876 and 918; see ASC ii p.171; also S 893 for Aethelsin.
70 ASC ibid.; see HRH entry for Abingdon.
71 MD p.396 (EHD 231 and C&S 36).
72 WMVD p.313.
73 S 876 and 918; cf. Keynes, op. cit. on these charters.
74 MD p.372f.
75 ASC s.a. 986.
76 The passage is quoted extensively in Keynes, op. cit. p.178; cf. O p.117.
77 Osbern, VD ibid.
78 S 893 (cf. also S 885).
79 MD pp.378–81; there are some acrostic poems addressed by Abbo to Dunstan, ibid. p.410f. (cf. VO p.460f.).
80 Ad p.53.
81 MD p.xxii f. on the possible identity of the author 'B'; cf. letters on pp. 374, 385 and 390; this work by 'B' was clearly known and respected by the first biographer of Oswald: cf. VO p.457 and MD p.lx n.1.
82 MD p.lix.
83 The text of '*Kyrie rex splendens*' is printed in MD, p.357f.; cf. Ad p.63; it is discussed by Dom Cuthbert Butler in DR, 1885; cf. also the tradition in E p.207.
84 B p.41f.
85 ibid. and also p.44.
86 ibid. p.48f.
87 ibid. p.49 (EHD 234 p.902).

88 ibid. p.50 (another translation is available in EHD 234).
89 Ad p.64f.
90 ibid. p.65.
91 B p.51: cf. Ad ibid.
92 Ad ibid.
93 B p.52 (MD p.lix discusses the later insertion into the first life of Dunstan in one of the manuscripts of a fabulous miracle at the saint's deathbed.)
94 Ad p.66; cf. Stubbs' translation on p.lxii, and also Plummer's comments in ASC ii p.172.

Chapter 10: The successors

1 There is a useful summary of Oswald's life and work in ODS (also DNB).
2 VO p.466.
3 ibid. p.470f. (abridged translation); cf. ASC ii p.176.
4 'Manual' (ed. Crawford, EETS, 1929), p.212; cf. LVH p.92 where Oswald is referred to as a 'saint'.
5 Translation from EHD 239: p.927f., ed. Skeat (EETS, 1966), i, p.471).
6 VO p.455 (EHD 236 p.916); cf. ASE p.375f.
7 EHD 230 (C&S 38); the text is also in MD p.397f.
8 EHD 10; cf. VO p.455 (EHD 236); also LE chapters 62 and 63: his widow commissioned a tapestry of his noble deeds to be hung in Ely Abbey.
9 cf. the treaty (II Ethelred) (EHD 42); also ASC ii p.174f.; but the payment of Danegeld was not without precedent: there is similar provision in the will of Eadred, for example (EHD 107).
10 ASC 994 (C).
11 See 'The collection of Danegeld and Heregeld in the reigns of Ethelfred II and Cnut', M.K. Lawson (EHR, 1984).
12 In EHD 127; cf. ASC s.a. 1002.
13 See ASE p.380 n.2; cf. also N. Lund, art. cit. (*Medieval Scandinavia*, 1976).
14 ASE ibid.; and appropriate entries in ASC (EHD 1).
15 ASE ibid. p.386.
16 ibid. p.394; also Lawson, art. cit.
17 See MO appendix IV; also ASC ii p.172.
18 cf. Brooks, op. cit. p.278f.
19 MD p.384f.
20 *Liber de Hyde*, ed. Edwards (RS, 1866), p.359f.
21 MD p.385f. (cf. C&S 37).
22 Sigeric's itinerary to Rome is preserved: MD p.391f.; cf. B. Peschi, art. cit. (*Rivista di archaeologica cristiana*, XIII, 1936).
23 MD p.400f.
24 ibid. p.406 (C&S 41).
25 HRH p.51.
26 ASC ii p.173 (see chapter 11 below).
27 cf. Brooks, op. cit. p.278 n.56.
28 EHD 117.
29 ASC ibid. p.177.
30 EHD 1 p.236 n.3.
31 HRH p.65; cf. Brooks, op. cit. p.279 n.64.
32 See ASC ii p.179.
33 B p.3 (prologue); cf. VO p.452.
34 Brooks, op. cit. p.259; cf. ASC ii p.178 on the inserted tradition in ASC about the conversion of Christ Church into a proper monastery at this time; the matter is weighed up in MO appendix III.
35 See note 103 below; ASC ibid. p.179.
36 EHD 121; and discussion in Brooks, op. cit. p.286f.
37 EHD 126.
38 EHD 122.
39 ASC s.a. 1005; cf. ASC ii pp.183–5.
40 Ad p.53 (proem).
41 See entry in ODS; the limited reliability of Osbern's 'Life of Alphege' is discussed in R.W. Southern, *St Anselm and his Biographer*, (Cambridge, 1963), p.250f.; cf. also Brooks, op. cit. p.285f.
42 This is from EHD 1 p.244 (Whitelock's translation of ASC); in 1023, Alphege was duly translated from London to Canterbury – ASC (D) s.a. 1023.

43 EHD 27; curiously the writer calls Alphege 'Dunstan'. There is another instance of a foreigner latching onto the name of Dunstan in this way – cf. Mrs J. Tait's article on the legend of St Ursula in *Historical Essays*, ed. Tait and Tout (Manchester, 1907).
44 See note 103f. below.
45 EHD 1 p.252 (ASC s.a. 1020).
46 HRH p.38; cf. F. Barlow, *The English Church: 1000–1066* (Longman, 1979 edition), p.73 n.6 for a caveat concerning Lyfing's background.
47 WMDA p.137 (this is Scott's translation); cf. MO p.70 n.3.
48 See *Chronicle of Aethelweard*, ed. Campbell (1962), p.xvi n.3 for discussion of the possible kinship ties here; also Barlow, op. cit. p.72 n.3, 4 and 5.
49 ASC ii p.216.
50 The best summary is in MO pp.57–69; see also Barlow, op. cit. chapter 1.
51 D. Whitelock, *Anglo-Saxon Wills* (Cambridge, 1930) is indispensable.
52 EHD 116.
53 EHD 122.
54 EHD 129.
55 S 876, 881, 884, 888, 889, 891, 896, 899, 903, 904, 909, 913, 916, 918, 919, 921, 933, 935, 937.
56 S 893.
57 S 889 and 891; also 918 and 935.
58 S 947 and 948.
59 Brooks, op. cit. p.261f. for a full discussion of this matter.
60 ibid.
61 ibid. p.274.
62 WMDA p.131f.
63 ibid. p.139 (this is Scott's translation).
64 LE p.290f.
65 ibid. p.137.
66 VO p.463f.
67 HRH p.24.
68 See chapter 11 below.
69 LVH – introduction by Birch, p.xi f.
70 MO pp.74–8; see R.R. Darlington, 'William of Malmesbury's Life of Wulfstan', (CS XL, 1928).
71 MO ibid. p.59f.
72 cf. VO p.474f. for the death of Aethelwine; ASC 991 for death of Brihtnoth.
73 See Campbell's introduction to *Chronicle of Aethelweard* (1962), p.xv.
74 EHD 239a; cf. HRH p.37.
75 S 911; Aelfric's letter to Eynsham was edited by M. Bateson in *Obedientiary Rolls of St Swithun's*, ed. Kitchin (HRS, 1892); (cf. MO p.66 n.2 for a possible colony from this house at Stow in Lincolnshire).
76 HRH p.71; cf. ASC ii p.179; also H.P.R. Finberg, 'The house of Ordgar and the foundation of Tavistock Abbey' (EHR LVIII, 1943); ASC (C) 997 for evidence of its considerable wealth and endowment.
77 EHD 122.
78 cf. Farmer's entry in ODS; also C.H. Talbot, 'The Life of St Wulsin of Sherborne by Goscelin' (*Revue Bénédictine*, LXIX, 1951); Aelfric's letter is in C&S 40; cf. also MD p.406f. (C&S 41), and mention in WMVD p.304.
79 VO p.466; in 1006, Eadnoth became bishop of Dorchester and he died at the battle of Ashingdon in 1016 (cf. ASC s.a. 1006 and 1016, and ASC ii pp.190 and 198).
80 See C. Hart, 'Eadnoth of Ramsey and the founding of Chatteris Nunnery', (*Proceedings of the Cambridge Antiquarians' Society*, 1964); and LE p.140 n.5.
81 EHD 125 (S 1536); cf. S 906; cf. 'The charters of Burton Abbey', P. Sawyer (*Northern History*, x, 1975).
82 HRH p.30.
83 MO p.70; also Barlow, op. cit. appendix II, which treats fully of the state of the monasteries after AD1000; cf. 'The legends and traditions concerning the origin of the abbey of Bury St Edmunds', A. Gransden (EHR, 1985).
84 ASC 1020.
85 cf. LE p.155.
86 S 980; cf. also S 984.
87 This matter is best approached through MO p.67f. and ASE p.462f.; also Barlow, op. cit. pp. 15 n.4, 228 and 233.
88 For Haakon at the court of Athelstan see note 9 of chapter 3.
89 See especially the 'Northumbrian Priests' Law', EHD 52 (C&S 63).

90 cf. MO p.67 n.2 remains a valuable bibliography: Adam of Bremen is in MGH SS 7; cf. too F. Birkeli, 'The missions to Norway' (*Nottingham Medieval Studies*, XV, 1971).
91 WMDA p.139; cf. MO p.67 n.3.
92 ASE p.463; cf. Barlow, op. cit. p.233 for English bishops in the Orkneys.
93 Farmer's entry in ODS is a useful summary; there is a valuable map in ASE p.400 and discussion on p.404f.
94 ASE ibid. p.463; and MO ibid. p.68 n.7.
95 See L. Gjerløw, *Adoratio Crucis: the Regularis Concordia and the Decreta Lanfranci* (Norwegian University Press: Oslo, 1961).
96 C.E. Fell, *Dunstanus Saga* (Copenhagen, 1963).
97 See Barlow, op. cit. p.15 n.4 for full details; also MO ibid.
98 LE p.168f. and n.5.
99 MO p.69.
100 cf. Barlow, op. cit. p.228.
101 The presence of German and other continentals in Scandinavia in the eleventh century may well indicate that the English missions began to spur the German Church into similar activities.
102 ASE p.396f.
103 LE ii chapter 87 (p.155f.) is a brief review of Wulfstan's career; for a general introduction see D. Bethurum, *Homilies of Wulfstan* (Oxford, 1971), p.54f.; also Barlow, op. cit. p.68f.
104 See Bethurum p.59f. for the importance of the continuity of learning at Worcester in the tenth century for Wulfstan's early work.
105 ibid. p.61 n.1 (cf. EHD 1 pp.225 and 228).
106 ibid. p.63 n.3 (cf. S 1384–5; 1459; also 1845–7).
107 ibid. pp.63–4.
108 ASC s.a. 1020.
109 C&S 62 p.449.
110 Bethurum, op. cit. pp.64–5 (Wulfstan lies buried in Bishop West's chapel in Ely Cathedral).
111 EHD 47 (C&S 59); cf. ASC 1018 – the addition in chronicle D which is discussed in ASC ii p.202.
112 Bethurum, op. cit. p.69f. is an excellent introduction to this aspect of his work; see too the various articles by D. Whitelock listed in the Bibliography.
113 cf. H.R. Loyn, art. cit. (1975); also Bethurum, op. cit. pp.70 and 98f.
114 EHD 41.
115 EHD 44 and its introductory note by D. Whitelock (C&S 49).
116 EHD 45 (C&S 50).
117 EHD 46 (C&S 52).
118 EHD 48 (C&S 60).
119 EHD 49 (C&S 64).
120 EHD 53 (this is Whitelock's translation) (C&S 60); cf. also C&S 61 (this text may be found in H&S III pp.559–61 and also in Levison, op. cit. appendix III where there is a pertinent discussion of its significance); for other examples of more routine papal correspondence see Bethurum, op. cit. appendix II.
121 EHD 51.
122 C&S 47 where there is a valuable discussion; cf. Bethurum, op. cit. p.73.
123 'Canons of Edgar', ed. R. Fowler (EETS, 1972) (C&S 48).
124 Fowler, op. cit. introduction p.xxvii (cf. MD p.cvii for a notable example of this older error in attributing these canons to Dunstan).
125 Fowler, op. cit. p.xxviii.
126 ibid. p.xli f.
127 ibid. p. xlvii f.
128 D. Whitelock, 'Archbishop Wulfstan, homilist and statesmen' (TRHS, 1942), p.35; cited in Fowler, op. cit. p.1.
129 EHD 52 (C&S 63).
130 Bethurum, op. cit. p.85f.
131 ibid. p.87.
132 EHD 240 (cf. edition by Whitelock, 1963).
133 For Aelfric see chapter 11.
134 Bethurum, op. cit. pp.69, 79 and 85.
135 'Institutes of Polity', ed. Jost (1959); cf. Bethurum, op. cit. p.76f.
136 See note 83 of chapter 8.
137 Bethurum, op. cit. p.78.
138 cf. H.R. Loyn, art. cit. (1975), p.101: the image is derived from Sedulius Scottus – see Jost's discussion of the text in his 'Institutes'.

139 This three-fold division was deeply traditional by the time of Wulfstan and Aelfric: cf. EHD
p.928 n.1. cf. D. Dubuisson, *'L'Irlande et la théorie médiévale des "trois ordres"*, (*Revue de l'Histoire
des Religions*, clxxxviii, 1975, pp.35–63) for the suggestion that this idea may have come to
England from Ireland.
140 cf. Loyn, art. cit. p.101; quoted above as an apposite picture of Dunstan as bishop; cf. C&S 53–7
for other documents reflecting Wulfstan's vision of episcopacy.

Chapter 11: The flowering of the tenth century

1 See chapter 1; cf. the prologue and part I of GA, ed. Backhouse, Turner and Webster (British
Museum, 1984), pp.11–19. This invaluable compendium affords the best picture of the whole
range of artistic achievement in this period.
2 Quoted from Aelfric's preface to his 'Grammar', ed. Zupitza (Berlin, 1880), by D.A. Bullough,
'The educational tradition in England from Alfred to Aelfric: teaching "utriusque linguae"'
(*Settimane di studio del Centro italiano di studi sull'alto medioevo*, Spoleto, 1972), p.493; cf. also K.
Sisam, *Studies in the History of Old English Literature* (Oxford, 1953), p.301.
3 See note 125 of chapter 10; cf. P. Clemoes, 'The Old English Benedictine office: CCCC. MS 190;
and 'The relations between Aelfric and Wulfstan – a reconsideration' (*Anglia*, 1960), p.281:
'The number of works by Aelfric that we know Wulfstan used for his own writings grows, and
no doubt will continue to grow as further work proceeds.' See too C&S 46 for Aelfric's first
pastoral letter for Wulfstan with a close discussion; also Bethurum, *Homilies of Wulfstan*
(Oxford, 1971), p.24f.
4 VE (EHD 235); 'Homily on St Swithun' in *Lives of the Saints*, I, p.441f., ed. Skeat (EETS, 1966
reprint); cf. 'Aelfric's saints' lives and the problem of miracles', M.R. Godden (*Leeds Studies*, xvi,
1986, p.83).
5 ASE p.457f.; cf. MO pp.61f. and 493f.; the important introduction to the study of Aelfric's
writings is by P. Clemoes, 'The chronology of Aelfric's works', (in *The Anglo-Saxons. Studies . . .
presented to Bruce Dickins*, ed. P. Clemoes (London, 1959), pp. 212–47 (cf. extracts in EHD 239).
6 Bullough, art. cit. p.488f.; cf. Aelfric's 'Grammar', ed. Zupitza (1880); also R.L. Thomson,
'Aelfric's Latin Vocabulary' (*Leeds Studies in English*, new series, vol.12, p.155).
7 Bullough, ibid. p.491; cf. E.R. Williams, 'Aelfric's grammatical terminology' (*Publications of the
Modern Language Association of America*, LXXIII, 1958).
8 Bullough, ibid. p.489.
9 ibid. p.488; *Colloquium: Aelfric's Colloquy*, ed. G.N. Garmonsway (London, 1939).
10 ibid. introduction, especially p.11f.
11 Ed. H. Henel (EETS, 1942); cf. introduction p.xlii f.
12 ibid. p.lv; cf. note also on p.96.
13 See EHD 239 a, from which this translation is taken; cf. also his own introduction to the second
series of homilies, ed. M. Godden (EETS 1979), p 1
14 ASE p.458.
15 Godden, op. cit. p.xciii; cf. the supplementary collection of these homilies, ed. J.C. Pope (EETS,
1967 and 1968).
16 Pope, op. cit. p. 105f.
17 ed. W.W. Skeat (EETS, 1966 reprint).
18 ed. R. Morris (EETS, 1967 reprint).
19 MO p.494; cf. Pope, op. cit. p.136f.
20 cf. Godden op. cit. p.lxii and Pope's introduction.
21 Pope, op. cit. p.150f.
22 P.G. Caraman, 'The character of the late Saxon clergy' (DR LXIII, 1945), p.189; also R.R.
Darlington, art. cit. (EHR, 1936).
23 Ed. S.J. Crawford (EETS, 1969 reprint); cf. MO p.62.
24 Crawford, op. cit. p.15f.; also MO ibid. p.63.
25 Crawford, op. cit. p.71f.; cf. EHD 239 (h): Aelfric concludes with a personal admonition against
excessive drinking!
26 See Bethurum, *Homilies of Wulfstan* (Oxford, 1957), p.96 n.2.
27 His pastoral letters are edited by B. Fehr, *'Die Hirtenbriefe Aelfrics'* (Hamburg, 1914; reprinted
Darmstadt, 1966); cf. C&S 40, 45 and 46; see also Bethurum, op. cit. p.304f.
28 Aelfric's letter to the monks of Eynsham is edited by M. Bateson in the *Obedientiary Rolls of St
Swithun's*, ed. Kitchin (HRS, 1892); the other treatises are printed by B. Assmann in
Angelsächsische Homilien und Heiligenleben (Kassel, 1889; reprinted Darmstadt, 1964).
29 Ed. S.J. Crawford (EETS, 1929; reprinted 1966); cf. Henel, op. cit. p.96 for a comment on the role
of priests as computists.
30 For Abbo's visit to England cf. Aelfric's homily on St Edmund the martyr (*Saints' Lives*, II, ed.

Skeat, EETS, 1966 reprint), p.315; this is largely a translation into English of Abbo's 'Life of St Edmund' in Latin, ed. M. Winterbottom (Toronto, 1972); Abbo's letter to Dunstan which prefaces this life is in MD p.378f.

31 Bullough, art. cit. p.483f.

32 Printed in MD p.410f.; also in VO p.459f.; for another example of Abbo's verse see VO p.431 (cf. MD p.376 and note for a letter from Fleury to Dunstan).

33 *Byrhtferth's Manual* ed. Crawford (1929), p.233; behind this work stands a common-place book which Byrhtferth compiled during Abbo's sojourn at Ramsey: see P.S. Baker, 'Byrhtferth's "Enchiridion" and the Computus in Oxford – St John's MS 17' (A/S 10, 1981).

34 Bullough, art. cit. p.486.

35 See G.F. Forsey, 'Byrhtferth's Preface' *(Speculum*. 1928), p. 505f.; also bibliography on p.22 of *Manuscripts at Oxford: R.W. Hunt Memorial Exhibition* (Bodleian Library, 1980) in chapter IV 'The revival of Latin learning in late Anglo-Saxon England', by M. Lapidge.

36 'Manual', ed. Crawford, p.135 (also p.151 – cf. MD p.xx); cf. John 16: 13.

37 'Manual' p.15; cf. the many diagrams and their symbolic significance in this text.

38 'Manual', appendix I (Byrhtferth's preface to Bede's *'De Temporibus'*), p.246.

39 This is discussed by J.A. Robinson, 'Byrhtferth and the life of St Oswald' (JTS, 1929) and by S.J. Crawford, 'Byrhtferth and the anonymous life of Oswald' (in *'Speculum Religionis' – Essays Presented to C.G. Montefiore* (Oxford, 1929), p.99f.); see also P.S. Baker, 'The Old English Canon of Byrhtferth of Ramsey' *(Speculum*, 1980).

40 VO p.457; its significance was first discussed by Stubbs in MD p.xviii.

41 See M. Lapidge, 'Byrhtferth of Ramsey and the early sections of the "Historia Regum" attributed to Simeon of Durham' (A/S 10, 1982); also C. Hart, 'Byrhtferth's Northumbrian Chronicle' (EHR, 1982) (cf. MD p.xx).

42 See Farmer's entry in ODS; also EHD 236, introduction by Whitelock, and M. Lapidge, 'The "hermeneutic style" in tenth-century Anglo-Latin literature' (A/S 4, 1975), p.91f.

43 The verdicts of MO p.494 and of ASE p.450 (cf. 457 also).

44 M. Forster, 'Über die Quellen von Aelfrics exegetischen Homiliae Catholicae' *(Anglia*, XVI, 1894) and Über die Quellen von Aelfric's Homiliae Catholicae', I, *Legenden* (Berlin, 1892); there is a valuable discussion in Pope, op. cit. p.150f.

45 ibid. p.156f.; cf. Smalley, op. cit. p.39f.; see also C.L. Smetana, 'Aelfric and the early medieval homiliary' *(Traditio*, XV, 1959) and 'Aelfric and the Homiliary of Haymo of Halberstadt' *(Traditio*, XVII, 1961).

46 See *Aldhelm – The Prose Works*, ed. M. Lapidge and M. Herren (Ipswich, 1979); also M. Lapidge, art. cit. (R.W. Hunt exhibition: Oxford, 1980), p.20f.

47 MD p.388.

48 M. Lapidge, 'Hermeneutic style' (A/S 4, 1975), p.67.

49 ibid. p.73.

50 There is a valuable list in Pope, op. cit. p.163f.; cf. Crawford's footnotes for the sources of Byrhtferth's 'Manual' (op. cit., 1929).

51 Bethurum, op. cit. p.61.

52 There is a full discussion of the contents of the library at Christ Church, Canterbury, in Brooks, op. cit. p.266f.

53 Alcuin's list of the contents of the library at York is in S. Alott, *Alcuin of York* (York, 1974), p.165; cf. discussion of Bede's library in *Bede – His Life, Times and Writings*, ed. A. Hamilton Thompson (Oxford, 1935), by M.L.W. Laistner (chapter IX; p.237f.).

54 The most penetrating study of the early medieval monastic approach to learning is by J. Leclerq, *The Love of Learning and the Desire for God* (SPCK, 1978).

55 Wulstan's *Life of Ethelwold*, ed. M. Winterbottom (Toronto, 1972).

56 MD p.369 for the letter of Lantfrith to the monks at Winchester.

57 See note 24 of chapter 10; cf. his letter in MD p.400f.

58 The 'Life of St Grimbald' may be found in *The Monastic Breviary of Hyde Abbey* (i.e. New Minster), ed. J.B.L. Tolhurst (HBS, 1932); see P. Grierson, 'Grimbald of St Bertin's' (EHR LV, 1940) and ODS entry.

59 MO p.64f.

60 See Brooks, op.cit. for the change at Canterbury Cathedral, p.263f.; there is a valuable discussion of tenth-century English psalters in general in *The Salisbury Psalter*, ed. Sisam (EETS, 1959) appendix I, p.47f.

61 See F. Wormald, *English Kalendars before 1100* (HBS, 1934); also H. Gneuss, 'The origin of standard Old English' (A/S 1, 1972) for the wider intellectual influence of the Winchester school.

62 *The Salisbury Psalter*, ed. Sisam, p.75.

63 ibid. p.52f.
64 M. Lapidge, 'Hermeneutic style' (A/S 4, 1975); see also his article, 'Three Latin poems from Ethelwold's school at Winchester' (A/S 1, 1972).
65 H. Gneuss, art. cit. (1972), p. 82.
66 cf. K. Young, *The Drama of the Medieval Church* (Oxford, 1933).
67 cf. Caraman, art. cit.; also C.P. Wormald, 'The uses of literacy in Anglo-Saxon England and its neighbours' (TRHS, 1977), p.113.
68 See discussion in MD p.cxix (see note 51 of chapter 8); cf. 'Canons of Edgar', ed. Fowler (EETS, 1972), p. 39 for note on chapter 61 (C&S 48).
69 e.g. GA 162 and 163; cf. M. Cameron, 'Sources of medical knowledge in Anglo-Saxon England' (A/S 11, 1983).
70 LVH p.260 (appendix D) and *Nunnaminster Codex*, ed. Birch (HRS, 1889), p. 109f. (appendix A).
71 'Manual', ed. Crawford, pp. 11 and 205.
72 'Homily against auguries', in *Lives of the Saints*, I, ed. Skeat, p.364.
73 Oda: canon ix (C&S 20).
74 VO p.471; VE chapter 19 (EHD 235 p.909); O p.131.
75 RC chapters 62 and 63; 'Life of Edith' chapter 6 (AA.SS.Sept V (1755) p.364f.).
76 EHD 107, 106, 116; cf. the manumissions at Bodmin: EHD 140–50.
77 EHD 129.
78 See EHD 6; also Asser's *Life of Alfred*, ed. Keynes and Lapidge (1983), p.22; cf. ASC ii p.94, and also p.138: discussed in JAR p.53f.; cf. EHD 3 s.a. 934 (Symeon of Durham).
79 See Abbo's letter to Dunstan: MD p.379; LVH p.96 recounts another testimony to the state of Cuthbert's body in the middle of the eleventh century.
80 ASE p.435; cf. Barlow, op. cit. pp. 34 and 105; also MO p.165f.; cf. *The Relics of St Cuthbert*, ed. C. F. Battiscombe (Oxford, 1956).
81 EHD 3 comprises extracts from the *'Historia Regum'* attributed to Symeon of Durham; EHD 6 comprises extracts from the anonymous 'History of St Cuthbert'; cf. GA 48 and 139 for glimpses of the cultural life at Durham.
82 Ethelwold had been tutor to Edgar (EHD 238 and RC proem 1); Sideman, bishop of Crediton, had taught Edgar's sons (VO p.449).
83 *Chronicle of Aethelweard*, ed. Campbell (1962), p. xii; cf. ASE p.461.
84 ibid. pp.21 and 51.
85 e.g. the lay correspondents of Aelfric (see note 5 etc. above).
86 C.L. Wrenn, *Beowulf* (London, 1973 edition, by W.F. Bolton), where there is a careful introduction and full bibliography; cf. GA 155.
87 GA 156 (EHD 10); cf. LE pp.133–6 for the tapestry commemorating him at Ely.
88 GA 153 and 154.
89 ibid.152.
90 cf. K. Sisam, *The Structure of Beowulf* (Oxford, 1965), conclusion p.60f.
91 E. John, 'War and society in the tenth century: the Maldon campaign' (TRHS, 1977); also D. Whitelock, 'Anglo-Saxon poetry and the historian' (TRHS, 1949).
92 RC epilogue; cf. sundry wills, notably EHD 122.
93 LVH p.47f., where there is a long note on confraternities: the idea (unlike the formalities) was not restricted to clergy and religious, and the very existence of a *'Liber vitae'* (here and at Durham) indicates the place of the laity too.
94 cf. G. Zarnecki, *The Early Sculpture of Ely Cathedral* (London, 1958).
95 See F.A. Gasquet and E. Bishop, *The Bosworth Psalter* (London, 1908); also P.M. Korhammer, 'The origin of the Bosworth Psalter' (A/S 2, 1973).
96 See note 60 of chapter 10 and note 78 of chapter 6 for the relations between Christ Church and St Augustine's, Canterbury; also Brooks, op. cit. p.264f.
97 GA p.88 provides a valuable introduction to this area of art.
98 'Canons of Edgar', ed. Fowler (1972), chapter 11: 'It is right that every priest in addition to learning learn a handicraft' (from C&S 48 p.318).
99 GA p.19f.
100 GA pp.135–8; cf. *Archaeology of Anglo-Saxon England*, ed. Wilson (1976), chapter 6 by D.M. Wilson.
101 GA 161; cf. W.H. Frere, *The Winchester Troper* (HBS, 1894).
102 MO p.552f.
103 ibid. p.557 and n.1 for discussion of the significance of tropers.
104 VO p.464; cf. MO ibid. p.559 n.1; see J. Handschin, 'The two Winchester Tropers' (JTS, 1936).
105 MO ibid. p.560; cf. WMVD pp. 257 and 301; cf. M. Lapidge, 'Dunstan's Latin poetry' for a further discussion of Dunstan's musical gifts (*Anglia*, 1980).

106 Wulstan's prologue to his metrical 'Life of St Swithun' (AA.SS. OSB p.630).
107 VO p.417; not all the monks' musical talents found expression in purely religious performance however: see C. Page, 'The Boethian metrum "Bella bis quinis" – a new song from Saxon Canterbury' (in *Boethius: His Life, Thought and Influence*, ed. Gibson (1981).
108 VO p.459; cf. article by Dom C. Butler, 'St Dunstan's Kyries' (DR, 1885).
109 Text in MD p.357f.; cf. MO p.552 n.1; E p.207; cf. Ad p.63.
110 B p.21; cf. MO ibid. p.555f. for the background to these developments in the monastic plainchant.
111 B p.41.
112 ibid.48f.
113 ibid. p.44.
114 Ad. p.65.
115 See B. Ward, 'Charismatic prayer and monastic liturgy' (*Cistercian Studies*, 1974).
116 GA 115; cf. J.J.G. Alexander, 'The Benedictional of St Ethelwold and Anglo-Saxon illumination of the reform period' (*Tenth Century Studies*, ed. D. Parsons, 1975).
117 ibid. p.176.
118 ibid.: Alexander's treatment of this benedictional is fascinating and full.
119 See note 144 of chapter 7; also R. Deshman, '"Christus rex et magi reges": kingship and Christology in Ottonian and Anglo-Saxon art', (*Frühmittelalterliche Studien*, (Münster: Berlin, 1976), p.393f.
120 MD pp.384 and 388 (cf. C&S 37).
121 cf. Deshman, art. cit. p.391f.
122 *Chronicle of Aethelweard*, ed. Campbell (1962), introduction; also JAR p.154.
123 MD p.359f.
124 See also note 76 etc. of chapter 8.
125 See full discussion in Deshman, art. cit.
126 ibid. p.399.
127 ibid. p.403f.

Chapter 12: St Dunstan

1 From Farmer's entry on Dunstan in ODS.
2 *Life of St Martin of Tours*, Sulpitius Severus, chapter X.
3 cf. RC p.xxvii f.; also EHD 239 (g) (Aelfric's homily on Swithun); see MD p.cv.
4 cf. RC p.xxviii n.1 (here translated).
5 VO pp.420, 455 and 457; cf. Symons, 'St Dunstan in the Oswald tradition' (DR, 1972).
6 VO p.457; cf. Wulstan VE, chapter xx; also in xiv, xxxviii and xl.
7 MD p.359f.
8 EHD 121.
9 MD p.409.
10 EHD 49 n.1 (C&S 64): I Cnut (ecclesiastical) chapter 17.1.
11 MD p.440 (cf. last page of *Byrhtferth's Manual*, ed. Crawford.)
12 EHD 239 (g) (*Lives of the Saints*, ed. Skeat, I, 468–71).
13 LVH p.91.
14 See P.M. Korhammer, art. cit. (1973) and Gasquet and Bishop, op. cit. on the Bosworth Psalter; also F. Wormald, *English Kalendars before 1100* (HBS, 1934) for the emergence of the cult of Dunstan in the pre-conquest kalendars of the English Church.
15 For Mayfield, see MD p.204: for Supperton, ibid. p.144 n.3.
16 See B. Ward, *Miracles and the Medieval Mind* (Scolar Press: London, 1982).
17 cf. VO p.448 for a comparison with Cuthbert.
18 Life 'B' passim; cf. VO p.457f.
19 Life by Adelard passim, but especially 'Lectiones' I and VI: cf. VE, chapters 2, 11 and 23 (EHD 235) for similar instances in the tradition about Ethelwold.
20 VO p.405; though the prayer of Oswald which rescues storm-stricken monks on p.448 might rank as a lifetime miracle.
21 Osbern's life, passim; Eadmer's life, passim.
22 William of Malmesbury's life, passim.
23 MD p.313; see note 72 of chapter 9.
24 See respective entries in ODS; the life of Grimbald was probably drawn up for liturgical use at Winchester in the tenth century. It is printed in *The Monastic Breviary of Hyde Abbey*, ed. J.B.L. Tolhurst (HBS, 1939).
25 This has been fully explored by H. Delehaye in *Les Légendes Hagiographiques* (2nd edition, Brussels, 1905).

26 See P. Brown, *The Cult of the Saints* (SCM: London, 1981).
27 e.g. Osbern 'Miracles of Dunstan', 12 (MD p.138).
28 Eadmer's 'Miracles of Dunstan' are in MD p.233f.
29 See R.W. Southern, *St Anselm and his Biographer* (Cambridge, 1963), p.260f.; cf. 'Religious sentiment and church design in the later Middle Ages', C. Brooke (in *Medieval Church and Society*, C. Brooke, London, 1971).
30 Eadmer's *Life of St Anselm*, ed. R.W. Southern (Oxford, 1962), p.154f.
31 Eadmer's 'Miracles of St Oswald' are appended to his 'Life of Oswald', *Historians of the Church of York*, ed. Raine (RC, 1874, ii p.1f.
32 A similar pattern occurs at the end of the 'Life of Edith' and also the 'Passion of St Edward'.
33 Southern, *St Anselm and his Biographer*, p.250 n.2.
34 Aelfric's *Lives of the Saints*, ed. Skeat, I, p.441f.
35 MD pp.129 and 161.
36 ibid p.150.
37 ibid. p.442f.
38 ibid. p.424f.
39 ibid. p.450f.; cf. B. Ward (ed.), *The Prayers and Meditations of St Anselm* (Penguin: London, 1973), especially appendix.
40 MD p.454f.; cf. Ad p.66f.
41 ibid. p.412f.
42 ibid. p.422.
43 ibid. p.xxxv.
44 ibid. p.426f.
45 ASC ii p.xxvi.
46 E p.163; cf. MD p.422 also.
47 O pp.128 and 160; cf. Stubbs' discussion in MD p.lxvi n.7.
48 VO p.457; cf. MD p.lx.
49 Stubbs' analysis of the character and provenance of the first biographer remains invaluable: MD pp.x f. and lvi f.; cf. B pp. 5 and 49.
50 MD p.387f. and Stubbs' notes on this letter.
51 ibid. pp.374 and 390.
52 Stubbs in MD p.xxvi f.; Wulfric's letter to Abbo of Fleury is on p.409.
53 ibid. p xxx.
54 C.E. Fell, *Dunstanus Saga* (Copenhagen, 1963); cf. various liturgical propers printed in MD p.444f.
55 R.W. Southern, 'The sense of the past' (TRHS, 1973); cf. *St Anselm and his Biographer*, part II.
56 On Sulcard of Westminster, see B.W. Scholz, art. cit. (*Traditio*, XX, 1964).
57 Southern, op. cit. p.281f.
58 MD p.xxxv f. and lxix f.; see J. Scott's masterly introduction to his edition of '*De Antiquitate Glastonie Ecclesie*' (1981).
59 Letter from Pope John XII is in MD p.296f. (C&S 25); EHD 238 is the English document which William refers to in WMVD p.290.
60 e.g. MD p.321f.
61 ibid. p.lxxi f.
62 ibid. p.325f.
63 JW; cf. JAR p.93.
64 MD p.xxxviii f.
65 ibid. p.cxvii f.
66 JAR p.90.
67 ibid. p.91.
68 JAR, also articles by J. Armitage Robinson.
69 MO and RC.
70 ASE and Whitelock – see bibliography.

BIBLIOGRAPHY

Introduction

The bibliographies at the end of F.M. Stenton's *Anglo-Saxon England* (Oxford, 1971) and of D. Knowles' *Monastic Order* (Cambridge, 1966), and also in *English Historical Documents*, vol. I, ed. D. Whitelock (London, 1979 edition) remain fundamental to this subject. So too do *The Bibliography of English History to 1485*, ed. E.B. Graves (Oxford, 1975) and *An Anglo-Saxon and Celtic Bibliography, 450–1087*, ed. W. Bonser (Oxford, 1957). Also of great value are the bibliographies in *Anglo-Saxon Charters*, ed. P.H. Sawyer (Royal Historical Society: London, 1968), in *The Archaeology of Anglo-Saxon England*, ed. D. Wilson (Cambridge, 1976), and *Anglo-Saxon Manuscripts*, ed. E. Temple (London, 1976). Extensive bibliographies may also be found in *Councils and Synods: 871–1204*, ed. Whitelock, Brett and Brooke (Oxford, 1981), in *The Heads of Religious Houses in England and Wales: 940–1216*, ed. Knowles, Brooke and London (Cambridge, 1972), and in *The Golden Age of Anglo-Saxon Art*, ed. Backhouse, Turner and Webster (London, 1984). The regular publication, *Anglo-Saxon England* (Cambridge, 1972 onwards) contains reviews of all recent work in this field, together with articles on historical and literary topics and topical bibliographies.

Where the date of a second or later edition is indicated in this bibliography, it is to that edition that footnote references in the book relate.

Printed primary sources

Abingdon, Chronicon Monasterii de, ed. J. Stevenson, RS 2, 2 vols (1858)
Acta Sanctorum Bollandiana (Brussels and elsewhere, 1643 onwards)
Acta Sanctorum Ordinis S. Benedicti, ed. L. D'Archéry and J. Mabillon (Paris, 1668–1701)
Adam of Domerham, Historia de Rebus Gestis Glastoniensibus, ed. T. Hearne (Oxford, 1727)
Adami Bremensis Gesta Hannaburgensis Ecclesiae Pontificum, in MGH, SS, VII

Aelfric
'Homilies' in *Liber Sermonum Catholicorum*, ed. B. Thorpe (London, 1844)
Grammatik und Glossar, ed. J. Zupitza (Berlin, 1880; reprinted 1966)
'Letter to monks at Eynsham', ed. M. Bateson, in *Obedientiary Rolls of St Swithun's, Winchester*, ed. Dean Kitchin (HRS, 1892)

Lives of the Saints, ed. W. Skeat (EETS, 1881, 1885, 1890 and 1900; reprinted 1960)
Die Hirtenbriefe Aelfrics (Pastoral Letters), ed. B. Fehr (Hamburg, 1914; reprinted 1966)
The Heptateuch, ed. S.J. Crawford (EETS, 1922; reprinted 1969)
'Grammar', in 'Early Scholastic Colloquies', *Anecdota Oxoniensia: Medieval and Modern Series*, part 15 – 1929, ed. W.H. Stevenson
De Temporibus Anni, ed. H. Henel (EETS, 1942)
Colloquy, ed. G.N. Garmonsway (London, 1939; 2nd edition, 1947)
   Homilies, a supplementary collection, ed. J.C. Pope (EETS, 1967 and 1968)
'Life of St Ethelwold', ed. M. Winterbottom, in *Three Lives of English Saints* (Toronto, 1972)
Catholic Homilies (Second Series), ed. M. Godden (EETS, 1979)

Aethelweard, Chronicle of, ed. A. Campbell (London, 1962)
Aethelwulf's 'De Abbatibus', ed. A. Campbell (Oxford, 1967)
Alcuin of York (select letters), ed. and trans. S. Alott (York, 1974)
Aldhelm's Prose Works (including *De virginitate*), ed. and trans. M. Lapidge and M. Herren (Ipswich, 1979)

Alfred the Great
King Alfred's West-Saxon Version of Gregory's 'Pastoral Care', ed. H. Sweet (EETS, 1871)
King Alfred's Translation of Boethius' 'De Consolatione Philosophiae', ed. W.J. Sedgefield (Oxford, 1899 and 1900)
King Alfred's Translation of St Augustine's 'Soliloquies', ed. H.L. Hargrove (Yale Studies in English XIII and XXII, 1902 and 1904)
Asser's Life of, ed. W.H. Stevenson (Oxford, 1904; reissued with introduction by D. Whitelock, 1959)
Alfred the Great (Life by Asser and other texts), ed. and trans. S. Keynes and M. Lapidge (Penguin: London, 1983)

'Alphege, Life of, by Osbern', in *Anglia Sacra*, ed. H. Wharton, ii, pp.122–47 (1691)
Anglia Sacra, ed. H. Wharton (1691)

Anselm of Canterbury
Opera Omnia, ed. F.S. Schmitt, 6 vols (Edinburgh, 1946–61)
Prayers and Meditations, ed. B. Ward (London, 1973)
Eadmer's Life of, ed. R.W. Southern (Oxford, 1962)

Bede
Opera Historica, ed. C. Plummer, 2 vols (Oxford, 1896)
The Old English Version of Bede's Ecclesiastical History of the English People, ed. T. Miller (EETS, 1890–8)
Ecclesiastical History of the English People, ed. B. Colgrave and R.A.B. Mynors (Oxford, 1969)

Benedict
Rule of (Latin and Old English text), ed. H. Logeman (EETS, 1888; reprinted, 1975)
Rule of, translated by Dom Bernard Basil Bolton (Ealing Abbey, London, 1969)
Life and Miracles of (Book ii of the Dialogues of St Gregory the Great), translated by O.J. Zimmerman and B.R. Avery (Liturgical Press: Minnesota)

Beowulf, ed. W.F. Bolton (London, 1973 edition)
Byrhtferth's Manual, ed. S.J. Crawford (EETS, 1929)
Chrodegang, Rule of, with the Capitula of Theodulf and an Epitome of Benedict of Aniane – (Old English version with Latin text), ed. A.S. Napier (EETS, 1916)

Charters (editions of)
Codex Diplomaticus Aevi Saxonici, ed. J.M. Kemble, 6 vols (London, 1839–48)
Cartularium Saxonicum, ed. W. de Gray Birch, 3 vols (London, 1885–93)

The Crawford Collection of Early Charters and Documents, ed. A.S. Napier and W.H. Stevenson (Oxford, 1895)
Select Charters of English Constitutional History, ed. W. Stubbs (Oxford, 9th edition, 1913)
The Sunbury Charter, ed. W.H. Tapp (Sunbury-on-Thames, London, 1951)

Chronicles
The Anglo-Saxon Chronicle, ed. C. Plummer and J. Earle (Oxford, 1892; 1952 edition)
The Parker Chronicle and Laws (facsimile of Corpus Christi College, Cambridge MS 173), ed. R. Flower and H. Smith (EETS, 1941; reprinted 1973)
Councils and Ecclesiastical Documents relating to Great Britain and Ireland, ed. W. Stubbs and A.W. Haddan, 3 vols (Oxford, 1869; reprinted 1964)
Councils and Synods: 871–1204, ed. D. Whitelock, M. Brett and C.N.L. Brooke, 2 vols (Oxford, 1981)

Dunstan
Memorials of St Dunstan, ed. W. Stubbs, RS, 63 (London, 1874; Kraus reprint, 1965) (contains the five 'Lives of Dunstan': by the anonymous 'B', Adelard, Osbern, Eadmer and William of Malmesbury; also one by Capgrave and sundry related texts and letters)
St Dunstan's Classbook from Glastonbury (Codex Bibl. Oxon. Auct. F.4.32: Umbrae Codicum Occidentalium), ed. R.W. Hunt (Amsterdam, 1961)
Dunstanus Saga, ed. C.E. Fell (Copenhagen, 1963)

'Edith, Life of, by Goscelin', in *Acta Sanctorum* (1755), Sept. V. pp.364–72; also in '*La légende de Ste Edith en prose et vers par le moine Goscelin*', A. Wilmart, *Analecta Bollandiana*, LVI (1938), pp.5–101 and 265–307

Edmund, King and Martyr
'Life and Passion of, by Abbo of Fleury', in *Memorials of St Edmund's Abbey*, ed. T. Arnold, RS (London, 1890); also in *Three Lives of English Saints*, ed. M. Winterbottom (Toronto, 1972)
Life by Aelfric, in *Lives of the Saints*, ed. W.W. Skeat (EETS, 1900), vol. ii, pp. 315–34
Edward, King and Martyr, Passion of, ed. C.E. Fell (Leeds, 1971)

Einhard, Life of Charlemagne, Latin text, ed. E.S. Firchow (Stuttgart, 1968); translated by L. Thorpe (Penguin: London, 1969)
Eliensis, Liber, ed. E.O. Blake, CS, Third Series, vol. XCII (London, 1962)
English Historical Documents, vol. I (*c.500–1042*), ed. D. Whitelock (London and Oxford, 2nd edition, 1979)
'Ethelwold, Life of, by Aelfric, and another life by Wulstan the Cantor', ed. M. Winterbottom, *Three Lives of English Saints* (Toronto, 1972)
Frithegodi Monachi Breviloquium Vitae Beati Wilfredi, et Wulstani Cantoris Narratio Metrica de S. Swithuno, ed. A. Campbell (Turin, 1950)
'Grimbald of St Bertin, Life and Legend of', in *The Monastic Breviary of Hyde Abbey* (8 July), ed. J.B.L. Tolhurst (HBS, 1939)

Homilies
The Blickling Homilies, ed. R. Morris (EETS, 1874, 1876, 1880; reprinted, 1967)
Angelsächsische Homilien und Heiligenleben, ed. B. Assmann, Bibliothek der angelsächsischen Prosa III (Kassel, 1889; reprinted Darmstadt, 1964)

Laws
Die Gesetze der Angelsachsen, ed. F. Liebermann, 3 vols (Halle, 1903–16)
The Laws of the Earliest English Kings, ed. F.L. Attenborough (Cambridge, 1922)

Liber Pontificalis, ed. L. Duchesne (Paris, 1886–92; reprinted in 1955, with supplementary volume by C. Vogel in 1957)

Monumenta Germaniae Historica, ed. G.H. Pertz *et al.*, *Scriptores*, vols I–XXXII (Hanover, 1826–1913) and *Epistolae*, vols I–VII (Berlin, 1887–1912)

'Oda, Archbishop of Canterbury, Life of, by Eadmer', in *Anglia Sacra*, ed. H. Wharton (1691), ii pp.78–87

Oswald
'Life of, by Byrhtferth', in *Historians of the Church of York*, ed. J. Raine, vol. I, RS, London, 1874), pp.399–475

'Life of, by Eadmer', ibid. vol. II (1886), pp.1–59

Patrologiae Cursus Completus, Series Latina, ed. J.P. Migne (Paris, 1844–64)

Psalters
The Oldest English Texts (Vespasian Psalter), ed. H. Sweet (EETS, 1885)

The Bosworth Psalter, ed. F.A. Gasquet and E. Bishop (London, 1908)

The Salisbury Psalter, ed. C. and K. Sisam (EETS, 1959)

Eadwine's Canterbury Psalter, ed. F. Harsley (EETS, 1889; Kraus reprint, 1975)

Ramsey Abbey, Chronicle of, ed. W.D. Macray, RS (London, 1886)

Regularis Concordia, ed. T. Symons (London, 1953)

Symeon of Durham, Opera Omnia, ed. T. Arnold, RS (London, 1882–5)

Wallingford, John of, Chronicle, ed. R. Vaughan, Camden Miscellany, vol. XXI (London, 1958)

William of Malmesbury
Gesta Pontificum, ed. N.E.S.A. Hamilton, RS (London, 1870)

Gesta Regum, ed. W. Stubbs, RS (London, 1887–9)

'Life of Dunstan', ed. W. Stubbs in *Memorials of St Dunstan* (London, 1874)

'Life of Wulfstan', ed. R.R. Darlington, Camden Series, vol. XL (London, 1928)

Early History of Glastonbury (De Antiquitate Glastonie Ecclesie), ed. J. Scott (Boydell Press: Ipswich, 1981)

William of Thorne's 'Chronicle of St Augustine's Abbey, Canterbury', ed. A.H. Davis (Oxford, 1934)

Winchester
Liber Monasterii de Hyde, ed. E. Edwards, RS (London, 1866)

An Ancient Manuscript (Nunnaminster Codex), ed. W. de Gray Birch (HRS, 1889)

Liber Vitae of Newminster and Hyde Abbey, ed. W. de Gray Birch (HRS, 1892)

Obedientiary Rolls of St Swithun's, ed. Dean Kitchin (HRS, 1892)

The Winchester Troper, ed. W.H. Frere (HBS, 1894)

The Monastic Breviary of Hyde Abbey, ed. J.B.L. Tolhurst (HBS, 1932)

Worcester, Florence of, Chronicle, ed. B. Thorpe (London, 1848–9)

Wulfstan
Homilies of, ed. D. Bethurum (Oxford, 1957; reprinted, 1971)

'Die "Institutes of Polity, Civil and Ecclesiastical"', ed. K. Jost, *Swiss Studies in English*, XLVII (Berne, 1959)

Sermo Lupi ad Anglos, ed. D. Whitelock (London, 3rd edition, 1963)

Wulfstan's 'Canons of Edgar', ed. R. Fowler (EETS, 1972)

'Wulsin, Life of', by Goscelin, in 'The Life of St Wulsin of Sherborne by Goscelin', C.H. Talbot, *Revue Bénédictine*, LXIX (1959), pp.68–85

Secondary sources

Andre, J.L. *Widows and Vowesses* (Royal Archaeological Institute, 1892)

Armitage Robinson, J. *The Times of St Dunstan* (Oxford, 1923)

Backhouse, J., Turner, D.H. and Webster, L. (eds) *The Golden Age of Anglo-Saxon Art: 966–1066* (British Museum: London, 1984)

Baker, D. (ed.) *Medieval Women* (Oxford, 1978)

Barlow, F. *The English Church: 1000–1066* (London, 2nd edition, 1979)

Barraclough, G. *Medieval Germany* (Oxford, 1938)

Battiscombe, C.F. *The Relics of St Cuthbert* (Oxford, 1956)

Bishop, E. *Liturgica Historica* (Oxford, 1918)

Bishop, T.A.M. *English Caroline Minuscule* (Oxford, 1971)

Blackburn, M.A.S. (ed.) *Anglo-Saxon Monetary History* (Leicester, 1986)

Bonser, W. *The Medical Background to Anglo-Saxon England* (London, 1964)

Brooke, C. *Medieval Church and Society* (London, 1971)

Brooks, N. (ed.) *Latin and the Vernacular Languages in Early Medieval Britain* (Leicester, 1982)

—*The Early History of the Church of Canterbury* (Leicester, 1984)

Brown, P. *The Cult of the Saints* (London, 1981)

Campbell, J. (ed.) *The Anglo-Saxons* (Oxford, 1982)

Campbell, J. *Essays in Anglo-Saxon History* (London, 1986)

Cheney, W.A. *The Cult of Kingship in Anglo-Saxon England* (Manchester, 1970)

Chrimes, S.B. *Kingship and Law in the Middle Ages* (Oxford, 1939)

Clapham, A.W. *English Romanesque Architecture before 1066* (Oxford, 1930)

Clemoes, P. (ed.) *The Anglo-Saxons: Studies in some Aspects of their History and Culture* (London, 1959)

Clemoes, P. and Hughes, K. (eds) *England Before the Conquest* (Cambridge, 1971)

Cross, F.L. and Livingstone, E. (eds) *The Oxford Dictionary of the Christian Church* (Oxford, 2nd edition, 1974)

Deanesly, M. *The Pre-Conquest Church in England* (London, 2nd edition, 1963)

—*Sidelights on the Anglo-Saxon Church* (London, 1962)

De la Mare, A.C. and Barker-Benfield, B.C. (eds) *Manuscripts at Oxford: R.W. Hunt Memorial Exhibition* (Bodleian Library, Oxford, 1980)

Delehaye, H. *Les Légendes Hagiographiques* (Brussels, 2nd edition, 1905)

Dolley, R.H.M. (ed.) *Anglo-Saxon Coins* (London, 1961)

Duckett, E.D. *St Dunstan of Canterbury* (London, 1955)

Dumville, D.N. *Wessex and England from Alfred to Edgar* (Ipswich, forthcoming)

Ekwall, E. *Oxford Dictionary of English Place-names* (Oxford, 4th edition, 1960)

Ellard, G. *Ordination Anointings before 1000* (Medieval Academy of America, XVI, 1933)

Farmer, D.H. (ed.) *Benedict's Disciples* (Leicester, 1980)

—*Oxford Dictionary of Saints* (Oxford, 1978)

Fell, C.E. *'Dunstanus Saga'* (Copenhagen, 1963)

—*Edward, King and Martyr* (Leeds, 1971)

—*Women in Anglo-Saxon England and the Impact of 1066* (London, 1984)

Gatch, M. *Preaching and Theology in Anglo-Saxon England: Aelfric and Wulfstan* (Toronto, 1977)

Gibson, M. (ed.) *Boethius: His Life, Thought and Influence* (Oxford, 1981)

Gilson, E. *History of Christian Philosophy in the Middle Ages* (London, 1955)

Godfrey, C.J. *The Church in Anglo-Saxon England* (Cambridge, 1962)

Gougaud, L. *Christianity in Celtic Lands* (London, 1932)

Gransden, A. *History Writing in England: 550–1307* (London, 1974)

Hamilton Thompson, A. *Bede – His Life, Times and Writings* (Oxford, 1935)

Hanson, R.P.C. *St Patrick, His Origins and Career* (Oxford, 1968)

Harmer, F.W. *Anglo-Saxon Writs* (Manchester, 1952)

Haslam, J. (ed.) *Anglo-Saxon Towns in Southern England* (Chichester, 1984)

Hill, D. (ed.) *Ethelred the Unready (Millenary Conference)* (British Archaeological Reports, V, 1978)

Hodgkin, R.H. *A History of the Anglo-Saxons* (Oxford, 1935)

James, E. *The Origins of France* (London, 1982)

James, M.R. *The Ancient Libraries of Canterbury and Dover* (Cambridge, 1903)

John, E. *Land Tenure in Early England* (Leicester, 1964)

—*Orbis Britanniae* (Leicester, 1966)

Kelly, J.N.D. *Early Christian Creeds* (London, 3rd edition, 1972)

—*The Oxford Dictionary of Popes* (Oxford, 1986)

Ker, N.R. *Catalogue of Manuscripts containing Anglo-Saxon* (Oxford, 1957)

—*Medieval Libraries of Great Britain* (RHS: London, 2nd edition, 1964)

Keynes, S. *The Diplomas of Ethelred the Unready 978–1016* (Cambridge, 1980)

Knowles, D. *From Pachomius to St Ignatius* (Oxford, 1966)

—*The Monastic Order in England, 940–1216* (Cambridge, 2nd edition, 1966)

Knowles, D., Brooke, C.N.L. and London, V.C.M. (eds) *The Heads of Religious Houses in England and Wales: 940–1216* (Cambridge, 1972)

Lampe, G.W.H. (ed.) *The Cambridge History of the Bible*, vol. II (Cambridge, 1969)

Latham, R.E. *Revised Medieval Latin Word-List* (British Academy: London, 1965)

Leclercq, J. *The Love of Learning and the Desire for God: a Study of Monastic Culture* (London, 1978)

Levison, W. *England and the Continent in the Eighth Century* (Oxford, 1946)

Loyn, H.R. *The Governance of Anglo-Saxon England* (London, 1984)

Maitland, F.W. *Domesday Book and Beyond* (Cambridge, 1897)

Mayr-Harting, H. *The Coming of Christianity to Anglo-Saxon England* (London, 1972)

McKitterick, R. *The Frankish Kingdoms under the Carolingians: 751–987* (London, 1983)

Miller, E. *The Abbey and Bishopric of Ely* (Cambridge, 1951)

Moore, W.J. *The Saxon Pilgrims to Rome and the 'Schola Saxorum'* (Freiburg, 1937)

Myres, J.N.L. *The English Settlements* (Oxford History of England) (Oxford, 1986)

Oakley, T.P. *English Penitential Discipline* (New York, 1923)

Oppermann, C.J.A. *The English Missionaries in Sweden and Finland* (London, 1937)

Oppermann, O. *Die älteren Urkunden des Klosters Blandinium und die Anfänge der Stadt Gent* (Utrecht, 1928)

Parsons, D. (ed.) *Tenth Century Studies* (London, 1975)

Poole, R.L. *Studies in Chronology and History* (Oxford, 1934)

Powicke, F.M. and Fryde, E.B. (eds) *Handbook of British Chronology* (RHS: London, 2nd edition, 1961)

Sawyer, P.H. *Anglo-Saxon Charters – an annotated List and Bibliography* (RHS: London, 1968)

Schramm, P. *The History of the English Coronation* (Oxford, 1937)

Sisam, K. *Studies in the History of Old English Literature* (Oxford, 1953)

—*The Structure of 'Beowulf'* (Oxford, 1965)

Smalley, B. *The Study of the Bible in the Middle Ages* (Oxford, 1952)

Southern, R.W. *St Anselm and his Biographer* (Cambridge, 1963)

—*Western Society and the Church in the Middle Ages* (London, 1970)

Stenton, F.M. *The Early History of Abingdon* (Oxford, 1913)

—*The Latin Charters of the Anglo-Saxon Period* (Oxford, 1955)

—*Anglo-Saxon England* (Oxford History of England) (Oxford, 3rd edition, 1971)

Stubbs, W. *Constitutional History of England* (Oxford, 1891)

—*Registrum Sacrum Anglicanum* (Oxford, 2nd edition, 1897)

Sweet, H. *Anglo-Saxon Primer* (Oxford, revised edition, 1953)

—*Anglo-Saxon Reader* (Oxford, revised edition, 1967)

Taylor, H.M. and J. *Anglo-Saxon Architecture* (Cambridge, 1965)

Temple, E. *Anglo-Saxon Manuscripts: 900–1066* (London, 1976)

Thomas, A.C. *Britain and Ireland in Early Christian Times* (London, 1971)

Thomson, R.M. *William of Malmesbury – a study* (Ipswich, 1987)

Ullmann, W. *The Carolingian Renaissance and the Idea of Kingship* (London, 1969)

—*A Short History of the Papacy in the Middle Ages* (London, 1972)

Ure, J. *The Benedictine Office: an Old English Text Ascribed to Wulfstan* (Edinburgh, 1957)

Wallace-Hadrill, J.M. *The Barbarian West* (London (3rd. edition, 1967)

—*Early Germanic Kingship in England and the Continent* (Oxford, 1971)

Ward, B. *Miracles and the Medieval Mind* (London, 1982)

Whitelock, D. *Anglo-Saxon Wills* (Cambridge, 1930)

—*The Audience of 'Beowulf'* (Oxford, 1951)

—*The Beginnings of English Society* (London, 1952)

Wilson, D.M. (ed.) *The Archaeology of Anglo-Saxon England* (London, 1976)

Wood, M. *Domesday: a Search for the Roots of England* (London, 1986)

Wormold, F. *English Kalendars before 1100* (HBS, 1933)

—*Studies in Western Art: I: Romanesque and Gothic Art* (Princeton, 1963)

Wright, C.E. *The Cultivation of Saga in Anglo-Saxon England* (Edinburgh, 1939)

Young, K. *The Drama of the Medieval Church* (Oxford, 1933)

Zarnecki, G. *The Early Sculpture of Ely Cathedral* (London, 1958)

Articles

Addleshaw, G.W.O. 'The beginning of the parochial system' (York, 1959)

Alexander, J.J.G. 'The Benedictional of St Ethelwold and Anglo-Saxon illumination of the reform period', *Tenth Century Studies*, ed. D. Parsons (1975), 169f.

—'Anglo-Saxon illumination in Oxford libraries' (Oxford, 1970)

Armitage Robinson, J. 'Flete's history of Westminster' (Cambridge, 1909)

—'Some memories of St Dunstan in Somerset', *Somerset Archaeological & Natural History Society Proceedings for 1916*, LXII xxvii–xxxvii and 1–25

—'The coronation order in the tenth century', JTS XIX, 1917, 50–72

—'The Saxon Bishops of Wells', *British Academy Supplementary Papers*, IV (Oxford, 1918)

—'St Oswald and the church at Worcester', *British Academy Supplementary Papers*, V (Oxford, 1919)

—'Somerset historical essays', *British Academy* (Oxford, 1921)

—'The early community at Christ Church, Canterbury', JTS XXVII, 1926, 225–40

—'Byrthferth and the life of Oswald', JTS XXX, 1929, 35–42

Atkins, I. 'The church of Worcester from the eighth to the twelfth centuries', *Antiquaries Journal*, XVII, 1937, 371–91

Baker, P.S. 'The Old English Canon of Byrhtferth of Ramsey', *Speculum* 58, 1980, 22–37

—'Byrhtferth's "Enchiridion" and the Computus at Oxford – St John's MS. 17', *Anglo-Saxon England*, X, 1981

Bately, J. 'Grimbald of St Bertin's', *Medium Aevum*, 35, 1966, 1–10

Bates, E.H. 'The cartularies of Muchelney and Athelney Abbeys', *Somerset Record Society*, XIV, 1899

Bateson, M. 'Rules for monks and secular canons after the revival under King Edgar', EHR IX, 1894, 690–708.

Bethurum, D. 'Archbishop Wulfstan's commonplace book', *Publications of the Modern Language Association of America*, LVII, 1942, 916f.

—'A letter of protest from the English bishops to the pope', *Philologica: the Malone Anniversary Studies*, 1949, 97–104

Biddle, M. 'Winchester: the development of an early capital', *Vor- und Frühformen der Europäischen Stadt im Mittelalter*, ed. H. Lankuhn (Göttingen, 1973), 229–61

—' "Felix urbs Winthonia": Winchester in the age of monastic reform', *Tenth Century Studies*, ed. D. Parsons (1975), 123f.

Binchy, D.A. 'Celtic and Anglo-Saxon kingship' (Oxford, 1970)

Birkeli, F. 'The missions to Norway', *Nottingham Medieval Studies*, XV, 1971, 27–37

Bishop, T.A.M. 'An early example of insular-caroline script', *Transactions of the Cambridge Bibliographical Society*, IV, 1963, 396–400

Bitterman, H.R. 'The organ in the early Middle Ages', *Speculum*, 4, 1929, 390–410

Blunt, C.E. 'The St Edmund memorial coinage', *Proceedings of the Suffolk Archaeological Institute*, XXXI, 1969, 234–5

Boase, T.S.R. 'English Romanesque illumination' (Oxford, 1951)

Böhmer, H. 'Das Eigenkirchentum in England', *Texte und Forschungen zur englischen Kulturgeschichte: Festgabe für Felix Liebermann* (Halle, 1921), 301–53

Bullough, D.A. 'The educational tradition in England from Alfred to Aelfric: teaching "utriusque linguae" ', *Settimane di studio del Centro italiano di studi sull' alto medioevo*, Spoleto, XIX (1972), 453–554

—'The continental background of the reform', *Tenth Century Studies*, ed. D. Parsons (1975), 20f.

Butler, C. 'St Dunstan's "Kyries" ', DR V, 1885, 49–51

Cameron, M. 'The sources of medical knowledge in Anglo-Saxon England', *Anglo-Saxon England*, XI, 1983

Caraman, P.G. 'The character of the late Saxon clergy', DR LXIII, 1945, 171–89

Clemoes, P. 'The chronology of Aelfric's works', *The Anglo-Saxons*, ed. P. Clemoes (1959), 212–47

—'The Old English Benedictine Office: Corpus Christi, Cambridge MS 190, and the relations between Aelfric and Wulfstan – a reconsideration', *Anglia*, LXXVIII, 1960, 265–83

—'Aelfric', *Continuations and Beginnings – Studies in Old English Literature*, ed. E.G. Stanley (London, 1966), 176–209

—'Late Old English literature', *Tenth Century Studies*, ed. D. Parsons (1975) 103f.

Cooper, J.M. 'The last four Anglo-Saxon archbishops of York' (York, 1970)

Cramp, R. 'Anglo-Saxon sculpture of the reform period', *Tenth Century Studies*, ed. D. Parsons (1975), 184f.

Crawford, S.J. 'Byrhtferth and the anonymous life of Oswald', *Speculum Religionis: Essays presented to C.G. Montefiore* (Oxford, 1929), 99–111

D'Alverny, M.T. 'Le symbolisme de la Sagesse et le Christ de St Dunstan', *Bodleian Library Review*, V (Oxford, 1956), 232f.

Darlington, R.R. 'Ecclesiastical reform in the late Old English period', EHR LI, 1936, 385–428

Deanesly, M. 'The "familia" of Christ Church, Canterbury', *Essays in Medieval History Presented to T.F. Tout*, ed. A.G. Little and F.M. Powicke (Manchester, 1925), 1–14

—'The archdeacons of Canterbury under Archbishop Ceolnoth', EHR XLII, 1927, 1–11

Deshman, R. '"Christus rex et magi reges": kingship and Christology in Ottonian and Anglo-Saxon art', *Frühmittelalterliche Studien* (Münster: Berlin, 1976), 367–405

Dhondt, J. 'La donation d'Elftrude à St Pierre de Gand', Académie Royale de Belgique, *Bulletin de la Commission Royale d'Histoire*, CV, 1940, 117–64

Dubuisson, D. 'L'Irlande et la théorie médiévale des "trois ordres" ', *Revue de l'Histoire des Religions*, CLXXXVIII, 1975, 35–63

Farmer, D.H. 'The progress of the monastic revival', *Tenth Century Studies*, ed. D. Parsons (1975), 10f.

Finberg, H.P.R. 'The house of Ordgar and the foundation of Tavistock Abbey', EHR LVIII, 1943, 190–201

—'Sherborne, Glastonbury and the expansion of Wessex', TRHS 5th series III, 1953, 101–24

—'Yniswitrin', *Lucerna* (London, 1964)

—'St Patrick at Glastonbury', *West Country Historical Studies* (Newton Abbot, 1969, 70–88

Fisher, D.J.V. 'The early biographers of St Ethelwold', EHR LXVII, 1952, 38–91

—'The anti-monastic reaction in the reign of Edward the Martyr, *Cambridge Historical Journal*, X, 1952, 254–70

Fleming, R. 'Monastic lands and England's defence in the Viking Age', EHR C, 1985, 243–65

Forsey, G.F. 'Byrhtferth's Preface', *Speculum* 3, 1928, 505–22

Forster, M. 'Über die Quellen von Aelfrics Homiliae Catholicae – I: Legenden' (Berlin, 1892)
—'Über die Quellen von Aelfrics exegetischen Homiliae Catholicae', Anglia, XVI, 1894, 1–61
Galbraith, V.H. 'The East Anglian see and the abbey of Bury St Edmunds', EHR XL, 1925, 222–8
Gem, R.D.H. 'The Anglo-Saxon cathedral at Canterbury', Archaeological Journal, CXXVII, 1970, 196–201
Gerould, G.H. 'Aelfric's legend of St Swithun', Anglia, XXXII, 1909, 347–57
Gjerløw, L. '"Adoratio crusis": the "Regalaris Concordia" and the "Decreta" of Lanfranc' (Oslo, 1961)
Gneuss, H. 'The origin of standard Old English', Anglo-Saxon England, 1, 1972
—'Dunstanus und Hrabanus Maur', Anglia, XCVI, 1978, 136–48
Godden, M.R. 'Aelfric's saints' lives and the problem of miracles', Leeds Studies in English, XVI, 1985, 83f.
Gransden, A. 'The legends and traditions concerning the origin of the abbey of Bury St Edmunds', EHR C, 1985, 1–24
Green, B. 'St Dunstan and the monastic reform', Benedict's Disciples, ed. D.H. Farmer (1980)
Gretsch, M. 'Ethelwold's translation of the Rule of St Benedict and its Latin exemplar', Anglo-Saxon England, III, 1974
Grierson, P. 'Grimbald of St Bertin's', EHR LV, 1940, 529–61
—'Relations between England and Flanders before the Norman Conquest', TRHS Fourth Series XXIII, 1941, 71–112
Hall, J.R. 'Some liturgical notes on Aelfric's letter to the monks at Eynsham', DR XCIII, 1976, 297–304
Handschin, J. 'The two Winchester Tropers', JTS XXXVII, 1936, 34–49 and 156–72
Hart, C. 'Eadnoth, first abbot of Ramsey and the foundations of Chatteris and St Ives', Proceedings of the Cambridge Antiquarians' Society, LVI/LVII, 1964, 61–7
—'The Ramsey "Computus"', EHR LXXXV, 1970, 29–44
—'Some Danelaw charters and the Glastonbury scriptorium', DR XC, 1972, 125–33
—'Byrhtferth and his "Manual"', Medium Aevum, 41, 1972, 95–109
—'Athelstan "Half-king" and his family', Anglo-Saxon England, II, 1973
—'Byrhtferth's Northumbrian Chronicle', EHR XCVII, 1982, 558–82
Harty, C. 'The Icelandic life of St Dunstan', Saga-Book of the Viking Society, XV, 1961, 263–93
Higgitt, J. 'Glastonbury, Dunstan, monasticism and manuscripts', Art History, 2, 1979, 275–90
Hinton, D.A., Keene, S. and Qualmann, K.E. 'The Winchester Reliquary', Medieval Archaeology, XXV, 1981, 45–77
Hohler, C.E. 'Some service books of the later Saxon church', Tenth Century Studies, ed. D. Parsons (1975), 60f.
Horden, J.N.P.B. 'The Norman Conquest of medicine', Travaux du Centre d'Histoire dans les Iles Britanniques, Université de Paris IV Sorbonne, VI Migrations, 1986, 7–22
Hunt, R.W. 'Manuscript evidence for knowledge of the poems of Venantius Fortunatus in later Anglo-Saxon England', Anglo-Saxon England, VIII, 1979
John, E. 'War and society in the tenth century: the Maldon campaign', TRHS Fifth Series XXVII, 1977, 173–95
Jones, A. 'The significance of the regnal reconsecration of Edgar in 973', Journal of Ecclesiastical History, XXXIII, 1982, 375–90
Jost, K. 'Wulfstanstudien', Swiss Studies in English, XXIII (Berne, 1950)
Keynes, S. 'King Athelstan's books', Learning and Literature in Anglo-Saxon England, ed. M. Lapidge (Cambridge, 1985)
—'A tale of two kings: Alfred and Ethelred the Unready', TRHS Fifth Series XXXVI, 1986, 195–217
Korhammer, P.M. 'The origins of the Bosworth Psalter', Anglo-Saxon England, II, 1973
Lapidge, M. 'Three Latin poems from Ethelwold's school at Winchester', Anglo-Saxon England, I, 1972

—'The hermeneutic style in tenth-century Anglo-Latin literature', *Anglo-Saxon England*, IV, 1975

—'St Dunstan's Latin poetry', *Anglia*, XCVIII, 1980, 101–6

—'The revival of Latin learning in Anglo-Saxon England', *Manuscripts at Oxford*, ed. A. De la Mare, 1980

—'Some Latin poems as evidence for the reign of Athelstan', *Anglo-Saxon England*, IX, 1980

—'The cult of St Indracht at Glastonbury', *Ireland in Medieval Europe: Studies in Memory of Kathleen Hughes*, ed. D. Whitelock (Cambridge, 1981) 179–212

—'Byrhtferth of Ramsey and the early sections of the "Historia Regum" attributed to Symeon of Durham', *Anglo-Saxon England*, X, 1982

Lawson, M.K. 'The collection of Danegeld and Heregeld in the reigns of Ethelred II and Cnut', EHR XCIX, 1984, 721–38

Loomis, L.H. 'The holy relics of Charlemagne and Athelstan', *Speculum*, 25, 1950, 447f.

Loud, G.A. 'A re-examination of the "coronation" of Symeon of Bulgaria in 913', JTS XXIX, 1978, 109–20

Loyn, H.R. 'Church and state in England in the tenth and eleventh centuries', *Tenth Century Studies*, ed. D. Parsons (1975), 94f.

—'Wales and England in the tenth century: the context of the Athelstan charters, *Welsh Historical Review*, X, 1980–1, 283–301

Lund, N. 'King Edgar and the Danelaw', *Medieval Scandinavia*, IX, 1976

Meyer, M.A. 'Women and the tenth-century English monastic reform', *Revue Bénédictine*, 87, 1977, 34–61

Nelson, J.L. 'Inauguration rituals', *Early Medieval Kingship*, ed. P.H. Sawyer and I.N. Wood (Leeds, 1977), 50–71

—'The earliest surviving royal "Ordo": some liturgical and historical aspects', *Authority and Power*, ed. B. Tierney and P. Lineham (Cambridge, 1980), 29–48

—' "A king across the sea": Alfred in a continental perspective', TRHS Fifth Series XXXVI, 1986, 45–68

Page, C. 'The Boethian metrum "Bella bis quinis": a new song from Saxon Canterbury', *Boethius – His Life, Thought and Influence*, ed. M. Gibson (1981)

Parker, M.B. 'The Parker MS of the Chronicle, laws and Sedulius, and historiography at Winchester in the late ninth century, *Anglo-Saxon England*, V, 1976

—'A note on MS Vatican Bibl. Apost. Lat. 3363', *Boethius – His Life, Thought and Influence*, ed. M. Gibson (1981)

—'A fragment of an early tenth-century Anglo-Saxon manuscript', *Anglo-Saxon England*, XII, 1983

Parsons, D. 'The pre-Conquest church at Canterbury', *Archaeologica Cantiana*, LXXXIV, 1969, 175–84

Peers, C.R. and Clapham, A.W. 'St Augustine's Abbey Church before the Norman Conquest', *Archaeologia*, LXXVII, 1927, 201–18

Pesci, B. 'L'itinerario romano di Segerico, arcivescovo di Canterbury, e la lista dei papa da lui portata in Inghilterra', *Rivista di archaeologica cristiana*, XIII, 1936, 43–60

Pontifex, D. 'St Dunstan in his first biography', DR LI, 1933, 20–40, 309–25

Quirk, R.N. 'Winchester Cathedral in the tenth century', *Archaeological Journal*, CXIV, 1957, 26–68

Radford, C.A.R. 'Excavations at Glastonbury, 1954', *Antiquity*, XXIX, 1955, 33–4

—'Excavations at Glastonbury, 1951–4', *Somerset & Dorset Notes*, XXVII, 1961, 21–4, 68–73, 165–9

—'Excavations at Glastonbury, 1962', *Somerset & Dorset Notes*, XXVIII, 1968, 114–17

—'Pre-Conquest minster churches', *Archaeological Journal*, CXXX, 1973, 120–40

Rahtz, P.A. 'The Saxon and medieval palaces at Cheddar: an interim report of excavations in 1960–1962', *Medieval Archaeology*, VI–VII, 1962–3, 53–66

—'Glastonbury Tor excavations, 1964–6', *Archaeological Journal*, CXXVII, 1970, 1–81

Rankin, S. 'Bishop Ethelwold and liturgical drama at Winchester', Brochure for the Millenial celebrations – 1984: Dean and Chapter of Winchester Cathedral

BIBLIOGRAPHY 197

Reuter, T. 'The "Imperial church system" of the Ottonian and Salian kings: a reconsideration', *Journal of Ecclesiastical History*, XXXIII, 1982, 347–74

Robinson, J.L. 'St Brigid and Glastonbury', *Journal of the Royal Society of Antiquaries of Ireland*, LXXXIII, 1953, 97–9

Rollason, D.W. 'The cults of murdered royal saints in Anglo-Saxon England', *Anglo-Saxon England*, XI, 1983

—'Relic cults as an instrument of royal policy: c.900–1051 A.D.', *Anglo-Saxon England*, XV, 1986

Sawyer, P.H. 'The charters of Burton Abbey and the unification of England', *Northern History*, X, 1975 (Leeds), 28–39

—'Charters of the reform period: the Worcester Archive', *Tenth Century Studies*, ed. D. Parsons, 1975, 84f.

Schoebe, G. 'The chapters of Archbishop Oda and the canons of the legatine councils of 786', *Bulletin of the Institute of Historical Research*, XXV, 1962, 75–83

Scholz, B.W. 'Sulcard of Westminster: "Prologus de Construccione Westmonasterii"', *Traditio*, XX, 1964, 59–92

Schutt, M. 'The literary form of Asser's life of Alfred', EHR LXXII, 1957, 209–20

Sheerin, D. 'The dedication of the Old Minster, Winchester, in 980', *Revue Bénédictine*, 88, 1978, 261–73

Slover, C.H. 'Glastonbury Abbey and the fusing of English literary culture', *Speculum*, 10, 1935, 147–60

Smetana, C.L. 'Aelfric and the early medieval homiliary', *Traditio*, XV, 1959, 163–204

—'Aelfric and the homiliary of Haymo of Halberstadt', *Traditio*, XVII, 1961, 457–69

Smith, R.A.L. 'The early community at Rochester', EHR LX, 1945, 289–99

Somers Cocks, E.M. 'Baltonsborough – Somerset' (Baltonsborough, 1972)

Southern, R.W. 'English origins of the "Miracles of the Virgin"', *Medieval and Renaissance Studies*, IV, 1958, 176–216

—'Aspects of the European tradition of historical writing: 4: the sense of the past', TRHS Fifth Series XXIII, 243–63

Stacpoole, A. '"Regularis Concordia Millenium Conference" – a preliminary report' (Leicester, 1971)

Stafford, P. 'The laws of Cnut and the history of Anglo-Saxon royal promises', *Anglo-Saxon England*, X, 1982

Stenton, F.M. 'Aethelweard's account of the last years of Alfred's reign', EHR XXIV, 1909, 79–84

—'The south-western element in the Old English Chronicle', *Essays Presented to T.F. Tout*, ed. Little and Powicke (Manchester, 1925), 15–24

—'The founding of Southwell Minster', *Collected Papers of F.M. Stenton*, ed. D. Whitelock (Oxford, 1970)

Stevenson, W. 'The great commendation to King Edgar in 973 A.D.', EHR XII, 1898, 505–7

—'Trinoda necessitas', EHR XXIX, 1914, 689–703

Stutz, U. 'Die Eigenkirche als Element des mittelalterliche germanischen Kirchenrechtes' (Berlin, 1895)

Symons, T. 'The monastic reforms of King Edgar', DR XXXIX, 1921, 38–51

—The "Regularis Concordia"', DR XL, 1922, 15–30

—'The monastic observance of the "Regularis Concordia"', DR XLIV, 1926, 157–71 and DR XLV, 1927, 146–64

—'The introduction of monks at Christ Church, Canterbury', JTS XXVII, 1926, 409–11

—'Monastic observance in the tenth century', DR L, 1932, 449–64 and LI, 1933, 137–52

—'Sources for the "Regularis Concordia"', DR LIX, 1941, 14–36, 143–70, 264–89

—'English monastic reform in the tenth century', DR LX, 1942, 1–22, 196–222, 268–79

—'Looking back on the "Regularis Concordia"', DR LXXVII, 1959 and DR LXXVIII, 1960, 286–292

—'Some notes on English monastic origins', DR LXXX, 1962, 55–69, 286–92

—The "Regularis Concordia" and the Council of Winchester', ibid. 140–56

—'Notes on the life and work of St Dunstan', ibid. 250–61, 355–66

—'St Dunstan in the Oswald tradition', DR XC, 1972, 119–24

—' "Regularis Concordia": history and derivation', *Tenth Century Studies*, ed. D. Parsons (1975), 37f.

Taylor, C.S. 'Bath: Mercian and West Saxon', *Transactions of the Bristol & Gloucester Archaeological Society*, XXIII 1900, 129–61

Taylor, H.M. 'The Anglo-Saxon cathedral at Canterbury', *Archaeological Journal*, CXXVI, 1969, 107–30

—'Tenth-century church building in England and the continent', *Tenth Century Studies*, ed. D. Parsons (1975), 141f.

Thomson, R.L. 'Aelfric's Latin vocabulary', *Leeds Studies in English*, XII, 1981, 155–61

Toke, L.A.St.L. 'The date of Dunstan's birth', appendix to *The Bosworth Psalter*, ed. Gasquet and Bishop (1908), 131–43

Tolkien, J.R.R. ' "Beowulf" – the monsters and the critics', *Proceedings of the British Academy*, XXII, 1936

Tout, M. 'The legend of St Ursula and the 11,000 virgins', *Historical Essays*, ed. J. Tait and T.F. Tout (Manchester, 1902), 17–56

Van Dijk, P. 'Origins of the Latin feast of the Conception', *Dublin Review*, 1954, 251–67, 428–42

Ward, B. 'Charismatic prayer and monastic liturgy', *Cistercian Studies*, 1974, 366–75

Ward, P.L. 'The coronation ceremony in medieval England', *Speculum*, 14, 1939, 160–78

—'An early version of the Anglo-Saxon coronation ceremony', EHR LVII, 1942, 345–61

Whitelock, D. 'A note on the career of Wulfstan the Homilist', EHR LII, 1937, 460f.

—'Wulfstan and the so-called "Laws of Edward and Guthrum" ', EHR LVI, 1941, 1f.

—'The conversion of the eastern Danelaw', *Saga-book of the Viking Society*, XII, 1941, 159–76

—'Archbishop Wulfstan, homilist and statesman', TRHS Fourth Series XXIV, 1942, 25f.

—'Wulfstan and the laws of Cnut', EHR LXIII, 1948, 453f.

—'Anglo-Saxon poetry and the historian', TRHS Fourth Series XXXI, 1949, 75–94

—'Recent work on Asser's "Life of Alfred" ', 1959 edition of Stevenson's *Asser* (Oxford), cxxxii–clii

—'The Old English Bede', *Proceedings of the British Academy*, XLVIII, 1962, 57–90

—'The prose of Alfred's reign', *Continuations and Beginnings: Studies in Old English Literature*, ed. E.G. Stanley (London, 1966), 67–103

—'The genuine Asser' (Reading, 1967)

—'Fact and fiction in the legend of St Edmund', *Proceedings of the Suffolk Archaeological Institute*, XXXI, 1969, 217–33

—'The authorship of the Old English account of King Edgar's establishment of the monasteries', *Philological Essays in Honour of H.D. Merritt*, ed. J.L. Rosier (1970), 125–36

—'The appointment of Dunstan as archbishop of Canterbury', *Otium et Negotium: Studies Presented to O. von Feilitzen*, ed. F. Sangren (Stockholm, 1973), 232–47

—'The importance of the battle of Edington', *From Bede to Alfred: Studies in Early Anglo-Saxon Literature and History* (D. Whitelock collected papers) (London, 1980)

Wickham, G.W.G. 'The Romanesque style in medieval drama', *Tenth Century Studies*, ed. D. Parsons (1975), 115f.

Williams, A. ' "Princeps merciorum gentis": the family, career, and connections of Aelfhere, ealdorman of Mercia (956–83)', *Anglo-Saxon England*, X, 1982

Williams, E.R. 'Aelfric's grammatical terminology', *Publications of the Modern Language Association of America*, LXXIII, 1958, 453–62

Wilson, D.M. 'The Vikings' relationship with Christianity in northern England', *Journal of the British Archaeological Association*, Third Series XXX, 1967, 437–47

—'Tenth-century metalwork', *Tenth Century Studies*, ed. D. Parsons (1975), 200f.

Wood, M. 'The making of King Athelstan's empire', *Ideal and Reality – Festschrift for J.M. Wallace-Hadrill*, ed. P. Wormald (Oxford, 1984)

Wormald, C.P. 'The uses of literacy in Anglo-Saxon England and its neighbours', TRHS Fifth Series XXVII, 95–114

Wormald, F. 'The Winchester school before St Ethelwold', *England before the Conquest*, ed. Clemoes and Hughes (Cambridge, 1971)

—'The liturgical kalendar of Glastonbury abbey', *Festschrift for Bernhard Bischoff*, ed. J. Autenrieth and F. Brunhölzl (Stuttgart, 1971), 325–45

Wormald, P. 'Bede, "Beowulf", and the conversion of the Anglo-Saxon aristocracy', *Bede and Anglo-Saxon England*, ed. R.T. Farrell, *British Archaeological Reports*, XLVI, 1978, 32–95

INDEX

Abbo of Fleury, scholar, 19, 32, 39, 59, 65, 75, 84, 103, 106, 111, 114, 132–3, 143, 147, 148, 156

Abingdon, abbey of, 18, 35, 37–40, 41, 46, 57, 63, 66–7, 68, 69, 72, 75, 84, 101, 105, 114, 117–18, 121, 135, 137, 142

Adam of Bremen, chronicler, 120

Adelard, monk and second biographer of Dunstan, 10, 12, 30, 35, 37, 43, 45, 47, 53, 56, 57, 60, 105, 106, 147, 149–50, 155, 156, 158

Adelolf, abbot of St Bertin's and count of Boulogne, 16, 45, 46

Aelfflaed, queen of Edward the Elder, 29

Aelfgar, bishop of Elmham, 57, 58, 107, 149

Aelfgifu, queen of Edmund and saint, 26, 36, 79, 87

Aelfhere, ealdorman of Mercia, 41, 46, 75, 87–8, 100–3, 104–5

Aelfric, scholar and homilist, 21, 68, 81, 116, 118, 125, 126, 129–132, 135–6, 137, 139

  'Grammar', 31, 130

  'Colloquy', 130

  'Life of Ethelwold', 20, 21, 32, 34, 37–8, 39, 56, 66, 68, 70, 72, 129, 135, 142, 147, 150

  'Life of Swithun', 53, 70–2, 89, 112, 130, 152

  'Catholic Homilies', 114, 131–2

  'Lives of Saints', 132

  'Heptateuch', 132

  'De temporibus anni', 130–1, 132

Aelfric, abbot of St Augustine's, 59

Aelfric, archbishop of Canterbury, 58, 103, 114, 117, 118, 119, 122, 156

Aelfric, abbot of Malmesbury and bishop of Crediton, 64

Aelfric, ealdorman of Hampshire, 54, 105

Aelfric 'Bata', 135, 153

Aelfstan, bishop of London, 35, 55, 60

Aelfstan, abbot of Glastonbury and bishop of Rochester, 56–7, 60

Aelfstan, bishop of Ramsbury, 57, 63

Aelfweald, bishop of Sherborne, 55

Aelfwold, bishop of Crediton, 35, 36, 115, 117, 118

Aelfwold, son of Athelstan the half-king, 73, 100, 102

Aelsige, 'abbot' of Glastonbury, 43, 63

Aescwig, bishop of Dorchester, 57, 114

Aescwy, abbot of Bath, 65

Aethelflaed of Damerham, queen of Edmund, 29

Aethelflaed Candida, queen of Edgar, 80, 87, 99

Aethelfleda, patron of Dunstan, 22–3, 24, 149

Aethelgar, abbot of New Minster and archbishop of Canterbury, 57, 67, 69, 105, 113–4, 140, 156

Aethelgar, bishop of Crediton, 36

Aethelgifu, daughter of Alfred and abbess of Shaftesbury, 4

Aethelgyfu, mother of Edwy's queen, 42–3, 46

Aethelmaer, founder of Cerne abbey, 116, 118, 130, 131, 137

Aethelmaer, ealdorman of Hampshire, 105

Aethelnoth, abbot of St Augustine's, 59

Aethelnoth, archbishop of Canterbury, 116, 117, 120, 121, 122, 130, 140

Aethelsige, son of Athelstan the half-king, 73

Aethelsige, bishop of Sherborne, 57

Aethelthryth, abbess of Nunnaminster, 69, 80

Aethelthryth, second queen of Edgar, 67, 79, 80, 87, 99, 100, 103, 104

Aethelweard, ealdorman and chronicler, 11, 41, 78, 99, 112, 118, 130, 131–2, 137–8

Aethelwin, founder of Ramsey abbey, 73, 74–5, 77, 78, 100–1, 102, 111, 118

Aethelwold, ealdorman of East Anglia, 41, 46, 87

Aethelwynn, patron of Dunstan, 23

Alan Twisted-Beard, of Britanny, 16

Alcuin, scholar, 55, 114, 126, 134, 135

Aldhelm, scholar, 24, 64–5, 133–4, 156

  'On virginity', 18, 32, 140

Alfred the Great, king, 3–8, 11, 12, 15, 16, 18, 19, 20, 21, 27, 29, 38, 43, 45, 67, 79, 90, 129, 131, 137–8, 141, 145

Alphege, bishop of Lichfield, 57